THE RULE OF LAW IN SINGAPORE

This book examines the operation of the rule of law in the non-liberal democracy of Singapore.

The rule of law in Singapore has been both lauded for anchoring efficient and effective government and lambasted for being procedural and statist. 21st-Century Singapore has experienced modest political liberalisation, manifesting a paternal democracy where the governor-governed relationship is evolving, from a 'father knows best' paternalistic mindset to a more consultative approach to governance, where dialogue rather than diktat is the norm in a post-deferential era.

The Singapore case study helps pluralise the rule of law as a universal principle which moderates power, and may be variously implemented. The book examines the reception of the rule of law within the Singapore legal order, and how it interacts with constitutional principles like the separation of powers and democracy in the design of constitutional institutions and forging of structural and rights-oriented judicial review. It considers how the rule of law, contoured by legal communitarianism, sustains a managed democracy in relation to legislation governing internal security, public assemblies, religious harmony and online falsehoods. It interrogates whether the chilling of political speech by strict laws on political defamation and contempt of court has been significantly defrosted by important developments which seek ordered liberty through a more calibrated form of review.

Lucid and engaging, this book will be of interest to researchers working in constitutional law.

Volume 4 in the series Rule of Law In Context

Rule of Law In Context

By exploring the rule of law in different jurisdictions around the world, the series makes an original and insightful contribution to the rule of law scholarship by moving past intractable debates over what the rule of law should mean to find out what it actually means and how it works 'on the ground', with an implicitly comparative objective as it explores these issues in the context of different legal systems.

Series Editors

Lorne Neudorf
Gabrielle Appleby

Associate Editors

Rosalind Dixon
David Landau
Lawrence McNamara
Arun Thiruvengadam

Recent titles in this series:

The Rule of Law in the United States: An Unfinished Project of Black Liberation
Paul Gowder

The Rule of Law in Brazil: The Legal Construction of Inequality
Juliano Zaiden Benvindo

The Rule of Law in Germany
Hannah Birkenkötter and Dana Burchardt

The Rule of Law in Singapore: Legal Communitarianism, Paternal Democracy and the Developmentalist State
Li-ann Thio

The Rule of Law in Singapore

Legal Communitarianism, Paternal Democracy and the Developmentalist State

Li-ann Thio

•HART•
OXFORD • LONDON • NEW YORK • NEW DELHI • SYDNEY

HART PUBLISHING
Bloomsbury Publishing Plc
Kemp House, Chawley Park, Cumnor Hill, Oxford, OX2 9PH, UK
1385 Broadway, New York, NY 10018, USA
29 Earlsfort Terrace, Dublin 2, Ireland

HART PUBLISHING, the Hart/Stag logo, BLOOMSBURY and the Diana logo are trademarks of Bloomsbury Publishing Plc

First published in Great Britain 2025

A catalogue record for this book is available from the British Library.

Library of Congress Cataloging-in-Publication data

Names: Thio, Li-ann, author.

Title: The rule of law in Singapore : legal communitarianism, paternal democracy, and the developmentalist state / Li-ann Thio.

Description: Oxford ; New York : Hart Publishing, 2025. | Series: The rule of law in context ; volume 4 | Includes bibliographical references and index. | Summary: "This book looks at the Rule of Law in the context of Singapore and reflects on what the Singapore case study contributes to the understanding of the rule of law. This book reflects on what the Singapore case study contributed to understandings of the rule of law. It explores the reception and development of the Singapore Local System, its constitutional order and institutions, the political dimensions, judicial review, and the context of democracy and civil rights. This lucid and engaging book will be of interest to researchers with an interest in constitutional law"—Provided by publisher.

Identifiers: LCCN 2024036756 (print) | LCCN 2024036757 (ebook) | ISBN 9781509951390 (hardback) | ISBN 9781509951406 (Epub) | ISBN 9781509951413 (ebook)

Subjects: LCSH: Rule of law—Singapore. | Communitarianism—Singapore. | Democracy—Singapore. | Singapore—Politics and government.

Classification: LCC KPP169.7 .T45 2025 (print) | LCC KPP169.7 (ebook) | DDC 340/.11—dc23/eng/20240813

LC record available at https://lccn.loc.gov/2024036756

LC ebook record available at https://lccn.loc.gov/2024036757

ISBN: HB: 978-1-50995-139-0
ePDF: 978-1-50995-141-3
ePub: 978-1-50995-140-6

Typeset by Compuscript Ltd, Shannon

Acknowledgements

THE COMPLETION OF a book is always cause for celebration and gratitude, not only because it denotes the terminus of an arduous journey, but also as it provides the occasion to remember those who have contributed in some manner along the way.

To that end, I am grateful to the Hart Rule of Law in Context book series editors Gabrielle Appleby and Lorne Neudorf for their invitation, which provided me with an experience I knew I would relish, to write a monograph-length treatment on the subject of the rule of law in Singapore. This invitation came prior to the COVID-19 pandemic which disrupted all our lives, ushering in a strange new world with its strictures on wearing masks, social distancing and discrimination on the basis of vaccine status. This all seems now like a fast-fading memory, despite the toll and costs it exacted and the scars it inflicted. More pertinently, it showed how even liberal democracies in the West can turn authoritarian and how the rule of law is not absolute but qualified by other important social values, whether this be higher moral principles, equity or the exigencies of managing a pandemic crisis. The question of when and if this is justified remains a constant to be grappled with.

The rule of law is a majestic ideal, a universal prescription for political justice. It is a topic I have researched and written about for much of my academic career, both in terms of the theory and competing conceptions of the rule of law, and how it is applied and experienced in the Singapore context. Although the rule of law is central to Singapore's development narrative and economic success, Singapore has been both criticised and celebrated for its rule of law-related achievements and failings. The same could be said for almost every, if not all, jurisdictions, but the Singapore model, based on a brand of legal communitarianism, is troubling to those who have a Fukuyaman faith in Western liberal democracy as the end of history. It stands as a rebuke to the orthodoxy that conflates the rule of law with the processes and institutions of liberal democracies by demonstrating that economic liberalisation within an advanced capitalist society does not invariably lead to political liberalisation along liberal lines. The Singapore case study underscores the universality of the rule of law principle and the variability in how it is understood and implemented; it provides the occasion for interrogating whether rule of law values can be meaningfully implemented in different constitutional contexts, particularly of the non-liberal or communitarian variety, without descending into the black hole of an authoritarian apology for power. This exercise promotes the pluralisation of visions of the rule of law, which are united in resisting autocratic rulers and rules. It is my hope that this book will be informative, insightful with respect to the Singapore context, warts and all, perhaps even a wee bit provocative when it comes to assessing whether and how rule of law values are realised.

I owe thanks to Kate Whetter, Linda Goss and the wonderful team at Hart Publishing. This is not my first project with Hart – my association with them dates back more than a decade, to the publication of *Constitutionalism in Asia: Cases and Materials* in 2014, and continues as one of the series editors of the Hart Constitutionalism in Asia series. Their professionalism, high standards, encouragement and cheerful dedication to their task makes this collaboration a rare pleasure.

Thanks also is owed to Lim Jia Rong for cheerfully rendering valued research assistance. This is an opportunity, too, to convey my appreciation to my colleagues at the National University of Singapore, with whom I teach constitutional and administrative law – Kevin Tan, Jaclyn Neo, Tan Hsien Li, Dian Shah and Marcus Teo: thank you for sustaining an intellectually vibrant academic environment, a safe haven for venting exasperations and extolling the joys of milo cubes, for the insights I gain from your scholarship and for being fellow travellers along the road of public law, with all its dreams of human flourishing, in a context of gritty realism and principled pragmatism.

Todah rabah, Ariel and Judah, constant sentinels.

Li-ann Thio
Singapore, 10 July 2024
SDG

Table of Contents

Abbreviations

AB	Advisory Board
AG	Attorney-General
AGC	Attorney-General's Chambers
AJPA	Administration of Justice (Protection) Act
AMLA	Administration of Muslim Law Act
BEIC	British East India Company
CA	Court of Appeal
CASE	Consumer Association of Singapore
CD	Correction Direction
CIL	customary international law
CJ	Chief Justice
CLAS	Criminal Legal Aid Scheme
CLTPA	Criminal Law Temporary Provisions Act
CPA	Council of Presidential Advisors
CPIB	Corrupt Practices Investigation Bureau
CRI	Community Remedial Initiative
DOL	Declared Online Location
EBRC	Electoral Boundaries Review Committee
ECHR	European Convention on Human Rights
ECtHR	European Court of Human Rights
EP	elected presidency
FIA	Freedom of Information Act
FICA	Foreign Interference (Countermeasures) Act
FPP	first past the post
FRNJ	fundamental rules of natural justice

GCD	General Correction Direction
GRC	group representation constituency
HIC	hostile information campaign
HKCFA	Hong Kong Court of Final Appeal
HRA	Human Rights Act (UK)
ICCPR	International Covenant on Civil and Political Rights
IMDA	Infocomm Media Development Authority
IMF	International Monetary Fund
ISA	Internal Security Act
ISD	Internal Security Department
JC	judicial commissioner
JI	Jemaah Islamiyah
JSC	Judicial Service Commission
LKY	Lee Kuan Yew
LPA	Legal Professions Act
LSC	Legal Services Commission
LSO	legal service officers
MCI	Minister/Ministry of Communications and Information
MDA	Misuse of Drugs Act
MDP	mandatory death penalty
MHA	Minister/Ministry for Home Affairs
MND	Minister/Ministry of National Development
MOA	Miscellaneous Offences (Public Order and Nuisance) Act
MOH	Ministry of Health
MOM	Minister/Ministry for Manpower
MP	Member of Parliament
MRHA	Maintenance of Religious Harmony Act
MRHWP	white paper on Maintaining Religious Harmony
MRT	Mass Rapid Transport

NCMP	Non-constituency Member of Parliament
NGO	non-governmental organisation
NIR	net investment returns
NMP	Nominated Member of Parliament
NParks	National Parks Board
OC	ouster clause
PAP	People's Action Party
PATI	prohibition against torture and inhuman treatment
PCAOJ	public confidence in the administration of justice
PCMR	Presidential Council of Minority Rights
PCRH	Presidential Council of Religious Harmony
PEA	Parliamentary Elections Act
PEC	Presidential Elections Committee
PEMA	Public Entertainments and Meeting Act
PM	Prime Minister
POA	Public Order Act
POFMA	Protection from Online Falsehoods and Manipulation Act
POHA	Protection from Harassment Act
PP	Public Prosecutor
PPSO	Preservation of Public Security Ordinance
PR	proportional representation
RCT	'reasonable classification' test
RO	restraining order
RoL	rule of law
RRG	Religious Rehabilitation Group
RRH	racial and religious harmony
SCL	soft constitutional law
SD	Stop Communication Direction

SICC	Singapore International Commercial Court
SDP	Singapore Democratic Party
SLE	substantive legitimate expectation
SMC	single member constituency
SM	Senior Minister
SoP	separation of powers
TCD	Targeted Correction Direction
TOC	The Online Citizen
UDHR	Universal Declaration of Human Rights
WB	World Bank
WP	Workers' Party

JOURNAL/REPORT ABBREVIATIONS

ACHPR	African Court of Human and Peoples Rights
AHRLR	African Human Rights Law Reports
AIR	All Indian Reports
AJCL	Asian Journal of Comparative Law
Am U Int'l L Rev	American University International Law Review
Asian YBIL	Asian Yearbook of International Law
BCCA	British Columbia Court of Appeal
CJAL	Columbia Journal of Asian Law
CJCCL	Canadian Journal of Comparative and Contemporary Law
CLJ	Current Law Journal
CLR	Commonwealth Law Reports
DJCIL	Duke Journal of Comparative and International Law
DLR	Dominion Law Report
FEER	Far Eastern Economic Review

Harv JLPP	Harvard Journal of Law and Public Policy
Harv L Rev	Harvard Law Review
IACHR	Inter-American Court of Human Rights
ICJ Rep	International Court of Justice Reports
ICON	International Journal of Constitutional Law
IHT	International Herald Tribune
IYCL	Indian Yearbook of Comparative Law
JMBRAS	Journal of the Malaysian Branch of the Royal Asiatic Society
Loy LA Int'l & Comp L Rev	Loyola of Los Angeles International and Comparative Law Review
LSI	Law and Social Inquiry
Mal LJ	Malayan Law Journal
Mal L Rev	Malaya Law Review
Mich L Rev	Michigan Law Review
NTU L Rev	National Taiwan University Law Review
NULR	Northwestern University Law Review
NYU JL & Liberty	NYU Journal of Law and Liberty
NZLR	New Zealand Law Reports
PL	Public Law
OJLR	Oxford Journal of Law and Religion
OJLS	Oxford Journal of Legal Studies
OUCLJ	Oxford University Commonwealth Law Journal
SAcLJ	Singapore Academy of Law Journal
SCR	Canada Supreme Court Reports
SJICL	Singapore Journal of International & Comparative Law
SJLS	Singapore Journal of Legal Studies
SL Rev	Singapore Law Review
SLR	Singapore Law Reports

SLR(R)	Singapore Law Reports (Reissue)
SPR	Singapore Parliament Reports
SYBIL	Singapore Yearbook of International Law
UBCLR	University of British Columbia Law Review
UCLAPBLJ	University of California in Los Angeles Pacific Basin Law Journal
UTLJ	University of Toronto Law Journal

Table of Cases

States

Singapore

Foreign Courts

Australia

Canada

Hong Kong

India

Malaysia

New Zealand

UK

USA

International/Regional Courts

ICJ

ACHPR

ECtHR

IACHR

Table of Legislation

Treaty

Legislation

Rules

Introduction: Rule of Law in Singapore – A Provisional Orientation

THAT SINGAPORE HAS been both lauded and lambasted for vindicating and subverting the rule of law (RoL) reflects how this universal prescription for political justice and constitutionalism remains an essentially contested concept.[1] This ideal, as the 'jurisprudential equivalent of motherhood and apple pie',[2] has both descriptive and normative dimensions. It is deployed in political rhetoric and legal discourse to buttress and erode government legitimacy, which is possible given there is no universal consensus of its content and what it requires, as the term is used to 'designate somewhat different ideals'.[3] Disagreement exists as to whether it is an 'unqualified human good' in effectively inhibiting power's all-intrusive claims',[4] as distinct from being a tool of violence and domination.[5] Indeed, it bears a paradoxical quality: it sometimes sides with the state in the name of public order and the effective enforcement of the majoritarian will and sometimes allies with the constitutionalist project of limiting state power, through counter-majoritarian mechanisms like judicial review of fundamental rights.

A conception of the RoL needs a theory of law if it is not to become a synonym for whatever is considered a desirable government trait; this will be shaped by the particular socio-political environment. However, foundational questions about the source and *telos* of the RoL, as a form of 'higher law'[6] housing principles positive law must conform to, are frequently eschewed. Instead, a functional

[1] Jeremy Waldron, 'The Rule of Law as an Essentially Contested Concept' in Jens Meierhenrich and Martin Loughlin (eds), *The Cambridge Companion to the Rule of Law* (Cambridge University Press, 2021) 121–36.

[2] Lord Bingham, 'Rule of Law' (2007) 66 Cambridge Law Journal 67, 69.

[3] Joseph Raz, 'The Law's Own Virtue' (2019) 39(1) OJLS 1, 2.

[4] EP Thompson, *Whigs and Hunters: The Origin of the Black Act* (Penguin Books, 1990) Afterword.

[5] Feminists critique the andro-centric nature of law which relegates women to the private sphere, while Marxists view law as serving bourgeois interests. See Mark Tushnet, 'Critical Legal Studies and the Rule of Law' in Meierhenrich and Loughlin (n 1) 328–39; Vanessa Munro, 'Feminist Critiques of the Rule of Law' in Meierhenrich and Loughlin (n 1) 340–56.

[6] Li-ann Thio, 'Higher Law/Rule of Law: The Sacred Roots and Secular Shoots of the Supreme Law' in Nicholas Aroney and Ian Leigh (eds), *Christianity and Constitutionalism* (Oxford University Press, 2022) 193–215.

or pragmatic approach is favoured, which posits a laundry list of legal rules, processes and institutions considered necessary to realising the RoL ideal.[7]

The official view is that Singapore's commitment to the RoL 'resting on a strong judiciary' has been central to 'Singapore's development narrative' and 'emergence as a modern economic miracle'.[8] Thus, the Singapore variant is primarily viewed in terms of securing law and order, which grounds a strong business environment and services global economic integration. It does not reflect 'the individualistic, liberty-maximising democracy most in the West conjure when they hear that term';[9] critics peg improvement in terms of a movement towards 'a thicker, more rights-laden RoL with a more robust separation of powers (SoP)' after Montesquieu.[10] They wag their finger against the Singapore brand of 'authoritarian constitutionalism',[11] its formal or 'thin' rule of law conception which, while securing legality or rule-following, is considered deficient in lacking muscular mechanisms to ensure public power accountability, and strong judicial review to secure rights. The varying RoL models deployed in political and legal discourse makes the dialogue of critique and rebuttal one that operates at cross purposes.

Without attempting a comprehensive definition of the elusive RoL ideal, a working understanding of what it entails is needed so it can serve as a useful guide in interrogating how it has been invoked and utilised, and how it fares and operates in practice as a social imaginary[12] in Singapore. It can be seen not in abstract but concrete terms, as 'what actors make of it'.[13] To this provisional orientation we now turn.

[7] The 'anatomical' as opposed to teleological approach to RoL: Martin Krygier, 'Rule of Law' in Michel Rosenfeld and Andras Sajo (eds), *The Oxford Handbook of Comparative Constitutional Law* (Oxford University Press, 2012); Alvaro Santos, 'The World Bank's Uses of the "Rule of Law" Promise in Economic Development' in David M Trubek and Alvaro Santos (eds), *The New Law and Economic Development: A Critical Appraisal* (Cambridge University Press, 2010) 253–300.

[8] Sundaresh Menon CJ, 'The Rule of Law: The Path to Exceptionalism' (2016) 28 SAcLJ 413, [23]. Brian Tamanaha argues that the relationship between RoL and economic development is 'decidedly murky': 'Functions of the Rule of Law' in Meierhenrich and Loughlin, (n 1) 231.

[9] Gordon Silverstein, 'Singapore: The Exception that Proves Rules Matter' in Tom Ginsburg and Tamir Moustafa (eds), *Rule by Law: The Politics of Courts in Authoritarian Regimes* (Cambridge University Press, 2012) 77.

[10] ibid 76. See Montesquieu, *The Spirit of the Laws* (Hafner Pub Co 1949) ch 6.

[11] Mark Tushnet, 'Authoritarian Constitutionalism' [2015]100 Cornell Law Review 391, 396; Kevin YL Tan, 'Is Singapore an Authoritarian Constitutional Regime? So What if It Is?' in Weitseng Chen and Hualing Fu (eds), *Authoritarian Legality in Asia; Formation, Development and Transition* (Cambridge University Press, 2020) 187–202.

[12] Charles Taylor, *Modern Social Imaginaries* (Duke University Press, 2004) 23 defined a social imaginary as 'that common understanding that makes possible collective endeavours and which is reinforced by them', that is, how people fit together in their social existence, the expectations between them and their normative underpinnings. This is both factual and normative, and focuses on practice and not merely principles associated with the rule of law.

[13] Jens Meierhenrich, 'What the Rule of Law Is … and Is Not' in Meierhenrich and Loughlin (n 1) 621.

I. RULE OF LAW: CORE VIRTUES AND CONTESTED CONCEPTIONS

The RoL is a key architectonic pillar in constitutional government, judicially recognised as an unwritten constitutional principle.[14] It is not an absolute value existing in splendid isolation; it interacts with and is qualified by other principles such as democracy and the SoP between co-equal government branches.[15] As an ideal, it is to be approximated, not perfectly achieved. This requires some evaluative criteria for assessing its success or failure.

Although there are proliferating and competing RoL conceptions, there is broad agreement about the core values or virtues it espouses. This would include the supremacy of law over arbitrary exercises of power and the equality of all before the law.[16] Legislation should be general, prospective, publicly accessible, clear and stable. The decision-making process should be transparent, and an independent judiciary should observe fair procedures and reasonableness in adjudicating disputes.

These basic requirements accord with prescriptions articulated by jurists such as Joseph Raz and Lon Fuller,[17] and are associated with a 'thin' or formal rule of law, which relate to values inherent in the concept of 'law' itself, not any comprehensive political theory. These values are essentially negative and may be considered deficient, the hallowing of a hollow standard which, in its minimalist approach, may be 'compatible with gross violations of human rights',[18] and extensive poverty. This points to the 'rule of state law' as opposed to the rule of law state,[19] which cannot guarantee just law.

Those preferring a richer soup than this thin gruel may articulate substantive RoL conceptions,[20] adding 'various content specification', drawn from an economic and political philosophy; this supports a 'distinctive concept of law'[21]

[14] *Chng Suan Tze v MHA* [1988] 2 SLR(R) 525, [86].

[15] *Vellama d/o Marie Muthu v AG* [2012] SGHC 155, [117] (Pillai J), citing Thio Li-ann, *A Treatise on Singapore Constitutional Law* (Academy Publishing 2012) 164.

[16] Peter Westen, 'The Empty Idea of Equality' (1982) 95 Harv L Rev 537 ('equality' is parasitic on an exterior philosophy).

[17] Joseph Raz, 'The Law's Own Virtue' (2019) 39(1) OJLS 1; Lon Fuller, *The Morality of Law*, rev edn (Yale University Press, 1969) ch 2 identified eight criteria composing the various aspects of formal legality, which he considered a moral ideal. The law must be: (1) general; (2) public; (3) non-retroactive; (4) comprehensible; (5) non-contradictory; (6) possible to perform; (7) relatively stable; and (8) administered in ways congruent with the rules as announced.

[18] Joseph Raz, 'The Rule of Law and Its Virtue' in J Raz (ed), *The Authority of Law: Essays on law and morality* (Oxford University Press, 1979) 219; see also Randall Pereenboom, 'Human Rights and Rule of Law: What's the Relationship?' (2005) 36(1) Georgetown Journal of International Law 815.

[19] Robert Cooter, 'The Rule of State Law versus the Rule of Law State' in E Buscaglia, W Ratliff and R Cooter (eds), *The Law and Economics of Development* (JAI Press, 1997) 101–48.

[20] Paul Craig, 'Formal and Substantive Conceptions of the Rule of Law: An Analytical Framework' [1997] PL 467.

[21] TRS Allan, 'The Rule of Law' in David Dyzenhaus and Malcolm Thorburn (eds), *Philosophical Foundations of Constitutional Law* (Oxford University Press, 2016) 201.

as normatively just, shaping the RoL's content and effect. Ronald Dworkin, for instance, championed a 'rights-based' over a 'rule-book' RoL conception[22] in service of enforcing 'moral rights' and his idiosyncratic view of 'equal respect and concern', which individuals enforced through courts; this was to be judicially discerned not from metaphysical abstraction, but from community understandings. There is 'no uncontroversial way to determine what these rights entail';[23] a rule of *good* law based on particular substantive values lacks analytical value, as it merges with the 'complete social philosophy' it incorporates.[24]

Detractors consider Dworkin's faith in courts to make authoritative determinations on polarised controversies misplaced, effecting social engineering through politicised judgments and threatening juristocracy.[25] Partial judges advancing partisan ideologies through values-based reasoning and advocacy undermine the RoL. Thicker RoL conceptions fall into the political thicket, as no uncontroversial theory of the Good exists, in a plural, postmodern age.[26]

The approach adopted here is to apprehend the RoL as a necessary but insufficient component of the ruling triumvirate of good government, together with human rights and democracy, which are related but not integral RoL features. The principles the RoL embodies in this understanding 'should be above political controversy, though their detailed implementation will not be'.[27] The RoL per se cannot guarantee just laws, insofar as it may be enlisted in the service of morally good or bad causes, although a focus on procedural requirements is not a 'morally neutral matter';[28] procedural fairness is part of substantive justice and has a social impact, affecting whether a legal system is, as Finnis puts it, 'legally in good shape'.[29]

To the individual, the chief RoL virtue is that it underpins personal, not political, freedom. By providing a stable, predictable legal environment, it affirms human dignity by treating 'humans as persons capable of planning … their future,[30] and avoiding unlawful conduct. The RoL should provide opportunities for argumentation about the law, such as before courts, treating citizens

[22] The legal system is to apply standards in accordance with 'rules explicitly set out in a public rulebook available to all': Ronald Dworkin, *A Matter of Principle* (Harvard University Press, 1985) 11.

[23] Brian Tamanaha, *On the Rule of Law: On the Rule of Law: History, Politics, Theory* (Cambridge University Press, 2004) 103, 104.

[24] Raz (n 18) 211.

[25] James Grant, 'The Rise of Juristocracy' (2010) 34(2) Wilson Quarterly 16.

[26] The cosmopolitan RoL vision entails respects for human rights and international law, although the criteria for making and interpreting international norms is unidentified: Tom Bingham, *The Rule of Law* (Penguin, 2011) 66–84, 110–29.

[27] Joseph Raz, 'The Law's Own Virtue' (2019) 39(1) OJLS 1, 8.

[28] Robert George, 'Reason, Freedom and the Rule of Law: Their Significance in Western Thought' (2002–03) 15 Regent University Law Review 187, 188.

[29] John Finnis, *Natural Law and Natural Rights* (Oxford University Press, 1980) 9–18.

[30] Raz, 'The Rule of Law and Its Virtue' (n 18) 221.

'with respect as active centers of intelligence',[31] tempering power by allowing them to question or be heard by power-holders.[32]

From the constitutionalist project's perspective, it is accepted that the RoL is against autocracy and arbitrariness, absolutist rulers and rules presiding over a 'totalising' state. Confidence in the legal system is promoted where individuals and groups are protected against abuses of power and assured the government acts 'to protect and advance the interests of the governed'.[33] Authoritarianism and concentrated power are opposed by the core RoL idea that state power is 'subject to legal limits',[34] primarily through judicial enforcement. Arbitrariness connotes rules and decisions based on personal whim or caprice, not reason. Thus, legal *constraints* on the exercise of power, *consistency* in implementing law and clear laws promoting legal *certainty* are RoL virtues.

The RoL ideal would not be attained in the event of official illegality,[35] where rules are ignored, exposing the populace to the 'all too familiar human tendencies and temptations'[36] to whim, bias and spite. Insofar as the RoL requires government fidelity to the law in its generation and application, this is a 'moral doctrine'.[37]

However, vague laws and procedures for changing the law do not always constitute RoL deficits. Precise rules, such as time limits, may be arbitrary if contrary to the reasons on which a law ought to be based. An obsession with generality of law renders it unable to effect distributive justice or address social inequalities.[38] Vagueness may undermine the RoL where it enables official action to be divorced from the law's purpose, conflating the law with official will.[39] However, vagueness may not undermine the RoL where an official is statutorily obliged to do something 'within a reasonable time' but is conditioned by required accounting for undue delay. This allows for 'various degrees of compliance'.[40] The view that judicial review of administrative action as constraint is a necessary aspect of the RoL discounts the possibility that people may follow rules without a review process, which Endicott argues is

[31] Jeremy Waldron, 'The Concept and the Rule of Law' (2008) Sibley Lecture, Paper 29, http://digitalcommons.law.uga.edu/lectures_pre_arch_lectures_sibley/29.

[32] Martin Krygier, 'Tempering Power' in Maurice Adams et al (eds), *Constitutionalism and the Rule of Law* (Cambridge University Press, 2017) 41.

[33] Raz, 'The Law's Own Virtue' (n 27) 13. Raz calls this the 'core idea' identifying the RoL (8).

[34] *Tan Seet Eng v AG* [2015] SGCA 59, [1].

[35] However, going by the book may generate its own form of arbitrariness, where the law is 'inflexible, insensitive or justified only by history or precedent'. P Selznick, 'Legal Cultures and the Rule of Law' in M Krygier and A Czarnota (eds), *The Rule of Law after Communism* (Ashgate, 1999) 26.

[36] Tamanaha, 'Functions of the Rule of Law' in Meierhenrich and Loughlin (n 1) 231.

[37] Above n 27, 5.

[38] On how the RoL services neo-liberal reforms in Western commercial law, see Brian Tamanaha, 'The Dark Side of the Relationship Between the Rule of Law and Liberalism' (2008) 23 NYU JL & Liberty 537.

[39] Timothy Endicott, 'The Impossibility of the Rule of Law' (1999) 19 OJLS 1, 3.

[40] Raz, 'The Law's Own Virtue' (n 27) 5.

symptomatic of Dicey's confusing the RoL with the rule of the High Court.[41] The RoL ideal does not require that all official decisions be subject to judicial control; indeed, it may be undermined by a partial court.

A further account is needed of what the law ought to regulate, and when the RoL is legitimately qualified by considerations like national security or legal pluralism. The muscularity of judicial review as a mechanism to enforce fundamental rights turns on the underlying philosophy, whether liberal, communitarian or statist. This will entail varying degrees of judicial law-making, whether interstitial and modest or fulsome and overreaching.

Every legal system within a modern state necessarily has vague laws[42] and broad discretionary powers. As such, the lack of constraint, inconsistency in rule-application and unpredictability may not in themselves be RoL deficits; objectivity, rationality and determinacy in relation to rules may be a myth to critical scholars and a noble lie,[43] but remain a worthy aspiration. The RoL may be 'unattainable' but not 'inconceivable',[44] to be measured[45] by degrees, on the basis of identified premises and a phenomenological study of practices.

With the intent to realistically apprehend the RoL phenomenon 'in its social totality',[46] the approach here starts with a formal RoL conception as operated in Singapore, and considers how it interacts with other constitutional principles such as the SoP, democracy and rights. It examines how the RoL is shaped and indigenised by contextual factors such as history, political philosophy, economic development and culture, which contour the law's purposive enterprise.

Singapore is significant as a case study into what the RoL looks like and how it functions in a non-liberal setting which practices legal communitarianism, and whether it is able to contribute to constitutional government. It challenges the regnant RoL conception which conflates what it requires with the normative premises underlying Western liberal democracy and liberal legalism.

Chapter one examines how the RoL was received and has developed within the legal order, from colonial times to independent statehood, and delineates the official narrative of how the RoL serves the developmentalist agenda. Chapter two examines how the RoL shapes Singapore's constitutional architecture, whether the political and legal institutions sustain limited government and what constitutional exceptions there are to the RoL. Chapter three deals with structural judicial review, and how the interplay of the RoL, SoP and democracy shapes the delineation of institutional boundaries. Chapter four examines how primary legislation in the selected fields of security, religious harmony,

[41] Endicott (n 39) 10.

[42] ibid 6.

[43] Ian Harden and Norman Lewis, *Noble Lie: The British Constitution and the Rule of Law* (Hutchinson, 1986).

[44] Endicott (n 39) 13.

[45] Whether the RoL is measurable is disputed: Svend-Erik Skaaning, 'Measuring the Rule of Law' (2010) 63(2) Political Research Quarterly 449.

[46] Brian Tamanaha, *A Realistic Theory of Law* (Cambridge University Press, 2017) 1.

public assembly and internet speech impacts the health of civil-political rights within a 'managed democracy'. Chapter five considers the RoL in relation to the 'green light' model of the Singapore administrative state, how it impacts the scope and intensity of review and how standing rules affect citizen participation in addressing public wrongs. Chapter six examines judicial review and rights jurisprudence, noting the three 'waves' of interpretive approaches, incorporating statist and communitarian values and rejecting the values and methods of liberal individualism. Particular focus is paid to the importance of political speech and how this may be unduly restricted by the law on political libel and contempt of court. Singapore public law has attracted the most criticism in these fields, framed in terms of a 'compliant' judiciary failing to safeguard speech rights. Many of these criticisms have not considered later developments, which are interrogated, to evaluate whether the 'chilling effect' has significantly thawed. Chapter seven offers concluding observations.

1

The Reception and Development of the Rule of Law within the Singapore Legal System: From Colony to State

I. INTRODUCTION

BRITISH COLONIALISM USHERED in the common law, which frames the operation of the rule of law (RoL) in Singapore. In 1819, Sir Stamford Raffles persuaded the Johor Sultan to allow the British East India Company (BEIC) to establish a trading post in Singapore, to counter Dutch regional influence.[1] A thriving seaport called Temasek had existed there since the fourteenth century, but this event 'set this island on a trajectory'[2] converting 'a fishing village into a humming centre for commerce, communication and industry'.[3] Singapore became 'a British colony, a free port, and a modern city'.[4]

British control over Singapore as part of the Straits Settlement (1826–1942) and Crown Colony (1946–63) ended in 1959, when it became self-governing. It joined the Federation of Malaysia on 16 September 1963, seceding and gaining Independence on 9 August 1965. The common law was imported[5] into the Straits Settlement as a uniform law through the 1823 Charter of Justice, 'a foundational legal document of the first order',[6] terminating the state of 'legal chaos'.[7]

The common law is 'the basic law of Singapore';[8] through *stare decisis*, a predictable legal order was established, although the common law has a normative dimension transcending the precedential accretion of 'historical judicial

[1] RH Hickling, 'The Origins of Constitutional Government in Singapore' in *Essays in Singapore Law* (Peladuk Publications, 1992) 3.

[2] Prime Minister (PM) Lee Hsien Loong, Launch of the Singapore Bicentennial, 28 January 2019, www.pmo.gov.sg/ (Bicentennial).

[3] PM Lee Kuan Yew, Speech, '150th Anniversary of the Founding of Singapore', Singapore International Chamber of Commerce, 6 February 1969, www.nas.gov.sg/archivesonline.

[4] PM Lee Hsien Loong, 'New Year Message' *Straits Times* (31 December 2017) www.pmo.gov.sg.

[5] Andrew Phang, *From Foundation to Legacy: The Second Charter of Justice* (Singapore Academy of Law, 2006).

[6] Andrew Phang, Goh Yihan and Jerrold Soh, 'The Development of Singapore Law: A Bicentennial Retrospective (2020) 32 SAcLJ 804, [15].

[7] ibid [10].

[8] *Cheong Seok Leng v PP* [1988] 1 SLR(R) 530, [57].

wisdom'.[9] To Lord Diplock, it embodies an ethos seeking 'fair dealing' between citizens and between citizen and government',[10] which judges in rapidly developing countries should apply to meet changing needs, 'which might diverge' from English developments.[11] TRS Allan considered the RoL a juristic principle embodying 'the liberal and individualistic bias of the common law in favour of the citizen'.[12]

Arguably, the individualistic common law principles of liberty and dignity did not take root in Singapore. First Prime Minister (PM) Lee Kuan Yew (LKY) declared that 'We shook ourselves free from the confines of English norms', which prioritise individual rights, as these ran contrary to 'the customs and values of Singapore', where 'our Asian traditional value system'[13] prioritised community interests over individual concerns. The RoL was experienced not as a force of freedom in the mother country, but in the anaemic rule-following form applied to overseas British territories, servicing the illiberal imperial project. As a tool of governance, the RoL in the colonies legitimated the sometimes brutal law and order measures.[14] Today, the common law may not be entirely common, being modified by local values, which indigenises the RoL.

This chapter first examines the historical reception of RoL ideals from the colonial era to its post-Independence judicial recognition as a constitutional principle. It then identifies the socio-political–legal matrix to frame and contextualise the discussion. The official government narrative is set forth, setting the stage for comparing non-official, alternative RoL discourses or invocations in later chapters. The developmentalist state project of securing economic development is founded on the centrality of the RoL, facilitating Singapore's evolution from a manufacturing hub to a leading international and regional centre for trade, financial services and dispute settlement. Given the RoL's legitimating power as key to good government, the intent is to evaluate whether an autochthonous non-liberal version of RoL has emerged that moderates state power or negates RoL values by serving statist values. Core values associated with the dominant RoL conception are identified, to provide grist to the mill in reflecting on how Singapore practice contributes towards apprehending the RoL.

[9] *UKM v AG* [2019] 3 SLR 874, [130].

[10] Lord Diplock, 'Judicial Control of Government' [1979] Mal LJ cxl, cxli. Earlier views linked the common law with natural law, specifically the law of God perceived by human reason, such that a 'manifestly absurd or unjust' decision is not law: William Blackstone, *Commentaries on the Law of England*, vol 1 (Clarendon Press, 1765) 63.

[11] Lord Diplock (n 10).

[12] TRS Allan, 'Legislative Supremacy and the Rule of Law: Democracy and Constitutionalism' (1985) 44 Cambridge Law Journal 111, 119. In New Zealand, the common law is treated as a type of fundamental law whose values shape common law rights, some which 'presumably lie so deep that even Parliament could not override them'. *Taylor v NZ Poultry Board* [1984] 1 NZLR 395, 398 (Cooke J).

[13] PM Lee Kuan Yew, 'Speech, Opening of the Singapore Law Academy' (1990) 2 SAcLJ 155, 156.

[14] Jens Meierhenrich, 'What the Rule of Law Is … and Is Not' in Jens Meierhenrich and Martin Loughlin (eds), *Cambridge Companion to the Rule of Law* (Cambridge University Press, 2021) 575.

II. RECEPTION OF THE RULE OF LAW: FROM COLONY TO INDEPENDENT REPUBLIC

From British colonial rule, Singapore inherited 'a strong belief in the RoL' and built on it, earning respect for its 'strong adherence' to the RoL domestically and in foreign policy as 'one of the hallmarks of Singapore'.[15] The RoL, together with parliamentary democracy, constitute the 'decisive and indelible imprint the British left on Singapore',[16] as Euro-American civilisational values which Singapore 'rightly adopted'[17] and adapted.

There is, however, growing disenchantment with the image of a benign British colonialism, where the liberal forms of government were 'nominally established' in British 'colonial outposts',[18] operating within racist, anti-democratic societies. Here, public order was imperilled by the inability to control gangsters and secret societies; political liberty was lacking, with no free press and the legal suppression of views critical of the colonial masters.

A. The Raffles Minute: Common Law Rule of Law Values and Regulating Regulation

Upon arrival, Raffles entered into a series of treaties[19] with the Johor Sultan, who ceded Singapore Island in 1824.[20] At the Sultan's request, Raffles wrote a 'Memorandum' in June 1823 providing that the judicial regulation of 'English law' would give 'due consideration' to Malay customary law, which 'shall be enforced where not contrary to reason, justice or humanity', with the Sultan and Temenggong (local chieftain) sitting on the bench. The Advocate-General of Bengal opined that English law could 'operate with effect and without injustice'.[21]

This Memorandum prompted Raffles to draw up six Regulations, which were the only body of judicial regulations in Singapore until the island became part of the Penang Presidency in 1826;[22] among other matters, this established a two-tier court system. Given 'the long want of government in these Islands', Raffles felt obliged to provide 'law and regulation' regarding police and judicial

[15] Tommy Koh, 'The British Rule of Singapore: An Evaluation' *Law Gazette* (July 2019) https://lawgazette.com.sg/.

[16] Bicentennial (n 2).

[17] 'White Paper on Shared Values' (Cmd 1, 1991) [29].

[18] Lee Kuan Yew, Speech, University of Singapore Law Society Annual Dinner, 18 January 1962, nas.gov.sg/lky19620118.

[19] MB Hooker, 'Raffles' Singapore Regulations' (1968) 10(2) Mal L Rev 248.

[20] Treaty of Friendship and Alliance, 2 August 1824.

[21] Hooker (n 19).

[22] These Regulations were technically illegal as the BEIC did not obtain sovereignty over Singapore until the 1824 Treaty.

administration, which was not to be administered by native authorities, to secure the 'security and comfort' of the people[23] and property.[24]

Raffles authored a Minute containing principles to inform framing regulations to run Singapore as a free port, beneficial to British trade interests.[25] The tension between universal values and solicitude for local circumstances is evident in the recommendation that 'the general principles of British Law' apply equally to all, subject to modifications giving due weight to local customs and peculiarities, including the natives' 'weaknesses and prejudices'.[26] Respect was to be given to native institutions dealing with religious observances, marriage and inheritance, provided these were not inconsistent 'with justice and humanity, or injurious to the peace and morals of society'.[27] Legal pluralism was thus an incipient aspect of the Singapore legal order, and the intent to preserve local laws and customs was later statutorily embodied in section 3(2) of the Application of English Law Act 1993.[28]

This Minute was described as 'a remarkable exposition on the RoL' by a non-lawyer,[29] involving key ideas like equal treatment by the law, not being a judge in one's own cause, trial by peers and requiring cause for liberty deprivation. Government administration should serve the 'protection and happiness' of inhabitants and not tyrannise them. To avoid vigilante justice, public officials should address grievances. Punishment must relate to the 'reasoning powers' of the Malays and Chinese, 'however weak', and the moral principle which 'still exists in the consciences of all men'.[30]

Raffles invoked the 'constitution of England' to protect the 'absolute rights' of 'all classes of people' living under the 'British flag'[31] in three respects: (i) the right to personal security relating to 'his life, his limbs, his body, his health and his reputation'; (ii) the right of personal liberty, consisting of the power of locomotion and requiring imprisonment or restraint to be by due process; and (iii) the right of property, as regulated by law. This reflects the Blackstonian understanding of common law liberties, which the Court of Appeal (CA) invoked in 2015.[32]

[23] Hooker (n 19) [23].
[24] ibid [17].
[25] CH Wake, 'Raffles and the Rajas: The Founding of Singapore in Malayan and British Colonial History' (1975) 48(1) JMBRAS 47, 65.
[26] Para 18, Report on the Administration of Justice to Holt Mackenzie, Secretary to Government (Fort William) from TS Raffles, 6 June 1823: (December 1968) 10(2) Mal L Rev 248, 281.
[27] ibid [24].
[28] Andrew Phang, 'Cementing the Foundations: The Singapore Application of English law Act 1993' [1993] UBCLR 246.
[29] Kevin YL Tan, 'Two Centuries of British Rule of Law: A Look Back to 1819' *Law Gazette* (July 2019).
[30] Hooker (n 19) [2].
[31] ibid.
[32] *Yong Vui Kong v PP* [2015] 2 SLR 1129, [18] (*Yong* 2015).

This common law heritage is reflected in tracing the roots of Article 9 (life and personal liberty) to clause 39 of the Magna Carta, which dealt not only with unlawful incarceration but property seizure and use of force.[33] These three principal Articles on the rights of Englishmen shows the primacy of historical intent in interpreting Article 9 of the Constitution,[34] which encompassed personal security and personal liberty but not private property, which was excluded from the Independence Constitution to avoid impeding the developmentalist project.[35] The CA considered the Article 12 equality guarantee as 'part of the wider doctrine of the RoL', genetically derived from clause 40 of the Magna Carta,[36] reflecting the influence of English common law values on Singapore public law.

B. Singapore Courts: The Reception and Development of the English Common Law and Rule of Law Values

When Singapore was part of the Straits Settlements, RoL virtues were applied as public law principles. In *ex parte Sim Soo Koon*,[37] Earnshaw J held that even if a liquor-licensing statute appeared to confer absolute discretion, this had to be exercised 'according to law and not in an arbitrary manner'. The relevant decision-maker contravened 'two cherished maxims': that nobody be judge in his own case and that 'the King (licensing board) ought not to be subject to an individual but to God and the Law'.[38] This refers to the RoL ideals of impartiality and the RoL as a higher law, beyond law promulgated by the political state, as a source of normativity providing criteria for evaluating positive law. Executive discretion was to be 'done according to the rules of reason and justice … it is not to be arbitrary, vague and fanciful, but legal and regular'.

After Independence, the courts continued to apply a non-literalist approach to statutory interpretation by applying natural justice rules to administrative power. Indeed, these procedural fairness norms were constitutionalised when 'law' in Article 9 was read to refer to 'fundamental rules of natural justice'.[39]

In 1988, the CA first explicitly recognised the RoL as a constitutional principle in *Chng Suan Tze v Minister of Home Affairs (MHA)*;[40] it rejected as invalid and contrary to the RoL the exercise of subjective executive discretion under the

[33] ibid [17].
[34] ibid [18].
[35] ibid [21].
[36] *PP v Taw Cheng Kong* [1998] 2 SLR(R) 489, [52].
[37] [1915] SSLR 2.
[38] Derived from Henri Le Bracton, *De Legibus et Consuetudinibus Angliae* (1235).
[39] *Ong Ah Chuan v PP* [1980–1981] SLR 48. The Court of Appeal (CA) later affirmed this Privy Council decision, eg in *Yong Vui Kong v PP* [2010] 3 SLR 489.
[40] [1988] 2 SLR(R) 525, [86].

Internal Security Act (ISA): 'All power has legal limits and the RoL demands that the courts should be able to examine the exercise of discretionary power.' What has become known as the *Chng* principle is today the architectural cornerstone of contemporary Singapore public law.[41] The RoL also anchors the judicial invalidation of unconstitutional laws.[42]

Has the common law 'served the purpose of making the basic principles of a western view of the RoL understood and appreciated?'[43] It would be realistic for English common lawyers to anticipate adaptations to the RoL, perhaps producing a 'synthesis of western-derived law and custom and procedures of the villages'.[44] This observation is replete with assumed superiority of Western RoL standards, as a prescription for less civilised societies. Rutter's critique centred on whether retaining the common law 'shell' which conveyed a 'vicarious respectability' was accompanied by adherence to individualist dignitarian values.[45] This complements the suggestion that only liberal democracies have the RoL or even constitutionalism itself; this unjustifiably stuffs into the RoL 'contestable normative presuppositions to produce a desired … outcome', imposed 'by definitional fiat'.[46]

To pluralise conceptions of the RoL, the dominant RoL version must be decoupled from its liberal presuppositions. For example, while it is agreed that the RoL is against political absolutism, this can be addressed not only through rights as expressions of normative individualism, but also through other norms, institutions and processes based on non-liberal public philosophies.

In relation to the judicial review of ISA preventive detention powers, the issue of whether the common law is 'common' came under question in *Chng Suan Tze*, where the CA overturned the subjective review approach expressed in *Lee Mau Seng v MHA*[47] in adopting an objective review approach, drawing support from English and Commonwealth jurisdictions. This vindicated Lord Atkin's famous dissent in *Liversidge v Anderson*, where his brother judges were chastised for being 'more executive minded than the executive'[48] in applying a subjective review test. The detention order was quashed on a technicality.

This principled judicial path was disrupted by legislative intervention when the discomfited government swiftly amended the Constitution and ISA

[41] Aside from security law, where the courts have not struck down a constitutionally authorised ouster clause limiting judicial review of detention orders to procedural non-compliance: see *Yong Vui Kong v AG* [2011] 2 SLR 1189, [79].

[42] *PP v Taw Cheng Kong* [1998] 2 SLR(R) 489, [89].

[43] LC Green, 'Native Law and the Common Law: Conflict or Harmony' (1970) 12 Mal L Rev 38, 59.

[44] ibid.

[45] MF Rutter, 'The Future of the Common Law' in *The Applicable Law in Singapore and Malaysia: A Guide to the Reception, Precedent and Sources of Law in the Republic of Singapore and Federation of Malaysia* (Malayan Law Journal, 1989) 575.

[46] Brian Z Tamanaha, 'The History and Elements of the Rule of Law' [2012] SJLS 232, 234.

[47] [1971–1973] SLR(R) 135.

[48] [1942] AC 206, 244.

in January 1989, limiting judicial review to procedural non-compliance, under section 8(2) ISA. Section 8B(1) enigmatically provided that the law governing judicial review under the ISA 'shall be the same as was applicable and declared in Singapore on the 13th day of July 1971', the date *Lee Mau Seng* was decided. Critics argued that the common law could not be frozen as it does not stand still. When these amendments were challenged, a chastened judiciary did not address this issue and evaded the question of whether the ISA ouster clause was contrary to the RoL. These ISA amendments normalised exceptional law authorising preventive detention, and were criticised as 'harkening back to sometime before King John issued the Magna Carta in the year 1215, which is to say the Middle Ages'[49] – a law dating beyond the colonial to the imperial era!

Before Parliament, Law Minister Jayakumar justified these amendments, opining that the CA in *Chng Suan Tze* had been unduly influenced by foreign cases decided by interventionist courts on security matters, and that Singapore could not be 'governed by cases decided abroad',[50] given the UK and Singapore's divergent socio-political and economic conditions. Matters pertaining to defence and security had to be 'interpreted by our own judges' aware of Singapore history and local conditions, not 'a body of UK judges sitting in the UK thousands of miles away', unfamiliar with 'our circumstances'.[51]

Subsequently, Singapore cut off ties with the Privy Council as the apex court in 1994, ostensibly because the 'safety net' it provided as a body immune from undue influence was no longer needed, as investors had sufficient confidence in the maturing Singapore legal system. A permanent Court of Appeal was established, issuing a Practice Statement on Judicial Precedents.[52] This set the tone for developing a legal system suited to social needs; seeking harmonisation with global best practices, commercial law precedents would be departed from 'sparingly', to safeguard legal certainty and predictability. However, there was no compelling imperative to follow English public law approaches, where the RoL operated within a liberal democratic setting. Instead, Singapore public law should give effect to 'the fundamental values of Singapore society'.

This inaugurated the 'second wave' of judicial review, under the steerage of second Chief Justice (CJ) Yong Pung How (1990–2006), distinct from the 'first wave' under Wee Chong Jin CJ (1963–90), where the Bench was 'well schooled in the English common law traditions' and made decisions 'against the backdrop of a system of parliamentary supremacy', discounting the supreme written constitution. Great deference was paid to parliamentary will and most decisions were 'workmanlike', being limited to the immediate dispute, rather than developing long-term principles. The 'second wave' was dominated by statist imperatives, utilitarianism and valorising efficiency over justice

[49] 'Medieval Singapore' *Wall Street Journal* (15 February 1989) 14.
[50] S Jayakumar, SPR, 25 January 1989, col 468.
[51] ibid cols 471–73.
[52] Issued 11 July 1994: (1994) 2 SLR 689.

and rights.[53] This severely diminished the potential for the courts to protect individual liberties or curb government excesses. However, the twenty-first century saw the advent of the 'third wave' of communitarian judicial review under the benches of Chief Justices Chan Sek Keong (2006–11) and Sundaresh Menon (2011–present). The attention turned to the intrinsic values of the law in balancing justice and efficiency, while according greater weight to collective interests than liberal democracies would. Singapore common law should be judicially developed 'for the common good';[54] the task was to 'build up a large body of local jurisprudence' so local decisions could be cited first before English decisions.[55] This would require 'a sustained intellectual effort by the courts'.[56]

Singapore courts have distinguished between English common law before and after it was influenced by European Court of Human Rights jurisprudence and altered 'in a liberal direction'[57] to weigh rights more heavily.[58] Developments relating to Europeanised English law, such as proportionality review,[59] have been rejected. This turn towards autochthony is also evident in administrative law.

Through judicial review, Singapore courts discharge their 'ultimate responsibility' to maintain an RoL-based system as 'the bedrock on which our society was founded on which it has thrived'.[60] However, the normative weight assigned to the RoL is shaped by local particularities, such as communitarian readings of liberties. The CA in *PP v Kwong Kok Hing* expressly identified 'communitarian values' as including the 'preservation of morality, the protection of the person, public peace and order, respect for institutions and the preservation of the state's wider interests'.[61] Official national ideology also favours communitarianism.[62] The courts, in developing 'an autochthonous or indigenous legal system',[63] havw not become insular or denied that universal values exist, such as the neighbour principle in tort law;[64] instead, a 'particularism without parochialism'[65] is

[53] Li-ann Thio, 'Principled Pragmatism and the "Third Wave" of Communitarian Judicial Review in Singapore' in Jaclyn Neo (ed), *Constitutional Interpretation in Singapore: Theory and Practice* (Routledge, 2016) 75–116.

[54] *Nguyen Tuong Van v PP* [2005] 1 SLR 103, [88].

[55] Supreme Court of Singapore, Practice Direction No 1 of 2008 (Citation of Judgements) [4].

[56] Chan Sek Keong CJ, Opening Address, 'Developments in Singapore Law 2006–2010', Singapore Academy of Law Conference 2011, 24 February 2011, [6].

[57] *AG v Wain (No 1)* [1991] SLR 373, 393F-G.

[58] See, eg *Yong Vui Kong v PP* [2010] 3 SLR 489, [61] (unlike various Caribbean states, the Singapore Bill of Rights was not modelled after the European Convention of Human Rights).

[59] *Chee Siok Chin v MHA* [2006] 1 SLR(R) 582, [87].

[60] *Tan Seet Eng v AG* [2016] 1 SLR 779, [1].

[61] [2008] 2 SLR(R) 684 (CA) [17].

[62] White Paper (n 17) [30].

[63] *Tang Kin Hwa v TCMPB* [2005] 4 SLR(R) 604, [27].

[64] *See Toh Siew Kee v Ho Ah Lam Ferrocement* [2013] 3 SLR 284, [22]–[24], finding this rooted in the Bible, the Confucian Gold Rule and the Kantian Categorical Imperative.

[65] Li-ann Thio (with David Chong SC), 'The Chan Court and Constitutional Adjudication: "A Sea Change into Something Rich and Strange"' in Chao Hick Tin et al (eds), *The Law in His Hands: A Tribute to CJ Chan Sek Keong* (Academy Press, 2012) 87–119.

evident in the regular consideration of international and comparative public law as a model, anti-model or inspiration in crafting novel solutions.[66]

The courts have identified their judicial role with the 'green light' theory.[67] In contrast, 'red light' English courts are more adversarial and interventionist in seeking to stop bad administrative practices through judicial review, which can spawn a legalistic, rights-based, merits-intrusive form of control. The 'green light' theory sees the courts and executive as partners in the collaborative enterprise of promoting good administrative practices, where law is seen more as a tool to facilitate governance, than to control government (see chapter five).[68]

The positive contribution of English law to Singapore law in relation to trade and commerce is valued. While the Singapore legal system seeks to achieve 'just and fair results' based on universalisable principles of logic and common sense,[69] the common law and RoL continue to acquire distinctive Singapore characteristics. This includes conceptualising mediation as an RoL value. Menon CJ considers "unduly"[70] restrictive' the view that adjudicative process is the essence of the RoL. He has extrajudicially championed a 'broader vision'[71] of the RoL suited to Singapore's 'socio-political and historical context'[72] and changing realities. Mediation, in promoting access to justice, was an 'essential ingredient'[73] of the RoL, whose 'normative content is capable of multiple incarnations', united by the 'ascendancy of law and of legal institutions in a system of governance'.[74] To adopt a 'more user-centric approach' towards dispute resolution, attention should be paid not only to adjudication,[75] but also to non-adjudicative processes. The latter, by promoting ideals like affordability, flexibility, accessibility and efficiency, served as a 'necessary complement' to more traditional RoL understandings.[76] Singapore has championed alternative international dispute resolution, particularly of mediation, which preserves harmonious business relationships, resonant with many Asian cultures. Nonetheless, this informal dispute resolution method is complemented by a mechanism to enforce mediated settlements in the Singapore Convention on Mediation.[77] This combination of diplomacy and

[66] eg how the UK test of responsible journalism for political libel might be locally adapted: *Review Publishing Co Ltd v Lee Hsien Loong* [2010] 1 SLR 52, [297].

[67] *Nagaenthran v AG* [2018] SGHC 112, [123].

[68] Chan Sek Keong, 'Judicial Review – From Angst to Empathy' (2010) 22 SAcLJ 469, 480.

[69] Phang, *From Foundation to Legacy* (n 5) [5].

[70] Chief Justice Sundaresh Menon, 'Mediation and the Rule of Law', Keynote address, The Law Society Mediation Forum, 10 March 2017, [14] at [2].

[71] ibid [3].

[72] ibid [5].

[73] ibid [3].

[74] ibid [11].

[75] Issues like litigation costs, technical formalities, delays, restricted court time and professional domination posed 'barriers to the individual user of the legal process'. ibid [14]–[15].

[76] ibid [1]–[15].

[77] 'Singapore Convention on Mediation to Come into Force on Sept 12' *Straits Times* (13 March 2020).

third-party dispute settlement seeks to uphold the international RoL through a rules-based international order.[78]

III. CONTEXTUALISING CONSTITUTIONALISM AND THE RULE OF LAW

A. Constitutional Text

Various constitutional provisions contour the RoL, as an implied fundamental norm. First, the Article 4 supremacy clause resonates with the Diceyan RoL understanding of the supremacy of law and 'predominance of regular law', over absolute power.[79] Second, Part IV safeguards fundamental liberties which, in limiting legislative power, has been described as 'the elevation of the RoL concept to its highest level'.[80] The Diceyan principle of subjecting all persons to the general law administered by ordinary law courts is entrenched in Article 93, which vests judicial power in the Supreme Court, and the Article 12 equality guarantee. Third, Article 149 demonstrates the RoL is not an absolute value, as it validates anti-subversion legislation which authorises exceptions to due process; Article 149(3) further immunises a law from judicial review challenges under Article 93. Fourth, the RoL virtue of generality of laws is qualified through Articles 152 and 153, providing for weak legal pluralism within a legally centrist strong state.

When Singapore was part of the Malaysian Federation, People's Action Party (PAP) leaders resisted the objective of a 'Malay Malaysia', where *bumiputera* (sons of the oil) received special privileges, as opposed to a 'Malaysian' Malaysia. At Independence, Singapore embraced a secular democratic identity, where no ethnic or religious group enjoyed privileged status, endorsing civic citizenship and a 'Singaporean Singapore'. Given geopolitical sensitivities, the minorities question demanded attention. Rather than recognising minority rights, Article 152(1) imposes a non-justiciable constitutional obligation mandating the government take constant care of the 'racial and religious minorities in Singapore'. Article 152(2) recognises the indigenous status of Malays and enjoins the government to promote and protect their political, educational, religious, economic, social, cultural and linguistic interests. Article 153 authorises the enactment of the Administration of Muslim Law Act (AMLA), which establishes an Islamic religious council, syariah courts and the limited application of Islamic law over personal law matters. The syariah courts only have jurisdiction over Muslims, and Muslims may resort to civil courts to resolve ancillary matters.

[78] Sundaresh Menon CJ, S Rajaratnam Lecture 2019, 'The Rule of Law, the International Legal Order and the Foreign Policy of Small States', 15 October 2019, https://mfa.gov.sg.

[79] AV Dicey, *An Introduction to the Study of the Constitution*, 7th edn (Macmillan, 1908) 198.

[80] Paul Kauper, 'The Supreme Court and the Rule of Law' (1961) 59 Mich L Rev 531, 531.

These provisions recognise the distinct identity of predominantly Muslim Malays,[81] and promotes inclusion by ensuring their treatment as equal citizens, who in fact enjoy certain privileges such as having an Islamic religious council and Muslim Affairs Minister to oversee matters like mosque-building programmes, *halal* certification and *haj* regulation. To accommodate the AMLA, reservations were made to treaties like the Convention for the Elimination of All Forms of Discrimination against Women (CEDAW) such that religious freedom prevailed over gender equality.[82] This is because Islam, contrary to the Women's Charter, permits polygamy and prohibits women from occupying certain religious offices, for example. While qualifying the generality of law, these minority protection provisions embody RoL values in ensuring racial and religious minorities 'are protected from the arbitrary whims of the majority'.[83]

B. Constitutional Context: Rule of Law and Legal Communitarianism in a Non-liberal Setting

Singapore political culture is generally non-liberal in orientation, with mixed statist, communitarian and liberal elements,[84] a free market managed economy committed to international trade and a distaste for social welfarism within an ethnically and religiously plural polity. In contrast, liberal forms of constitutionalism prioritise maximising individual autonomy, often through a rights-oriented court-centric constitutionalism. These favour strong checks against executive power, predicated on a 'liberalism of fear';[85] the state is allegedly 'neutral', but promotes a latent liberal theory of good, based on personal desire and individual choice,[86] made by rational actors.[87] This promotes Millian experiments in living and individualist, cosmopolitan values, downplaying local customs and communal bonds. Ironically, where yoked to progressivism, the 'liberal' state transformed into a powerful remoralised state with illiberal elements, opposing

[81] 98.8% of Malays are Muslim: 'More S'poreans Have No Religious Affiliation: Population Census' *Straits Times* (16 June 2021).

[82] Sixth Periodic Report: Singapore, CEDAW/C/SGP/6 (21 December 2021), [221]–[223].

[83] AG Lucien Wong, Speech, 'The Rule of Law and the Duty of the Legal Service', Opening of the Legal Year 2023, 9 January 2023, [12].

[84] Li-ann Thio, 'Constitutionalism in Illiberal Polities' in Andras Sajo and Michel Rosenfeld (eds), *Oxford Handbook on Comparative Constitutionalism* (Oxford University Press, 2012) 133–52; Graham Walker, 'The Idea of Nonliberal Constitutionalism' in Ian Shapiro and Will Kymlicka (eds), *Ethnicity and Group Rights* (NYU Press, 1977) 154–84.

[85] Judith Shklar, *Political Thought and Political Thinkers* (Stanley Hoffman ed, University of Chicago Press, 1998) 3.

[86] James Kalb, *Tyranny of Liberalism: Understanding and Overcoming Administered Freedom, Inquisitorial Tolerance and Equality by Command*, 2nd edn (Intercollegiate Studies Institute, 2008); Stephen Macedo, *Liberal Virtues: Citizenship, Virtue and Community in Liberal Constitutionalism* (Oxford University Press, 1990) ch 5.

[87] John Rawls, *A Theory of Justice* (Harvard University Press, 1971) 235–43 considers the legal order a set of public rules addressed to rational persons to whom it is impartially administered.

communal norms resistant to its own programme of control.[88] The PM has stated that Western liberal democracy is not 'the pinnacle of human achievement and the solution for the whole of the world'.[89]

The RoL in Singapore subsists within a non-liberal communitarian democracy,[90] where reasonably free periodic elections are held; a strong 'activist' government steers economic and human development. Tensions exist between the appreciated need for accountability mechanisms to check corruptible governors, and the politics of virtue or neo-Confucianist trust in governors;[91] the latter suits a 'deference' society which is waning in an increasingly post-deferential, repoliticised age.[92] The government actively articulates a vision of the common good and good citizenship.

Political constitutionalism,[93] which emphasises political checks on power, is a prominent feature, coexisting with legal processes like judicial review, associated with legal constitutionalism. In adjudicating rights, the courts are allergic to juristocratic impulses, and situate rights discourse in conversation with responsibilities and social harmony.

The role of the law transcends the 'command and control' model in preserving public order; it encompasses an educative and symbolic role which affirms common values, herds expectations and promotes conciliation where racial and religious disharmony incidents erupt. This serves the object of relational constitutionalism to maintain social cohesion through sustainable relationships. Maintaining racial and religious harmony (RRH) is a facet of public order transcending the absence of civil disorder; it speaks to a quality of relational

[88] Patrick Deene, *Why Liberalism Failed* (Yale University Press, 2018).

[89] PM Lee Hsien Loong's Interview with Frankfurter Allgemeine Zeitung (24 July 2009) www.pmo.gov.sg.

[90] Li-ann Thio, '"We Are Feeling Our Way Forward, Step by Step": The Continuing Singapore Experiment in the Construction of Communitarian Constitutionalism in the 21st Century's First Decade' in Albert Chen (ed), *Constitutionalism in Asia in the Early Twenty-First Century* (Cambridge University Press, 2014) 270–94.

[91] Trust may well be fraying, despite Singapore's consistently high global rankings in the Edelman Trust Barometer: 'Government Remains Most Trusted Institution in Singapore, Amid Global Trend of Societal Polarization: Survey' (Channel News Asia (CNA), 15 March 2023). The loss of moral authority and its corrosive effect on trust is evident from events in July 2023 impelling the PM to issue a ministerial statement concerning the adulterous affairs of PAP MPs, the investigation of the Transport Minister for corruption and the investigation of two ministers, later cleared, of allegedly receiving preferential rental rates for state-owned heritage bungalows: 'PM Lee's Ministerial Statement on CORRUPTION PROBE INVOLVING ISWARAN and MPs' Resignations over Affair' (*CNA.com*, 2 August 2023); 'Ridout Road Debate a Reminder that Public Perception Matters' (*CNA.com*, 5 July 2023). Further, the government's investment arm made substantial investment losses: 'Temasek's "Disappointing" $377 Million Loss in FTX Caused Reputational Damage, Says Lawrence Wong' (*Asiaone*, 30 November 2022).

[92] This stems from the loss of a Group Representation Constituency (GRC) for the first time since its introduction in 1988, in the 2011 General Elections, with the PAP winning 81 of 90 elective seats. In the 2020 General Elections, the opposition won two GRCs, with the Worker's Party (WP) securing nine of 92 elective seats.

[93] Marco Goldoni and Christopher McCorkindale, 'Political Constitutionalism' in *Encyclopedia of the Philosophy of Law and Social Philosophy* (Springer, 2018) 1–8.

well-being between distinct religious and ethnic communities, a vision of covenantal community beyond transactional coexistence.[94] In this respect, liberal legalism, which focuses on rights and legal sanction, is inapt in repairing relational breaches; instead, we see the rule of *soft* constitutional law,[95] which support RoL values insofar as these hortatory norms, found in executive-authored white papers or declarations, have some legal effect and provide guidance on socially desirable behaviour (see chapter two).

Within a dominant party state, the *existence* of constraints does not denote their efficacy. Rule-following is a foregone conclusion, which may sustain a culture of bare legality, with weak formal checks and the default position being 'ownself check ownself'.[96]

C. Rule of Law and Paternal Democracy: Between Thick and Thin?

Where the RoL is praised, this primarily relates to maintaining security and strong private law protection of commercial and property rights, which is global capital's primary concern. This can be secured by adherence to a thin, formal RoL or 'rule by law'.[97] The RoL is hailed as an intangible 'economic asset', yielding 'good returns from the MNCs … the banks, the financial institutions and the flood of capital to buy up properties in Singapore'.[98] RoL related criticism is directed at Singapore's 'public law record'[99] in terms of insufficient rights protection or lack of robust separation of powers. The metric deployed is predicated on a liberal, substantive RoL conception.

Decoupled from Anglo-American style limited government and individual rights guarantees after Lockean liberalism, there is always a danger that the RoL may devolve into an authoritarian apology for power, where law does not limit but serves the interests of state elites, in the name of the collective. This perpetuates a politically hegemonic status quo, where punctilious observance of legal procedure 'occludes erasure of rights in legal substance'.[100]

[94] Li-ann Thio, 'Relational Constitutionalism and the Management of Inter-religious Disputes: The Singapore "Secularism with a Soul" Model' (2012) 2 OJLR 446.

[95] Li-ann Thio, 'Soft Constitutional Law in Non-liberal Asian Constitutional Democracies' (2010) 8 ICON 766; Stephen Daly, 'The Rule of (Soft) Law' (2021) 32(1) King's Law Journal 3.

[96] Term coined by WP MP Pritam Singh, referring to a situation where the ruling party is its own check. The government has spun this as a virtue: Ong Ye Kung, '"Ownself check ownself" Is a Virtue, S'pore in Trouble if Govt Can't Ensure Public Accountability' *Today* (13 January 2022).

[97] Gordon Silverstein, 'Singapore: The Exception that Provides Rules Matter' in Tom Ginsburg and Tamir Moustafa (eds), *Rule by Law: The Politics of Courts in Authoritarian Regimes* (Cambridge University Press, 2008) 73–101.

[98] Lee Kuan Yew, 'Independence and Integrity of Singapore's Judiciary', 65 SPR, 11 February 1995, cols 223, 236.

[99] Observations of Kevin Tan, 'Is S'pore Legal System Getting a Bad Name?' *Straits Times* (25 October 1997).

[100] Jothie Rajah, 'Punishing Bodies, Securing the Nation: How Rule of Law Can Legitimate the Urbane Authoritarian State' (2011) 36(4) LSI 945, 946.

The government unapologetically accords paramountcy to security and public order, particularly in the early days of nation-building, facing communist insurgency and communal riots. The focus was not on 'the greatness or grandeur' of ideal legal concepts, but on pragmatically delivering results producing 'order and justice' in social relationships.[101] Today, the RoL's strong law and order component is celebrated for sustaining a 'low crime rate'[102] and public safety, facilitated by popular support for the death penalty[103] and corporal punishment to handle serious crimes like drug-trafficking and firearm offences.

Sited along the spectrum bookended by liberal individualism and illiberal statism, the RoL in Singapore may occupy a non-liberal third space, in the practice of legal communitarianism, whose normative orientation elevates community interests above the self, where rights are balanced against 'moral and social obligations'.[104] This emphasises the instrumental role of law in securing governance, which upholds a culture of authority, while appreciating the role of rules, penalties and adjudication in sustaining a culture of legality.

A commitment to 'communitarianism as solidarity' may be an authentic expression of a socio-political culture where shared public norms are developed by consultation and consensus-seeking. In terms of governance styles and the evolving governor–governed relationship, the descriptor 'paternal democracy' captures the shift from barking diktats to seeking dialogue. While 'paternal' is a relational term, 'paternalistic' is a 'father knows best' mindset or ideology.

While PM LKY was a 'Stern Father' during the early developmentalist phase, PM Goh Chok Tong saw himself as the 'Elder Brother' tasked with persuading Singaporeans to accept the family's house rules.[105] PM Lee Hsien Loong was a quiet reformer, firm but admonishing his MPs to discard a feudal overlord mentality[106] and be public servant-leaders.[107] Following this, MPs urged their residents not to greet them deferentially with lion dances, garlands or excessive fanfare.

In the 1990s, ministers admonished Singaporeans not to adopt an attitude of '*boh tua boh sway*' (no big no small) in public debate, but to treat government leaders as the senior party.[108] By 2024, when PM Lee left office, the ethos was more egalitarian, framed in terms of 平起平坐 (*pinquipingzuo* – to be on an equal footing), of speaking to another with mutual respect, as equals.[109]

[101] Lee Kuan Yew, Speech, University of Singapore Law Society Annual Dinner (n 18).
[102] DPM Jayakumar, Keynote Address, IBA Rule of Law Symposium, 19 October 2007, [25], www.mlaw.gov.sg.
[103] 'Strong, Growing Support for Death Penalty Reflected in Surveys of Singapore, Neighbouring Countries: Shanmugam' *Today* (8 May 2024).
[104] *Taw Cheng Kong v PP* [1998] 1 SLR(R) 78, [54].
[105] 'PM Goh on His Role as Elder Brother' *Straits Times* (20 October 1994).
[106] 'MPs Tell Residents: No Need to Stand, Clap for Us' (*Yahoo News*, 19 June 2011).
[107] PM Lee, Letter to MPs on Rules of Prudence, 28 May 2011.
[108] 'Debate Yes, but Do Not Take on Those in Authority as "Equals"' *Straits Times* (20 February 1995) 19. Minister George Yeo stated that one must remember one's place in society before engaging in public debate. Yeo was voted out in the 2011 General Elections.
[109] PM Lee Hsien Loong, May Day Rally, 1 May 2024.

This idea of an evolving governor–governed relationship was baked into the 'trade-off' model of law and development associated with the 1990s Asian values debate: strict control of civil-political rights and social discipline was initially necessary to secure the political stability needed to attract trade and foreign investment. Once economic development was achieved, it was understood that political liberalisation would ensue, with an educated electorate demanding viewpoint diversity and robust political debate. Holding 'national conversations'[110] is now the norm, denoting an incipient culture of justification. However, political liberalisation is not a linear process, and 'communitarianism as muscular majoritarianism' may be invoked regressively to advance state-defined collective interests in authoritarian fashion, pressuring a minority group. This was evident during the COVID-19 pandemic years, where harsh discriminatory measures were imposed against the unvaccinated minority, who were demonised as 'free-riders', impeding the interests of the overwhelmingly vaccinated majority.[111]

Context must be borne in mind in examining the state of the RoL in Singapore, such as whether the field of inquiry is in public or private law. The RoL's paradoxical quality in both bolstering and restraining state power must be appreciated; attention should be paid to indigenised elements such as hitching the RoL to the project of maintaining RRH and associating access to justice with mediation.[112] Given that the politico-legal culture is in flux, and that the RoL is 'an ever-evolving configuration of structures, social attitudes and traditions',[113] a temporal element is worth noting in considering whether the critiques made in the twentieth century that the 'RoL' was mere autocratic legalism, more akin to the 'rule of Lee',[114] still hold (equal) force in the twenty-first century.

D. The Official Government Rule of Law Narrative

(i) Rule of Law: As Restraint on Government and as a Tool of Effective Governance

The features of the 'RoL with Singapore characteristics' may be discerned through examining ministerial and extrajudicial speeches. Since Independence, the emphasis has rested on maintaining a strong law-and-order model, where the RoL took centre stage as an effective tool of governance to deal with security

[110] 'Our Singapore Conversation Themes Identified, Dialogue to Continue' *Today* (15 July 2013).

[111] Li-ann Thio, 'Legal Communitarianism and Pandemic Regulation in Singapore' in Stefan Braum (ed), *Experimental Law: The Rule of Law and the Regulation of the Corona Pandemic in Europe*, Luxembourg Legal Studies (NOMOS 2023) 388–91.

[112] The 2021 Rules of Court empower court to order parties to attempt mediation for complex cases: Order 5, rule 3(1).

[113] VK Rajah, 'Panel Discussion: Measuring the Rule of Law' [2012] SJLS 331, 331.

[114] Attributed to exiled former Solicitor-General Francis Seow: 'Parliament to Debate Chee Soon Juan Issue' *Straits Times* (30 October 1995) 1.

threats and the economic development imperative in the face of high unemployment and homelessness, rather than as a restraint on government. This was driven by the fear of chaos, for 'if the state disintegrates, then the rules of all laws must vanish'.[115] Colonial-era preventive detention laws were retained and applied to new threats like terrorism, itself 'a flagrant disregard'[116] of the RoL.

Centralising state power was integral to maintaining the strong state able to govern without institutional gridlock or confrontational politics. Trade unions were leashed through Tripartism, under which unions, employers and the government collaborate to promote workers' interests. While authorised strikes are legal, they are rare,[117] and harmonious labour–management relations are projected as a competitive economic advantage.

To some, like founding father PM LKY, the RoL was more important than democracy in sustaining a free market and foreign investment; it is a key pillar in Singapore's development narrative, emerging from 'third world to first',[118] from 'mudflat' to 'metropolis'[119] within a generation. While the GDP per capita was US$500 in 1965, it had risen to US$50,000 by 2011.[120] In 2024, it rose still further to $88,000,[121] with Singapore becoming the world's fourth wealthiest city.[122]

An attitude of pragmatic realism which adapts forms and principles to suit 'our given sociological and economic milieu'[123] is evident in Lee's declaration that he focused on producing results, not theoretical prescriptions: 'social peace and stability within the country, no fight between the races, between religions, fair shares for all, everybody is a homeowner'.[124] Buoyed by performance legitimacy and a proven economic success track record, Lee declared that RoL was not an 'empty slogan'.[125] A global financial hub with respected courts upholding the commercial RoL, low corruption and generally strong economic growth has cemented the social compact with 'We the Economic Beneficiaries', based on fairness and meritocracy. Although Singapore has attracted 'considerable criticism' for not conforming to 'some of the conventional thinking' of what the RoL requires in relation to civil-political rights and political accountability, the Law Minister asserted that 'our approach is defensible'.[126]

[115] Lee Kuan Yew, Speech, University of Singapore Law Society Annual Dinner (n 18).

[116] ibid [30].

[117] 'Explainer: What Is the Role of Unions in Singapore, and Are Strikes Legal?' *Today* (31 July 2020); Anthony Woodiwiss, *Globalisation, Human Rights and Labour Law in Pacific Asia* (Cambridge University Press, 1998) ch 6.

[118] Lee Kuan Yew, *From Third World to First: The Singapore Story: 1965–2000* (Harper, 2000).

[119] Lee Kuan Yew, Speech, Sree Narayana Mission, 12 September 1965, www.nas.gov.sg.

[120] K Shanmugam, 'The Rule of Law in Singapore' [2012] SJLS 357, 358.

[121] 'Singapore Has Achieved Astonishing Economic Success' *The Economist* (8 May 2024).

[122] 'Singapore is World's 4th Wealthiest City, Overtaking London: Report' *Straits Times* (7 May 2024).

[123] Lee Kuan Yew, Speech, University of Singapore Law Society Annual Dinner (n 18).

[124] 'No Prescription Needed: MM' *Straits Times* (23 September 2008).

[125] Lee Kuan Yew, 'Speech, Opening of the Singapore Law Academy' (n 13).

[126] Lee Kuan Yew, Speech, Sree Narayana Mission (n 119) 360.

(ii) Minimum Core and a Thick Cultural Overlay

Government ministers have generally given a formal RoL account:

> [T]he Rule of Law refers to the supremacy of law, as opposed to the arbitrary exercise of power. The other key tenet is that everyone is equal before the law. The concept also includes the notions of the transparency, openness and prospective application of our laws, observations of the principles of natural justice, independence of the Judiciary and judicial review of administrative action.[127]

Project Singapore is built on the idea of the RoL, which is 'central to our ideas of fairness, equality and justice', having cultivated 'a society based on equality and racial harmony'[128] which avoids Chinese majority chauvinism and protects racial and religious minorities. Singapore would 'lose its cohesion' if a significant section of society believed the system privileged the economic elite and no longer provided 'equal opportunities'.[129] The RoL means that no one is above the law,[130] that 'individuals can get redress for their grievances', including against 'persons in high position, or the Government',[131] through impartial courts, without undue impediment.[132] The High Court's acquittal of Parti Liyani, a foreign domestic worker accused by her wealthy employer of theft, was held up as illustrating 'how the RoL applies' irrespective of 'what the parties are'. Where power is abused, 'swift decisive action' follows.[133] During the COVID-19 pandemic, trust was sustained by ensuring the mask-wearing rule applied to all, upholding the RoL virtue of equality, whether minister or road sweeper.[134] Foreign leaders exposed for not wearing masks were cast as anti-models.[135]

RoL virtues support 'a transparent and rational business environment' where confidence in law enforcement and protecting commercial rights provides 'the foundation for our economic and social development'.[136] In later incarnations, the RoL entailed 'upholding individual rights' while 'carefully balancing them

[127] PK Ho (Law Minister of State), 'Rule of Law' motion, 71 SPR, 24 November 1999, cols 569, 592.

[128] Law Minister K Shanmugam, New York State Bar Association Rule of Law Plenary Session, 28 October 2009, mlaw.gov.sg.

[129] 'Why Singapore Insists on Equality before the Law: Shanmugam' *Straits Times* (6 November 2020).

[130] AV Dicey, *Introduction to the Study of the Law of the Constitution*, 8th edn (Macmillan, 1915) 114.

[131] PM Lee Hsien Loong, 150th Anniversary of the AGC, 31 March 2017, www.pmo.gov.sg/Newsroom/pm-lee-hsien-loong-150th-anniversary-attorney-generals-chambers.

[132] AG VK Rajah, Opening of the Legal Year, 5 January 2015, [5].

[133] Ministerial Statement, Review of the Case of *Parti Liyani v PP* (2020) Part 2, [11]–[21], 4 November 2010, www.gov.sg.

[134] Lee Hsien Loong (Secretary General), Speech, PAP Convention, 28 November 2021, para 17, www.pap.org.sg.

[135] eg 'Boris Johnson's Lockdown Partygate' *The New Yorker* (11 January 2022; 'Biden, Other Politicians Chided for Lapses in Mask Protocols' *Las Vegas Review Journal* (28 October 2021). In contrast, Singapore's PM wore two masks in public: 'PM Lee Seen Wearing 2 Masks at Jakarta ASEAN Summit' (*sporeuncensored.com*, 25 April 2021).

[136] Chief Justice PH Yong, President, Legal Services Commission, 1st Singapore Legal Service Annual Dinner, 6 April 2001.

against society's need to maintain law and order, fostering harmony and social cohesion among people of diverse races and religions'.[137] The central judicial role in upholding RoL by 'ensuring legality and defending rights'[138] is recognised; however, the RoL does not 'spell out what this balance must be',[139] what metric to apply in weighing rights claims, which contextual factors will shape.

The RoL is thickened up by two framing factors in structuring 'a modern civilised society'.[140] First, the people have 'the sovereign right to elect their Government'; the health of the RoL is maintained by government accountability at elections. As the 'normal product' of the legislative branch which is 'most responsive to the people',[141] the general rule of law has 'special claim to preference', which the government follows and amends, pursuant to its democratic mandate.

Second, laws 'must not offend that society's norms of fairness and justice'. The government actively seeks to cultivate in citizens moral solidarity and a common identity, as 'governance subject to laws that resonate with society's values nurtures community cohesion'[142] and expectations of safety and security. Fairness 'implies moderation and proportionality in the content and enforcement of our laws'.[143] Beyond the legal framework, an RoL culture needs to be 'actively nurtured and fostered'.[144] Law has an educative role[145] and a signalling function in supporting social values, even when perfect enforcement is impossible or difficult. For example, the government banned a limited number of internet sites promoting pornography or adultery as a symbolic statement of content 'which the community is opposed to'.[146] Given the primacy of RRH as part of 'public order', certain offences under the Maintenance of Religious Harmony Act (MRHA) were given extraterritorial effect, despite enforcement difficulties, as this 'signals our commitment to protect our religious harmony, even when threats originate beyond our shores'.[147] Law also has a role in securing RRH by promoting conciliation under an MRHA mechanism, discussed in chapter two.

[137] PM Lee Hsien Loong (n 131).

[138] Sundaresh Menon, 'The Rule of Law: The Path to Exceptionalism' (2016) 28 SAcLJ 413, 417 [15].

[139] S Jayakumar, 'Applying the Rule of Law' (2009) 43(1) The International Lawyer 83, 84.

[140] PK Ho (n 127) [7].

[141] Antonin Scalia, 'The Rule of Law as a Law of Rules (1989) 56(4) University of Chicago LR 1175, 1176.

[142] Menon, 'The Rule of Law (n 138) 86.

[143] PM Lee Hsien Loong (n 131).

[144] Lee Kuan Yew, Speech, University of Singapore Law Society Annual Dinner (n 18) [23].

[145] Brian Buti-Hendrix, 'The Educative Function of Law' in Michael Freeman and Ross Harrison (eds), *Law and Philosophy* (Oxford University Press, 2007) 243.

[146] Lui Tuck Yew (Minister for Information, Communications, Arts), 'Blocking Pornographic Sites (Review of Policy)', 87 SPR, 11 January 2011, cols 2174–77; 'Registration of Extramarital Dating Website in Singapore', 90 SPR, 11 November 2013; 'Promotion of Pro-Marriage Values', 90 SPR, 11 November 2013.

[147] Sun Xueling, Senior Parliamentary Secretary MHA and MND, Second Reading, MRHA [Amendment] Bill, 7 October 2019, www.mha.gov.sg.

In its commitment to secular democracy within a multi-religious plural society where different communities hold deep moral values based on religious or irreligious grounds, the RoL as the rule of secular general law is integral to the social solidarity project. While respecting religious identity and religious freedom guarantees, the RoL has an integrative role to play in establishing 'common ground rules of engagement and conflict resolution' and securing a 'large common secular space' for citizen interaction.[148]

A third aspect of the cultural overlay is an 'emphasis on *communitarian* over individualist values'. This includes values like 'dialogue, tolerance, compromise and placing the community above self',[149] which have modulated how the courts approach the RoL. Neo-Confucian ideals also inform the political culture, such as by promoting the rule of elected governors, who, as 'honourable men 君子' (*junzi*), are duty bound to 'do right for the people' and whom the people trust and respect. This is distinct from the 'Western idea of distrusting governors' and giving them limited powers.[150] Considerations of honour have impelled the resignations of politicians committing adultery, and also influence higher awards for political defamation (see chapter six).

IV. CONCLUSION

The official RoL narrative in Singapore thus encompasses the elements of a formal RoL, thickened by values derived from non-liberal, communitarian democracy. It is qualified by necessity and local particularities, and coexists with the idea of a strong state run by elected governors who are presumptively trusted, in tension with the need to hold public power to account.

[148] Lee Kuan Yew, Speech, University of Singapore Law Society Annual Dinner (n 18) [17]–[19].
[149] Menon, 'The Rule of Law (n 138) [24].
[150] White Paper (n 17) [41].

2

Rule of Law, the Constitutional Order and Institutions

I. INTRODUCTION

THE RULE OF law (RoL) and constitutionalism are ideas concerned with channelling and limiting public power to secure the common good and fundamental rights. While the RoL articulates standards of constitutional government, constitutionalism 'usually refers to various constitutional devices and procedures' to realise these standards and values,[1] resisting arbitrary rule. Other items in the constitutional toolbox include the separation of powers (SoP) and democracy, which interact with the RoL in both its Lockean and Hobbesian incarnations; the former emphasises rule by limited government and the latter, rule by an empowered sovereign government.[2]

This chapter examines how the RoL as a legal principle shapes and is reinforced by the Singapore constitutional architecture. Constitutional law must prevail against inconsistent legislation for the RoL to be respected and realised.[3] Constitutional supremacy is key to ensuring that constitutional institutions are 'governed by the RoL', constitutional purposes are secured and fundamental liberties are guaranteed.[4]

In designing institutions, attention must be paid to how public power is distributed to ensure rules are conducive to enacting general laws beneficial to the common good. RoL values like transparency are promoted through public debate and the promulgation of prospective,[5] clear and accessible legislation able to guide individual conduct. Accountability is served through coordinating enforcement action through legal and political checks to ensure public officials do not transgress their powers.

[1] CL Ten, 'Constitutionalism and the Rule of Law' in Robert E Goodin, Philip Pettit and Thomas Pogge (eds), *A Companion to Contemporary Political Philosophy* (Blackwell Publishing, 1993) 493.

[2] Gabor Toth, 'Illiberal Rule of Law? Changing Features of Hungarian Constitutionalism' in Maurice Adams et al (eds), *Constitutionalism and the Rule of Law* (Cambridge University Press, 2017) 389.

[3] Singapore Constitution, Art 4.

[4] *Tan Eng Hong v AG* [2012] 4 SLR 476, [60].

[5] Art 11 prohibits retrospective criminal laws.

Part II of this chapter examines whether the Constitution provides effective safeguards for an independent judiciary as a functional RoL component to ensure adjudication is based on law, not political influences. Part III discusses the evolution of parliamentary institutions and the electoral system, and whether this has secured constitutional government that goes beyond majoritarian rule, curbing populist, Chinese chauvinism.[6] Part IV considers the introduction of autochthonous institutions such as the elected presidency (EP), with veto powers over primarily fiscal matters, to curb the Cabinet's untrammelled powers. This is an expression of intra-branch SoP and is bent towards political constitutionalism, where non-legal checks are meant to control aspects of executive power; whether this is an effective constraint is evaluated. Part V considers key constitutional provisions which represent an exception to or moderate the RoL by ousting review or signalling judicial restraint over matters meant primarily for political management. In particular, clauses relating to the authorisation of anti-subversion legislation (Article 149 of the Constitution) and the definition of marriage (Article 156). Part VI reflects on the brand of 'mixed' Singapore constitutionalism.

Two preliminary points merit mention. First, Singapore has experienced a long, uninterrupted period of political stability with no political turnover since Independence. This has enabled the ruling People's Action Party (PAP) government, within a dominant party state, to engage in long-term planning spanning generations and to follow this through effectively.[7] As the PAP easily commands the two-thirds parliamentary majority needed to effect constitutional amendments, this facilitated a spate of constitutional experimentation producing an ever-evolving hybrid of constrained parliamentarianism.[8]

Second, legally trained Prime Minister Lee Kuan Yew (PM LKY), as the chief founding father, formulated Singapore 'with precise portions of Plato's Republic, Anglophile elitism, unwavering economic pragmatism, and old-fashioned strong-arm repression'.[9] Despite LKY's charismatic authority sustaining rule by the virtuous wise, this was moderated by majoritarian democracy, supporting a form of legal-rational authority predicated on electoral success. Democratic legitimacy undergirds the PAP's broad popularity, and what it characterises as a 'high trust society'[10] in both vertical (the government and people) and horizontal (where the people trust each other 'regardless of race, language or religion'[11]) dimensions. The higher the trust, the greater the disposition to place the Hobbesian RoL, with its capacity for authoritarian rule, ahead of the Lockean RoL.

[6] The Chinese constitute 74.3% of the population, the other main groups being Malays (13.5%), Indians (9%) and Others (3.2%): Department of Statistics Singapore, Key findings, singstat.gov.sg.

[7] Message, Secretary-General Lee Hsien Loong, 1 July 2020, pap.org.sg.

[8] As of 2023, there have been 62 constitutional amendments acts after Independence.

[9] Mark Jacobson, 'The Singapore Solution', *National Geographic* (January 2010).

[10] PM Lee Hsien Loong, National Day Rally Speech, 20 August 2023, www.pmo.gov.sg.

[11] National Heritage Board, 'National Pledge', www.nhb.gov.sg.

II. THE JUDICIARY AND THE RULE OF LAW

An independent judiciary maintains the RoL by policing the legal limits of public power. This is particularly important in Westminster parliamentary government models, given the 'near complete fusion' between the Cabinet and the legislature, which it controls through the party whip.[12] This may produce an 'elective dictatorship',[13] where the parliamentary executive agenda is resisted only by the minority parliamentary opposition. This system is centred on political constitutionalism, ie political checks and balances.

Lord Diplock deemed it 'crucial' that the judicial branch should have 'exclusive power to interpret all written law' and 'to declare the unwritten common law and rules of equity'.[14] The Court of Appeal (CA) affirmed this nod to legal constitutionalism, as judges bear the 'ultimate responsibility' of ensuring 'a system which abides by the RoL',[15] for which the judiciary must not be handmaiden to powerful political actors.

A. Judicial Independence: Personal and Corporate

To that end, Part 8 of the Constitution contains safeguards applicable only to Supreme Court judges. Judges, who wield neither sword nor purse, must be able to operate 'free from fear',[16] and be seen to resolve disputes fairly and effectively as impartial arbiters, to earn legitimacy and public confidence in the courts as 'reliable truth-finders seeking to do justice according to law'.

Confidence in the judiciary can be undermined by both a subservient judiciary and a hubristic one where judges champion their political preferences;[17] thus, 'judicial modesty' must unite with 'judicial courage' in service of the RoL,[18] which underwrites the legitimacy of political institutions. Judges must make independent decisions, 'irrespective of what their fellow judges think',[19] and not succumb to 'group-think' when part of a panel, evidenced by separate concurring or dissenting opinions. Although rare before the twenty-first century,[20] the number of separate judgments is now steadily increasing.[21]

[12] Walter Bagehot, *The English Constitution*, 2nd edn (1894) [11].
[13] Lord Hailsham, *Elective Dictatorship*, Dimbleby Lectures (BBC, 1976).
[14] Lord Diplock, 'Judicial Control of Government' [1979] Mal LJ cvl, cxlii.
[15] *Tan Seet Eng v AG* [2015] SGCA 59, [1].
[16] See judicial oath, Constitution, First Schedule.
[17] If political ideology dominates adjudication, a judge is either a hero or a villain, depending on which political constituency the decision appeals to: Michael J Klarman, 'What's So Great About Constitutionalism' (1998) 93 NULR 145, 146–88.
[18] *Tan Seet Eng* (n 15) [94], quoting Lord Diplock (n 14) cxlvii.
[19] Chan Sek Keong, 'Securing and Maintaining the Independence of the Court in Judicial Proceedings' (2010) 22 SAcLJ 229, [30].
[20] Li-ann Thio, '*Lex Rex or Rex Lex*: Competing Conceptions of the Rule of Law in Singapore' (2002) 20 UCLAPBLJ 1, 18, fn 89.
[21] Lau Kwan Ho, 'A Study in Separate Judgments' in Goh Yihan and Paul Tan (eds), *Singapore Law: 50 Years in the Making* (Academy Publishing, 2015) 4.22–4.23, 4.70–4.88.

Singapore courts have won international accolades[22] for robustly securing property and contract rights, but have attracted criticism for not protecting fundamental liberties in the fashion of a liberal state. However, government action may be challenged through judicial review and the courts have ruled against government interests occasionally, though not as frequently as within liberal democracies. Within a non-liberal democratic setting, the courts have to some extent become sites of political resistance, insofar as a decade's worth of unsuccessful litigation was brought to overturn laws such as anti-sodomy legislation. Eventually, the government yielded to the pressure of sustained activism and repealed the law in 2022, while simultaneously appeasing social conservative concerns by staving off potential equality-based attacks against traditional marriage through adopting Article 156, explored below.

While formal safeguards provide judges with some insulation from public or private pressures, this may not suffice, particularly where judicial review is a weak check against authoritarian government.[23] Further, the personal and corporate independence of judges rest not only on competence and moral fortitude, but also on judicial culture, with the Chief Justice providing 'moral leadership'.[24] Thus, interrogating judicial independence within a non-liberal setting like Singapore should encompass examining whether judicial reasoning manifests excessive judicial deference evident in statist legalism or utilitarian ideology (conflating government and public interest), or whether courts have developed calibrated review which preserves the RoL by policing unlawful action and protecting rights without necessarily adhering to liberal values (see chapters five and six).

B. Constitutional Safeguards and the Judicial Code of Conduct

The political branches are involved in appointing Supreme Court judges, where the President, acting in his personal discretion, concurs with the PM, under Article 95(1). The PM must consult the Chief Justice before advising on judicial appointments,[25] and no public hearings are held, though the Chief Justice consults the profession; the 'general public perception' is that appointments are merit-based.[26] Judges enjoy tenure until the mandatory retirement age of 65,[27]

[22] Singapore topped the Heritage Foundation's 2021 Index of Economic Freedom for judicial effectiveness (www.heritage.org). The World Economic Forum's 2019 Global Competitive Index ranked Singapore first for efficient dispute settlement and 14th of 141 for judicial independence: 'Singapore Crowned World's Most Open and Competitive Economy' (WEF, 11 October 2019) www.weforum.org.

[23] The political-judicial accommodation of each country lies on a spectrum ranging from 'a completely unfettered judiciary to one that is completely subservient': J Cohen, 'The Chinese Communist Party and "Judicial Independence": 1949–1959' (1969) 82(5) Harv L Rev 967, 972.

[24] Chan Sek Keong, 'Securing and Maintaining the Independence' (n 19) [13].

[25] Art 95(6).

[26] Kevin YL Tan, 'As Efficient as the Best Businesses: Singapore's Judicial System' in JY Yeh and WC Chang (eds), *Asian Courts in Context* (Cambridge University Press, 2014) 234.

[27] Art 98(1A).

so they cannot be 'displaced should they make inconvenient decisions'.[28] Their remuneration and terms of office may not be disadvantageously altered after appointment.[29] Judges acting in their judicial capacity enjoy immunity from lawsuits;[30] Singapore judges are amongst the highest paid in terms of remuneration and benefits in the world today,[31] minimising corruption's lure. The strict anti-corruption stance as part of the 'Singapore psyche'[32] has been globally celebrated,[33] as this assault on equality and meritocracy was 'anathema to the RoL'.[34] Today, it is inconceivable to think of bribing a Singapore judge.[35] In recognising the role judges play in economic development as one of the world's 'best and most efficient' judiciary,[36] judges received a GDP bonus if the growth rate is more than two per cent.[37]

To protect judges who by convention in common law jurisdictions do not respond when they receive criticism, Parliament may not discuss a judge's conduct except on a substantive motion supported by 25% of all MPs.[38] The political executive cannot singlehandedly remove a judge; instead, either the PM or the Chief Justice after consulting the PM may make representations to the President, who may appoint a five-person peer tribunal the Chief Justice presides over, comprising other former or present Supreme Court judges, and possibly including an equivalent Commonwealth judge.[39]

There are concerns over provisions made for appointing non-tenured judges, in the form of contract judges and judicial commissioners (JCs), introduced by constitutional amendments in 1970 and 1979 respectively. Under Article 95(2), a former Supreme Court judge above 65 may be reappointed 'for a specified period' on a contractual basis, ie as a 'supernumerary' judge, to retain the experience of judges fit and willing to serve.[40] The JC scheme facilitated

[28] Sundaresh Menon CJ, 'The Rule of Law and the SICC', Singapore International Chamber of Commerce Distinguished Speaker Series (10 January 2018).

[29] Art 98(8).

[30] Supreme Court of Judicature Act (SCJA), s 79; State Court Act (SCA), s 68.

[31] This is regulated by the Judges Remuneration Act (1994, 2020 rev edn). Under the Judges Remuneration (Annual Pensionable Salary) Order (1 September 1994), the follow annual pensionable salaries are paid (SGD): Chief Justice ($347,400), Justice of the Court of Appeal ($253,200), Judge of Appellate Division ($244,200), Judge of the High Court ($234,600); Tan, 'As Efficient as the Best Businesses' (n 26) 233. Salaries were revised in 2022: '5–12% Pay Jump for Administrative Service Officers, Judicial and Statutory Appointment Holders from Oct: PSD' *Today* (12 September 2022).

[32] Sundaresh Menon, 'Inspiring Confidence in the Courts through Independence, Integrity and Competence', 5th Roundtable Meeting of the Asia-Pacific Judicial Reform Forum, Singapore, 31 October 2013, [25].

[33] 'IMF Chief Cites Lee Kuan Yew's "Zero Tolerance" Stance Towards Corruption as Example for Rest of World' *Today* (12 May 2016). See also 'Annex B: Singapore's Social and Economic Indicators', www.mlaw.gov.sg/files/news/others/2017/04/AnnexB-Rankings.pdf.

[34] Menon, 'The Rule of Law' (n 28) [21].

[35] ibid.

[36] Tan, 'As Efficient as the Best Businesses' (n 26) 262.

[37] Chan Sek Keong, 'Securing and Maintaining the Independence' (n 19) 238, fn 24.

[38] Art 99.

[39] Art 98(4).

[40] EW Barker (Law Minister), Constitution (Amendment) Bill, 29 SPR, 16 June 1969 cols 60ff.

appointments ranging from six months to three years;[41] the original rationale was to overcome the difficulty of attracting senior legal talent to the Bench, given the earnings disparity with top private sector legal practitioners, to assess a JC for suitability on the Bench and to help clear case backlogs. The judicial commissionership may be a prelude to full judgeship, or the JC can return to practice. This attracts concern that these judges without tenure may be induced not to render decisions disquieting to the government. Even perceptions of this state of affairs may be deleterious.

Subsequent amendments have provided under Article 95(4) that to facilitate the disposal of Supreme Court business, the President, concurring with the PM's advice, could appoint a JC, a senior judge (a person who has ceased to be a Supreme Court judge) or an international judge (a non-national who sits on the Singapore International Commercial Court (SICC), launched in 2015)[42] for a specific period, to hear a single case.[43] The Chief Justice may appoint a senior or international judge to hear a specific case or class of cases and the legislature may limit the classes of cases the latter may hear.[44] As of May 2024, the Supreme Court consists of 35 judges.[45]

Non-tenured judges lack security of tenure, which remains 'a challenge to full judicial independence', even absent concerns about politically motivated appointments.[46] It has been argued against such 'purist' concerns that 'theoretical comments' about risks that judges may rule in the government's favour on grounds other than law 'may not be significant in reality'.[47] Temporary judges may not be assigned 'political' cases and the quality of their legal reasoning remains open to the disciplining factor of scrutiny. High quality, timely decisions help sustain a high level of public trust in judges, their social stature and legitimacy. The converse is true.

In November 2020, the Supreme Court made public a Judicial Code of Conduct[48] to guide judges and manage public expectations, also covering post-judicial activities. Essentially, judges must not be influenced by print or social media to make 'popular' decisions; on appointment, judges must cease all

[41] Tan, 'As Efficient as the Best Businesses' (n 26) 235. Chief Justice Chan Sek Keong (2006–12) became the first Judicial Commissioner (JC) on 1 July 1986.

[42] The SICC is part of the High Court; the Chief Justice presides over a mixed bench of local and foreign judges, hearing international commercial disputes: Menon, 'The Rule of Law' (n 28) [28].

[43] Kevin Tan argued appointing a person to hear a single case is 'almost certainly unconstitutional' in allowing the President in concert with the PM to pick their preferred judge for that case: Tan, 'As Efficient as the Best Businesses' (n 26) 294.

[44] Art 95(9) (10). Under SCJA, s 5A, SICC judges only sit in the SICC; these *ad hoc* appointments enjoy no security of tenure, but senior practitioners and judges are unlikely to be swayed by extraneous forces.

[45] Including 21 international judges, four judicial commissioners and five senior judges: 'Our Judges', www.judiciary.gov.sg/who-we-are/our-judges.

[46] Tan, 'As Efficient as the Best Businesses' (n 26) 235.

[47] Chan Sek Keong, 'Securing and Maintaining the Independence' (n 19) [37]; Chan Sek Keong, 'The Courts and the 'Rule of Law' in Singapore' [2012] SJLS 209, 217.

[48] Judicial Code of Conduct, 6 November 2020, www.judiciary.gov.sg.

partisan political activities, act diligently, observe propriety and declare all gifts from external parties to the Supreme Court Office of Public Affairs. To maintain impartiality, judges should recuse themselves from cases where they have a pecuniary or intangible interest. Counsel from both sides were asked and did not object to Menon CJ sitting on a five-judge panel to hear a case concerning the elected presidency, having chaired a 2016 constitutional commission on this very institution.[49] To preserve fairness in an adversarial justice system, judges were not to interfere excessively by descending 'into the arena', adopting the compromising posture of advocacy, as opposed to seeking clarification.[50]

C. State Court Judges: Bifurcation of the Legal Services Commission and the Judicial Service Commission

Members of the lower judiciary deal with more than 95 per cent of judicial matters.[51] The Legal Service Commission (LSC) handles the appointment, promotion, discipline and dismissal of Singapore Legal Service members.

State (formerly subordinate) court judges do not enjoy security of tenure or remuneration, raising concerns in times past they were insufficiently shielded from extraneous pressure. As legal officers, they were routinely shuffled between the executive and judicial branch, and it was feared they would imbibe the executive's corporatist ethos.[52] As their career advancement depended on the LSC, headed by the Attorney-General (AG) and Chief Justice, it was possible that a lower judiciary member could be transferred to the Attorney-General's Chambers (AGC) or a government department if they did something displeasing.

It was alleged the executive interfered with the judiciary in transferring Senior District Judge Michael Khoo to the AGC in August 1984, after he heard a January 1981 criminal case involving opposition parliamentarian JB Jeyaretnam. Khoo SDJ imposed a fine for a fraud offence but acquitted Jeyaretnam on false statement charges, such that the fine did not rise to SGD$2000, which disqualifies someone from holding a parliamentary seat under Article 45(1)(e). This judgment was later overruled.[53]

[49] 'Five Judges to Hear Tan Cheng Bock's Case on Presidential Election in Court of Appeal' *Straits Times* (27 July 2017.

[50] *BOI v BOJ* [2018] SGCA 61 [111]–[112].

[51] Chan Sek Keong, 'Securing and Maintaining the Independence' (n 19) [38].

[52] Kanishka Jaysuriya, 'Corporatism and Judicial Independence within Statist Legal Institutions in East Asia' in *Law, Capitalism and Power in Asia: The Rule of Law and Legal Institutions* (Routledge, 1999) 173.

[53] The High Court ordered a rehearing of the false statement charges; Jeyaretnam was fined and lost his parliamentary seat. The AG raised a motion leading to Jeyaretnam being struck off the rolls for alleged moral turpitude under the Legal Professions Act (LPA). Jeyaretnam successfully appealed his debarment before the Privy Council: *JB Jeyaretnam v Law Society of Singapore* [1988] 1 SLR 137. Parliament later amended the LPA to abolish appeals arising from disciplinary cases

There was 'public disquiet'[54] over the transfer, which some considered a politically motivated punitive measure. The AG described the transfer as career development, determined by the LSC and Chief Justice, who had final say over judicial postings.[55] Rather than a parliamentary committee as initially explored,[56] the government convened a one-man inquiry commission to investigate these allegations, chaired by High Court Judge TS Sinnathuray, known for his pro-establishment judgments.[57] The conclusion was that the Chief Justice had initiated Khoo's transfer, and the executive had not interfered with the subordinate courts.[58]

Since 1986, there have been proposals to have a separate body to determine the promotion and transfer of districts judges, so they can 'be seen to be absolutely independent of the Executive in their decisions'.[59] The government preferred an integrated judicial and legal service, as they thought this would provide more diverse career pathways for a small talent pool, exposing legal officers to work at the Bar, Bench or AGC.[60] However, in 2022, the Constitution was amended to provide for a bifurcated judicial and legal services, ostensibly to promote future readiness and greater specialisation,[61] given complex legal developments. Both the legal and judicial branches share the same goal of 'advancing the RoL', but through 'different contributions'.[62]

to prevent interference in local politics, which opposition politicians criticised as 'childish pique to serious matters of principle': Lee Siew Choh, Legal Profession (Amendment) Bill, 52 SPR, 17 February 1989, col 753.

[54] JB Jeyaretnam, 'Legal Service Postings (PM Statement)', 47 SPR, 21 March 1986, cols 891, 894; Frank et al, '"The Decline of the Rule of Law in Malaysia and Singapore Part II – Singapore", A Report of the Committee on International Human Rights of the Association of the Bar of the City of New York' (1991) 46 The Record 65.

[55] Chan Sek Keong, 'Securing and Maintaining the Independence' (n 19) [38]. Chan suggested circumstances could make it impractical to have a separate judiciary and legal service. Arguably, a lower court judge could not be transferred out at the executive's behest, as the LSC independently decides on postings and promotions: Nathaniel Khng, 'Judicial Independence and the Singapore Judiciary' (2012) Lawasia Journal 53, 69.

[56] 'Legal Service Postings (PM Statement)', 47 SPR, 21 March 1986, cols 891, 913–16. Jeyaretnam criticised the Commission's changed terms of reference: 'Commission of Inquiring into Allegations of Executive Interference in the Subordinate Courts (Terms of Reference)', 48 SPR, 1 August 1986, cols 441ff. A later motion deplored Jeyaretnam's raising of parliamentary privilege to avoid giving evidence for his allegations as 'dishonourable': Report, Commission of Inquiry into Allegations of Executive Interference in the Subordinate Courts (Cmd 12, 1986), 48 SPR, 28 July 1986, col 128 (Report).

[57] eg *AG v Wain No 1* [1991] SLR 383, adopting a liberal approach in finding speech contemptuous.

[58] Report (n 56).

[59] Jeyaretnam (n 54) col 896.

[60] Constitutional Amendment Bill, 83 SPR, 16 July 2017: Sylvia Lim (col 1072), S Jayakumar (cols 1080–81).

[61] In July 2021, Government Parliamentary Committee for Law members raised a motion about the feasibility of setting up a Judicial Service Commission to nurture specialist judicial officers, which Parliament debated in November 2021; the amendments came into effect in January 2022.

[62] AG Lucien Wong, Opening of the Legal Year 2023, 'The Rule of Law and the Duty of Legal Service', 9 January 2023.

The move to specialist services became viable with the increase in numbers of legal service officers (LSOs),[63] the maturation of the legal and political branches providing 'diverse opportunities within each Branch'.[64] The Chief Justice and AG are Presidents of the Judicial Service Commission (JSC) and reconstituted LSC respectively; lending a 'human resource perspective',[65] the Public Service Commission Chair is vice-president of both. The President in his discretion appoints JSC and LSC members, who cannot have 'formal political links'.[66]

This amendment received bipartisan support, for different reasons. The sole opposition Member of Parliament underscored the need for judicial independence, while the five government members focused on equipping legal and judicial officers to handle complex matters like smart contracts and cryptocurrency, and to learn empathy in ensuring the equal treatment of all persons. The amendment effected 'a cleaner separation of powers', as judicial officers no longer engage in public prosecution, while pragmatically supporting a qualified 'separation of functions'[67] by facilitating cross-postings between legal and judicial officers. Overall, this amendment should have a depoliticising effect, better insulating judicial officers insofar as the AG is part of the executive branch[68] and is no longer involved in their appointment, promotion and dismissal.

D. The Exclusivity of Judicial Power and its Content: The Article 93 Vesting Clause

If the source of judicial power is legislative rather than constitutional, the courts' jurisdiction and powers could be statutorily diminished. Thus, Article 93 vests the judicial power 'in a Supreme Court and in such subordinate courts' as the written law may provide. Subordinate courts derive their power from the State Courts Act, while the Supreme Court is constitutionally vested with judicial power, which is 'co-equal'[69] in status with legislative and executive power.

The Supreme Court consists of the Court of Appeal and the High Court (Appellate and General Division), and its jurisdiction is organised under the Supreme Court of Judicature Act. Up until 8 August 1994, the Privy Council was the final court of appeal for civil and criminal cases; it was retained at Independence to ensure that judicial processes in Singapore would be reviewed by a tribunal insulated from undue influence, as this would serve 'the interests

[63] There were 45 LSOs at independence, rising to 589 and 800 in 2014 and 2021 respectively.
[64] Edwin Tong (Second Law Minister), Constitution Amendment Bill, 95 SPR, 3 November 2021.
[65] ibid.
[66] ibid.
[67] ibid.
[68] Art 35.
[69] *Mohd Faizal bin Sabtu v PP* [2012] 4 SLR 947, [16].

of the administration of justice',[70] aside from reassuring foreign investors. By 1994, the Privy Council safety net was thought unnecessary, given the credibility and confidence in the legal system, and its removal would facilitate developing an autochthonous jurisprudence.[71]

The judicial power is exclusively vested in the courts, subject to constitutional limitation, consonant with the SoP, which is considered part of the 'basic structure' of Singapore's Westminster-style Constitution.[72] 'Judicial power' is understood to have a core meaning, given the 'reasonably clear judicial consensus'[73] about the judicial function, from historical and jurisprudential hallmarks.[74] At heart, it entails a controversy between the state and its subjects, or between two or more subjects; the courts make factual findings[75] and apply the relevant law, 'determining the rights and obligations of the parties concerned' to govern their future relationship.[76] To determine if the SoP is violated, the scope of 'judicial power' must be identified. This excluded sentencing power, which the legislature delegated to the courts to apply, reflecting 'the functional efficiency of this constitutional arrangement'. Thus, if the legislature deems it appropriate, non-judicial actors like penologists, psychologists, or social workers may exercise sentencing powers to punish offenders.[77]

Akin to the approach in *Marbury v Madison*,[78] the Supreme Court has asserted the power to strike down unconstitutional laws, although it has never done so.[79] The power to adjudicate on the constitutionality of law and executive action is a claim the government has accepted, and which the court has grounded on the RoL.[80] Critics argue that not taking a decision against the state by striking down rights-restrictive laws indicates a lack of judicial independence. The counter-argument is it would be more rational to examine not just outcomes, but 'the exact rationale and methodology' informing judicial reasoning.[81]

The High Court exercises unlimited original and supervisory jurisdiction over inferior tribunals and administrative bodies at common law, including

[70] Lee Kuan Yew, 24 SPR, 22 December 1965, col 430, 442.

[71] Jayakumar, Judicial Committee (Repeal) Bill, 62 SPR 23, February 1994, cols 388–89.

[72] *Mohd Faizal* (n 69) [11].

[73] ibid [27].

[74] ibid [19].

[75] Jury trials were abolished in 1970 as Lee Kuan Yew, after successfully securing the acquittal of four murder suspects, considered it a foolish foreign system: George P Landau, 'Lee Kuan Yew's Opposition to Trial by Jury', www.postcolonialweb.org/singapore/government/leekuanyew/lky2.html.

[76] *Mohd Faizal* (n 69) [27].

[77] ibid [63].

[78] 5 US (1 Cranch) 137 (1803), cited in *Tan Seng Kee v AG* [2022] 1 SLR 1347, [14].

[79] The High Court in *Taw Cheng Kong v PP* [1998] 1 SLR(R) 78 struck down s 37(1) of the Prevention of Corruption Act for allegedly violating the Art 12 equality guarantee. The CA overturned this in *PP v Taw Cheng Kong* [1998] 2 SLR(R) 489, holding that Parliament could adopt extraterritorial legislation and that s 37(1) did violate Art 12 in differentiating between citizens and non-citizens.

[80] *Taw(CA)* (n 79) [89]; *Chng Suan Tze v MHA* [1988] 2 SLR(R) 525, [86].

[81] Chan Sek Keong, 'Securing and Maintaining the Independence' (n 19) [41].

powers of contempt, examined in chapter six. There is no provision for pre-promulgation review, although the President, on the Cabinet's advice, may request an advisory opinion on any constitutional provision from a Tribunal of Supreme Court judges,[82] established under Article 100. Practically moribund, President Ong invoked this once in 1994, concerning the scope of presidential powers.[83] This mechanism is not open to citizen complaints, only to government actors seeking the non-adversarial resolution of actual or potential disputes.[84]

As an adversarial forum, the court does not engage in abstract review or comment on 'hypothetical issues'[85] but hears actual cases. Nonetheless, unlike the US equivalent (Article III, section 2), Article 93 does not refer to a need for a controversy. The CA has stressed courts should be slow to read in jurisdictional requirements restricting access to justice or shrinking judicial power.[86] Exceptionally, the court may choose to hear a hypothetical case, if it serves the public interest; this entails a real legal interest and 'debatable points of law',[87] as distinct from a mere socio-political question.[88] The RoL requires that law be capable of guiding behaviour, and this is advanced by 'clear judicial pronouncements on what the law is', especially to matters of 'high constitutional importance'.[89] The court will be more inclined to hear hypothetical issues if all sides of the argument are fully made, approximating adversarial contestation, as a determination could affect many people.[90]

Access to justice is shaped by judge-made rules on standing. In Singapore, the approach is generally restrictive, as the aggrieved applicant must have a sufficient personal interest in the matter, as distinct from being interested in the matter. However, it would be unthinkable for the courts, as 'the guardians of the RoL', to allow a situation where citizens lack legal recourse to stop unlawful public conduct.[91] While cautious towards the prospect of an influx of frivolous, vexatious litigation, courts want to ensure accountability for public wrongs.

To have standing, an individual must show his private right, such as a constitutional right, has suffered 'actual or arguable' violation.[92] This encompasses challenging a law under which one has not been prosecuted, but where there is

[82] Although the Constitutional Tribunal is not part of the Supreme Court, it has similar procedural rules: Order 30, Rules of Court 2021, rule 8.
[83] *Constitutional Reference No 1 of 1995* [1995] 1 SLR(R) 803.
[84] Chan Sek Keong, 'Judicial Review – From Angst to Empathy' (2010) 22 SAcLJ 469, [4]. Opposition politician Jeyaretnam twice wanted the President to ask the tribunal whether the Public Entertainments Act was constitutional and whether the government needed certain approvals before making sizeable loans: 'Constitutional Tribunal Plea Rejected' *Straits Times* (30 January 1999) 54; 'Send US$5b Loan Case to Constitutional Court, Says Jeya' *Straits Times* (24 November 1997) 28.
[85] *Nicky Tan v Meta Eco Solutions* [2021] 1 SLR 1135, [62].
[86] *Tan Eng Hong v AG* [2012] 4 SLR 476, [142].
[87] ibid [16], [137]–[138].
[88] ibid [143].
[89] This related to the constitutionality of anti-sodomy legislation.
[90] *Tan Eng Hong* (n 86) [145]–[146].
[91] *Jeyaretnam Kenneth Andrew v AG* [2014] 1 SLR 345, [60]–[61].
[92] *Tan Eng Hong* (n 86) [73].

a credible threat of future prosecution. In *Tan Eng Hong v AG*, Tan challenged the constitutionality of section 377A of the Penal Code, which criminalises male homosexual conduct. Standing was granted on the basis of an arguable violation of Tan's constitutional right not to be prosecuted and deprived of liberty under an allegedly unconstitutional law. If a public right is involved, which public authorities hold and vindicate, the applicant must show he has suffered specific damages because of the public act and has a genuine private interest to protect.[93]

The test for standing for constitutional rights cases was the same as that applicable to ordinary private rights, not more relaxed. This applicant must have a 'real interest' in bringing the action, a 'real controversy' must exist between the parties for the court to resolve and the declaration sought must relate to the applicant's violated personal right and be enforceable against an adverse party to the litigation.[94] Public interest litigation or *actio popularis* is not recognised, for fear of open floodgates. Judicial review in Singapore manifests an ethos based on 'vindicating personal rights and interests through adjudication, rather than determining public policy through exposition'; otherwise, in departing from 'the fundamental precepts of adversarial litigation', courts could be misused 'as a platform for political point-scoring'.[95] Over-liberal standing rules would seriously impair executive efficiency.[96]

Nonetheless, the CA in *Jeyaretnam Kenneth Andrew v AG* recognised there may be cases where a person brings a claim, in the public interest, of government actors breaching public duties,[97] without generating correlative public or private rights.[98] Such cases could be conceptualised as involving a type of 'special damages' justifying standing to constrain public wrongs. This could potentially liberalise standing rules, but the CA hastened to add that such cases would be 'extremely exceptional', wanting to avoid a scenario where taxpayers engaging in public interest litigation questioned 'all nature of administrative acts'. The efficient running of the courts should not be undermined by Singapore citizens acting on 'whims and fancies', and 'running amok' in invoking the 'public interest'.[99]

The RoL's paradoxical quality, as an impulse to maintain control and order and an impulse to challenge public actors, is evident. In striking the balance, the CA affirmed that in most cases, an individual must show 'sufficient stakes',[100]

[93] ibid [69].
[94] *Karaha Bodas v Pertamina Energy* [2006] 1 SLR(R) 112.
[95] *Vellama v AG* [2013] 4 SLR 1, [33]–[34].
[96] Chan Sek Keong (n 84) 480.
[97] *Jeyaretnam Kenneth Andrew* (n 91) [51]: Art 144 was allegedly breached as the government made a loan to the IMF during the 2012 Eurozone crisis, without obtaining presidential and parliamentary approval.
[98] ibid [47].
[99] ibid [62].
[100] ibid [63].

limiting the role of courts as a vehicle for popular participation in public affairs, where concerned citizens may vindicate general public wrongs.

E. Judicial Practice and Reform: Efficiency, Expertise, Access and Leveraging the Legal Ecosystem

The RoL in Singapore is closely tied to the faith in its symbiotic relation with economic growth, based on 'a fair, respected and efficient legal system',[101] which facilitates global commerce and develops Singapore as a regional dispute resolution hub.[102] This is seen in such initiatives as the SICC, launched in 2015, and a 2020 agreement enabling the International Tribunal of the Law of the Sea to sit in Singapore, burnishing its reputation as a neutral venue for resolving inter-state disputes, buttressing the peace architecture of the rules-based international legal order.

Central to this project was the need to clear the cases backlog plaguing the courts in the 1970s–1980s, as justice delayed is justice denied. At its worst, the Supreme Court faced a backlog of more than 2000 pending cases, with available trial dates being at least three years away.[103] Under Yong CJ's leadership in the 1990s, through appointing more judges, streamlining judicial processes and expanding inferior court jurisdiction, the backlog was cleared in three years.[104]

By 2016, the Supreme Court achieved a clearance rate of 97 per cent, where the number of matters disposed of was almost equal to the number of new matters filed.[105] Between 2018 and 2020, the state courts achieved a total case clearance rate of over 100 per cent per year, that is, the number of cases cleared was greater than the number of new cases filed each year.[106] Today, the Supreme Court sets waiting periods for various court processes: in 2022, at least 90 per cent of High Court trials were heard within eight weeks, while originating summons were heard within six weeks.[107]

Under the Yong Bench, the RoL underpinned an attractive investment environment[108] solicitous of 'common business sense'.[109] His successors have

[101] PM Lee Hsien Loong, '150th Anniversary of the AGC' (31 March 2017) www.pmo.gov.sg.

[102] The Singapore International Arbitration Centre was founded in 1991, while the Singapore International Mediation Centre commenced operations in 2014.

[103] Tan, 'As Efficient as the Best Businesses' (n 26) 237.

[104] WH Malik, *Judiciary-Led Reforms in Singapore: Framework, Strategies, and Lessons* (World Bank Publications, 2007).

[105] Menon, 'The Rule of Law' (n 28) [13]. Singapore was ranked first of 140 countries in terms of 'efficiency of its legal framework in settling disputes' by the World Economic Forum: Global Competitiveness Report 2016–2017, 319.

[106] Edwin Tong (n 64).

[107] Supreme Courts Annual Report 2022, 31, www.judiciary.gov.sg/news-and-resources/publications/publication-details/singapore-courts-annual-report-2022.

[108] Yong CJ, Legal Service Dinner Speech, 6 April 2001, www.supcourt.gov.sg/speechesm.

[109] Menon, 'The Rule of Law' (n 28) [8].

continued to pursue efficiency, but not at the expense of justice, as 'the fair administration of justice must ultimately trump efficiency and convenience'.[110] Attention is directed to internal legal values like fairness and reasonableness, beyond an instrumentalist evaluation of the quality of law in terms of speed in hearing a case. A 'modified docking system' ensures that cases are assigned to judges with relevant subject expertise. The turn to specialisation is also evident in how family and youth courts are structured under the 2014 Family Justice Act, where decisions are heard on appeal by the High Court Family Division. Innovative developments manifesting an ethos of care include the launch in 2022 of the Panel of Therapeutic Specialists. Through specialised interventions by mental healthcare professionals directed at litigants, a bespoke model of therapeutic justice is facilitated.

The prevailing ethos is to be a user-centric court system, which helps to 'secure public trust and legitimacy'.[111] For example, night courts are held to deal with minor regulatory and traffic offences outside working hours.[112] The 2021 Rules of Court modernises language, facilitates active judge-led case management and seeks to keep costs reasonable, ensuring fair access to justice.[113] To be future ready, technology is leveraged upon, such as through the e-litigation platform, as 'a single platform and access point' for managing civil cases.[114] While the pandemic made it 'essential … to delink the idea of access to justice from physical access to the courts', there are efforts to meet 'the needs of modern society'[115] by identifying which processes and hearing can be conducted virtually or through asynchronous hearings.

To ensure that access to justice does not remain the preserve of the privileged few, public outreach efforts to discharge an 'assistive responsibility'[116] towards users navigating the system have been made by providing legal information and practical assistance, online case summaries, guidebooks for accused persons in Singapore's four official languages and a Family Orders guide to assist self-representation and demystify family justice.[117]

Competence is needed to sustain public trust. The judiciary is well resourced,[118] receives 'generous' funding[119] with resources dedicated to modernising infrastructure, judicial reform and continuing education as a necessary part of a

[110] Chan Sek Keong CJ, Welcome Reference (22 April 2006) [5], [14], http://app.supremecourt.gov.sg/.

[111] Sundaresh Menon CJ, Inaugural Supreme Court of India Day Lecture, 'The Role of the Judiciary in a Changing World' (4 February 2023) [37], www.www.judiciary.gov.sg.

[112] 'Other Types of Criminal Courts in Singapore': www.singaporecriminaldefencelawyer.com/other-types-of-criminal-courts-in-singapore/.

[113] SG Courts, 'Media Release: New Rules of Court to Transform and Modernize Singapore's Civil Justice System' (1 December 2021) www.judiciary.gov.sg/.

[114] Sundaresh Menon CJ, 'Judging and the Judiciary: Challenges and Lessons in the Age of Technology', Korea-Singapore Legal Technology Seminar, 19 October 2020, [33] See Chan Sek Keong CJ, 'Pursuing Efficiency & Achieving Court Excellence – The Singapore Experience', Speech, 14th Conference of Chief Justices of Asia and the Pacific, Seoul, South Korea, 13 June 2011.

[115] Sundaresh Menon CJ, Speech, Official Opening of the State Court Towers, 14 July 2023.

[116] Menon, 'The Role of the Judiciary' (n 111) [38].

[117] ibid [39].

[118] Tan, 'As Efficient as the Best Businesses' (n 26) 237–38.

[119] ibid 238.

judicial career. In 2015,[120] the Singapore Judicial College[121] was launched to build judicial capabilities, specialist subject-matter knowledge and practical skills.

The work of the Bar and the government is needed to help overcome 'the many barriers that persist in the way of accessing justice',[122] which, if unremedied, can weaken confidence in the legal system. The Chief Justice has encouraged new lawyers to undertake pro bono work,[123] and the profession and the public at large lauded the dedicated efforts of one lawyer, Anil Balchandani, in defending pro bono an Indonesian domestic worker accused by her rich employer of theft.[124] In 2022, the Public Defender's Office was created to promote equality of arms, a key facet of the RoL.[125]

While the government has funded civil legal aid through the Legal Aid Bureau, it has not done the same for criminal cases; some such funding has, however, been provided through the Law Society-run Criminal Legal Aid Scheme (CLAS) since 1985. In 2013, the government decided to provide direct legal assistance and support to criminal law defendants.[126] Through an enhanced CLAS scheme launched in May 2014 in partnership with the Law Society, the government provided substantial funding to cover, for example, lawyer honorariums. This positive contribution to access to justice also marks a shift from 'mistrust to a working relationship' manifesting an evolving 'government and lawyer dynamic'.[127]

While historically associated with adjudication,[128] Chief Justice Menon has advanced a broad vision of the RoL, reimagined to encompass non-adversarial methods of dispute resolution such as mediation, which is third party-facilitated negotiation. Under Order 5r3(1), judges are empowered to order the parties to attempt mediation to help contain disputes. The RoL is complemented

[120] 'Singapore Judicial College launched' *Today* (5 January 2015).

[121] Menon, 'The Role of the Judiciary' (n 111).

[122] Response, Sundaresh Menon CJ, Opening of the Legal Year, 10 January 2022, [26] www.judiciary.gov.sg.

[123] 'Chief Justice Urges New Lawyers To Do Pro Bono Work, as Pandemic Reduces Lower Income Groups' Access to Justice' *Today* (25 August 2020).

[124] Chan J, *Parti Liyani v PP* [2020] SGHC 187, [205]. See Jothie Rajah and Arun Thiruvengadam, 'Of Absences, Masks and Exceptions: Cause Lawyering in Singapore' (2014) 31(3) Wisconsin ILJ 646, 658.

[125] Wong (n 62) [39]; Statement, Minister of Law, Establishment of a Public Defender's Office, 95 SPR, 4 April 2022.

[126] Law Minister K Shanmugam, Speech, 'Association of Muslim Lawyers Inaugural Lecture', 6 December 2013, [16]–[22].

[127] Helena Whalen-Bridge, 'Access to Justice in Singapore: A Government and Lawyer Dynamic' in Helena Whalen-Bridge (ed), *The Role of Lawyers in Access to Justice: Asian and Comparative Perspectives* (Cambridge University Press, 2022) 177. The mistrust stemmed from changes to the Legal Professions Act (Cap 217) in 1987, which confined the Law Society to commenting on legislation or legal matters submitted to it: s 56(1), precluding initiative. This came after a Law Society press statement criticised a law which would control foreign press reporting on Singapore.

[128] Lon Fuller, 'The Forms and Limits of Adjudication' (1979) 92 Harv L Rev 353.

insofar as court-connected mediation[129] helps address access to justice concerns. Mediation presents an alternative to adjudication with its adversarial bent, formalities, dominance by the professional tribe of lawyers, rising litigation costs and limited amounts of court time available. In serving the values of affordability, efficiency, accessibility, flexibility and effectiveness, mediation may be seen to support traditional RoL values associated with adjudication.[130]

From the perspective of individual disputants, mediation may be more accessible and user-friendly, as it is less technical, faster and cheaper, and allows for a broad range of issues to be raised, unencumbered by pleading rules. Mediation may not provide justice according to law in the form of authoritative public guidance, but it does provide access to 'a quality of justice that is distinct and reconcilable with legal structures'.[131]

Diversifying the suite of dispute resolution options allows disputants to choose that which best suits their case particularities. Insofar as parties in non-judicial dispute resolution processes operate within the parameters of existing legal rights and obligations, at least as a starting point, this may foster stronger respect for norms established by the adjudicative process. From a systemic perspective, mediation may be seen not as oppositional, but as complementary to adjudication and the RoL if it aids, as part of the 'dispute resolution toolkit' in delivering fair outcomes to disputants,[132] without precluding access to a judicial remedy.

III. WESTMINSTER PARLIAMENTARIANISM WITH SINGAPORE CHARACTERISTICS

Under the constitutional order founded on the Westminster parliamentary government model, sovereign power is divided among the 'trinity'[133] of constitutional organs: the legislature, the executive and the judiciary. Unlike the strict separation of the executive and the legislature under presidential systems, the

[129] If court-ordered mediation fails, the disputes return to the courts. In 2012, the presumption of alternative dispute resolution was introduced into civil disputes: State Court Practice Directions, [25]. The Mediation Act (2017) strengthens the enforceability of mediated settlements: Sundaresh Menon CJ, 'Mediation and the Rule of Law', Law Society Mediation Forum, 10 March 2017, [28]–[29], [32].

[130] Conversely, mediation may undermine the RoL as it is private, informal and, unlike the public norm-setting function of adjudication, does not yield precedents: JR Sternlight, 'Is Alternative Dispute Resolution Consistent with the Rule of Law? Lessons from Abroad' (2006–07) 56 DePaul LR 569.

[131] Michael Barlet, 'Mandatory Mediation and the Rule of Law' (2019) 1(1) Amicus Curiae Series 2 50, 60.

[132] See Dorcas Quek Anderson, 'The Evolving Concept of Access to Justice in Singapore's Mediation Movement' (2020) 16(2) International Journal of Law in Context 128. Barlet argued that mandatory mediation dilutes the RoL and violates the separation of powers in the judicial delegation of a non-delegable duty to private mediators: ibid 76–77.

[133] *Mohd Faizal* (n 69) [11].

'efficient secret' of the English constitution is reproduced in Singapore. This is 'the nearly complete fusion of the executive and legislative power' through the 'connecting link' of the Cabinet, which is 'a committee of the legislative body selected to be the executive body'.[134] This coexists with the 'dignified' institution, the head of state, which commands respect as a unifying national symbol – in this republic, the President.

Parliamentary systems are general thought of as prioritising effective government, while presidential systems emphasise accountability, sometimes at the cost of institutional gridlock.[135] Judicial and parliamentary powers are kept separate, and the parliamentary democracy system relies heavily on political checks, such as parliamentary and public debates and scrutiny, no-confidence votes, ministerial responsibility and the ballot box. This requires the support of expressive freedoms, a vibrant media and equal voting rights. The judicial ability to hold elected and public officials to account for illegal actions is an RoL virtue.

Two key points are noteworthy. First, the Westminster model was adopted with incipient modifications, such as a unicameral legislature and a justiciable bill of rights; it has subsequently been indigenised through constitutional experimentation, producing autochthonous institutions.[136] This includes two classes of unelected parliamentarians, presidential councils with limited legislative oversight powers, multi-member electoral constituencies and an EP with limited 'veto' powers over specific matters.

Second, the PAP government, which wields the two-thirds parliamentary majority needed for constitutional amendments, has engineered a constitutional system it considers suited to national purposes. Whether the purposes were to promote multiracialism or political pluralism, the general effect of these amendments have been to perpetuate a politically dominant 'strong state'.

In the 1970s, somewhat self-serving government rhetoric maintained that a one-party state was just as able as a two-party state to secure democracy, as a parliamentary opposition composed of 'bums, opportunists and morons'[137] could endanger democracy through engendering chaos and repelling foreign investment. During that time, PAP backbenchers were organised to play the role of an ersatz opposition, which has obvious limitations. This requires too sanguine a view of corruptible human nature, as a one-party Parliament helmed by incompetent, unaccountable governors may also wreck democracy. The risk of this appeared distant to the PAP, whose leaders had such self-perception

[134] Walter Bagehot, *The English Constitution* (1894) [11].

[135] It is argued both these typical systems share functional similarities: see Richard Albert, 'The Fusion of Presidentialism and Parliamentarianism' [2009] 57 American Journal of Comparative Law 531.

[136] English law remains relied upon for matters like parliamentary privileges: Parliament (Privileges, Immunities and Powers) Act, s 3.

[137] S Rajaratnam, quoted in Chan Heng Chee, *The Politics of One Party Dominance: PAP at Grassroots* (Singapore University Press, 1976) 228.

or aspiration that they governed as trustworthy Confucian *junzi* or virtuous honourable gentlemen, in contrast with the Humean idea that in politics 'every man ought to be supposed a knave'.[138]

After JB Jeyaretnam won the Anson by-election in 1981, breaking the PAP parliamentary monopoly (1968–81), PAP leaders began to speak of the danger of 'freak elections',[139] where voters, while wanting a PAP government, cast protest votes and inadvertently vote the incumbent government out. A spate of constitutional experiments followed, to manage the perceived desire of citizens for greater political participation and accountability, while curbing the dangers of voter 'irresponsibility' and 'freak elections'. This likely decelerated the momentum towards a two- or multi-party system.[140]

A. Unelected Parliamentarians

Two classes of non-government unelected parliamentarians with limited voting powers were introduced in 1984 and 1990 respectively: the Non-Constituency Member of Parliament (NCMP) and the Nominated Member of Parliament (NMP). These were ostensibly designed to sate the popular desire for some parliamentary opposition and to banish the one-party state from Singapore's political landscape. It reversed the prior stand that the sole route to Parliament was by way of elections, which was a central democratic tenet for post-colonial governments.[141]

PM Goh Chok Tong candidly observed in the 1990s that 'the system we want is actually one-party and many small parties to keep us on our toes'.[142] This is a recipe for managed democracy, where non-government parliamentarians could provide alternative viewpoints, but not an alternative government. This projected more consultative governance, while solidifying the political status quo. Today, the rhetoric has shifted, as the PAP no longer assumes it will always form the government.[143]

If the fundamental distinction in the political branches is between the parliamentary majority, which the Cabinet controls, and the parliamentary minority,

[138] David Hume, 'Of the Independency of Parliament' in *Essays Moral, Political and Literary* (1741–58) https://press-pubs.uchicago.edu/founders/documents/v1ch11s4.html.

[139] 'Opposition in Parliament', 51 SPR, 29 July 1988, cols 460, 464; First DPM Goh Chok Tong, Constitution (Amendment No 2) Bill, 54 SPR, 29 November 1989, cols 695, 704.

[140] Ten opposition parties and the PAP contested the 2020 General Elections; all were registered as 'political associations' under the Societies Act. See 'Four Opposition Parties to Form New Alliance Ahead of the Next GE' *Straits Times* (1 June 2023).

[141] *Report of the Constitutional Commission* (1966) [47].

[142] 'PAP Loss Would Be "Hard to Contemplate Given the Grave Consequences"' *Straits Times* (10 December 1992) 22. See Li-ann Thio, 'The Right to Political Participation in Singapore: Tailor-Making a Westminster-Modelled Constitution to Fit the Imperatives of "Asian" Democracy' (2002) 6 SJICL 181.

[143] PM Lee Hsien Loong, President's Address, 27 January 2016; 'DPM Lawrence Wong's Interview with the Economist' (6 May 2024) pmo.gov.sg.

these amendments would go some way towards filling the 'parliamentary gap' in ensuring the role of parliamentary opposition was discharged by non-government MPs.

The NCMP scheme sought to ensure 'the representation in Parliament of a minimum number of Members' from political parties not forming the government. NCMPs would sharpen the flabby debating skills of government MPs, provide an outlet for raising government malfeasance and educate voters on the limits of the parliamentary opposition role.[144] Originally, if no opposition candidates were elected, up to six NCMPs could be selected from the top losing opposition politicians with the largest voting shares, securing a minimum of 15 per cent of the vote in the contested ward. If five opposition politicians were elected, one NCMP seat would be offered, and so on.

Opposition politicians broadly decried this as an exercise in tokenism, but pragmatically took up these 'second class' seats, and the heightened profile and parliamentary experience the position offered; some NCMPs have subsequently been successfully elected. While certain government ministers used to congratulate themselves for being so democratic as to let 'losers' into Parliament,[145] a humbler tone is evident in the post-deference era, after the post-Independence high of six opposition MPs were directly voted into Parliament in 2011. This marked the waning of a culture of feudal hubris and the government's discovery of the ability to apologise for mistakes made.[146] The number of NCMPs were later raised from six to nine and then to 12 in 2016.

The NMP scheme was presented as a response to the opposition's supposed inability to present adequate alternative views; NMPs could not belong to any political party and nine would be selected by a parliamentary select committee from distinguished members of various communities, such as the arts, sports, academia, the professions, community service or the labour movement,[147] ensuring that NMPs 'reflect as wide a range of independent and non-partisan views as possible'. NMPs could contribute constructively to parliamentary debate without political grandstanding, enriching discussions through their expertise or distinct perspective.

NMPs would be drawn from people having 'good reasons' for not wanting to enter politics or look after a constituency, such as the under-represented group of women.[148] By offering Singaporeans another vehicle 'to participate

[144] Li-ann Thio, 'The Post-Colonial Evolution of the Singapore Legislature' [1993] SJLS 80, 97–99.

[145] Minister Wong Kan Seng rejected a proposed independent elections commission, declaring: 'We even allow a loser to be in Parliament and make speeches attacking the government. Where could you find such a democracy in other countries?': 'Conflict in a City of Consent' *Asiaweek* (30 November 2000).

[146] While Lee Kuan Yew admonished voters in Aljunied Ward that they would have five years to 'repent' if they voted in the opposition, his son Lee Hsien Loong adopted a humbler tone in apologising for mistakes made: 'PM Says His Apology Resonates with People' *Straits Times* (5 May 2011).

[147] Fourth Schedule, Singapore Constitution.

[148] Goh Chok Tong, Constitution (Amendment No 2) Bill, 54 SPR, 29 November 1991, cols 696–97.

in actively shaping their future',[149] the government projected a willingness to accommodate constructive dissent – implicitly characterising opposition MPs as purveyors of 'destructive' dissent. The scheme attracted much criticism, as NMPs lack the power base and burden of representing a constituency, and the scheme was viewed as a vehicle for co-opting critics, harking back to the colonial era, where the governor appointed members of various chambers of commerce to the legislative assembly.

Originally, the scheme had a built-in sunset clause, and each Parliament had to decide whether to have NMPs, who serve for 2.5 years. The government has consistently praised NMPs for raising the quality of public debate, although the necessity of the scheme, which embodies a form of consultation without contestation, remains questionable.[150] Both NCMPs and NMPs had lesser voting powers and could not vote on constitutional amendments, supply bills and no-confidence motions.

The PAP government declared the success of these schemes by making the NMP scheme permanent in 2012,[151] at a time competitive politics was gaining ground. In 2016, the number of NCMPs was raised to 12, and, unlike the NMPs, the NCMPs were now vested with full voting powers, to be 'equal in powers although not in responsibility and scope to constituency MPs', to diminish critiques they were second-class parliamentarians. As the 'best losers', NCMPs ensured opposition voices in Parliament, and had 'at least as much right to be in Parliament' as MPs elected by a party list under a proportional representation (PR) system, having earned sizeable electoral support.[152] The NCMP scheme was supposedly meant to 'moderate the extreme outcomes' of a first-past-the-post (FPP) system.

The government now presents the scheme as one where the right 12 people 'will be able to hold the Government to account' and who might, after gaining experience and valuable public exposure as NCMPs, successfully contest and win seats at the next elections.[153]

While non-government MPs can question bills and policies and place things on the political agenda by initiating adjournment motions or raising non-orthodox, embarrassing or irritating criticisms, they remain a weak accountability mechanism. For example, when an NCMP raised the disproportionate

[149] President's Address, 52 SPR, 9 January 1989, cols 11, 15.

[150] 'Quality Debate v Democratic Ideals' *Straits Times* (5 September 2009).

[151] 'The Big Read: 30 Years of NMP Scheme – Are Non-partisan, Unelected Voices Still Needed in Parliament?' (*CNA.com*, 25 January 2021). NMP applicants have dropped from 62 (2020) to 30 (2023) nominations: 'Lowest Number of Names Proposed for Nominated MP Role in Two Decades' *Straits Times* (24 April 2023).

[152] Government candidates won by extremely narrow margins in certain wards eg in Potong Pasir, the PAP candidate won 7992 votes (50.36%) to the Singapore People's Party 7878 votes (49.64%). Elections Department (Singapore) 2011 Parliamentary General Elections Results: www.eld.gov.sg/elections_past_parliamentary2011.html.

[153] 'Not wise to purposely let the opposition grow bigger, says PM' *Straits Times* (6 April 2018). See PM Lee Hsien Loong, Debate on President's Address, 27 January 2016, www.pmo.gov.sg.

harshness of discriminatory measures taken against the unvaccinated during the COVID-19 pandemic years, implicating bodily integrity, autonomy and livelihood, this elicited no policy change.[154]

Thus, by the twenty-first century's second decade, the preferred PAP model of a dominant party kept on its toes by small parties was in place. As such, '12 plus 9, we will now have at least 21 non-ruling MPs in the House',[155] which constitutes 22.5 per cent of seats within Parliament. The 'strong state' is maintained if the PAP continues to command a predominant parliamentary majority, which seems likely in the medium term. In the 2020 General Elections, the PAP's national voting share was 61.24 per cent, down from 69.9 per cent in 2015, translating into 83 of 93 elective seats.

B. The Electoral System, Multiracialism and Preserving the 'Strong State'

Constitutional democracy is not unrestrained majoritarianism, being concerned with minority protection. Without the RoL, 'Singapore would cease to be a functional democracy', terminating the project 'to organise ourselves as a multiracial, democratic nation, governed by law'.[156] Electoral systems and the democratic values espoused or downplayed will influence the practical outworkings of an institutional SoP.

The desire to increase ethnic representation within a predominantly Chinese city-state to ameliorate fears of majoritarianism while maintaining an effective government has driven alterations to the electoral scheme. This was organised around single member constituencies (SMCs) operating under the FPP system, where the victor candidate wins the most seats and the number of seats a political party secures is not proportionate to voting shares. The FPP system tends to produce decisive majorities, squeezing out smaller parties. PR schemes, which favour democratic representation over political stability, have been proposed as a way of securing minority interests and ensuring an effective parliamentary opposition.[157] The PAP government consistently rejects PR systems, which tend to produce multi-party parliaments, where many smaller parties serving factional interests may gain parliamentary seats according to the aggregate vote obtained. This produces weaker coalition-based governments, anathema to the 'strong state'. Further, PR systems threaten the intensification of race-based political parties and tribal politicking.

The uniquely Singaporean solution to guaranteeing ethnic minority legislative representation without resorting to rigid quotas[158] or compromising the

[154] Rahayu Mahzam (Health Parliamentary Secretary), Vaccine Differentiated Safe Management Measures, 95 SPR, 10 January 2022.
[155] See Debate (n 153).
[156] Wong (n 62).
[157] Thio, 'The Post-Colonial Evolution' (n 144) [48].
[158] Electoral scheme details are set out in the Parliamentary Elections Act (PEA).

PAP's political dominance took the form of the group representation constituency (GRC), introduced in 1988. Article 39A provided for multi-member teams, originally featuring three candidates,[159] who would contest an upsized constituency; one member must belong to the stipulated Malay, Indian or 'Other' minority,[160] which assumes that representation is primarily based on ethnicity. The GRC would induce a brand of multiracial politics, and paternalistically school voters in the importance of returning 'a racially balanced party slate of candidates'.[161]

Opposition parties were concerned, given human resource constraints, with being unable to muster sufficient candidates to contest GRCs. They were partially assured by the retention of SMCs, which pose lower entry barriers, where they had experience of electoral success. Their fears were subsequently realised as the number of SMCs steadily declined and that of GRCs increased, leaving many GRCs uncontested, with the law requiring a minimum of eight SMCs (see Table 1).[162]

Table 1 General Elections: number of SMC and GRC seats

Year of General Election	SMCs (number of parliamentary seats)	GRCs (number of parliamentary seats)	PAP popular vote (per cent)
1988	42	13 GRCs (3-person team)–39 seats	63.17
1991	21	16 GRCs (up to 4-person team)–60 seats	60.97
1997	9	15 GRCs (up to 6-person team)–74 seats	64.98
2001	9	14 GRCs – 75 seats	75.29
2006	9	14 GRCs – 75 seats	66.60
2011	12	15 GRCs – 75 seats	60.14
2015	13	16 GRCs – 76 seats	69.86
2020	14	17 GRCs – 79 seats	61.23

The reasons for expanding GRC sizes up to six members were unrelated to the constitutional purpose of entrenching multiracialism. Unsurprisingly, opposition politicians cried foul as this development demonstrably benefitted the

[159] Malay leaders expressed disdain for the original 'twinning' proposal', pairing a Malay with another candidate to contest a ward, as this implied an inability to win apart from having a 'so-called "strong" twin brother to lean on': Ahmad Matter, quoted by Goh Chok Tong, 50 SPR, 11 January 1988, cols 180–81.

[160] The government has adopted a CMIO (Chinese–Malay–Indian–Others) model of ethnic classification, around which certain policies are constructed: 'Singapore's CMIO Race Model an Administrative Tool to Manage Policies: IPS Panel' *Straits Times* (24 January 2022).

[161] Goh Chok Tong (n 159) cols 180–81.

[162] PEA, s 8A(1A).

incumbent party, even if the electoral scheme was 'theoretically neutral',[163] raising RoL and democracy concerns.

As no ethnic quotas were set, the increase in GRC sizes meant that with fewer GRCs, there would be fewer guaranteed minority MPs. The proffered justification for enlargement was to facilitate town council management or promote local governance through community development councils.[164] The apparent intent was to stabilise the political system from 'temporary swings in popular opinion',[165] impelling voters to consider not just political rhetoric, but a candidate's ability to run a housing estate.

Politically speaking, larger-sized GRCs favoured the incumbent PAP government, as the under-resourced opposition were unable to assemble sufficient teams with the requisite minority candidate,[166] resulting in many undesirable electoral walkovers. Empirically, it was certainly easier for the PAP to win GRCs seats and, indeed, for 23 years since 1988, they won all the GRC seats, consolidating PAP rule. Political competition is essential in providing a salutary reminder to elected officials that they serve the public; its absence harms the public good.

Given the near certitude of winning all GRCs, the PAP's political renewal strategy was to field political newcomers who needed some guarantee of winning 'at least their first elections'[167] in GRCs, riding the coat-tails of the 'anchor' candidate who was a potential or sitting minister.[168] At one fell swoop, winning a GRC could carry six MPs into Parliament.

PAP self-renewal is unrelated to the GRC's constitutional purpose. Since the GRC scheme derogates from certain constitutional norms, amendments should not lightly depart from the original purpose, certainly not for reasons of partisan advantage or administrative convenience. The GRC scheme potentially violated the Article 12 equality clause, as recognised by the Article 39A9(3) 'notwithstanding' clause, which validates any GRC-related law even if it contravenes Article 12. RoL values may be qualified by other important objectives: giving preferential treatment to minority groups may contravene equality, but may be justified in servicing multiracialism as part of national identity. From the voter's perspective, the RoL value of political equality may also be negatively implicated: while every voter casts one vote,[169] each vote carries variable

[163] PM Goh asserted the GRC scheme was 'theoretically, if you like, scientifically neutral. The key is who can produce the better team': 'GRC Changes: Are They Intended to Fix the Opposition?' *Straits Times* (29 October 1996) 20.

[164] Li-ann Thio, *A Treatise on Singapore Constitutional Law* (Academy Publishing, 2012) 335–51.

[165] Goh Chok Tong, 51 SPR, 28 June 1988, col 384.

[166] eg Jufrie Mahmood (WP) 'switched' and ran as an SDP candidate in Aljunied GRC in 1988.

[167] Goh Chok Tong, Senior Minister, Remarks, South-East CDC Appointment Ceremony, 26 June 2006, [3].

[168] Kevin YL Tan, 'The Constitutional Implications of Singapore's 1991 General Elections' (1992) 13 SLR 25, 49.

[169] PEA, s 42.

voting power which can send one to six candidates to Parliament, depending on geographical residence.

Further, as the RoL requires clear laws able to guide citizens and officials alike, there were 'gerrymandering' concerns over the frequent changing of electoral boundary lines and the swallowing up of opposition strongholds into other constituencies,[170] which affects the certainty need for campaigning strategies. Opposition resources spent 'stomping the ground' were wasted when the ground was literally pulled out from under them.[171] The boundary lines are drawn by the ad hoc Electoral Boundaries Review Committee (EBRC), composed of five senior civil servants the PM appoints, on the basis of objective factors like size and residential distribution of the electorate.[172] The government rejected the idea of an independent elections agency which would transparently delimit boundaries,[173] according to demographic shifts, logic and attention to democratic principles, as it believes the current system 'works well',[174] being operated by honest people with integrity. However, this trust in civil servants fails to cater for all contingencies related to systemic failures, such as the possibility that civil servants will make the process less creditable by being unduly influenced by their political masters.

The current system is advantageous to the ruling party, as they know beforehand the lay of the electoral landscape; the PM may call elections at short notice, giving opposition candidates little time to prepare. The Parliamentary Elections Act mandates a 10-day campaigning period,[175] from the close of nominations to the eve of Polling Day. The day before elections is designated a 'cooling off' day,[176] which precludes campaigning, presumably to promote voting based on rational reflection rather than emotions, to avoid 'freak elections'.[177]

After the PAP lost their first GRC ward in 2011, further losses were sustained in 2020 when the opposition seized Aljunied and Sengkang GRCs, proving the GRC scheme's theoretical neutrality. No longer could the GRC scheme be counted on to shore up the strong state or PAP political renewal. After the 2020

[170] Anson SMC was absorbed into Tanjong Pagar GRC and the boundary lines were redrawn, resulting in the disappearance of Cheng San and Eunos GRCs, which the PAP won marginally in 1997 and 1998 respectively. Thio, 'The Right to Political Participation' (n 142) 211–12.

[171] Sin Kek Tong contested Braddell Heights SMC in 1988 (41%) and 1991 (47.7%), and intended to do so again in 1997. However, two months before polling day, this SMC was absorbed into Marine Parade GRC, the PM's constituency. Mr Sin did not want to challenge the PM, noting there were 'no common boundaries' between the two constituencies: 'Change to Electoral Boundaries "Expected"' *Straits Times* (22 November 1996) 55.

[172] 'Who's on the Electoral Boundaries Review Committee and How It Draws Up GE Battle Lines' *Today* (5 September 2019).

[173] Opposition politician Sylvia Lim said the entire EBRC process is one 'shrouded in secrecy': Constitution (Amendment) Bill, 87 SPR, 26 April 2010.

[174] Wong Kan Seng, 70 SPR, 15 April 1999, col 1211.

[175] PEA, s 34(6)(d).

[176] PEA, s 80.

[177] On how drawing electoral boundaries can impact equality, see Kevin YL Tan and Terence Lee, *Voting in a Time of Change: Singapore's 2020 General Election* (Ethos Books, 2021).

elections, the PM designated Pritam Singh, the secretary-general of the Workers' Party (WP), which held 10 parliamentary seats, as Singapore's first Leader of the Opposition, with additional privileges and allowances. This recognised that the desire for greater political pluralism was a trend that was 'here to stay', and this initiative enabled 'our political system to evolve in a way that maintains our sense of national purpose'.[178]

Politics remains in a state flux and there is evidence of a modest degree of political liberalisation, in relation to normalising viewpoint diversity, competitive politics and the desire for a more effective parliamentary opposition to hold the government accountable.[179] At this stage in history,[180] opposition parties posture themselves as checks against PAP dominance, rather than offering an alternative government, seeking to block arbitrary constitutional amendments by securing one-third of parliamentary seats. PAP leaders accept that as Singapore democracy matures, both 'serious government and serious opposition' are needed, and that the latter should 'offer serious alternatives' rather than 'opportunistic or populist ideas'.[181]

Institutional developments and practices are unapologetically set along an autochthonous trajectory which mitigates the strictness of authoritarian rule, while prioritising government stability over deepening democratic representation, with no aspiration to mimic Western liberal forms of government.

C. Responsive Government within a Party-centric Dominant Party System

The impulse to maintain the strong state is reflected in legal provisions upholding a party-centric parliamentary system, such as the anti-hopping mechanism in Article 46(2)(b). Under it, an MP elected under the ticket of political party A loses her seat if she switches to party B.

The institutional checks on legislation are relatively weak. For example, the Presidential Council of Minority Rights (PCMR) is constitutionally tasked with reviewing legislation and issuing adverse reports where a bill contains a 'differentiating measure',[182] which prevents the giving of presidential assent.

[178] Speaker of Parliament and Leader of the House Joint Press Statement, 'Duties and Parliamentary Privileges of the Leader of the Opposition' (28 July 2020) www.parliament.gov.sg/.

[179] Popular support is increasing for opposition parties: eg the WP crowd-funded more than a million dollars in a few days to cover the legal fees for a lawsuit contesting alleged improper payments made by WP town councilors: 'Worker's Party MPs End Fund-Raising Appeal as Public Donations Cross Million-Dollar Mark', *Straits Times* (28 October 2018).

[180] 'WP Chief Pritam Singh on Opposition Replacing the Government: "I Don't Think It's Possible at All"' *Asiaone* (4 July 2020).

[181] 'Opposition Has a Role to Play in Singapore's Maturing Democracy, DPM Wong Says to Pritam Singh'; 'Pritam Singh Rejects Criticisms That WP Has No Serious Policies or Advances Populist Ideas' (*CNA.com*, 21 April 2023).

[182] Art 68 provides that 'differentiating measure' is one which in its practical application is disadvantageous to persons of any racial or religious community.

This is not a veto, and the PCMR's chief power is to cause the government to consider the public odium it would incur 'for enforcing majority rule to the disadvantage of a minority, although this is normal democratic practice'.[183]

Three key points demonstrate this scheme's weakness. First, the PCMR report is only given after a bill's third reading, whereas the second reading is the main occasion for parliamentary debate. Second, PCMR review does not apply to a money or security bill, or PM-certified 'urgent' bill. Third, an adverse report may be overridden by a motion supported by a two-thirds parliamentary majority. Since its inception in 1968, the PCMR has issued no adverse report – unsurprisingly, as its members are not independent persons as originally proposed;[184] many are politically affiliated, including the PM and the Law Minister, while the politically unaffiliated include the Chief Justice and religious and minority group representatives.[185]

Unsurprisingly, the PCMR has been criticised for being toothless, merely symbolic in providing psychological assurance to minorities by inspiring a sense of security and fair play. Its role does not imperil legislative supremacy.

While Article 24 affirms that the Cabinet is collectively responsible to Parliament, the government overwhelmingly commands the confidence of a PAP-dominated Parliament, and PAP MPs are beholden to Cabinet ministers for political advancement. This tempers the effectiveness of the ministerial responsibility doctrine, where Parliament seeks to check the Cabinet through question time and debating motions. Whether the government is responsible and responsive to the public will depend much on ministerial good faith and an accurate taking of the national pulse.

For example, after the government received its lowest share of votes at the 2011 General Elections, it sought to appease voter anger over the extraordinarily high salaries of government ministers and other senior public officials. An independent committee was appointed, producing a white paper[186] with recommendations leading to downward salary adjustments.[187] The government also conducts periodic surveys on hot button topics, such as imposing the mandatory death penalty for drug offences which has 'very strong support' among Singaporeans; this indicates the high level of public confidence in the criminal justice system, deterrence and having adequate safeguards in capital cases.[188]

[183] EW Barker (Law Minister), 29 SPR, 12 June 1969, cols 60, 62–63.

[184] *Report of the Constitutional Commission* (n 141) [59].

[185] PCMR members are listed at www.sgdi.gov.sg/organs-of-state/parl/departments/pcmr.

[186] 'Salaries for a Capable and Committed Government', white paper (Cmd 1, 2012).

[187] Under the new benchmarks, annual salaries fell by 37% to $1.1 million for ministers, the PM's salary fell by 36% to $2.2 million and the President's salary was cut by 51% to $1.54 million. These elected officials' salaries remain amongst the highest globally: World Population Review, 'What Government Has the Highest Paid Government Leader 2023', https://worldpopulationreview.com/country-rankings/what-country-has-the-highest-paid-government-leader.

[188] 'Strong Support in S'pore, Regional Cities for Death Penalty for Serious Crimes: Studies' *Straits Times* (19 October 2022).

Such studies fuel Singapore's continued resistance to criticism from external actors like UN officials.[189]

The government has moved rapidly to rectify certain errors that have surfaced. For example, during the COVID-19 pandemic, privacy concerns were raised regarding TraceTogether, a smartphone Bluetooth app. A petition opposing the device garnered 30,000 signatures within three days.[190] Citizens were persuaded to download the app by government assurances that it was not a tracking device, as the data would only be used to serve public health. However, Minister Balakrishnan, who oversaw the Smart Nation initiative, made a key oversight in not realising that TraceTogether data was not exempt from section 20(1A) of the Criminal Procedure Code, which empowers the police to order anyone to produce 'data' to facilitate criminal investigations or trial proceedings. The minister apologised before Parliament in January 2021, promising the police would judiciously utilise such data only for serious offences. This provoked widespread outrage and a sense of betrayal.[191] In response, the minister accepted full responsibility and introduced an urgent bill in February 2021 (all three readings taking place in a single sitting), confining data use to seven categories of serious offences, such as murder and terrorism. Rather than doubling down on errors, this ministerial *mea culpa* demonstrated a healthy transparency and responsiveness; it went some way to restoring public trust in using the app for pandemic management and belief the police would act lawfully.[192]

In other matters, opposition politicians have urged the PAP not to demonise their ideas but to constructively counter-argue with evidence to show why proposed policies were unworkable.[193] As getting information from the government was like 'squeezing blood out of a stone',[194] opposition MPs urged the establishment to be more receptive to their informational requests, to enable them to discharge their role in checking the government.

Much ground remains to be traversed towards developing more muscular forms of political accountability. The government still prefers promoting 'consensus without contention'.[195] The 'strong state' is maintained by institutional

[189] UN Press Release, 'Singapore: UN Experts Condemn Continued Use of Death Penalty for Drug-Related Crimes' (28 April 2023).

[190] 'TraceTogether: Singapore Turns to Wearable Contact-Tracing Covid Tech' (*BBCnews.com*, 4 July 2020).

[191] 'More than 1,100 Users Have Deregistered from TraceTogether: Vivian' *Straits Times* (11 May 2021).

[192] 'TraceTogether: PAP MPs Say Proposed Legislation Addresses Concerns; PSP Suggests Data Should only Be Used for Contact Tracing' (*CNA.com*, 11 January 2021).

[193] 'WP, PSP Say They Offer "Rational" Alternative Policies, Urge PAP not to "Demonise" Opposition's Ideas with Labels' *Today* (18 April 2023).

[194] Pritam Singh related this to the difficulty of getting information about the number of intra-corporate transferees from India who worked in Singapore based on the Comprehensive Economic Cooperation Agreement, an emotionally charged issue: 'WP not Opportunistic, Populist since Govt Adopted Its Policy Ideas, PAP Should Change Approach to Opposition: Pritam Singh' *Today* (21 April 2023).

[195] This is one of five declared shared values: white paper (Cmd 1, 1991).

adaptation and processes facilitating citizen participation in collective common good deliberation.[196]

Despite being assessed an 'electoral autocracy' according to V-Dem indicators,[197] the PAP government enjoys democratic legitimacy from relatively free and fair elections and performance legitimacy. A parliamentarian opined that a key feature of Singapore democracy was taking 'real action' to secure the future, with unity of purpose.[198] For example, the omnibus COVID-19 (Temporary Measures) Act was adopted at breakneck speed after three readings on 7 April 2020 to meet pandemic exigencies.[199] The effectiveness of government remains paramount, with secondary emphasis on accountable government.

IV. THE EXECUTIVE GUARDS THE EXECUTIVE: INTRA-BRANCH SEPARATION OF POWERS

The introduction of the elected presidency (EP) in 1990 represented a significant departure from the primarily ceremonial role played by the Head of State within the Westminster system. The EP, which cannot belong to any political party, was transformed into a directly elected office, invested with both political and moral authority to oppose certain Cabinet decisions, through a 'veto' power over certain budgets, fiscal transactions and key public sector appointments. This hybrid institution, ushering in duallist democracy, would safeguard national reserves, guard against corruption and nepotism, and exercise supervisory powers over certain fundamental liberties.

PM LKY first mooted the idea in 1984, after the PAP suffered a 12.6 per cent negative swing in votes at the General Elections. Although the PAP controlled 77 of 79 parliamentary seats, this was disquieting to a party which had enjoyed a parliamentary monopoly from 1968 to 1981. Lee feared that profligate future governments could wipe out 25 years-worth of hard-earned national reserves through fiscally imprudent decisions, such as where a coalition government pandered to populist pressures and offered free public transport, or a powerful Cabinet might otherwise act incompetently. A 'blocking mechanism'[200] to brake the government's untrammelled power was needed to ensure built-up reserves could not be spent without the consent of the EP and a committee of advisors;

[196] 'Youth Panels Being Set Up for Young S'preans to Suggest Policy Ideas that May Be Tabled in Parliament: Edwin Tong' *Today* (21 April 2023).

[197] This is defined as 'de jure multiparty elections for the chief executive and the legislature, but failing to achieve that elections are free and fair, or de facto multiparty': Pew Research Center, 'Citizens in Advanced Economics Want Significant Changes to Their Political Systems' (21 October 2021) Appendix A. On Varieties of Democracy (V-Dem) indicators, see https://v-dem.net/.

[198] Murali Pillai, Constitution (Amendment) Bill, 95 SPR, 3 November 2021.

[199] 'Necessary for Singapore to Fast-Track Covid-19 Laws amid Unprecedented Situation: Lawyers' (*CNA.com*, 13 April 2020).

[200] PM Lee Kuan Yew, National Day Rally 1984 (1:02) nas.gov.sg.

free buses would have to be funded by taxes, which exacts a political cost. It would be a 'fatal naivety' to bank on there being a 'good and honest' government in perpetuity.[201]

Conversely, opposition politicians insisted a robust parliamentary opposition and the courts as final arbiter in disputes would furnish 'a better safeguard than a one-man Elected President'.[202] The better route was to allow democracy to mature by relaxing controls over political liberties.

Nonetheless, the government preferred to resort to law to institutionalise checks and balances through a 'two key' scheme to protect *past* reserves[203] accumulated by the government, statutory boards and government companies holding substantial government assets. The basic mechanism is based upon empowering the EP, in consultation with an unelected Council of Presidential Advisors (CPA), to withhold assent to supply bills and transactions drawing down on 'past reserves'.[204] The past reserves vault would only be opened if the keys held by the Cabinet and the President were deployed simultaneously.

This reflects a shift away from trusting to distrusting governors who are not Madisonian angels. This is distinct from the 'liberalism of fear'[205] in Western liberal orders preoccupied with safeguarding individual freedoms from intrusive governments. Instead, it is rooted in the fear of future squandering of wealth amassed under the PAP's watch.[206] At first glance, the EP as an institutional check imports some degree of inefficiency into the system, short of portending institutional gridlock.

This scheme is unique as a form of moderated parliamentarianism where Parliament holds the purse, while the Cabinet has the 'general direction and control of the Government'.[207] The EP, in whom executive authority is invested,[208] checks the Cabinet. This is distinct from Ackerman's model of constrained parliamentarianism,[209] where independent agencies help the

[201] First DPM Goh Chok Tong, Constitution (Amendment No 3) Bill, 56 SPR, 4 October 1990, col 462.

[202] Lee Siew Choh, 56 SPR, 4 October 1990, cols 459, 491.

[203] The president has no role over expenditure financed out of current reserves the sitting government accumulates. The rationale was political parties running for office should not 'have the luxury' of 'promising to spend reserves' past governments accumulated: 'Safeguarding Financial Assets and the Integrity of the Public Service' (Cmd 11, 1990) para 12.

[204] Past reserves means reserves (the excess of assets over liabilities) not accumulated by the government during its current term of office: Arts 2, 142, Singapore Constitution.

[205] Judith Shklar, *Political Thought and Political Thinkers* (Stanley Hoffman ed, University of Chicago Press, 1998) 3.

[206] This attitude may account for conflating party and state, where PAP leaders have dangled the carrot of prioritising the ward upgrading programmes for wards voting for the PAP, which involves deploying state resources for partisan benefit: 'SDA Distances Itself from Chee's Behaviour' *Straits Times* (1 November 2001) H4. When an opposition MP asked whether a PM should look after party rather than national interests, the response was that since the government accumulated Singapore's reserves, the electorate could choose to vote PAP and get PAP programmes, or not: Low Thia Khiang, 71 SPR, 24 November 1999, col 622.

[207] Art 24(2).

[208] Art 24(1).

[209] Bruce Ackerman, 'The New Separation of Powers' (2000) 113(3) Harv L Rev 633.

legislative body check the executive, although there are elements of this in the form of independent constitutional actors like the Auditor-General, who audits government accounts and presents his findings in a public report, with the expectation that relevant bodies will remedy lapses and correct course.[210] The EP has a role in appointing the Director of the Corrupt Practices Investigation Bureau (CPIB) and may refuse an appointment, which a two-thirds parliamentary majority may overrule by resolution.[211] If the PM refuses, the CPIB Director may nevertheless proceed to carry out any investigation with the EP's concurrence.[212]

Overall, the institutional scheme preserves the strong state as the EP's powers are subject to a counter-checking mechanism, so that when the EP, contrary to the CPA's recommendations,[213] refuses to assent to a supply bill, a two-thirds parliamentary majority vote could neutralise the presidential veto; presidential assent is deemed given from the date that the parliamentary resolution is passed.[214] This system is distinct from semi-presidential models, which involve dividing the executive into two co-equal independent constitutional institutions; such power sharing can lead to clashes, as has been seen between the President and the PM of France's Fifth Republic.[215]

The government stresses the EP is not an alternative centre of power or executive president; EP powers are reactive, custodial and not agenda-setting. While the Cabinet, with the PM as *primus inter pares*, has general powers, the EP's power are specific and narrow, moderated by the duty to consult the CPA and vulnerable to parliamentary overriding when the EP and CPA disagree. Indeed, presidential powers have been rolled back and reduced since 1990, through amendments removing the EP's role in relation to defence spending bills and the transfer of past reserves between the government and statutory boards/government companies.[216]

Although the EP is directly elected, the presidential elections scheme is oriented towards pro-establishment candidates. This is due to twin filters in the form of stringent qualifying criteria and the need for candidates to be issued a certificate of eligibility by the Presidential Elections Committee (PEC) which is

[210] Art 148F. See 'Auditor-General Flags Lapses in Govt Agencies, Including Transfer of Official Funds to Personal Bank Accounts' *Straits Times* (19 July 2023).

[211] Arts 22(n), 37IA, 37IF.

[212] Art 22G.

[213] The CPA comprises eight members who are appointed in staggered terms, with the EP, PM and Chief Justice all having a role in the selection process: Art 37B.

[214] Arts 148A, 37IF.

[215] Matthew Shugart, 'Semi-Presidential Systems: Dual Executive and Mixed Authority Patterns (2005) 3 French Politics 323; Tarunabh Khaitan, 'Balancing Accountability and Effectiveness: A Case for Moderated Parliamentarianism' (2021) 7 CJCCL 81.

[216] Arts 148I, 151A. Li-ann Thio, 'Past Imperfect, Future Tense: The Elected Presidency and the Constitutional Development of an "Ever Evolving Hybrid"' in Jaclyn L Neo and Swati S Jhaveri (eds), *Constitutional Change in Singapore: Reforming the Elected Presidency* (Routledge, 2019) 41–66.

'not subject to appeal or review in any court'.[217] The PEC has no duty to give reasons and has denied certificates to financially highly qualified private sector candidates.[218] Stipulated high public office-holders are automatically eligible (ministers, Chief Justice, Speaker, Attorney-General, Accountant-General, Auditor-General, etc),[219] while private sector candidates have to be CEOs of companies worth over $500 million in shareholder equity.[220] Potential candidates who automatically qualify have the unfair advantage of making campaign preparations earlier, such as where the only candidate putting up posters nationwide was the eventual winner of the 2023 elections, former Deputy PM Tharman Shanmugaratnam.[221]

In the six presidential elections since 1993, only three have been contested. No 'private sector' presidents have emerged. There is a sense of 'all in the PAP family', insofar as three presidents have been former deputy PMs.[222] One was the House Speaker who had no competitors in a 'reserved' election, introduced in 2017 as an admittedly 'unpopular decision'[223] to ensure multiracialism.[224]

Any expectation the EP would be an aggressive muscular check has waned, particularly after a robust exit interview in 1999 where President Ong Teng Cheong critically identified obstacles encountered, including uncooperative government agencies.[225] Disquieted ministers addressed the President's concerns through ministerial statements before Parliament.[226] Subsequently, a

[217] Presidential Elections Act, s 8C.

[218] Most notably, businessman George Goh, founder of Harvey Norman Ossia, was denied a certificate to run in the 2023 presidential elections. He criticised the PEC decision for taking a 'very narrow' interpretation of the requirements in relation to the shareholders' equity and profitability criteria, as he was the most senior executive managing five companies (rather than a single one) which cumulatively met the criteria: 'George Goh Says "Shocking News for S'pore" He Didn't Qualify for Presidential Elections 2023' (*Mothership.sg*, 18 August 2023).

[219] Art 19(3).

[220] This was amended in 2017, whereby a candidate formerly had to be Chair or CEO of companies with minimum paid-up capital of $100 million.

[221] '"Seeing Tharman's Posters and Banners Around the Island Just Makes My Blood Boil", daughter of Tan Kin Lian Frustrated at Limited Time for Campaign' *The Independent SG* (25 August 2023).

[222] Ong Teng Cheong (1993), Tony Tan (2011) and Tharman Shanmugaratnam (2023). SR Nathan (1999, 2005) was a senior diplomat and civil servant. This is not to say that former PAP ministers cannot act independently, but perceptions matter.

[223] 'Will Reserved Election Promote Multiracialism?' *Straits Times* (3 September 2017). Critics argued that this amendment, which reserved the 2017 elections for Malays, blocked strong non-Malay candidates from running: 'Tan Cheng Blocked Again: Dr Tan Rubbishes REACH's Claims That He Didn't Sign Up for Presidency Forum' (*Redwiretimes.com*, 30 September 2016).

[224] Art 19B reserves presidential elections for a particular racial group if there has been no President from it for five continuous terms (30 years). This was driven by multiracial symbolism, although it is arguably unmeritocratic. Only House Speaker Halimah Yacob got a certificate of eligibility; two other candidates, with greater financial expertise and market knowledge, did not: 'Rejected Hopefuls Disappointed, but Want to Continue Service' *Today* (12 September 2017).

[225] '"I Had a Job to Do" Whether the Government Liked It or Not, Says ex-President Ong' *Asiaweek* (10 March 2000); 'The Ong Presidency' *Straits Times* (29 August 1999) 32.

[226] PM and Finance Minister Statements, 'Issues Raised by President Ong Teng Cheong at His Press Conference on 16th July 1999' 70 SPR, 17 August 1999, col 2018.

'convention' of non-binding or soft constitutional law norms[227] authored by the government, which the President accepted, was expressed in a white paper.[228] This contained principles on technical matters like accounting methodology and general commitments that both parties would seek a 'harmonious working relationship', which is how all EPs have subsequently characterised their relationship with the parliamentary executive.[229] This denotes a relationship as cooperative partners rather than adversarial combatants, joined in the task of public governance. The requirement that presidential elections be conducted in a 'dignified'[230] manner, reflects the unifying role of the EP; the discouragement of 'divisive' election rallies[231] reflects a brand of patrician, rather than populist, democracy. In this view, the EP should 'remain above the political fray', not pursue a political agenda and not 'support or oppose' the government.[232]

The 'two-keys' system has apparently not impeded efficiency, such as when the government sought President SR Nathan's approval, which he gave after 11 days of deliberation, to draw $4.9 billion from past reserves to fund job-saving and credit-easing schemes during the 2008–09 global financial crisis.[233] President Halimah Yacob approved budgets drawing down on past reserves amounting to $69 billion over three years to handle the COVID-19 pandemic, after 'extensive, robust and thorough discussions',[234] which were 'rigorous but not antagonistic'.[235]

Overall, the scheme has pivoted from Westminster parliamentarianism, removing some matters from parliamentary control and inserting technocratic elements, such as calculating the 'net investment returns (NIR)': under Article 142, the spending limit ceiling is 50 per cent of NIR, as a matter of intergenerational equity. The Finance Minister must calculate the NIR using the 'long term real rates of return' formula, which refers to the average returns expected over 20 years; the EP must concur with this figure, after consulting

[227] Li-ann Thio, 'Soft Constitutional Law in Non-liberal Asian Constitutional Democracies' (2010) 8 ICON 766. The principles in the 1999 white paper did not bind future successors who could unilaterally repudiate them.

[228] 'Principles for Determining and Safeguarding the Accumulated Reserves of the Government and the Fifth Schedule Statutory Boards and Government Companies' (Cmd 5, 1999).

[229] 'President Nathan Calls It a Day, after 12 Years' *Today* (2 July 2011); 'President Tony Tan: Elected President Is Symbol of National Unity, Must Be Able to Work with Government' *Straits Times* (7 November 2016); 'Signing Off as President, Halimah Calls for "Unity and Purpose" in an Era of Economic Rivalries, Geopolitical Alliances' *Today* (13 September 2023).

[230] Elections Department, 'Campaigning', www.eld.gov.sg/candidate_presidential_campaign.html.

[231] 'Rallies "May Be Divisive", Not Encouraged for Presidential Election: Elections Department' (*CNA.com*, 12 August 2023).

[232] Elections Department, PM's Office Press Release, 'Campaigning Guidelines for the Presidential Elections' (29 August 2017).

[233] 'Turning of the Second Key Went Smoothly' *Straits Times* (20 February 2009) 2.

[234] 'Signing Off as President' (n 229).

[235] PM Lee Hsien Loong, Speech, Farewell Ceremony for President Halimah Yacob, 13 September 2023, Istana, pmo.gov.sg.

with the CPA and any investment experts.[236] This is a complex public finance matter beyond the ken of the average person. The choice was taken to insulate this process from populist pressures by not submitting it for parliamentary evaluation; instead, reliance was placed on internal checks amongst experts and government bodies. It is not envisaged that the courts will play a role in determining these constitutional terms, such as where the Finance Minister must certify to the EP a financial year's net investment income, of which at least 50 per cent shall be saved and stored as past reserves. Under Article 142(3), this certificate constitutes 'final and conclusive evidence' of this amount, and courts will probably not review what is not a question of law.

Faith is placed in having 'the right people in charge … within the system'; reliance is placed on professional, rather than political, judgement and popular accountability, the former being less prone to overspending.[237] This reflects to some degree the rule of the virtuous wise and trust in the technocrats. While birthed in the desire to restrain imprudent government, the EP has evolved in a manner where power holders are trusted and distrusted.

The EP scheme has altered the nature of the head of state from a ceremonial office to a 'ceremonial plus' office, with some presidential oversight powers, which are quite weak and dependent on the financial acumen, independence and common sense of the EP and CPA. It is a modest corrective to the possible abuses of a dominant party state in wasting national reserves, although the EP has no role over foolish policy choices financed out of current reserves. The EP scheme does not threaten a real loss of political power, although the EP's public disagreement with the Cabinet is a high-profile event, bringing to bear a high degree of publicity and political pressure. As things stand, where the government controls a parliamentary supermajority, if the EP withholds assent to a government budget, this may still be overruled by parliamentary resolution. Curiously, this means that when a strong government maintains a minimal two-thirds parliamentary majority, the EP's role as a check is weaker. When the government is weak, the EP's role and powers assumes real force, ministering to RoL values of holding government actors accountable.

V. CONSTITUTIONAL NORMS IMPACTING THE RULE OF LAW AND THE JUDICIAL ROLE

A. Article 149: Security

While the Constitution is supreme under Article 4, it provides for regimes of exception to the RoL, where the normal legal order is of necessity suspended

[236] The Constitution does not envisage that the EP and CPA must be 'their own lawyers or accountants'. PM and Finance Minister Statements (n 226) col 2025.

[237] Finance Minister, Tharman Shanmugaratnam, Constitution (Amendment No 2) Bill, 85 SPR, 20 October 2008.

to preserve state survivability. Article 149 authorises the enactment of anti-subversion and emergency legislation, reintroducing a limited degree of parliamentary supremacy by truncating or precluding judicial review, where Part 4 fundamental liberties are concerned.[238]

Legislation like the Internal Security Act (ISA), addressing matters 'prejudicial to the security of Singapore', is a nightmare to limited government proponents. It authorises detention without trial and is valid 'notwithstanding' its inconsistency with specific fundamental liberties, including life and liberty, equality, free movement and free speech, and would otherwise transgress legislative power. This exception to rights and due process severely denudes the detainee's arsenal of protection, heightening executive power.

The ISA was originally designed to address the communist threat in the 1950s–1960s and its retention was justified by PM LKY in the need to depart from British patterns developed during 'two centuries of peaceful, non-revolutionary England'. While the RoL spoke of habeas corpus, rights of assembly and peaceful demonstrations, these were not without limitations, as, blindly applied, such ideals 'can work towards the undoing of organized society'.[239] To insist on open trials and strict evidentiary rules for subversive agents or triad members who intimidated potential witnesses would be to invite chaos.

While law cannot operate without order, abusive appeals to 'order' may be attempted to justify egregious rights violations. The ISA has been used to detain political dissidents, although, in the twenty-first century, it is primarily directed at religiously motivated terrorists.[240] The ISA has been celebrated as part of the nation-building project, with the creation of the Internal Security Department Heritage Centre in 2002, which highlights the security threats Singapore faces seeking support for the law, in the face of calls to repeal it.[241] As governments in the West have 'grudgingly accepted' the necessity of preventive detention to address terrorist threats, international criticism is more muted.[242]

The ISA was notoriously used to detain 16 people for their involvement in the so-called 'Marxist conspiracy' of 1987.[243] After the CA quashed detention

[238] See Jaclyn Neo and Yvonne Lee, 'Constitutional Supremacy: Still a Little Dicey' in Li-ann Thio and Kevin Tan (eds), *Evolution of a Revolution: 40 Years of the Singapore Constitution* (Routledge, 2009) 153–92.

[239] Lee Kuan Yew, Speech, University of Singapore Law Society Annual Dinner, 18 January 1962, https://nas.gov.sg/lky19620118.

[240] See, eg 'The Jemaah Islamiyah Arrests and the Threat of Terrorism', white paper (Cmd 2, 2003). More recently, it has been used to detain individuals self-radicalised by online religious propaganda, with the hope of reintegrating them into society after religious counselling: Li-ann Thio, 'Securitisation and Solidarity in Singapore after 9–11', Verfassungsblog.de Online Symposium: Collateral Damage to Human Dignity in an Era of Securitization, March 2022, https://verfassungsblog.de/os5-singapore/.

[241] 'Think Centre Renews Call to Abolish ISA' (16 September 2011) www.thinkcentre.org/article.php?id=3099.

[242] 'Limits Needed for Internal Security Act: Ho Kwon Ping' *Straits Times* (5 February 2015).

[243] See Francis Seow, *To Catch a Tartar: A Dissident in Lee Kuan Yew's Prison* (Yale Southeast Asia Studies, 1994); Teo Soh Lung, *Beyond the Blue Gate: Recollections of a Political Prisoner* (SIRD, 2010).

orders on a technicality and espoused an objective test of review in *Chng Suan Tze v MHA*,[244] a flurry of constitutional and ISA amendments took place within a month[245] to overturn the case and, through Article 149(3), to immunise the ISA and ISA actions from judicial challenge by providing that 'nothing in Article 93 shall invalidate any law enacted pursuant to this clause'. The subjective review test was restored pursuant to a denuded, formalistic conception of the RoL as the rule of rules adopted by Parliament. Chapter four further examines the ISA's impact on fundamental liberties.

The justification for this was that the executive, rather than interventionist and ignorant foreign judges who influenced Singapore judges, should make security-related decisions.[246] Privy Council appeals were terminated[247] and significant judicial oversight over ISA powers 'virtually ousted',[248] confined to procedural non-compliance.[249] Legislatively overruling court decisions through constitutional amendments is disquieting to the constitutionalist project, and it is comforting that this has not happened since 1989.

Detention without trial is not detention without process, but the safeguards for detainees are relatively weak, such as the right under Article 151 to be informed of grounds for detention and to make representations before an Advisory Board (AB) within three months.

With the 1989 amendments, a clear gap in individual protection arose. It was decided to have a non-legal check against possible abuses, as judging whether a person was a security threat 'rested with the executive and not with the courts'.[250] As the EP scheme was then under discussion, the government decided to make the EP that political check over ISA powers, even if the EP's main purpose related to fiscal constitutionalism.

Thus, under Article 151, if the AB recommends a detainee's release and the Cabinet disagrees, further detention will require EP concurrence. At best, the EP's powers are weak; for example, the EP plays no role in guarding liberties of detainees if the AB never recommends release, as the EP must act in tandem with the AB, an intermediate unelected body. Ultimately, the primary if blunt check is the ballot box, as the Law Minister rhetorically asked: 'If we abuse the ISA, do you think a sophisticated electorate would tolerate it?'[251] Within a dominant party system, this is a chimerical prospect, a gap in the architecture of accountability. Even if the government considers sustained electoral success as proof of

[244] [1988] 2 SLR(R) 525.

[245] The amendment was debated and adopted on 25 January 1989: see Law Minister S Jayakumar, Constitution (Amendment) Bill, 52 SPR, 25 January 1989, col 463.

[246] ibid cols 467–74.

[247] Internal Security Act, s 8C, repealed in 1994 when the Privy Council ceased to be the apex court.

[248] HP Lee and Marilyn Pittard, 'The Challenge of Judicial Independence in the Asia-Pacific' in HP Lee and Marilyn Pittard (eds), *Asia-Pacific Judiciaries: Independence, Impartiality and Integrity* (Cambridge University Press, 2018) 398.

[249] Internal Security Act, s 8B.

[250] 'Safeguarding Financial Assets and the Integrity of the Public Services' (Cmd 11, 1990) para 24.

[251] Frank et al (n 54) 27.

the RoL's health, preventive detention laws operate under an exceptional 'non-law' realm, unhindered by weak political checks and muted procedural review.

B. Article 156: Safeguarding Social Goods Through Parliamentary Supremacy?

The government decided to repeal section 377A of the Penal Code, which criminalises male sodomy, after a decade of unsuccessful constitutional challenges. To avoid the future risk of it being struck down on equal protection norms, the government wanted to proactively negotiate a political settlement,[252] while realising that Singapore marriage laws could similarly be challenged. This would lead to 'the recognition of same-sex marriages', impacting other laws and policies based on marriage as a union between a man and a woman ('traditional marriage').[253]

Aware of the political sensitivities in repealing a high-profile Act in Singapore's 'culture wars', the government decided, in tandem with repealing section 377A in a 'controlled and carefully considered way',[254] to amend the Constitution to protect the institution of marriage. As marriage is based on a male–female union, it could now be challenged on equal protection grounds, as 'same-sex marriage' or redefining marriage has been a key goal of the homosexual rights agenda elsewhere.[255] PM Lee stated that if activists were to 'force the pace through litigation', this would detrimentally polarise society, and that courts should not decide such 'political issues'.[256]

Article 156 was the political compromise designed to 'protect the definition of marriage from being challenged constitutionally in the court', which is found in statutes like the Interpretation Act[257] and Women's Charter.[258] The government appealed to what 'most Singaporeans' found acceptable, which extended to decriminalising 'sexual relations between consenting men in private', being conscious that 'most Singaporeans' were concerned this might 'trigger a drastic shift' in social norms across the board, including the definition of marriage, sex education in public schools and entertainment standards.[259]

[252] Panel Discussion on Tan Seng Kee v AG and s 377A Penal Code – Opening Address, Law Minister K Shanmugam, 26 September 2022, www.mha.gov.sg/.

[253] 'S377A Repeal: Proposed Constitutional Amendment to Protect Marriage Definition Without "Hard-Coding" It, Says Edwin Tong' *Today* (22 August 2022); see also Walid Abdullah, 'The Politics of Compromise: Analyzing the Repeal of 377A in Singapore' (2023) 96(1) Pacific Affairs 105.

[254] PM Lee Hsien Loong, National Day Rally Speech, 21 August 2022, ITE Headquarters, www.pmo.gov.sg/Newsroom/National-Day-Rally-2022-English.

[255] There are restrictions on who may marry: marriage is between opposite sex couples who are not already married, are of sufficient age and not close blood relations: see Robert George, Sherif Girgis and Ryan T Anderson, 'What Is Marriage' (2010) 34(1) Harv JLPP 245.

[256] Lee Hsien Loong (n 254).

[257] s 2(1).

[258] s 12.

[259] Lee Hsien Loong (n 254).

The declared intent of this 'political accommodation' was to update 'current social mores' while reconciling this with the 'traditional mores of our society' to protect 'conservative social values', such as that 'marriage should be between a man and a woman, children should be born and raised within such families, [and] the traditional family should form the basic building block of our society'.[260] The government would maintain 'our current family-oriented approach' so 'even as we repeal s377A, we will uphold and safeguard the institution of marriage'. It clarified there was 'no intention' to change the definition of marriage or any national policies based on traditional marriage, including public housing and adoption rules. In a society with divisive polar views and the slow creep of 'cancel culture to brow-beat and shut up opponents … splitting society into warring tribes', it was best all groups show restraint in the interests of moving forward as 'one nation together'. The key point was that politically controversial issues would be politically managed, not legally determined or put to referenda, as the government knew best how to strike the 'right balance'. The PAP did not lift the whip when debating this amendment.[261]

The manner in which Article 156 is formulated is instructive. It does not provide maximum protection, which a substantive constitutional definition of marriage would.[262] Instead, Article 156(1) provides that the legislature may, by law, 'define, regulate, protect, safeguard, support, foster and promote the institution of marriage'. The government and public authorities under Article 156(2) may, subject to any written law, 'protect, safeguard, support, foster and promote the institution of marriage'. Article 156(3) and (4) provides that nothing in Part 4 of the Constitution, the fundamental liberties chapter which includes the equality guarantee, invalidates a law or exercise of executive authority respectively, which operates on the basis that marriage is 'a union between a man and a woman'.

While this apparently resembles a notwithstanding clause of sorts, in upholding laws which may contravene Part 4 liberties, Article 156 does not immunise challenges to the definition of marriage as such;[263] it does not go as far as Article 149(3), which provides that nothing in the Article 93 judicial power clause shall invalidate Article 149-authorised legislation. This signals to the court that judicial restraint is appropriate, reserving this issue exclusively

[260] ibid.

[261] ibid. Notably, Deputy PM Lawrence Wong, who became PM on 15 May 2024, stated the government has no plans to go further, such as recognising same-sex unions: 'Lawrence Wong & Edwin Tong on Potential Political Cost of 377A Repeal: Not How We Look at the Issue' (*Mothership.sg*, 22 August 2022).

[262] eg Hungarian Constitution (2011), Art L; Tuvalu Constitution (2023), Art 43. This could trump conflicting provisions in the same text.

[263] For example, the courts may have to interpret two presumably co-equal constitutional provisions such as Arts 12 and 156. Further, for a constitutional guarantee to be meaningful, it must arguably mean 'any citizen can complain to the courts if there is a violation of it': *Chan Hiang Leng Colin v Minister for Information and the Arts* [1996] 1 SLR(R) 294, [13].

or primarily for political management. This dampens the prospects of constitutional challenges, but does not definitively preclude it.

Article 156 does not entrench the current statutory definition of marriage, so a subsequent Parliament could choose not to foster traditional marriage and through a simple majority easily alter the statutory definition of marriage to include same-sex couples or polyamorous unions etc. Theoretically, traditional marriage enjoys no more protection than a dog-licensing law, subject to the fortunes of political expediency and pragmatism, rather than principle. This approach keeps the definition of marriage open-ended, for future contestation. It protects the legislature's power to define marriage, rather than protecting marriage as a constitutionally entrenched social good.[264] If those in power adopt the revisionist view of marriage as a social construct, to be renovated as society sees fit, this could be implemented through ordinary parliamentary politics.

Notwithstanding this, Article 156 arguably goes beyond mere symbolism, a sop to assuage social conservative concerns by pointing to the mention of marriage in the Constitution, as if that were a sufficient guarantee of what many consider a fundamental value and pre-social natural institution. It has some legal effect insofar as it protects existing laws and policies protective of traditional marriage, making it less likely the courts will strike them down. This constitutional bargain thus gives 'legal form' to the government's affirmation of the importance of the traditional family unit, demonstrating 'awareness that marriage occurs within a moral ecology'.[265] It ensconces the issue squarely within, not above, the realm of politics. Today's decision does not bind tomorrow's government, reflecting the tenet of parliamentary supremacy and the spirit of pragmatic agnosticism in relation to foundational moral questions.

VI. MIXED CONSTITUTIONALISM: LAW, POLITICS AND RELATIONISM

The Singapore system stands at an intermediate stage between parliamentary and constitutional supremacy, eschewing judicial supremacy. Singapore constitutionalism is a hybrid of Anglo-American influences, with an autochthonous normative commitment to communitarianism. This has informed constitutional experiments in institution-building where the rule and role of law are not only to

[264] The government did not want to constitutionally hard-code the definition of marriage, which would raise it to the same level as fundamental rights, fundamentally changing 'the whole complexion and the scheme' of the Constitution. 'S377A Repeal' (n 253). However, the Singapore Constitution does contain some substantive values by inference, such as inter-generational equity (Art 142) and minority protection (Art 152), so there is no legal bar to entrenching other fundamental values directly. The choice is clearly to keep the issue in the realm of ordinary, not extraordinary, politics.

[265] Tan Seow Hon, 'Strengthening the Institution of Marriage as the Union of One Man and One Woman' *Law Gazette* (March 2023) https://lawgazette.com.sg/.

ensure a government of laws, but to facilitate effective governance, implementing the developmentalist goals of a strong state. Reliance on judicial review and political checks reflects the mix of legal and political constitutionalism.

In addition, the goal of relational constitutionalism is a key feature, where a mix of legal and soft law norms, practices and institutions are utilised to manage ethno-religious diversity and potential disputes. A former Law Minister has stressed that in non-homogeneous societies the RoL is important in making expectations 'transparent', and helps reduce social conflict where communities with deeply held religious and moral beliefs are guided by these even if this breaks the law. The RoL is associated with general law and sustaining a 'large common secular space' where all citizens can interact, keeping their faith and public peace. Thus, 'maintaining racial and religious harmony has become an important tenet for us when approaching the RoL'.[266]

Beyond keeping order, relational constitutionalism seeks to nurture social harmony within multicultural societies, to secure

> the relational well-being of individuals and groups and to preserve sustainable relationships in a polity where disparate religious groups and their members are able to coexist, maintain their distinct identities, while being unified by a national identity and a shared commitment to the common good.[267]

This is centred around the soft constitutional law norm of religious harmony, which is not binding but has legal impact, in setting forth standards of normatively desirable social conduct. Effectively, these norms, contained in white papers and declarations, are an executive interpretation of the scope of a constitutional liberty, such as propagating faith in a manner which is non-denigratory, as set out in the Maintenance of Religious Harmony white paper. Within the statutory framework of the Maintenance of Religious Harmony Act, 'religious harmony' is a capacious understanding of 'public order', but with a focus on maintaining right relationships, not just rights, to sustain solidarity. While the law may provide legal sanctions, it may also be deployed as an instrument for reconciliation when social conflict erupts. This is explored further in chapter four.

Relational constitutionalism gives expression to cultural traits and conceptions of the common good, bringing to the table a broader vocabulary of purpose beyond rights, encompassing the matrix of duties, solidarity, commitment to conciliation as a pacific means of dispute resolution in speaking to what a good citizen is. This reflects the close association of the RoL with maintaining racial and religious harmony as part of the peace-making and -keeping architecture.

[266] DPM Jayakumar, 'The Meaning and Importance of the RoL', IBA RoL Symposium, 19 October 2007, [19], www.mlaw.gov.sg/.

[267] Li-ann Thio, 'Relational Constitutionalism and the Management of Religious Disputes: The Singapore "Secularism with a Soul" Model' (2012) 2 OJLR 446.

3

Rule of Law, Institutions and Structural Judicial Review

I. INTRODUCTION

THE RULE OF law (RoL) interacts with other constitutional principles, such as democracy and the separation of powers (SoP), when courts delimit the boundaries between constitutional organs. In exercising structural judicial review over provisions establishing 'the basic structure of government',[1] a balance is struck between institutional autonomy and accountability. This is evident in judicial doctrines of non-justiciability, presumptions of legality and interpretive approaches towards ouster clauses. This balance depends on whether emphasis is placed on legal or political checks, and the relational architecture between the courts and political branches.

This chapter explores the factors eliciting judicial restraint and shaping the contours of judicial review over legislation such as the criminalisation of male sodomy under section 377A, Penal Code, which has been 'a lightning rod for polarization'.[2] It considers how the courts vary the intensity of review over exercises of executive power in politically sensitive areas, such as foreign relations, prosecutorial discretion and elections law. It examines how courts approach legislative ouster clauses, including exceptional security legislation like the Internal Security Act (ISA), where review over preventive detention orders was constitutionally truncated in January 1989 and confined to procedural irregularities. This came swiftly after the Court of Appeal (CA) quashed a detention order in of *Chng Suan Tze v MHA*,[3] advocating a shift from a subjective to an objective approach towards reviewing executive power. This momentous executive reaction and desire to stymie what it viewed as judicial interventionism sent judicial review into the doldrums.[4] After the first decade of the

[1] Adrienne Stone, 'Judicial Review without Rights: Some Problems for the Democratic Legitimacy of Structural Judicial Review' (2008) 28(1) OJLS 1.

[2] *Tan Seng Kee v AG* [2022] 1 SLR 1347, [3].

[3] [1988] SLR 132.

[4] Michael Hor, 'Constitutionalism and Subversion: An Exploration' in Li-ann Thio and Kevin YL Tan (eds), *The Evolution of a Revolution: 40 Years of the Singapore Constitution* (Routledge-Cavendish, 2009) 286–87.

twenty-first century, it appeared to revive when the CA noted that, outside of security law, the 'full amplitude'[5] of the objective review of executive power was intact. This chapter examines how the courts have treated ouster clauses outside of ISA cases.

The contemporary approach towards the judicial control of government is investigated to ascertain whether this is one of *subservience*, which bodes ill for the RoL, or one of *deference* based on the SoP principle of institutional co-equality and comity. Unwritten constitutional principles like the RoL and SoP can speak in more than one voice, serving both accountability and autonomy. Judicial review is 'both the hallmark of the judicial enforcement of the RoL and essential to the RoL'.[6] As the means by which constitutional supremacy is upheld[7] and public power is 'subject to legal limits', the RoL is invoked to emphasise accountability through judicial control, while the SoP is frequently associated with institutional autonomy.

The interplay of these principles within the context of legal communitarianism shapes judicial restraint, not to be confused with judicial passivity or an abdicating 'no review' approach. Singapore courts prefer nowadays to speak in terms of calibrated review, a brand of 'principled pragmatism'[8] reflecting the tension between principled consistent recourse to objective values of what is just or good and a pragmatic relaxing of this where circumstances warrant. This may involve deferring to the competence of an elected government, or concerns that an 'activist' judicial decision could alienate the political branches and erode judicial legitimacy. The general allergy towards judicial adventurism resides in the view that judicial overreaching undermines rather than promotes democratic values through providing multiple pathways to public power. This flows from the Supreme Court's self-image not as an adversary, but as a constructive partner with the political branches in the constitutional democracy project.

In a non-liberal setting, faith in the primacy of political constitutionalism shapes the tenor of judicial deference. Here, the RoL is not primarily centred on the judicial role in checking public power; nor is majoritarian democracy invariably equated with arbitrary government driven by a populist impulse, which threatens the RoL.[9] Majoritarian excesses are tempered through managed forms of political participation and deliberative decision-making solicitous of minority concerns and multiracialism. This is supported by general trust in the

[5] *Yong Vui Kong v AG* [2011] SGCA 9, [79].

[6] AG VK Rajah, 'Judicial Review, Politics, Policy and the Separation of Powers', lecture at the Singapore Management University, 24 March 2016, [3].

[7] *Tan Seng Kee* (n 2) [1].

[8] Li-ann Thio, 'Principled Pragmatism and the "Third Wave" of Communitarian Judicial Review in Singapore' in Jaclyn Neo (ed), *Constitutional Interpretation in Singapore: Theory and Practice* (Routledge, 2016) 76.

[9] Roberto Gargerella, 'The Majoritarian Reading of the Rule of Law' in José María Maravall and Adam Przeworski (eds), *Democracy and the Rule of Law* (Cambridge University Press, 2003) 147–67.

wisdom of virtuous rulers, as a neo-Confucianist ideal,[10] or at least their demonstrated record of securing economic development.[11]

II. JUDICIAL RESTRAINT: MORALLY AND POLITICALLY SENSITIVE ISSUES

Where politically and morally controversial issues are at stake, judicial restraint is applied to avoid trespassing in the legislative or executive realm.

The supreme constitution divides sovereign power among the 'trinity of constitutional organs',[12] where the courts and executive are co-equal, not subordinate to Parliament. Distinct from the court-centric focus of liberal democracies, the courts as a counter-majoritarian check in working out the Singapore brand of legal communitarianism place great weight on legislative intent and the presumption that 'Parliament knows best' the needs of the citizenry, such that a responsible, reasonable Parliament is best placed to helm socio-political reform. The SoP requires the protection of the 'institutional space' of each government branch, within which their allocated powers are fully and fairly exercised.[13]

Judicial restraint is manifest in adopting a sober, technical style of judicial reasoning, even if a decision yields a robust legal outcome. A deferential tone of remonstrance or interlocution is adopted where courts suggest legislative change or hint a statute may be invalid.[14]

A. Moral Questions Doctrine: Judicial Review of Legislation

If reposing faith in majoritarian governments to resolve morally controversial issues is misplaced, placing faith in unelected judges to do so replaces one form of elite rule with another.

Singapore courts have consistently rejected juristocracy, or rule by judges, trading in personal moral values rather than legal concepts, as undemocratic and contrary to the RoL. The 'moral questions' doctrine appreciates that part of the trade-off for judicial independence is that judges demonstrate self-restraint over 'inherently legislative'[15] divisive issues involving societal values,[16] such as

[10] White paper on shared values (Cmd 1, 1991) para 41.

[11] Singapore may exemplify a form of majoritarian government 'compatible with a serious concern for judicious debates' rather than one producing 'irrational and immoderate norms which threaten minority rights': Gargerella (n 9) 152, 157.

[12] *Mohd Faizal v PP* [2012] 4 SLR 947, [11].

[13] *Tan Seng Kee* (n 2) [14].

[14] eg suggesting that Parliament adopt the effects doctrine as the basis of extraterritorial anti-corruption laws: *PP v Taw Cheng Kong* [1998] 2 SLR(R) 459, [88].

[15] Lord Sumpton, *R (Nicklinson) v Ministry of Justice* [2014] UKSC 38, [230]. For questions implicating 'moral and religious questions' where consensus is absent, Parliament should be afforded 'a wide margin of judgement': Lord Reed, [297].

[16] *Tan Eng Hong v AG* [2013] SGHC 199, [94]; *Yong Vui Kong v PP* [2010] 3 SLR 489, [49].

anti-sodomy legislation or the mandatory death penalty for serious drug-trafficking offences. If courts act as a 'mini-legislature'[17] and take sides in the 'culture war'[18] rather than safeguarding the rules of democratic engagement, they risk haemorrhaging legitimacy and their role as 'an independent, neutral and objective forum' for deciding controversies 'on the basis of objective legal rules and principles'.[19] Public debate is demeaned and judicial hubris displayed by removing a moral question from the democratic process, presuming voters cannot decide sensitive issues on 'decent and rational grounds',[20] ushering in 'social transformation without representation'.[21]

The SoP generally 'precludes courts from engaging in reviews of the substantive merits of legislative acts',[22] allowing Parliament to devise 'a pluralistic vision that accommodates divergent interests'.[23] After the Attorney-General (AG) advised the government of a 'high risk'[24] that anti-sodomy legislation might violate the equality guarantee, as the CA had suggested,[25] the government negotiated a political compromise in repealing the law while mitigating the downstream effect by providing some protection for the traditional definition of marriage under new Article 156,[26] discussed in chapter two.

By maintaining that moral questions belong to the legislative province and in refusing direct appeal to moral values,[27] the courts give Parliament the freedom to determine the trajectory of social reform, and to bear the political costs of their decisions. This judicial signalling that a law might be unconstitutional exerts a subtle pressure on Parliament while allowing Parliament to take the lead in devising solutions unavailable to the court.[28] This reflects the official view that moral questions are better suited to the realm of politics, not the empire of law.

The moral questions doctrine is predicated on the possibility of distinguishing between legal and extra-legal questions, keeping the latter within the realm of democratic decision-making, in resisting the judicial temptation 'to turn

[17] *Lim Meng Suang v AG* [2015] 1 SLR 26, [70], [77], [82], [84], [93], [101], [189] (*LMSCA*).
[18] Justice Scalia, *Lawrence v Texas* 539 US 558, 602 (2003).
[19] Lord Sumpton (n 15) [230].
[20] *Schuette v BAMN*, 572 US 291, 134 SCt 1623, 1637, 188 L Ed. 2d 613 (2014).
[21] Justice Scalia, *Obergefell v Hodges* 135 SCt 2574, 2629 (2015).
[22] *Xu Yuanchen v PP* [2023] SGHC 123, [87].
[23] *Tan Seng Kee* (n 2) [5].
[24] AG Lucien Wong, Opening of the Legal Year 2023, The Rule of Law and the duty of the Legal Service, 9 January 2023, [30]; 'Real Risk of Courts Striking Down s377A in Future if Law Is Not Repealed: Panellists' *Straits Times* (26 September 2022).
[25] In *Tan Seng Kee* (n 2) [324], the CA noted that whether the test of 'reasonable classification' in applying the equality guarantee would succeed or fail depended on how the statutory purpose was framed.
[26] PM Lee Hsien Loong, National Day Rally Speech, 21 August 2022, www.pmo.gov.sg; 'Leaving 377A Decision to Courts Would Be Path of Least Resistance, but also Irresponsible, Wrong: Shanmugam' (*CNA.com*, 28 November 2022).
[27] RH Fallon, 'A Constructivist Coherence Theory of Constitutional Interpretation' (1987) 100 Harv L Rev 1189, 1204.
[28] eg the legislature could repeal or partially delete a legislative provision: *LMSCA* (n 17) [180].

sociologist, economist and politicians'. Judges by training are not 'the ultimate repositories of human wisdom' in addressing the socio-political and economic policy issues 'which parliament and administrators' have to deal with, involving a range of reasonable choices. The political branches have access to a fuller range of expert views than what forensic litigation may supply, and can consider the views of groups otherwise unrepresented before a court. Judicial modesty must not disguise abdication, where judicial courage is required to invalidate ultra vires acts, to ensure 'the RoL will continue to be preserved'.[29]

While the legal/extra-legal distinction may be conceptually complicated, even heretical to a critical legal scholar for whom 'law is politics', Singapore courts have adopted a pragmatic working approach towards this. The CA in *Lim Meng Suang v AG*[30] noted the 'intensely controversial' nature of the law criminalising sodomy, eliciting intensely emotional responses 'in the extra-legal sphere'; it declared fealty to 'the voice of the law, which represents the voice of objectivity'.[31] If courts considered extra-legal arguments, this would 'efface the very SoP which confers upon the court its legitimacy in the first place'.[32] What fell within the 'extra-legal' and parliamentary purview included philosophical or jurisprudential debates such as the Millian harm principle or Lord Devlin's arguments about law and regulating social morality,[33] or rhetorical invocations about the dangers of majoritarian (and minoritarian) tyranny.[34] Courts were ill-equipped to assess 'empirical data' in surveys,[35] scientific matters,[36] public health or medical matters,[37] better addressed by Parliament as 'the right place to settle issues which the ordinary man regards as controversial'.[38] The legitimacy of a legislative object implicates 'extra-legal standards' which are 'quintessentially within the sphere of legislative review'.[39] Extra-legal considerations may be judicially referenced to the extent 'absolutely necessary' to enable the court to apply the 'relevant legal principles'[40] relating to constitutional liberties.

In relation to the Article 12 equality guarantee, a modest two-step 'reasonable classification' test (RCT) has been adopted, which permits a narrow assessment of legitimacy considerations as there are 'no legal standards'[41] capable of guiding the court on what is legitimate. This 'threshold'[42] test requires first that the

[29] The CA in *Tan Seet Eng v AG* [2016] 1 SLR 779, citing Lord Diplock, 'Judicial control of Government [1979] Mal LJ cxl, cxlvii, [94].
[30] *LMSCA* (n 17).
[31] ibid [5].
[32] ibid [189].
[33] ibid [162]–[166], [167]–[170].
[34] ibid [159], [172].
[35] ibid [173].
[36] ibid [176].
[37] ibid [177].
[38] ibid [178].
[39] ibid [85].
[40] ibid [6].
[41] ibid [85].
[42] ibid [65].

law provides an intelligible differentia which clarifies who falls within/without a category; second, the differentia must bear a rational nexus to the legislative purpose. This is distinct from more intrusive forms of review, such as tiered scrutiny or proportionality review.

The RCT incorporates 'a limited element of illegitimacy'[43] that operates to ascertain whether there is a 'serious flaw' in the intelligibility of the differentia, which must not be illogical and/or incoherent,[44] or 'a clear disconnect' between the differentia and its legislative purpose, such that the statute may contravene Article 12. Only 'very seldom' would a statute fail this test as 'intelligible' is pegged at 'a relatively low threshold that ought to avoid any consideration of substantive moral, political and/or ethical issues because these issues are potentially (and in most instances, actually) controversial'.[45] For the RCT to be violated, an overwhelming consensus on an ethical position is required; there must be 'no reasonable dispute' on a moral-political question,[46] which would be rare. To fail, the criteria must be 'so unreasonable as to be illogical and/or incoherent',[47] with the CA clarifying that this must be of 'an extreme nature' such that 'no reasonable person' could consider the differentia, even if clear, to be 'functional'.[48] The RCT is connected to 'the wider concept of the SoP', where constitutional interpretation must not dissolve into constitutional amendment. Actors seeking legal changes should resort to political processes, such as seeking constitutional amendment, which is politically possible.[49]

Thus, the moral questions doctrine directs social controversies based on 'incommensurable competing conceptions of the good'[50] to the legislature, as adjudication cannot resolve 'sincere disagreements over deep matters of social conscience' with any finality. Further, where Parliament debates and retains colonial era laws, such as exempting women from caning, this is treated as contemporary legislative endorsement of a choice differentiating between men and women, which the courts should not disturb.[51]

The appropriate division of labour between the legislature, the executive and the judiciary is itself a moral question,[52] as justice may require judicial intervention or self-restraint. The moral questions doctrine seeks to avoid the risk of courts being viewed as a site for 'the continuation of politics by other means'.[53] The emphasis on political constitutionalism is evident in the judicial

[43] ibid [84].
[44] ibid [66].
[45] ibid [65].
[46] ibid [67].
[47] ibid [67].
[48] ibid [67].
[49] ibid [92].
[50] Sundaresh Menon, 'Executive Power: Rethinking the Modalities of Control' [2019] 29 DJCIL 277, 297.
[51] *Yong Vui Kong v PP* [2015] 2 SLR 1129, [108]–[111].
[52] Aileen Kavanagh, 'Judicial Restraint in the Pursuit of Justice' (2010) 60(1) UTLJ 23, 32.
[53] Menon, 'Executive Power' (n 50).

response to a hypothetical raised about whether a law banning all women from driving on the road would contravene Article 12. Aside from opining that such law would fail the RCT as the sex-based differentia may be illogical or incoherent, the court noted this extreme law 'would probably not be enacted by a reasonable Parliament'.[54] Faith is placed in the sense and sensibility of electorally accountable legislative representatives,[55] and the US case of *Roe v Wade*[56] serves as an anti-model of heavy-handed judicial activism, short-circuiting 'the process of democratic, organic change' at state level, by declaring a constitutional privacy right to abortion. This deferred 'stable settlement of what has now become an intractable issue'.[57] This state of affairs continues even after a victory for the pro-life movement: *Roe* was overturned in June 2022 in a 5–4 opinion in *Dobbs v Jackson Women's Health Organization*.[58] This returned abortion regulation to the states, vindicating local democracy.

Deferential review does not necessarily connote milquetoast review nor preclude judicial innovation. This is evident in the limited adoption of substantive legitimate expectations (SLE), to attach legal consequences to an otherwise non-binding government promise or policy, where constitutional rights may be implicated. This related to the policy not to proactively enforce section 377 of the Penal Code, declared before Parliament in 2007 and reiterated by the AG's representations in 2018. The CA in *Tan Seng Kee v AG* adopted and applied an 'extremely limited'[59] version of SLE such that section 377A was 'unenforceable in its entirety' until the AG gave 'reasonable notice' of a change in prosecutorial policy.[60] This would address the concern of homosexual men who were 'unable to plan their lives adequately', not knowing with 'reasonable certainty' how section 377A would be applied; this was undesirable 'from a[n] RoL perspective' as law 'must be capable of guiding the conduct of those that it binds'.[61] This would enable homosexual men to enjoy the 'accommodation'[62] Parliament extended to them, protecting their expectation of not being subject 'to the grave threat of prosecution and the attendant deprivation of liberty',[63] without an express change of enforcement policy. Legal heft was given to a political promise, based on Parliament's intention to retain section 377A[64] without applying a 'living tree' interpretation.

[54] *LMSCA* (n 17) [114].

[55] Ariel Bendor and Zeev Segal, 'Constitutionalism and Trust in Britain: An Ancient Constitutional Culture, a New Judicial Review Model' (2002) 17 Am U Int'l L Rev 683, 700–02.

[56] 410 US 113 (1973): *Tan Seng Kee* (n 2) [6]. See Loh J, *Lim Meng Suang v AG* [2013] 3 SLR 118, [142], citing RB Ginsburg, 'Some Thoughts on Autonomy and Equality in Relation to Roe v Wade' (1985) 63 North Carolina LR 375, 385.

[57] *Tan Seng Kee* (n 2) [6].

[58] 597 US ___ (2022) (US Supreme Court).

[59] *Tan Seng Kee* (n 2) [132].

[60] ibid [150].

[61] ibid [109], citing Tom Bingham, *The Rule of Law* (Penguin Books, 2011) 91–95.

[62] ibid [134].

[63] ibid [133].

[64] ibid [112].

This unique judicial solution did not contravene the SoP; the courts did not evaluate the 'substantive merits' of the political compromise nor constrain future prosecutorial or legislative action, regarding section 377A.[65] It provided homosexual men with certainty and allowed the government flexibility to decide whether to retain or repeal the law 'at an appropriate time'.[66] This innovation reflects the primacy of political constitutionalism.

This relatively weak form of review is a form of dialogic review[67] where a conversation is initiated over a moral question but the political branches have the final say. It presumes a non-adversarial relationship, where the courts may help legislators avoid inconsistencies or the public 'embarrassment' of having legislation struck down. This exercise of judicial review does not entail judicial supremacy, in 'nudging' the legislature, while respecting its superior democratic legitimacy.

B. From Categorical Rejection to Calibrated Review: Judicial Review of Executive Power

Three main factors inform the calibrated review[68] of executive power. First, the matter may involve policy choices, which is a function of political preference. Second, polycentric considerations may be involved. Third, institutional propriety may mandate subjecting a decision to political forms of accountability. This recognises the need both to confront executive lawlessness and to respect the co-equality of institutions and their partnership in upholding RoL.

The doctrine of non-justiciability recognises the limited 'capabilities of the courts'[69] in considering 'where public decision-making responsibility should best reside'.[70] Primary justiciability relates to whether a decision is amenable to judicial review, while secondary justiciability assumes that judicial review is available, but on truncated grounds. While recognising that a subject matter is non-justiciable, the courts are reluctant to adopt a categorical rejection of review. This reflects the mutual qualification of SoP and RoL values, as examined in various fields of executive activity.

(i) Foreign Policy and Foreign Relations

The conduct of foreign relations and foreign policy is politically sensitive, affecting inter-nation comity. As the Constitution is silent, the Westminster practice

[65] ibid [135]–[136].

[66] ibid [151].

[67] Swati Jhaveri, 'Interrogating Dialogic Theories of Judicial Review' (2019) 17(3) ICON 811.

[68] Steven Chong J, *Yong Vui Kong v AG* [2011] 1 SLR 1, [29].

[69] BV Harris, 'Judicial Review, Justiciability and the Prerogative of Mercy' (2003) 62(3) Cambridge Law Journal 631, 631.

[70] ibid 634.

that Cabinet, in exercising executive authority under Article 23, engages in acts like treaty-making is followed. In this field, the courts recognise 'there are areas of prerogative power' entrusted to 'the democratically elected Executive and Legislature'[71] subject to ultimate electoral accountability. Judicial review may be inappropriate where specialist competence and non-legal factors dominate a field. For example, where the geopolitically sensitive issue of state recognition is concerned, the courts seek to avoid embarrassing the executive.

Thus, in *Civil Aeronautics Administration v Singapore Airlines*,[72] the court upheld the executive's 'one-China policy' that Taiwan was not a state and could not claim sovereign immunity. Under section 18 of the State Immunity Act, an executive certification is conclusive evidence of whether an entity is a state. A decision not to issue a certificate is treated as evidence of non-recognition,[73] not as an ambiguity inviting judicial assessment of statehood.[74] The CA noted that sovereign immunity was a matter within 'the exclusive province of the Executive', involving both policy and facts, some not 'within the public domain'.[75] The courts should not 'get themselves involved in international relations' or 'second-guess' the executive, but seek 'further clarification'[76] over uncertainties. Where the executive gives a 'reasonably clear' answer, it is 'vital … the Judiciary and the Executive should speak with one voice'.[77]

Other areas of executive decision-making 'that are, and should be, immune from judicial review'[78] include 'high policy' matters, like national defence, declaring war and international boundary disputes.[79] This is akin to the American 'political questions' doctrine. Nonetheless, the courts refuse to adopt a 'highly rigid and categorical' approach in deciding whether a case is justiciable. Instead, based on the SoP 'applied sensibly', the courts have sought to construct 'a sophisticated and nuanced doctrine of judicial deference' able to 'tailor' the intensity of review to the 'particular institutional circumstances and constitutional context' of the case.[80] The High Court in *Lee Hsien Loong v Review Publishing*[81] articulated a set of principles to apply in determining where the boundaries of unreviewable executive prerogative powers lay.

First, justiciability depended not on the source of power, but on the subject matter; while the 'forbidden areas' were not immutable, they would include

[71] Menon JC, *Lee Hsien Loong v Review Publishing Co Ltd* [2007] 2 SLR(R) 453, 491, [98].
[72] [2004] 1 SLR(R) 570, [12]–[28].
[73] ibid [11].
[74] Olufemi Elias, 'The International Status of Taiwan in the Courts of Canada and Singapore' (2004) 8 SYBIL 93.
[75] *Civil Aeronautics* (n 72) [22].
[76] ibid [27].
[77] ibid [41].
[78] ibid [95].
[79] ibid [96].
[80] Rajah (n 6) [47].
[81] [2007] 2 SLR(R) 453.

foreign policy and foreign deployment of armed forces.[82] Second, judges are ill-equipped by training and lack of access to materials, and should not review decisions involving competing policy considerations. Third, the courts should abstain from review to avoid embarrassing the government or hindering its capacity to conduct foreign policy. Lastly, courts exercise due restraint, being conscious that government branches are co-equal.[83]

Judicial review is available over prima facie non-justiciable matters, where the courts, on 'closer scrutiny', can isolate a pure question of law which may be justiciable, such as interpreting an international instrument which affects domestic law and litigants' legal obligations, as distinct from evaluating defence policy, where the people look to the government for 'wise and effective decisions'.[84] Limited judicial review over high-policy matters may avail, confined to matters like reviewing for bad faith.[85] Where prerogative powers involving 'national security' affect individual rights, such as deportation decisions or rejecting passport applications, these are nevertheless justiciable.[86]

Thus, context rather than categorical rules is emphasised for high-policy matters where judicial review may be available when questions of law can be separated from the morass of policy considerations, and where individual rights are gravely impacted.

(ii) Reviewing Constitutionally Allocated Executive Powers: Prosecutorial Discretion

The shift from a 'no review' to a limited review approach towards exercises of prosecutorial discretion under Article 35(8)[87] reflects the recalibration of review. This is underscored by the persistence of the presumption of constitutionality as applied in the prosecutorial context, where the AG, by dint of his constitutional status, presumably 'acts in the public interest'. This presumption of legality of acts of high state officials should 'not be regarded as the courts deferring to the Prosecution', as distinct from recognising institutional autonomy and the honour or trust due to the office-holder,[88] consonant with the neo-Confucianist trustworthy governor ideal.

[82] Kay J, *R (Campaign for Nuclear Disarmament) v PM* [2002] EWHC 2777 (Admin), [50], cited in *Review Publishing* (n 71) [87].

[83] *Civil Aeronautics* (n 72) [98].

[84] Law LJ, *R (on the application of Marchiori) v Environment Agency* [2002] EWCA Civ 3, [38].

[85] ibid [40], discussed in *Review Publishing* (n 71) [94].

[86] Citing Taylor LJ, *R v SS for Foreign and Commonwealth Affairs ex p Everett* [1989] 1 QB 811, 820, in *Review Publishing* (n 71) [91].

[87] Art 35(8) states: 'The AG shall have power, exercisable at his discretion, to institute, conduct or discontinue any proceedings for any offence.'

[88] *Ramalingam Ravinthran v AG* [2012] 2 SLR 49, [46]. A similar but weaker presumption of legality also applied to officials not holding constitutional office: [47].

Though very wide, prosecutorial discretion is not absolute, and courts have rejected the argument that it is not justiciable.[89] An executive power, 'even one with a constitutional status', cannot be allowed to override a constitutional liberty.[90] Executive powers are subject to legal limits, as the RoL demands, and must be exercised in good faith, not arbitrarily, respecting constitutional rights.[91] Judicial intervention in such matters would not contravene the principle of judicial non-interference with prosecutorial power, based on SoP considerations. Where an offender is able to prove a prima facie breach of a fundamental liberty, the burden then shifts to the Prosecution to justify its prosecutorial discretion.

In *Ramalingam Ravinthran v AG*,[92] two offenders involved in the same drug-trafficking criminal enterprise were charged differently – one with a non-capital and one with a capital offence. This did not involve judicial power, as preferring charges is an executive function. Both constitutional powers are 'distinct and separate'[93] but of equal status,[94] and to be harmoniously construed.[95]

While the courts could review the considerations informing the AG's decision, acting as Public Prosecutor (PP), this did not extend to determining what charge to prefer, irrespective of whether it involved a mandatory penalty, which removes sentencing discretion. The 'very essence of prosecutorial discretion' in formulating charges was to accord 'due weight' to 'all relevant circumstances or considerations',[96] after which judicial power over the criminal proceedings is triggered.

The decision was challenged as violating the equality guarantee. However, the court noted the 'treat like alike' test Article 12(1) required applied differently in the legislative and prosecutorial domains.[97] Regarding the former, the judicial function was to ensure equal treatment for similar legal guilt, applying the presumption of constitutionality.[98] In relation to the latter, the PP could consider legal guilt and many other factors, provided there was no bias and no irrelevant matters considered.[99] Relevant factors include the offender's moral

[89] *Sim Min Teck v PP* [1987] SLR(R) 65 and *Thiruselvam v PP* [2001] 2 SLR 125, as discussed critically in *Ramalingam* (n 88) [30], [36], [40], for its uncritical application of *Teh Cheng Poh*, which concerned only one offender.

[90] *Ramalingam* (n 88) [41].

[91] *Law Society of Singapore v Phyllis Tan* [2008] 2 SLR(R) 239.

[92] *Quek Hock Lye v PP* [2012] 2 SLR 1012.

[93] ibid [28].

[94] *Phyllis Tan*, [144], cited in *Ramalingam* (n 88) [43].

[95] *Quek Hock Lye* (n 92) [29].

[96] ibid [29].

[97] ibid [61].

[98] *Lee Keng Guan v PP* [1977–78] SLR(R) 78, discussed in *Ramalingam* (n 88) [48].

[99] Applying *Teh Cheng Poh* [1979] 1 Mal LJ 50, 56, which, like the CA in *Ramalingam* (n 88) [24] and [29], dealt with one offender whose criminal act was an offence under two different statutes.

blameworthiness, willingness to cooperate, gravity of harm or even showing compassion, matters not readily amenable to judicial supervision. Such factors could provide 'legitimate reasons'[100] justifying a decision to charge one offender differently from parties to the same criminal enterprise, so they would experience divergent penalties without violating Article 12. For example, the PP could reduce the drug quantity specified in the charge, presumably not acting on personal whim but 'for the greater good of society, to maintain law and order and "to uphold the RoL"'.[101] Given these 'manifold factors', it was 'wholly unrealistic' for the court to proceed on the basis that the PP would be unable 'to point to any relevant consideration' to explain his decision; thus, the court stated the PP was not obliged to provide reasons for making a particular prosecutorial decision.[102] On the facts, the co-accused's willingness to be prosecution witness was one such legitimate factor.

In reviewing executive power, a 'sliding scale' approach is evident. Courts more readily intervene where narrow questions of law and procedure, falling within their expertise, are concerned. Greater judicial reticence is apparent where a matter involves polycentric issues and domain expertise.

(iii) Judicial Intervention and By-elections Law

Calling by-elections mid-term to fill a vacated electoral seat is a politically sensitive matter, which can become a 'spectator blood sport'.[103] This was the case in pre-Independence Singapore when 13 PAP assemblymen broke off in 1961 to form the Barisan Socialis, leaving the ruling PAP government with a 26:25 majority; this became a nerve-racking 25:25 when a PAP minister died in 1962. Every no-confidence motion potentially spelt political turnover.

On Independence, the PAP government sought to diminish such political drama by decreasing the impact of individual Members of Parliament (MP) in two ways: first, by introducing an anti-hopping clause in Article 46(2)(b), vacating the seat of an MP who is expelled or resigns from his party; and second, by removing a clause mandating by-elections within three months of seat vacation,[104] and not specifying a time limit. The PAP leadership had been required to introduce such a clause in the state constitution when joining the Federation of Malaysia in 1963.

In 2008, Prime Minister (PM) Lee observed that these amendments resulted in 'less buying or intimidation of MPs to switch sides', preventing MPs from randomly forcing by-elections and 'distracting the country from other more

[100] *Quek Hock Lye* (n 92) [63], [65], [71].
[101] ibid [53].
[102] ibid [78].
[103] Lee Hsien Loong, Motion: Parliamentary Elections, 84 SPR, 27 August 2008.
[104] PM Lee Kuan Yew stated the three-month limit would no longer apply for reasons stemming from 'our own experience of elections and of government in Singapore'. 24 SPR, 22 December 1965, col 432. On the precursor clauses, see *Vellama v AG* [2013] 4 SLR 1, [58]–[60].

pressing concerns'.[105] This centralises power in a party-centric system[106] where individual MPs are disciplined by the party whip. While this conduces to stable government, it weakens political checks. The official view was that the political system is focused not on individual MPs, but on the ruling party delivering on its programmes. Thus, a vacant seat does not affect the government's five-year ruling mandate, and the PM has 'full discretion' over calling by-elections.[107]

The CA in *Vellama v AG*[108] rejected the idea that the PM enjoyed absolute discretion on whether to call by-elections in vacated single member constituencies (SMCs), but nonetheless softened the blow by underscoring that judicial intervention would be exceptional. This showed deferential regard for this polycentric policy decision, while standing sentinel against unchecked executive power.

Article 49 baldly provides that a parliamentary vacancy 'shall be filled by election' in accordance with the relevant legislation. Section 24 of the Parliamentary Elections Act only provides that the President, acting on Cabinet's advice, must issue election writs addressed to the Returning Officer, specifying the nomination day, within certain parameters. Article 49 provides neither substantive nor procedural norms regulating the exercise of the power to call by-elections. This would leave any future vacancies to 'the whims and fancies of the Party in power',[109] possibly imperilling the state of parliamentary democracy if by-elections are unreasonably delayed.[110]

However, Article 49 must be read against the matrix of constitutional principles. The CA, in examining parliamentary discussions, noted no one argued there was an unfettered discretion not to fill a vacancy, as distinct from the existence of a discretion to call by-elections.[111] Removing the time-limit clause in 1965 rendered the question of when to call by-elections 'more political', but the legal question of whether the PM had unfettered discretion under Article 49 remained.[112] Without a 'pre-determined time frame', the timing issue would be resolved by applying 'the general law relating to statutory construction'.[113]

The CA held that the PM was under a duty to call by-elections to fill empty parliamentary seats, even if no time limit was specified.[114] Section 52 of the Interpretation Act provided guidance, requiring that when no time period is

[105] Lee Hsien Loong (n 103).
[106] *Vellama* [2013] (n 104) [80]: 'our Constitution emphasizes the political party rather than the individual MPs'.
[107] Lee Hsien Loong (n 103).
[108] *Vellama* [2013] (n 104). This overruled the High Court decision in *Vellama v AG* [2012] 4 SLR 698.
[109] Ahmad Jabri, 21 SPR, 1 August 1963, col 689, cited in *Vellama* [2012] (n 108) [62].
[110] Lee Siew Choh, 20 SPR, 9 April 1963, col 350, cited in *Vellama* [2012] (n 108) [64].
[111] *Vellama* [2013] (n 104) [71]–[72].
[112] ibid [74].
[113] ibid [78].
[114] Art 49 only applied to SMC, not group representation constituency vacancies.

prescribed, a thing 'shall be done with all convenient speed'.[115] This phrase embodies 'the common law concept of a reasonable time', considering all relevant circumstances. This went beyond merely logistical or practical considerations, as the PM is allowed a 'measure of latitude' on the question of timing, which involved 'a polycentric matter' in a 'dynamic situation'. It was not possible to identify predetermined factors to assess the reasonableness of not calling a by-election. The PM could justifiably consider policy issues like public health threats caused by haze or pandemic.[116] Nonetheless, this discretion did not extend to indefinite deferral or refusal to call a by-election, absent an intention to soon call a general election.

The 'substantial measure of discretion' under Article 49 was to be balanced by 'an equally important consideration',[117] the constitutional value of democracy, representation and legitimation, and the prospect of voters facing a 'serious risk' of disenfranchisement through a seat left empty 'for an unnecessary prolonged period',[118] depriving them of an MP serving as 'the voice of the people of the constituency'.[119] Additionally, the limits of the PM's discretion not to call by-elections is subject to a test of reasonableness, serving the RoL value of accountability.[120] A deferential note is struck in recognising that judicial intervention 'would only be warranted in exceptional cases', given the 'fact-sensitive' context. Nonetheless, the PM has a continuing duty to review the circumstances 'from time to time',[121] and to call a by-election where circumstances change. Space is left for political judgement, while precluding unfettered discretion.

III. JUDICIAL REVIEW OF OUSTER CLAUSES

Courts have traditionally been hostile to ouster clauses (OCs), which represent legislative attempts to exclude judicial review. The RoL jealously guards the judicial role as the impartial arbiter of legal disputes, as effective OCs may shield power abuses and block access to justice. Judicial approaches towards OCs reveal understandings of institutional roles, and Singapore courts generally view OCs 'with circumspection',[122] and have in practice sometimes declined to give effect to them. Judicial notice has been taken of academic opinion that OCs may be 'incompatible with the RoL'[123] and unconstitutional.

[115] *Vellama* [2013] (n 104) [83].
[116] ibid [84]–[85].
[117] ibid [87].
[118] ibid [85].
[119] ibid [79].
[120] ibid [88].
[121] ibid [87].
[122] *Robin Per v HDB* [2015] SGCA 62, [64].
[123] ibid [65]. Reference was made to Thio Li-ann, 'Law and the Administrative State' in KYL Tan (ed), *The Singapore Legal System* (Singapore University Press, 1999) 195; Thio Li-ann, *A Treatise*

If judicial review is to implement parliamentary will, showing fidelity to parliamentary intent according to classic ultra vires theory,[124] then judicial review and OCs are set at tension. On closer examination, two contrasting legislative intents are discernible: first, the intent to preclude judicial review; and second, the intent that judicial review should prevent agencies from transgressing their allotted powers. Suspicion would be directed at courts ignoring clear statutory provisions and at attempts to oust judicial review, respectively. Ignoring either intent may violate the RoL, reflecting its paradoxical quality of being both statist and constitutionalist, affirming and constraining power.

A. Constitutionally Authorised Privative Clauses

A third intent may be identified when it comes to Article 149-authorised security legislation, which vindicates the will of a parliamentary supermajority in enacting legislation which may be contrary to constitutional norms.

As discussed in chapter one, Parliament introduced a constitutional amendment in 1989 after an ISA detention order was struck down in *Chng Suan Tze*.[125] The new Article 149(3) authorised amendments to the ISA, providing that 'nothing in Article 93' shall invalidate any law pursuant to Article 149 and such laws would be 'valid notwithstanding' inconsistency with various constitutional liberties, or which would be 'outside the legislative power of Parliament'. The RoL was severely diluted as judicial control of extraordinary anti-subversion laws was effectively denuded. While democratic means of accountability avail, this is illusory in a dominant party state. Indeed, the CA in *Chng* considered it 'no answer to refer to accountability to Parliament as an alternative safeguard', as the executive should be responsible to the courts for the lawfulness, and to Parliament for the 'efficiency and policy' of their actions.[126]

The amendment was ostensibly to 'restore the law on judicial review',[127] ousting substantive review while retaining review for procedural illegalities. When the constitutionality of these ISA amendments were challenged in

on Singapore Constitutional Law (Academy Publishing, 2012), [10.218]; Chan Sek Keong, 'Judicial Review – From Angst to Empathy' (2010) 22 SAcLJ 469, [19].

[124] This was developed in the parliamentary sovereignty context, after the Diceyan vision of unitary democracy: Paul Craig, *Administrative Law*, 4th edn (Sweet & Maxwell, 1999) 4–7. Arguably, given the supremacy of the Singapore Constitution, a modified ultra vires doctrine may be developed, indigenised by reference to constitutional principles: Thio Li-ann, 'The Theory and Practice of Judicial Review of Administrative Action' in TM Yeo et al (eds), *SAL Conference 2011: Developments in Singapore Law between 2006 and 2010: Trends and Perspective* (Singapore Academy of Law, 2011) 714–52.

[125] *Chng Suan Tze v MHA* [1988] 2 SLR(R) 525.

[126] Citing Lord Diplock, *IRC v National Federation of Self-Employed and Small Businesses Ltd* [1982] AC 617, 644 in ibid [86].

[127] S Jayakumar (Law Minister), Constitution (Amendment) Bill, 52 SPR, 25 January 1989, col 463.

Teo Soh Lung v MHA, the High Court stated that Parliament, in enacting an OC,[128] had not abolished the RoL nor usurped judicial power; it had 'done no more than to enact the RoL relating to the law applicable to judicial review'. The legislation did not direct the courts to enact a particular judgment and the amendments were designed to 'ensure the effectiveness of preventive detention',[129] leaving it to the executive's 'subjective satisfaction'[130] to decide whether preventive detention was necessary. There was nothing to stop Parliament from deciding that the subjective test of review 'should apply to all cases, past, present and future'.[131]

This parlous, positivist reading treats 'law' as 'rules properly enacted', without subjecting the content of law to objective principles. This reflects a spirit of judicial subservience, paying obeisance to legislative will and constitutional authorisation.

B. Reviewing Ouster Clauses Beyond the Internal Security Act

Beyond security law, OCs are not automatically deferred to, and may be circumvented in two primary ways.

First, OCs may be evaded by the common law interpretive technique the House of Lords developed in *Anisminic v Foreign Compensation Commission*,[132] where errors of law produced 'purported' rather than 'real' determinations; as the former are a legal nullity, OCs cannot apply to them and do not impede judicial review. This judicial technique of circumventing OCs 'has long been incorporated as a feature of our local administrative law jurisprudence'.[133] Thus, OCs have been ineffective in the face of jurisdictional errors of law relating to patent errors, natural justice violations, bad faith and irrationality.[134]

Second, an OC is arguably inconsistent with Article 93 and 'the supervisory jurisdiction of the courts cannot be ousted'.[135] This is linked to the RoL as a constitutional principle and the idea that judicial review applies to all executive decisions, even where this involves reading a statute countertextually, within the context of a supreme constitution. No court has unambiguously

[128] ISA, s 8B(2).

[129] *Teo Soh Lung v MHA* [1989] 1 SLR(R) 461, [48].

[130] ibid [49].

[131] ibid [53]. The CA left open future challenges to the ISA on grounds of statutory purpose, bad faith, unreasonableness or violation of the constitutional basic structure: *Teo Soh Lung v MHA* [1990] 1 SLR(R) 347–68.

[132] [1969] 2 AC 147 (UKHL).

[133] *Nagaenthran v AG* [2018] SGHC 112, [122].

[134] *Re Application by Yee Yut Ee* [1977–1978] SLR(R) 490, [18], [31]; *Stansfield Business v MOM* [1999] 2 SLR(R) 866, [21]–[22]; *Teng Fuh Holdings v Collector of Land Revenue* [2007] 2 SLR(R) 568.

[135] Chan (n 123) [19].

treated Article 93 as a categorical trump which would eviscerate all OCs as illegitimate legislative usurpations of judicial power.[136]

However, some consider that Menon CJ's obiter observations in *Nagaenthrean v AG* denote a 'judicial intent to forge a different path'[137] from that of the High Court, which sought to apply a 'reasonable balance' test. The CA in *Ridzuan v AG*[138] addressed the reviewability of the PP's determination, under section 33B(2)(b) of the Misuse of Drugs Act (MDA), whether to award an offender a substantive assistance certification for providing information useful to disrupting drug-trafficking activities. In addition to bad faith and malice, which section 33B(4) expressly provided for,[139] assuming it was a partial OC, the determination could also be challenged for violating constitutional rights. The CA in *Ridzuan* said it seemed intuitively inconceivable that an aggrieved person who could substantiate that the PP had considered irrelevant considerations, a ground section 33B(4) did not list, had no judicial remedy. This was 'especially compelling' where the accused's life was at stake.[140] Thus, the statutory text and parliamentary intent in scoping down the available grounds of review was not determinative of which grounds of review availed, where constitutional norms were involved.

While ultimately finding that section 33B(4) was not an OC but a statutory immunity clause,[141] the CA rejected the respondent's view that the court would be powerless to act if it was shown the PP considered irrelevant considerations. Menon CJ suggested that, to the extent section 33B(4) ousted judicial review, it would be 'constitutionally suspect' for violating Article 93 and the SoP.[142] This could be read to mean that any legislative preclusions of judicial review on grounds not listed in section 33B(4), like irrationality or natural justice, would be 'constitutionally suspect'. If any attempt to preclude grounds of judicial review is per se invalid, then only constitutionally authorised OCs may be valid. Menon CJ observed that judicial review as a 'core aspect of the judicial power and function' would not 'ordinarily be capable of being excluded by ordinary legislation such as the MDA'.[143] As Article 93 was part of the supreme law,

[136] Thio Li-ann, 'Ousting Ouster Clauses: The Ins and Outs of the Principles Regulating the Scope of Judicial Review in Singapore' [2020] SJLS 392; Kenny Chng, 'Microcontextual Considerations in Ouster Clause Analysis: A Comparative Study of Parallel Trends in the UK and Singapore' (2022) 20(3) ICON 1257.

[137] Kenny Chng, 'Reconsidering Ouster Clauses in Singapore Administrative Law' (2020) 136 Law Quarterly Review 40, 43.

[138] [2015] 5 SLR 1222.

[139] The High Court treated s 33B(4) MDA as an OC and noted determinations could also be challenged on the unlisted ground of 'unconstitutionality'. It described the clause not as a contravention of Art 93, but as 'an exemplar of the SoP principle in action': *Nagaenthran v AG* (n 133) [97].

[140] *Nagaenthran v PP* [2019] 2 SLR 216, [70].

[141] ibid [47]–[50], [63], [65], [67], [75].

[142] ibid [74]. Some may read Menon CJ's obiter as being categorical insofar as he considers any OCs, even partial OCs, 'constitutionally suspect'.

[143] *Nagaenthran v PP* (n 140) [71].

there would be 'few, if any' state and citizen legal disputes from which judicial power would be excluded in determining the legal limits of power,[144] consonant with 'any society that prides itself in being governed by the RoL, as our society does'.[145]

The obiter speaks to the *possibility* of excluding judicial review by ordinary legislation, while emphasising the *rarity* of such exclusion. This would host a non-categorical, contextual approach towards the degree of constitutional offensiveness required to invalidate an OC, a call to deferential review, not no review at all. On this understanding, partial OCs may pass constitutional muster. This aligns with the approach in *Tey Tsun Hang v AG*,[146] which the High Court in *Nagaenthran v AG*[147] endorsed.

In *Tey*, the OC in question was section 39A of the Immigration Act, which provides that 'there should be no judicial review in any courts' for a decision made under the Act except where there is non-compliance with statutory procedure. The case concerned the failed renewal application for a re-entry permit which permanent residents like Tey, a Malaysian citizen, needed to leave and return to Singapore.

It was not considered wrong per se to oust the court's jurisdiction, as there were 'good and self-evident reasons' why certain matters, such as land planning, immigration and defence, were 'best left to the executive arm'.[148] The intent behind section 39A was to prevent courts from reviewing the merits of an immigration decision and frustrating, eg the government's decision to expel aliens or deal with illegal entrants.

The High Court noted that section 39A was a partial, not a total, OC, representing a 'reasonable balance'[149] between competing RoL and institutional autonomy considerations; the OC was effective insofar as only non-compliance with statutory procedure was reviewable, which meant the decision-maker did not have unfettered discretion in this limited respect.[150] There have been other arguments that, applying *Anisminic*, judicial review may be available for other jurisdictional errors of law beyond those statutorily identified in a constitutionally valid statutory OC. If accepted, this favours

[144] Citing *Yong Vui Kong v AG* [2011] 2 SLR 1189, [31]; *Chng Suan Tze* (n 125) [86]; *Nagaenthran v PP* (n 140) [73].

[145] *Nagaenthran v PP* (n 140) [73].

[146] [2015] 1 SLR 856.

[147] [2018] SGHC 112, [92].

[148] *Tey Tsun Hang v AG* [2015] 1 SLR 856, [44].

[149] ibid [44]–[45]. The CA in *Nagaenthran v PP* [2019] SGCA 37 did not refer to a 'reasonable balance' test, but has not definitely overruled it. Some argue that balancing is inappropriate as Art 93 confers exclusive judicial power to the courts in absolute terms: BJ Ong, 'The Constitutionality of Ouster Clause: Nagaenthran v AG [2018] SGHC 112' (2019) 19 OUCLJ 157, 170. However, this discounts reading constitutional principles like the RoL, a key aspect of judicial power, against other principles like the SoP in a mutually modulating manner, shaping how OCs are interpreted.

[150] *Tey Tsun Hang* (n 148) [46].

RoL considerations based on accountability, drawing from common law principles, not the statutory text.[151]

To circumvent the evasive *Anisminic* technique, section 104 of the 2021 Foreign Interference (Countermeasures) Act (FICA) apparently attempts to create a judge-proof OC. It provides that any determination, order or decision of the relevant authority 'is final' and may only be challenged on grounds of procedural non-compliance. Section 104(2) provides that determinations include *purported* determinations, provided the error was not 'an excess of jurisdiction or a failure to exercise jurisdiction'. In other words, legal errors stemming from exercising jurisdiction one did not have or from abrogating or fettering discretion could produce purported determinations to which the OC would not apply. However, legal errors stemming from the abuse or misuse of jurisdiction one does possess, such as irrationality, would not be treated as legal nullities, and would be insulated from judicial review by the OC.[152]

Whether an OC would pass constitutional muster turns on a multifactor analysis involving the judicial negotiation of interacting constitutional principles. The first factor is whether the clause is a total or partial OC, in relation to grounds of review, time or remedies. A total OC runs the risk of making autocratic legal islands of public officials. Here, section 104 FICA is a partial ouster clause. Where Parliament, which in Singapore is not sovereign, states in clear terms its intent to preclude judicial review, the court will have to grapple with the RoL value of upholding constitutional principles and subject the court to the RoL in the sense of being obliged to give effect to parliamentary will, as embodied in OCs. The second factor is whether fundamental liberties or important individual interests, towards which the courts will be protective, are involved in ensuring a judicial remedy. The third is whether the subject matter is one of high policy, better suited to executive handling, involving 'sensitive and polycentric considerations' such as foreign manpower or handling xenophobic social tensions, where 'speed and efficiency' are 'critical considerations'.[153] Fourth, where controversial legal questions are at stake and are to be decided by an alternative regime like an administrative tribunal, which has expert knowledge and can act with expedition or secrecy, this may be a good reason for deferring to Parliament's choice to limit review. Where the tribunal is composed of independent judges, limiting judicial review may be

[151] In *Nagaenthran v AG* (n 133), the High Court held in principle that grounds of review not listed in s 33B(4) could still avail. It left open the question whether all legal errors are jurisdictional – if so, all errors of law would be reviewable even if there is an OC: [123].

[152] Notably, a similar OC in the Judicial Review and Courts Act 2022 relating to a 'purported decision' was given full effect by the High Court *in R (Oceana) v Upper Tribunal (Immigration and Asylum Chamber)* [2023] EWJC 79 (Admin). This appears at odds with the Supreme Court's decision in *R (Privacy International) v Investigatory Powers Tribunal*, where Lord Carnwath stated it fell to the courts, not the legislature, 'to determine the limits set by the RoL to the power to exclude review': [2020] AC 491, [3].

[153] Edwin Tong (Second Law Minister), 'Rule of Law, Judicial Review and the Sunlight of Scrutiny', 95 SPR, 4 March 2021.

less constitutionally objectionable. The subject matter of FICA is certainly politically sensitive, in that it deals with measures to counter foreign interference seeking to manipulate domestic politics through online hostile information campaigns (HICs) and through local proxies or 'politically significant persons'.

FICA empowers the government to order a tech company to disable access to certain content, to issue a Must Carry Direction informing the public of an ongoing HIC or a Transparency Directive to reveal an article's author where it is 'incendiary', such as urging Singapore civil servants to march on the streets like their Hong Kong counterparts.[154] An online location may be declared as proscribed. The recipient of HIC directions may appeal first to the minister, then to an independent three-person reviewing tribunal composed of Singapore citizens and chaired by a Supreme Court judge,[155] who all enjoy the immunities of a High Court judge.[156] The tribunal, applying a statutory proportionality test, may override the ministerial decision.[157] It may with finality dismiss the appeal or revoke the decision appealed against.[158] It has the power to ensure that information before it is not disclosed, where contrary to Singapore's national security, economic well-being or how the intelligence service functions.[159]

The justification for precluding judicial review is 'to protect sensitive information' which would have 'very serious' consequences if leaked.[160] It would be impossible to get foreign contacts who provide information to attend court, especially if revealing this information could imperil life. Even if heard in camera, the information would be exposed to many ears.[161] In terms of institutional design, a 'balancing exercise'[162] is undertaken whereby the courts are tasked with ensuring procedural compliance and a proper exercise of jurisdiction, without intruding into the merits. This entails weighing the risks of a 'rogue Government' versus 'rogue foreign interference'.[163]

Although RoL was the foremost consideration, it was acknowledged during parliamentary debates that the trial process was not suited for specific matters like maintaining religious harmony, land acquisition, regulating immigration and preventive detention laws, all of which are handled by tribunals wielding quasi-judicial powers, as an alternative external control mechanism. The Singaporean people as 'a highly educated literate population', who have the

[154] K Shanmugam (Law & Home Affairs Minister), 'Foreign Interference (Countermeasure) Bill, 95 SPR, 4 October 2021, www.mha.gov.sg.

[155] FICA, ss 92, 93.

[156] FICA, s 94. The degree to which a tribunal acts like a court informed Lord Sumption's views that the RoL was 'sufficiently vindicated' in *R (Privacy International)* (n 152) [172].

[157] FICA, ss 92, 93; Shanmugam (n 154) [129]–[152].

[158] FICA, s 97.

[159] FICA, s 99(g).

[160] FICA, ss 92, 93; Shanmugam (n 154) [186].

[161] ibid [300]–[306].

[162] ibid [316].

[163] ibid [360].

'final say', expressing their 'public opinion through elections'.[164] This shows the official preference for blunt political checks not substantively limiting a strong state, while securing broad popular support. Limits to judicial review require justification and continuing acceptance; thus, OCs should be subject to generational review of what the people find acceptable, 'under what circumstances, and towards what end', including a shift from authoritarian practices to 'greater checks and balances'.[165]

Cumulatively, the presence or absence of these factors denotes a kind of 'sliding scale' for grading an OC's degree of constitutional offensiveness. This invites inquiry into the substantive reasons for and against the effectiveness of an OC. Avoiding confrontation between Parliament and the courts, a 'reasonable balance' is sought between efficiency and accountability in calibrating the level of scrutiny the RoL requires. This is negotiated against the pull of the SoP, presumption of legality and democratic considerations as part of the constitutional matrix shaping the contours of judicial review, where courts ensure other government branches do not transgress their legal powers. It appears OCs are presumptively ineffective, in the absence of countervailing considerations.

C. Concluding Reflections: Of Trust and Constructive Balance

The basic constitutional architecture is composed of principles such as the RoL, SoP and democracy, which interact, qualify and shape each other. In Singapore, a 'constructive balance'[166] is sought between the three government branches, where the judiciary polices unlawful action while preserving effective governance, which enables decisive action and avoids gridlock; considerable weight in this scheme is given to political modes of accountability. The 'mutual trust and respect' for each branch's expertise and competence is emphasised,[167] as is cooperative partnership over confrontation 'informed by mutual distrust and self-preservation'.[168]

As an example of this spirit of mutual respect, Menon CJ recounted what happened after the CA found a detention order issued under the Criminal Law Temporary Provisions Act (CLTPA) to be unlawful in *Tan Seet Eng v AG*.[169] The criminal activities in the order did not impact public safety in Singapore, as required. Tan was released and rearrested six days later under a fresh CLTPA

[164] ibid [361].

[165] Muralli Pillai, 'Rule of Law, Judicial Review and the Sunlight of Scrutiny', 95 SPR, 4 March 2021. The Second Law Minister stated that OCs are regularly reviewed and repealed when no longer necessary.

[166] Shanmugam (n 154).

[167] ibid.

[168] ibid.

[169] [2016] 1 SLR 779.

order, indicating how Singapore's public order was affected by Tan's global football match-fixing activities.[170]

The Home Affairs Ministry, on its own initiative, reviewed the cases of three detainees in the light of the CA's decision, and released them. This executive commitment to respect judicial pronouncements was 'critical to the RoL and good governance' as the robustness of a nation's RoL framework depends on how 'the other branches view the Judiciary' and whether it, in turn, 'is able and willing to act honestly, competently and independently'.[171] The strong state acts decisively and fairly, and does not provoke judicial activism through egregious injustice.

A brand of judicial review conducive to this cooperative ethos may best suit Singapore's economic developmental needs, communitarian culture and governance priorities; ultimately, the government follows the law 'because it wants to',[172] out of political commitment. It may retaliate against a judicial decision it dislikes, such as where ISA decisions were insulated from substantive review by amending the Constitution after *Chng Suan Tze*; however, this is not something the government does frequently, which can impair judicial independence. ISA powers implicating national security are hived off from other areas of executive power implicating public order, which are reviewable. There has been no judicialisation of politics in Singapore, where there is a 'very activist, interventionist'[173] government; there is no need to resort to the courts as political leaders are able to drive law and social reform.[174]

Although the courts have the power to strike down legislation, they have not resorted to this as a regular way to discipline legislative processes, preferring to make recommendations to induce legal change as an interlocutor, not competitor. This flows from the belief that where other government branches respect the court, the court is able to 'effectively shape the debate', ensuring the legality of government action 'by setting out its concerns openly' and avoiding potential clashes between the judiciary and the executive.[175] In exercising structural judicial review and determining the parameters of institutional powers, courts make value judgements over competing conceptions of the nature of constitutional arrangements. Under Singapore legal communitarianism, where the elected government is pre-eminent, great trust is reposed in the government to take its constitutional commitments seriously, with the appreciation

[170] 'New Detention Order Issued Against Dan Tan' *Today* (5 December 2015). He was released in December 2019.

[171] Sundaresh Menon, 'The Rule of Law: The Path to Exceptionalism' (2016) 28 SAcLJ 413, 423.

[172] Wong (n 24) [17].

[173] K Shanmugam (Law & Home Affairs Minister), 'Regardless of Race – The Dialogue 2' (30 September 2019) [23], www.mha.gov.sg/.

[174] In contrast, the India Supreme Court adopted sexual harassment guidelines it declared were legally binding until 2013, when the legislature enacted the necessary law: *Vishaka v State of Rajasthran* AIR 1977 SC 3011.

[175] Menon, 'The Rule of Law' (n 171) 421.

that judicial review is generally available to redress public wrongs. The courts seek to nurture the view that they are constructive partners in the joint project of sustaining the RoL, constitutional democracy and a fair government; disagreement is expressed in a 'respectful, restrained and courteous way'[176] which avoids provoking embarrassment and retaliation. Thus, a collegial rather than aggressive brand of judicial review helps facilitate institutional comity and inter-branch cooperation.

[176] Kavanagh (n 52) 38.

4

Rule of Law, Managed Democracy and Civil and Political Rights

I. INTRODUCTION

THE RULE OF law (RoL) and the protection of civil-political rights such as religious liberty and freedom of expression, association and assembly are integral to the functioning of a free, democratic society. However, the government has long considered the over-exuberant exercise of such rights socially disruptive. An elected government with a popular mandate must be able to rule effectively, without pressures from foreign interference or local civil disobedience tactics.

Consequently, strict regulatory controls preclude street protests and the press does not act as an adversarial fourth estate but as a nation-building partner, supporting a cohesive, prosperous society.[1] Provisions in the Newspaper and Printing Presses Act guard against foreign control of local press companies and authorise restrictions on the circulation of foreign publications for 'interfering with domestic politics',[2] deploying the tool of financial disincentive, not outright bans.

The Societies Act 1996 regulates associational rights, operating a two-track system of automatic registration for 'innocuous' societies, and the normal track applicable to a 'specified society' dealing with 'sensitive' issues, listed in the Schedule. The Registrar may refuse registration if the society is likely 'to be used for unlawful purposes' or is prejudicial to public peace or the national interest.[3] What is telling is that topics considered 'sensitive' include martial arts

[1] PM Goh Chok Tong, 'The Singapore Press: Part of the Virtuous Cycle of Good Government and Good Society', Press Release No 26/JUL02-1/95/07/15 (15 July 2007) www.nas.gov.sg/archivesonline/data/pdfdoc/gct19950715.pdf.

[2] For example, the government restricted the circulation of *Asiaweek* from 10,000 to 500 copies per issue when it refused to publish an unabridged letter from the Home Affairs Ministry seeking to correct errors in a story entitled 'Battle Against Leftism': Jon ST Quah. 'Singapore in 1987: Political Reforms, Control and Economic Recovery' in M Ayoob and Ng Chee Yuen (eds), *Southeast Asian Affairs 1988* (ISEAS, 1988) 246–49.

[3] Societies Act 1966, s 4(2)(b) and (d). In 2023, the amended Act allowed the registrar to make further inquiries under the 'automatic registration' track to catch groups which masqueraded as eg historical interest societies, while planning to engage in racial group advocacy: Sun Xueling (Home Affairs Minister of State), Societies (Amendment) Bill, 95 SPR, 4 October 2023.

societies and, more to the point, political associations and societies whose object is to discuss or promote any language, any matter relating to the governance of society and 'any civil or political right (including human rights, environmental rights, and animal rights)'. It also lists societies addressing issues relating to 'any religion, ethnic group, clan, nationality or a class of persons defined by reference to their gender or sexual orientation'.[4] This encompasses a whole spectrum of politically charged topics, where the government instinct is to prioritise public order in trying to contain divisive 'culture wars'.[5]

Viewpoint diversity is key to a healthy democracy. Critics argue that the sum of such repressive laws creates 'a climate of fear' and self-censorship, silencing and discouraging dissent.[6] In 2009, a nominated Member of Parliament (MP) noted that the 'climate of fear' that loomed large until the late 1980s 'is not so evident today', given the government's ameliorative steps, although more could be done as such fear 'can erode our sense of ownership and affect our rootedness'.[7] Another assessed that while there was 'no longer a fear of reprisals', constraints remained which inhibit dissent.[8]

With the People's Action Party (PAP) government running all major state institutions and regulating potential interlocutors like the Law Society,[9] entering opposition politics requires a risk assessment for fear of political reprisals. Civil society activists regularly point to obstacles to their advocacy work, such as being denied licences for holding public meetings, being arrested for holding public meetings without licences[10] or being demonised and delegitimated for disloyalty.[11]

As a facet of paternal democracy,[12] things have clearly shifted from an ideological paternalism towards responding to increasing demands for political pluralism. Under previous rules of political engagement or 'out of bounds (OB) markers' in the mid-1990s, Singaporeans were admonished that only politicians,

[4] Societies Act, Schedule, s 1.

[5] Lawrence Wong, 'Gender Identity Issues "Bitterly Contested Sources of Division"; Singapore "Should Not Import These Culture Wars"' (*CNA.com*, 1 February 2021).

[6] Catherine Lim, An Open Letter to the PM, 26 November 2007, www.theonlinecitizen.com/2007/11/26/catherine-lims-open-letter-to-the-prime-minister/.

[7] Viswa Sadasivan, 'Nation Building Tenets' 86 SPR, 18 August 2009, cols 1107, 1015.

[8] Audrey Wong, Nation Building Tenets, 86 SPR, 18 August 2009, cols 1145ff.

[9] Jothie Rajah, *Authoritarian Rule of Law: Legislation, Discourse and Legitimacy in Singapore* (Cambridge University Press, 2012) ch 5.

[10] 'PAP's Overwhelming Dominance Makes Civil Rights Advocacy Challenging, Says Jolovan Wham' (*TOC*, 10 May 2023).

[11] 'S'porean Website Accuses PJ Thum & Kirsten Han of Treason: Character Assassination Is Part and Parcel of Singapore Politics' (*Mothership.sg*, 12 April 2018); 'Shanmugam on Thum Ping Tjin's Meeting with Mahatir: Whole Conduct Is "a Little Sad" and "a Bit Regretful"' *Straits Times* (3 September 2018). The Law Minister disclosed that the Accounting and Corporate Regulatory Authority had rejected Thum and Kirsten Han's attempt to register a company, OSEA Pte Ltd, on national security grounds, as it received funding from a George Soros-linked group, to promote democracy and human rights in Singapore.

[12] Thio Li-ann, 'Between Apology and Apogee, Autochthony: The "Rule of Law" beyond the Rules of Law in Singapore' [2012] SJLS 269, 282–87.

not armchair critics, who bore responsibility to the people should engage in political discourse.[13] Further, speakers should maintain respectful deference towards government leaders and be careful in discussing sensitive issues like race and religion. To be Singaporeanised was to be 'politically inert and economically dynamic'.[14] However, there are signs this political ennui is dissipating.[15]

Two factors in the twenty-first century have been significant in changing the political landscape. The first is electoral losses and the psychological impact of seeing PAP ministers voted out of office. In 1991, the parliamentary opposition presence peaked at four in an 81-seat house.[16] In the 'watershed'[17] 2011 General Elections, the PAP lost Aljunied GRC to the Workers' Party (WP), unseating two Cabinet ministers. In the 2020 General Elections, the WP won a post-Independence high of 10 of 93 elective seats, heralding a repoliticised environment.

The political rhetoric shifted from diktat or the didactic to one of inclusive dialogue and an expressed willingness to reconsider sacred cows.[18] Third Prime Minister (PM) Lee Hsien Loong had indicated a shift away from autocratic democracy where silenced dissent festers underground, encouraging citizens not to be 'passive bystanders' but to 'debate issues with reason, passion and conviction', based on 'facts and logic', not just on 'assertions and emotions'. While the government would respond dispassionately to 'constructive dissent', it would aggressively rebut the opposition's criticism to maintain moral authority.[19] The general practice now is broad consultation, such as the year-long engagement with 6000 Singaporeans and non-government organisations over women's issues that resulted in a white paper in 2022, containing 25 collective action plans ranging from flexible workplace arrangements to legalising elective egg freezing for any woman aged 21–35.[20]

However, in an authoritarian turn during the COVID-19 outbreak, those dissenting from official health policy by expressing concern about vaccine safety or the discriminatory effects of vaccine-differentiated measures regulating public spaces access were harshly criticised as misinformation purveyors or troublemakers.[21]

[13] '"Join a Party' if You Want to Contribute' *Straits Times* (9 September 1993) 33.

[14] Michael C Davis, 'Constitutionalism under Chinese Rule: Hong Kong after the Handover' (1998) 27 Denver Journal of International Law and Policy 275, 299.

[15] 'Politically Apathetic? Not Us, Say PAP and Opposition Youth Volunteers' *Straits Times* (23 April 2023).

[16] The breakdown for the 1991 General Elections: PAP, 77 seats; SDP, 3 seats; and WP, 1 seat, www.singapore-elections.com/parl-1991-ge/seats.html.

[17] PM Lee Hsien Loong, Speech, Swearing-In Ceremony, Istana, 21 May 2011, pmo.gov.sg.

[18] 'We Are Prepared to Relook Everything: Lawrence Wong on a Changing Society and His Hopes for S'pore' *Straits Times* (15 May 2024).

[19] DPM Lee Hsien Loong, Speech, Harvard Club of Singapore, reproduced 6 January 2004, https://petir.sg.

[20] 'White Paper on Singapore Women's Development: Towards a Fairer and More Inclusive Society', www.reach.gov.sg/participate/conversations-on-singapore-womens-development.

[21] Li-ann Thio, 'Legal Communitarianism and Pandemic Regulation in Singapore' in Stefan Braum (ed), *Experimental Law: The Rule of Law and the Regulation of the Corona Pandemic in Europe* (NOMOS 2023) 431–38.

The second factor is the rise of web-based and mobile technologies, raising a host of regulatory conundrums. The Internet has expanded citizen participation in public affairs. Anyone with minimal digital skills can share an opinion and email grievances to officials, either politely or in a 'very rude' fashion, as political habits coarsen.[22] The Internet is an inexpensive vehicle for lobbying, and digital platforms can host information, facilitate interactive exchanges, garner feedback and mount online petitions for or against policies The Internet and online social media as the fifth estate[23] can promote participatory democratic values, challenge official narratives through alternative sources of information and enhance political accountability. However, there is a dark side to this.

The Internet also carries misinformation, which distorts and degrades democratic deliberation. The facility to curate 'desirable' news creates echo chambers. Powerful technological companies like Google, Facebook and X have value biases and the power to determine whose voice to amplify or mute,[24] governing what we see and say through algorithms. Foreign entities can leverage on this technology to interfere with national politics.[25]

This problem is whether or not to regulate the Internet, with a light touch or heavy hand, assuming this capacity exists.[26] The Internet offers opportunities for free expression, but invites censorship, surveillance and 'horizontal chilling' when private citizens silence other citizens through intimidation and cyberbullying.[27] The virality, reach and longevity of online speech exacerbates the harm it can inflict. On new media, 'truth is buried by falsehoods, anonymity is often abused and strident voices crowd out moderate views'.[28]

As the government succumbs to social liberalism, provided it does not entail political liberalism or delegitimates their rule, there is hardly any topic beyond discussion in online public debate. Indeed, the government is keen to debate, challenging Richard Branson and non-governmental organisations (NGOs) like Human Rights Watch to live televised debates about the death penalty with the Law Minister,[29] or to give evidence before the Select Committee on the proposed 'fake news' legislation. These were declined as 'public grandstanding' rather than engaging in substantive debate.[30]

[22] Deputy PM Wong Kan Seng, 84 SPR, 28 February 2008, col 1125.

[23] William H Dutton, *The Fifth Estate: The Power Shift of the Digital Age* (Oxford University Press, 2023).

[24] CS Yoo, 'Free Speech and the Myth of the Internet as an Unintermediated Experience' (2010) 78 George Washington LR 697.

[25] *Wham Kwok Han Jolovan v PP* [2020] SGCA 111, [46].

[26] 'Singapore Bans Two Porn Websites in Symbolic Move' (Reuters, 23 May 2008).

[27] Thio Li-ann, 'The Virtual and the Real: Art 14, Political Speech and the Calibrated Management of Deliberative Democracy in Singapore' [2008] SJLS 25, 54–57.

[28] President Tony Tan's Address, Opening of 12th Parliament, 12 October 2011.

[29] 'Singapore Rebuts Richard Branson's Post on Drug Laws, Death Penalty, Invites Him to Debate with Shanmugam' *Straits Times* (22 October 2022).

[30] 'Invitation for Human Rights Watch to Give Evidence Remains Open: Select Committee' *Today* (27 March 2016).

Despite the modest liberalisation towards political speech, caution towards certain topics persists, where this might imperil geopolitical relations or social harmony. For example, the authorities have refused to grant Speakers' Corner permits, as required under the Public Order Act in relation to the conflict after Hamas's genocidal attack on Israel on 7 October 2023, given heightened domestic and regional religious tensions.[31]

This chapter examines the impact in four main areas of primary legislation and associated policies on the health of civil-political rights and 'managed democracy', with reasonably fair elections, although authoritarian constraints on rights may persist. The efficacy of democratic checks in a dominant party state must not be assumed, as competitive elections may ratify power structures. Although organisations like Freedom House have ranked Singapore as the least free among advanced economies, a 2021 Pew Research Centre Report surveying 17 advanced economies indicated than 82 per cent of Singaporeans were satisfied with the workings of democracy, compared to a 57 per cent median, hence the relatively low demand for political reform.[32] The fields relate to security, religious harmony, public assembly and Internet speech. The approaches adopted may differ from legal liberalism's focus on legal sanctions, rights and courts, revealing different perspectives on the role and rule of law. The Internal Security Act, Maintenance of Religious Harmony Act, Public Order Act and Protection from Online Falsehood and Manipulation Act will be analysed against RoL values like legal certainty, rights protection and control against regulatory overreach, to ascertain whether securing other values of contextual importance justify departures from RoL values.

II. THE INTERNAL SECURITY ACT

Preventive detention under the Internal Security Act (ISA) has gained a degree of notoriety, as a recognised exception to the RoL,[33] though such laws are not uncommon today, in an age of global terrorism and illegal immigration.[34] Detention orders are renewable every two years, and the most draconian application has been the 23-year detention of alleged communist and former

[31] 'No Events on Israel-Hamas War Approved at Speakers' Corner Amid Online Calls to Attend Them: Police' *Straits Times* (5 November 2023).

[32] 'S'poreans Most Satisfied among People Polled in 17 Economies with How Well Democracy Is Working' *Straits Times* (21 October 2021). For an opposing view, see Netina Tan and Cassandra Preece, 'Democratic Backsliding in Illiberal Singapore' (2022) 9(1) Asian Journal of Comparative Politics 25.

[33] Home Affairs and Law Minister, K Shanmugam, Speech, Judicial Executive Programme 2022, 21 November 2022, [38], www.mlaw.gov.sg/news/speeches/2022-11-21-speech-k-shanmugam-judicial-executive-programme/.

[34] Andrew Ashworth and Lucia Zedner, *Preventive Justice* (Oxford University Press, 2014) 171–95.

parliamentarian Chia Thye Poh.[35] Its colonial precursor was the Preservation of Public Security Ordinance (PPSO),[36] under which an Appeal Tribunal, comprising three sitting judges, could order a detainee's release over which the government had no further say.[37] This was distinct from the advisory role of similar appeal tribunals in neighbouring countries.[38] In 1959, PM Lee Kuan Yew (LKY) stated the judges had indicated their discomfort over their executive responsibilities under the PPSO.[39] The Tribunal then became an Advisory Committee, with recommendatory powers only. Today, no Singapore citizen shall be detained for more than three months unless the Advisory Board (AB) has considered his representations and recommended continued detention. There is a strong judicial element in the AB's composition, being chaired by a person qualified to be a Supreme Court judge, whom the President appoints in consultation with the Chief Justice.

The ISA has been criticised as a 'blatant negation of the RoL',[40] which is undermined on three levels. First, a detained person is not charged with any criminal offence, and does not have the procedural and evidentiary safeguards associated with open criminal trials. This is justified by the prospect of witness intimidation. As PM LKY asserted, the ISA served Singapore's political stability and he would not allow subversives to 'get away' by insisting on compliance with 'the strict rules of evidence in a court of law'.[41] The government would act if 'convinced of the truth of the matter', provided this was not obtained 'by torture, coercion, or distortion of the truth'.[42] This requires much to be taken on faith and trust, as governments are not above the temptation to abuse extensive powers for expedient purposes. While ISA powers are preventive, they can have a punitive effect where used by a predatory state to marginalise political opponents, breeding fear and political passivity, and muzzling dissent, which degrades democracy. Exceptions to legal processes are justified in terms of tempering doctrine with practical wisdom, as the choice is not 'between order and liberty', but 'between liberty with order and anarchy without either'.[43]

[35] 'Letters: Bogus Reasons for 22-Year Detention' *FEER* (16 November 1989).

[36] The Singapore government arrested 113 activists and opposition members under the PPSO on 2 February 1963, under the anti-Communist 'Operation Cold Store'. This decimated the political opposition and allowed the government to consolidate control: M Fernandez and KS Loh, 'The Left Wing Trade Unions in Singapore, 1945–1970' in M Barr and CA Trocki (eds), *Paths Not Taken: Political Pluralism in Post-War Singapore* (NUS Press, 2008) 206–27.

[37] Yee Chee Wai, Monica Ho and Daniel Seng, 'Judicial Review of Preventive Detention under the ISA' (1989) 10 SL Rev 66.

[38] Chief Minister DS Marshall, 'Preservation of Public Security Bill', Singapore Legislative Assembly Vol 1, 21 September 1955, cols 695, 706–07.

[39] PM Lee Kuan Yew, 'Preservation of Public Security (Amendment) Bill, Singapore Legislative Assembly Vol 11, 14 October 1959, cols 665, 668–69.

[40] JB Jeyaretnam, 'Rule of Law' Motion, 71 SPR, 24 November 1999, cols 569, 576.

[41] 'PM: Not Our Practice to Take Subversives to Court' *Straits Times* (3 June 1987) 10.

[42] 'Archbishop Accepts Evidence' *Straits Times* (3 June 1987) 1.

[43] Justice Jackson, *Terminiello v Chicago* 337 US 1, 37 (1949), quoted by Law Minister K Shanmugam, Keynote address, Rule of Law Symposium 2012, 14 February 2012, [53], www.mlaw.gov.sg.

Second, the exercise of coercive ISA powers violates fundamental liberties, such as personal liberty, under Article 9. Here, the RoL becomes the instrument of the strong to silence their critics, not the protector of fair process. It consolidates, not constrains, the asymmetries of power between citizen and executive.

Third, the power to detain is a legal power with legal limits, which the courts usually enforce; however, this was truncated to review for procedural non-compliance[44] after the 1987 Marxist Conspiracy. This legal check has been partially replaced with the weaker, less transparent check of the elected president's veto power; however, this is not triggered if the AB does not recommend release in the face of the detaining authority's objection.

Initially, the ISA was primarily used against communist insurgents and drug traffickers. However, its deployment under 'Operation Spectrum' in 1987 to detain 22 so-called Marxist conspirators, where no threat of violence was involved, remains for many a dark stain in the nation's history.[45] In 2015, the Catholic Archbishop described this as a 'dark period' in the Church's history.[46] The detainees were lay church workers, student organisers, lawyers and social activists, allegedly involved 'in a Marxist plot to subvert the political and social system of Singapore'.[47] They had allegedly infiltrated the Catholic Church, law society and theatre groups, all masterminded by Oxford graduate law student Tan Wah Piow. The decision to detain was framed in terms of not taking chances with Singaporean lives and not risking 'the prosperity', even if it was not entirely clear what the detainees had done.[48]

There remains scepticism that the detained were not Marxists[49] and that detention was unnecessary. Indeed, PM Lee's later description of the detained as 'do-gooders' wanting to help 'the poor and dispossessed'[50] does not square with former Cabinet Minister and President Tony Tan's acknowledgement that the ISA as a 'blunt instrument' should be reserved for the 'most extreme circumstances' where there is 'no choice'.[51] The alleged conspirators

[44] ISA, s 8B(2).

[45] Noting that among professional Singaporeans, there was a general lack of acceptance that 'various anti-government actions by disparate people constituted a grand Marxist Conspiracy': Michael Malkin, 'The Conspiracy Theory' *FEER* (22 October 1987) 22.

[46] 'Time to Move on from Marxist Conspiracy: Returning to Dark Period Won't Help in Nation-Building' *Straits Times* (28 March 2015).

[47] *Teo Soh Lung v MHA* [1990]1 S SLR(R) 347, [30].

[48] Rajah (n 9) 227–31.

[49] One detainee, Chew Kheng Chuan argued he was a capitalist not a Marxist, but after the arrest he declared he would become like other Singaporeans, 'eschew politics – and pursue wealth'. 'A Statement of Beliefs' *FEER* (22 October 1987) 26–28.

[50] ISD notes of the meeting between the PM and Catholic Church leaders on 2 June 1987, 3pm at the Istana: Michael D Barr, 'Marxists in Singapore? Lee Kuan Yew's Campaign against Catholic Social Justice Activists in the 1980s' (2010) 43(3) Critical Asian Studies 335, 353.

[51] 'Tony Tan, Tan Jee Say Clash over ISA' (*Yahoo News*, 19 August 2011).

have written books[52] providing important counter-narratives, and increasingly speak publicly about suffering physical abuse and psychological torture, making forced confessions, demonstrating how preventive detention laws can be abused to quash the civil-political rights of political opponents.[53]

After an on-site visit, an International Commission of Jurists delegation concluded that detention without trial and using 'brainwashing' interrogation techniques constituted human rights violations and abrogated the RoL; the detainees were merely exercising their civil rights, which would be 'applauded in a healthy democracy'. There was no evidence of a Marxist conspiracy, nor did the informal network of community groups and workers pose an imminent threat to Singapore security. The Commission's report asserted the state's evidence 'is simply too weak to stand up in court'.[54]

Chiam See Tong, the sole opposition parliamentarian in 1987,[55] moved a motion calling for the release of 15 'Marxist Conspiracy' detainees on humanitarian grounds. He chided the government for overreaching, causing anguish to family members, asserting the detentions were made for political purposes. Ministers had called the detainees novices and pawns, and there was 'no evidence' they were a real security threat, beyond their 'own confession' extracted after the 'torture' of 'continuous interrogation', which any court of law would 'throw out'. In sum, their only crime 'is that they are against the Party in power'. When his motives were questioned for bringing the motion, Chiam noted 'if it were not for me, there will be no public forum for these 15 persons arrested'.[56] Despite his courageous stand, his motion was amended to express support for the arrests and intent to release the detained once 'rehabilitated' and 'unlikely to resume their subversive activities'.[57] The weakness of political checks in a dominant party state is self-evident.

Many, including former detainees, have called for abolition of the ISA, as it impedes a 'mature and functioning democracy'.[58] Detainees testify the

[52] Tan Wah Piow, *Smokescreens and Mirrors: Tracing the 'Marxist Conspiracy* (Function 8 Ltd, 2012); Fong Hoe Fang (ed), *That We May Dream Again* (Ethos, 2012); Chng Suan Tze et al (eds), *1987 Singapore's Marxist Conspiracy 30 Years On* (Function 8 Ltd, 2017).

[53] 'Detention and Release; Arrested at Night, Some Detainees Claim Harsh Treatment' *FEER* (22 October 1987) 24–26.

[54] 'ICJ Mission to Singapore Dismisses Allegations of "Marxist Conspiracy"' (ICJ, 12 October 1987); *Report of the International Mission of Jurists to Singapore, July 1987* (ICJ, October 1987) www.icj.org/.

[55] Two opposition politicians were elected to the 79-seat house during the 1984 General Elections, but JB Jeyaretnam lost his parliamentary seat in 1986 after being convicted for making false statements about his party's funds, which was later overturned.

[56] Chiam See Tong, Marxist Conspiracy (Detentions under ISA), 49 SPR, 29 July 1987, cols 1431, 1433–34, 1442–43.

[57] ibid col 1514. PAP MP Chng Hee Kok reluctantly supported Mr Chiam's private member motion.

[58] Abolish Singapore's Internal Security Act, Letter of 19 September 2011 (16 signatories), www.theonlinecitizen.com/2011/09/19/abolish-singapores-internal-security-act/. An online petition dated 4 May 2012 to abolish the ISA, stating that more than 2500 Singaporeans have been detained

ISA has been 'absolutely abused' in Singapore',[59] describing it emotively as 'political rape'.[60] Prominent public figures like current President Tharman Shanmugaratnam and former Attorney-General (AG) Walter Woon[61] have reportedly doubted whether using the ISA in 1987 was justified, as the conspirators were merely social activists promoting press freedoms and migrant workers' rights, which is a key staple of contemporary civil society activism.[62] It later became known that Minister S Dhanabalan resigned from the Cabinet in 1992 over his discomfort with the detentions.[63]

The Catholic Archbishop has acknowledged that many people have been 'wounded and hurt'[64] by the 1987 incident, but has called for forgiveness, while others advocate setting up a Truth and Reconciliation Commission or a Commission of Inquiry[65] to examine the true reasons for the arrests and to bring closure 'to this sad episode of our recent history'.[66] Some former political prisoners have also demanded apologies.[67]

The government maintains the ISA is necessary for evolving security threats, seeking to dispel the image of the ISA as a tool of repression by projecting it as part of the nation-building narrative. Even some ex-detainees believe preventive detention laws are necessary, while urging more rigorous checks and balances. Former detainees have criticised as farcical the protection AB hearings are supposed to provide, revealing that in 1987 the AB did not examine witnesses or evidence against the detainees, that appearances lasted only a few minutes and that Internal Security Department (ISD) officers said appearing before the AB may jeopardise an early release.[68] The regime could be modified by reducing the

under it since the 1960s, garnered 14 supporters: www.change.org/p/singapore-pap-government-and-pm-lee-hsien-loong-abolish-the-internal-security-act-isa.

[59] Chew Kheng Chuan (Chair of Substation Theatre), quoted in 'Ex-ISA Detainee Sees Need for Act but Urges Changes' *Straits Times* (6 February 2015).

[60] Vincent Cheng, 'Persecuted for Justice's Sake' in '23 Years after Operation Spectrum: Ex-detainees Recall Mental and Physical Abuses' (*Singapore Rebel*, 24 May 2010) https://singaporerebel.blogspot.com/2010/05/23-years-after-operation-spectrum-ex.html.

[61] 'Operation Spectrum Was Political Rape' (*TOC*, 26 May 2009) theonlinecitizen.com.

[62] eg Cheah Wuiling, 'Migrant Workers as Citizens within the ASEAN Landscape: International Law and the Singapore Experience (2009) 8(1) Chinese JIL Law 205.

[63] Goh Chok Tong revealed this in his interview: Sonny Yap, Richard Lim and Leong Weng Kam, Men in *White: The Untold Story* of *Singapore's Ruling Political Party*, 2nd edn (Singapore Press Holdings, 2010) 468.

[64] 'Time to Move on from Marxist Conspiracy' *Straits Times* (28 March 2015).

[65] Teo Soh Lung, 'Time to Set Up a Truth and Reconciliation Commission and Abolish the ISA' (*Singapore Rebel*, 19 August 2011) https://singaporerebel.blogspot.com/2011/08/time-to-set-up-truth-and-reconciliation.html.

[66] Tan Jee Say, 'Abolish the ISA and Set Up a Commission on Inquiry to Foster National Unity' (*TOC*, 19 September 2011) www.theonlinecitizen.com/2011/09/19/abolish-the-isa-and-set-up-a-commission-on-inquiry-to-foster-national-unity/.

[67] 'Former Political Prisoners Calls for Abolishment of ISA and Apology from PAP Govt on 60th Anniversary of Operation Coldstore (*TOC*, 2 February 2023) www.theonlinecitizen.com/2023/02/02/former-political-prisoners-calls-for-abolishment-of-isa-and-apology-from-pap-govt-on-60th-anniversary-of-operation-coldstore/.

[68] Above n 58.

period of initial detention from two years to one, and installing more muscular checks for subsequent detention periods, such as involving two High Court judges or parliamentarians, and capping the maximum number of consecutive detention periods.[69]

Preventive detention laws, while upholding public order as an aspect of the RoL, downplay other RoL values of having effective checks against broad discretionary powers affecting personal liberties to sift genuine security considerations from self-interested political reasons.

In the post 9/11 security landscape,[70] the need for preventive detention powers is broadly accepted, with the debate being whether to repeal the ISA and adopt more tightly scoped anti-terrorist legislation.[71] Today, the ISA is not seen to be deployed against political dissenters, but against genuine terrorist threats from groups or self-radicalised individuals.[72] As threats of religiously motivated terrorism implicate physical violence and intangibles like social cohesion, the government has adopted a soft 'relational' hand to manage community relations.

This was evident after the discovery in December 2001 of the plot to bomb the Yishun MRT (Mass Rapid Transport) Station and US and Israeli embassies by the Al Qaeda-linked Jemaah Islamiyah (JI) group, which intended to build an Islamic caliphate in south-east Asia. Fifteen persons, all Malay Muslims, were detained.[73] While the alleged Marxist conspirators were demonised and testified to suffering abuse, the government took proactive steps to humanise the detained JI members.

After neutralising the physical threat, three significant steps were taken to address the psychological and spiritual harm upon social cohesion. First, to legitimate the detentions, the government transparently provided information on the arrests. It released reconnaissance video clips[74] taken by JI members of potential bombing sites and a white paper summarising the government's case against the detained, with photographic evidence.[75] This was extensively debated in Parliament.[76]

Second, the government proactively engaged the community through closed door and public dialogue sessions, in contrast to the 1987 detentions, when no

[69] 'The Next 50 Years of Singapore's Security and How NS, ISA and Caning Need to Change' *Straits Times* (6 February 2015).

[70] Michael Hor, 'Singapore's Anti-terrorism Laws: Reality and Rhetoric' in V Ramraj (ed), *Global Anti-terrorism Law and Policy* (Cambridge University Press, 2012) 271–89.

[71] eg the WP supports the idea of a dedicated anti-terrorism law, where detention orders would be reviewable: 'Worker's Party Position on the Internal Security Act' (The Workers' Party, 16 September 2011) www.wp.sg/workers-party-position-on-the-internal-security-act/.

[72] 'The Road to Redemption: How Two Radicalized Youths in Singapore Shed Violence and Extremism' (*CNA.com*, 30 April 2023).

[73] A total of 36 people were arrested in December 2001 and August 2002, most of whom were JI members.

[74] 'More Videotape Evidence of Terror Plot Here' *Straits Times* (2 March 2022) 3.

[75] White paper, 'The Jemaah Islamiyah Arrests and the Threat of Terrorism' (Cmd 2, 2003) (JI White Paper).

[76] Wong Kan Seng, Threat of Terrorism (Motion), 75 SPR, 20 January 2003, col 2036.

public meetings were held.[77] As majority–minority relations were at their post-Independence nadir, given the heightened suspicion of the Muslim community, even schools were briefed. In relational terms, the detainees and their families were demonstrably supported, through weekly familial visits and provision for performing religious obligations. The ISD formed family support groups, helping them find jobs and allaying fears of government persecution.[78]

Third, the government framed the situation in a way to promote healing, underscoring that terrorist groups sought to undermine Singapore by harming inter-ethnic peace. It distinguished between 'militant' and 'moderate' Muslims, asserting that most Singapore Muslims were moderate. JI members were a 'small and isolated group of misguided Muslims',[79] influenced by the chief villains, foreign radical teachers. The government noted that in neutralising radical teachers and foreign terrorist operatives, the 'legitimate practices'[80] and religious freedoms of Muslims must not be disrupted. It urged the Muslim community to develop a comprehensive self-regulatory scheme for detecting extremist teachings, which became the Asatizah Recognition Scheme.[81] To emphasise that the problem was Singaporean rather than Muslim, all citizens were exhorted to notify the authorities of suspicious activities. A 'soft' code on religious harmony to guide inter-religious relations was proposed, eventuating in the 2003 Declaration on Religious Harmony.[82]

Detention and averting physical violence is not the endgame; in recent years, a rehabilitative approach has evolved that seeks to deradicalise and socially reintegrate detainees.[83] As the Law Minister stated: 'We give them religious rehabilitation, we don't throw away the keys.'[84] This approach does not view the terrorist as an inveterate state enemy, but as a misguided prodigal son who may be redeemed and reinstated as a responsible citizen.

This is done through informal regulatory modes, in cooperation with non-state volunteers such as the faith-based Religious Rehabilitation Group (RRG), formed in 2003, composed of religious teachers. The government arranges for detainees to receive psychological counselling and to continue their education.

[77] 'Ministers Hold Sessions on ISA Arrests' *Straits Times* (25 January 2002) H5.

[78] 'ISA Detainees Co-operative, Coping Well' *Straits Times* (24 January 2002) H4; 'Don't View Muslims with Suspicion … Carry on Life as Before' *Straits Times* (1 February 2002) H10–11.

[79] JI White Paper (n 75) 23.

[80] ibid 22.

[81] Li-ann Thio, 'Irreducible Plurality, Indivisible Unity: Singapore Relational Constitutionalism and Cultivating Harmony through Constructing a Constitutional Civil Religion' (2019) 20(7) German Law Journal 1007, 1023–24.

[82] Li-ann Thio, 'Constitutional "Soft" Law and the Management of Religious Liberty and Order: The 2003 Declaration on Religious Harmony' [2004] SJLS 414.

[83] Shashi Jayakumar, 'Research Note: Singapore's "Deradicalisation" Model: Revolution – or Evolutions?' (2021) No 26 Journal for Deradicalisation 227, https://journals.sfu.ca/jd/index.php/jd/article/view/443/271.

[84] K Shanmugam (Law and Home Affairs Minister), Foreign Interference (Countermeasures) Bill, 4 October 2021, [344].

The Inter-Agency Aftercare Group, an informal network of Muslim associations, provides emotional and financial support to families of detainees, including giving their children pocket money, to motivate the detainees' will to rehabilitate, knowing their families are cared for. Through religious counselling, the RRG mission is 'to correct the misinterpretation of Islamic concepts' and 'dispel the extremist and terrorist ideologies' detainees have imbibed.[85] As this engages theology, which is beyond the competence of a secular state, this public–private partnership is part of a holistic approach towards security.

This resonates with relational constitutionalism's commitment to cultivating durable relationships in plural societies. It is important for respected religious teachers to build relationships with the detainees, to secure their cooperation and prevent recidivism. As the nature of the terrorist threat evolves, the ISD has adapted to address the needs of teenaged detainees by assigning them a mentor; the RRG now has female counsellors to advise female detainees.[86] When an Indian Protestant male was detained in 2021 for planning knife attacks at a mosque, the ISD worked with the National Council of Churches of Singapore to secure a suitable Christian counsellor.[87]

The securitisation of law and normalisation of exceptions to due process which diminish human rights observance and qualifies the RoL may certainly impair individual autonomy and human dignity. However, human dignity, of which they are variable conceptions, may also be vindicated by the Singapore process of 'detention, rehabilitate and release', restoring someone to good standing as a member of society. Unlike the harsh treatment reported by 'Marxist conspirators', JI detainees have reported being treated with 'dignity and respect', having halal food and regular doctor visits.[88]

This unique experiment in deradicalisation through public–private partnership has been successful, insofar as 88 per cent of the JI detainees were rehabilitated.[89] There is certainly a loss of liberty for those detained under the ISA, which the government retains to buttress its claim to legal exceptionalism based on new forms of vulnerability. However, this works with 'soft law' measures, seeking to educate and promote integration through early intervention.[90]

[85] Mohamad Ali, 'The Religious Rehabilitation Group (RRG): A Community–Government Partnership in Fighting Terrorism' in ZA Rasheed and Norshahril Saat (eds), *Majulah:50 Years of Malay/Muslim Community in Singapore* (World Scientific, 2016) 243–55.

[86] In 2017, the first woman was detained under the ISA: 'Radicalised Female Infant Care Assistant from PCF Sparkletots Detained under ISA for Pro-ISIS Activities' *Straits Times* (12 June 2017).

[87] '16-Year-Old Detained under ISA for Planning Mosque Attacks to Receive Religious, Psychological Counselling' *Straits Times* (27 January 2021).

[88] MHA Press Release, '20th Anniversary of ISD's Operations Against Jemaah Islamiyah in Singapore' (4 December 2021) 23.

[89] Successful rehabilitation is marked by the release and reintegration of a detainee back into society. For example, in relation to the JI plot, 52 of 56 detainees were released: 'How the Govt–Community Partnership Works in Tackling the JI Threat and Rehabilitating Its Members' *Today* (22 December 2021).

[90] Li-ann Thio, 'Securitisation and Solidarity in Singapore after 9–11' (*VerfBlog*, 31 March 2022) https://verfassungsblog.de/os5-singapore/, DOI: 10.17176/20220331-131302-0.

The value of preserving life may be a worthwhile trade-off, such as where the first young female detainee planning to go to an ISIS warzone was detained, had 'the roots' of her 'radical terrorist inclinations'[91] addressed, was released and today has 'the prospect' of living and achieving 'her full potential'.[92]

III. THE MAINTENANCE OF RELIGIOUS HARMONY ACT

A. Origins and Regulatory Powers

After the 1987 Marxist Conspiracy, the Maintenance of Religious Harmony Act (MRHA) was introduced in 1990, 'more in sorrow than in joy', to stem 'a retrogression or potential deterioration in religious harmony'.[93] It was recognised as an exception to the RoL, as MRHA restraining orders (ROs) are non-justiciable,[94] and potentially violate religious freedom (Article 15) and free speech (Article 14), removing an important layer of accountability.

In lieu of criminal prosecution, which might be 'too severe', the MRHA was meant to facilitate 'prompt action' to prevent the repetition of 'harmful, provocative acts'. Such pre-emptive executive power was preferable to an open trial, which might involve 'considerable delay' before judgment, and fears that the 'judicial proceedings' would, as in times past, exacerbate heightened emotions 'if the defendant turns them into political propaganda'.[95] Consent of the Public Prosecutor (PP)[96] was required to charge one with violating an RO, attracting a fine of $10,000 and/or two years' imprisonment. ROs have effect for up to two years, and are renewable.

Originally, under sections 8 and 9, the minister, if satisfied, could issue ROs against religious officials[97] or 'secular' conflict entrepreneurs instigating religious officials to commit the following acts:

(a) causing feelings of enmity, hatred, ill-will or hostility between different religious groups;
(b) carrying out activities to promote a political cause, or a cause of any political party while, or under the guise of, propagating or practising any religious belief;

[91] Sundaresh Menon, 'International Terrorism and Human Rights' (2014) Asian Journal of International Law 1, 31.

[92] Shanmugam, Foreign Interference (Countermeasures) Bill (n 84) [336].

[93] Goh Chok Tong (First DPM and Defence Minister), Maintenance of Religious Harmony Bill, 54 SPR Reports, 23 February 1990, cols 1145, 1159. Rajah (n 9) 227 notes that the Marxist conspiracy was 'almost certainly the event that precipitated' the MRHA.

[94] MRHA, s 18.

[95] Maintenance of Religious Harmony white paper (Cmd 21, 1989) (MRHWP) para 31.

[96] MRHA, s 17. See generally Li-ann Thio, 'Control, Co-optation and Co-operation: Managing Religious Harmony in Singapore's Multi-ethnic, Quasi-secular State' (2005) 33(2/3) Hastings Constitutional Law Quarterly 197.

[97] MRHA, s 8 refers to 'any priest, monk, pastor, imam, elder, office-bearer or any other person who is in a position of authority in any religious group or institution'.

(c) carrying out subversive activities under the guise of propagating or practising any religious belief; or
(d) exciting disaffection against the President or the Government while, or under the guise of, propagating or practising any religious belief.

The Home Affairs Minister is empowered to prohibit a religious personage who incites his congregation to hatred of another religious group 'from repeating such inflammatory or provocative statements',[98] from addressing any religious group or any topic or from participating in religious publications without prior permission.

Grounds (b)–(d) directly relate to state–religious group/person relations, while ground (a) relates to inter-religious group relations. The clauses on exciting disaffection and causing 'feelings of ill-will and hostility' bear similarity to a 'seditious tendency' under section 3(1)(a) and (e) of the now repealed Sedition Act.[99] The white paper on Maintaining Religious Harmony (MRHWP) provides insights into what constitutes a religious harmony threat, with an annexed ISD report giving examples.[100] While Article 15 of the Constitution safeguards religious freedom, this was subject to 'the over-riding considerations of the overall national interests'.[101]

These threats may be divided into two categories: first, the 'horizontal' threat of inter-group religious tensions; and second, the 'vertical' threat of religious challenges to state authority, either through mixing 'religion' and 'politics' or by using religion for subversive purposes, of which the 'Marxist conspiracy' was paradigmatic.

The first is an indirect threat to democracy, as sustainable democracy requires a culture of civility, distinct from silencing competing viewpoints through intimidatory tactics. There must be sufficient relational solidarity for citizens to recognise all have equal rights to participate in democratic discourse. Social cohesion in plural societies is jeopardised if 'enmity, hatred, ill-will or hostility' exists between different religious groups. This could be caused by 'aggressive and insensitive proselytization',[102] where 'religious sensitivities are offended, emotions are quickly aroused', which could 'inflame passions,

[98] MRHWP (n 95) [30].

[99] s 3(1)(a) relates to disaffection against the government, while s 3(1)(e) refers to causing ill-will etc 'between different races or classes'. Introduced to curb opposition to British colonial rule, the Sedition Act was repealed in 2021: 'Singapore Parliament Repeals Sedition Act after 83 Years' *Straits Times* (5 October 2021).

[100] 'Religious Trends – A Security Perspective', MRHWP (n 95) Annex, 13–19.

[101] MRHWP (n 95) [7].

[102] The ISD enumerated instances of complaints made to the government between 1985 and 1989, from Hindus and Muslims about Christian evangelical activities and Muslim counter campaigns. Other disputes relate to the burials of non-Muslims who had apparently converted to Islam, and Muslims protesting against the Ahmadis calling their building a mosque. Intra-religious tensions also existed between Hindu sects and between Protestants and Catholics: ibid 13–15, [2], [6], [9], [12], [30].

kindle violence'.[103] The category 'religion' is associated with emotions, which the secular state, a core liberal value,[104] dispassionately manages as part of its 'secular, rational and multiracial approach' to development.[105] While acknowledging the constitutional right to propagation, the MRHWP underscores the responsibility to exercise this 'very sensitively',[106] to avoid causing religious enmity 'by denigrating other faiths or by insensitively trying to convert those belonging to other religions;[107] this would provoke strenuous resistance from religious groups fearing their flocks are being poached. Further, sermons by an 'unrestrained preacher' which go beyond identifying differences in belief systems to denouncing other religionists as 'misguided infidels and lost souls'[108] could upset entire communities, provoking violent retaliation against persons and places of worship, thus breaching criminal law.[109]

However, controlling religion to avoid politicisation or subversion may itself potentially threaten democracy, by suppressing political criticism. The official fear is that if one religious group seeks political influence, or if political parties curry religious favour, others will follow suit. The 'end result' will be destabilising 'conflict between religions'.[110] While religious individuals may participate qua citizens in the political process, religious leaders are exhorted not to incite their co-religionists to 'actively oppose secular government policies'.[111] The prescription is that religious groups should mutually abstain from 'competitive political influence' to preserve 'religious tolerance and harmony'.[112] This includes not mounting political campaigns against the government or undertaking radical social action, thus heightening social tensions.[113]

While the security threat is framed in terms of religious groups jostling for political power, it discounts the possibility that religious groups could form inter-faith alliances[114] to support or challenge government policies. Hence, the

[103] ibid [11].

[104] Seven ineliminable political concepts associated with liberalism are: 'liberty, rationality, limited government, accountable government, sociability, the general interest and individuality': Michael Freeden, *Liberalism: A Very Short Introduction* (Oxford University Press, 2015) 15.

[105] Yang di Pertuan Negara's Speech, First Session, Legislative Assembly, 24 SPR, 8 December 1965, cols 5, 7.

[106] MRHWP (n 95) [15].

[107] ibid [13].

[108] ibid [16].

[109] Penal Code, s 295 (now repealed and ported over in 2019 to the MRHA).

[110] MRHWP (n 95) [19].

[111] ibid [20], [22]–[23].

[112] ibid [28].

[113] ibid [26(c)].

[114] eg Christian and Muslim groups united through the 2014 Wear White movement to defend family values in opposition to the homosexual rights Pink Dot campaign: 'Christians to Don White for Services as Hong Lim Park Hosts Pink Dot' *Straits Times* (12 June 2015); 'Religious Teacher Launches "Wear White" Online Campaign: Aim Is to Protest against Homosexuality, He Says' *Straits Times* (20 June 2014) (online campaign by Ustaz Noor Deros asking Muslims to support 'what is good and pure').

official prescription is that safeguards against a corrupt government should not be religious but 'secular', through 'public meetings, publicity in the media, debates and motions of no confidence in Parliament, actions in the Courts and finally by campaigning to oust such a government in a general election'.[115] Such political checks are somewhat feeble within a dominant party state. Judicial review of ROs is precluded under section 18 MRHA.

To moderate the power to issue 'gag' orders, the President may confirm or deny an order[116] where Cabinet advice is contrary to the Presidential Council for Religious Harmony[117] (PCRH)'s recommendation. However, the door to concentrated executive authority is open, as the President has no role if the PCRH and government are *ad idem*. Rajah argues the government looks to the secular PCRH members to be a 'modern moderating presence', diffusing inter-religious tensions by bringing to bear 'the rationality of secularism', a tenet of the liberal faith.[118] Trials are venues where a 'counter-narrative' can enter the public domain, and this is now cut off, privileging the state's preferred narrative.[119] PCRH proceedings are secret.[120]

The executive enjoys a remarkable amount of discretion in unilaterally determining what falls within the realms of 'religion' and 'politics',[121] which are not hermetically sealed categories, particularly where faiths do not recognise a secular-sacred divide.[122] Indeed, while the government recognises the impossibility of dividing voters' minds into secular and religious halves,[123] it reserves the prerogative to determine what falls within the realm of 'politics', which can be cavernous.[124] This fosters legal uncertainty, as religious leaders may be unsure when an activity is religious or political.

The MRHWP provides broad guidelines of 'acceptable', politically non-threatening religious practices, such as social work with the aged, disabled and children in health and education. It is explicitly permissible for Catholic medical personnel not to perform abortions as a matter of conscience, but unclear

[115] MRHWP (n 95) [21].

[116] Art 22I.

[117] MRHA, s 3: the President, on the President Council or Minority Rights' advice, appoints PCRH members, two-thirds being religious leaders and one-third being persons who have 'distinguished themselves in public service or community relations in Singapore'.

[118] Rajah (n 9) 248.

[119] ibid 243.

[120] MRHA, s 7.

[121] The Select Committee opposed allowing courts to determine what fell within 'religion' and 'politics' as this implicated public policy: Report of the Select Committee on the Maintenance of Religious Harmony Bill, October 1990, Parl 7 of 1990, vi–vii.

[122] MRHWP (n 95) [25], noting that Islam and some forms of Christianity see faith as impacting all of life.

[123] ibid [24].

[124] For example, 'politics' was defined in *Dow Jones Publishing v AG* [1989] 1 SLR(R) 637, [42] as encompassing 'the political system of Singapore and the political ideology underpinning it', including public institutions and government policies.

whether an 'unborn lives matter' campaign would cross the line.[125] However, the government clarified that engaging in public discourse about whether to construct a casino or maintain laws criminalising sodomy was permissible.[126] On the other hand, no conscientious objection exemption avails Jehovah's Witnesses refusing to perform compulsory military service, which is considered criminal conduct, threatening national security,[127] while it might elsewhere be considered part of religious freedom.[128] Secular determinations trump sacred understandings and restrain freedom of religious practices, though the government insists that in separating 'religion' from 'politics', the intent is not to determine the veracity of any belief system but to keep the peace.[129] The liberal RoL based on the liberalism of fear against governors gives way to an RoL where appeal is made to the communitarianism of trusting powerful governors.

The MRHA was designed to be a less severe response to non-subversive religious activity, not involving bloodshed and riots, which is the ISA's purview. The ISD report referred to the Marxist Conspiracy as an example of religion and subversion, as well as the goal of the Muslim Brotherhood to build an Islamic state and incite Muslims to use armed violence to demand Islamic laws.[130] The MRHA would empower the government to 'take quick but less severe action against a transgressor to head off a problem'.[131] ROs are not legal sanctions but pre-emptive 'cease and desist' warnings, though these may limit religious freedom in the name of religious harmony.[132]

Clearly, the RO's design contemplated the rise of the Catholic Church as a civil society leader which could pressurise the government. The powers to 'gag' a religious leader from giving a speech or handling religious publications were correlated with the activities of four Catholic priests which the ISD report referenced in discussing 'Mixing Religion and Politics'. They were described as social activists acting as 'a political pressure group', where the Church and Society

[125] MRHWP (n 95) para 26(a). See Seow Hon Tan, 'Religion in the Abortion Discourse in Singapore: A Case Study of the Relevance of Religious Arguments in Law-making in Multi-religious Democracies' (2010) 26(2) Journal of Law and Religion 505; Li-ann Thio, 'Religion in the Public Sphere of Singapore: Wall of Division or Public Square' in Bryan S Turner (ed), *Religious Pluralism and Civil Society: A Comparative Analysis* (Bardwell Press, 2008) 73–104.

[126] PM Lee Hsien Loong, National Day Rally Speech, 16 August 2009, www.pmo.gov.sg/.

[127] *Colin Chan v PP* [1994] 3 SLR(R) 209, [78].

[128] Singapore does not accept conscientious objection to military service is part of religious human rights, as it would 'compromise the defence of Singapore': Singapore Permanent Mission, 35th Session, Agenda Item 3, Human Rights Council, 13 June 2017, www.mfa.gov.sg. The Human Rights Committee has recognised that the right of conscientious objection to military service is part of religious freedom, which is enshrined under Article 18 of the International Covenant on Civil and Political Rights: see *Yeo-Bum Yoon and Myung Jin Choi v Republic of Korea* (CCPR/C/88/D/1321-1322/2004 of 23 January 2007).

[129] MRHWP (n 95) [27].

[130] 'Religious Trends' (n 100) [32]–[35].

[131] MRHWP (n 95) [32]–[33].

[132] Art 15(1) protects the right 'to profess and practise his religion and to propagate it#, while (4) authorises limitations 'relating to public order, public health or morality'.

Study Group published booklets criticising the government on 'various secular issues'[133] like workers' rights. The *Catholic News* contained articles criticising citizenship laws, media regulation and transnational corporations.[134] These priests agitated against the arrest of the 'Marxist conspirators', held masses and made statements 'to work up emotions and pressure the Government to release the detainees';[135] the detainees were painted as victims and the political climate as repressive, and declarations were made that God would punish the Home Affairs Minister and his officials.[136]

The ISD report referenced instances from the 1970s and 1980s, when Muslim theologians were banned from entering Singapore for making 'provocative political speeches' lambasting Malay/Muslims as stooges for not opposing the destruction of mosques and failing to convert the Chinese.[137] Hindu–Sikh tensions arose after Indira Gandhi's assassination, and the police stated that 'events in India did not concern Singaporeans' and 'foreign politics should not be imported'.[138] The MRHA is premised on Singapore's ongoing vulnerability, whether from communalists, communists or terrorists, giving rise to the securitisation of religion and government ambivalence in viewing religion as both a 'constructive social force'[139] and a destructive threat if politicised.

That no RO was ever issued before the MRHA was amended in 2019 is cited as proof of the MRHA's deterrent success.[140] Notably, warnings[141] have been issued and criminal prosecutions pursued under the Sedition Act[142] and the Penal Code[143] for acts which could fall within the MRHA's scope. The non-use of the MRHA was attributed to the 'active work behind the scene[s]' in building relationships and mutual confidence, where the PM held regular private

[133] 'Religious Trends' (n 100) [13].

[134] Rajah (n 9) 232–33, detailing the social issues raised eg minimum wage, foreign workers and elitist education schemes.

[135] 'Religious Trends' (n 100) [15].

[136] ibid [16]–[19], to which Minister Jayakumar declared he was a Hindu and unafraid of Catholic curses, asserting a secular polity would be harmed where religious leaders invoked 'the divine power of damnation upon secular authorities': 54 SPR, 6 October 1989, cols 636–37.

[137] 'Religious Trends' (n 100) [21]–[23].

[138] ibid 17, [25]–[27].

[139] Shared Values white paper (Cmd 1, 1991) para 45.

[140] Lee Kuan Yew noted that after the MRHA was passed, active Christian evangelism of Muslims and Catholic social activism subsided: Han Fook Kwang et al, *Lee Kuan Yew: The Man and His Ideas* (Times Edition, 1998) 190.

[141] See 'Maintenance of Religious Harmony Act (Number of Restraining Orders Issued)', 82 SPR, 12 February 2007, col 1319. The government almost issued ROs in three instances: see 'Govt Reins in Religious Leaders' *Straits Times* (12 May 2001) 1, such as where a Muslim leader criticised the belief that the Hindu deity Ganesha could drink milk offerings.

[142] *PP v Benjamin Koh* [2005] SGD 272 (for posting an online picture of a pig and a halal logo accompanied by anti-Malay and anti-Muslim remarks); *Ong Kian Cheong v PP* [2009] SGDC 163 (when a Protestant Christian couple were convicted for sending 'tracts' such as 'Who Is Allah?' to persons with Malay/Muslim names).

[143] Penal Code, s 298 relates to an utterance made with the deliberate intent of wounding religious feeling, though no actual impact is needed: *PP v Amos Yee* [2015] SGDC 215.

meetings with religious leaders, 'relying on mutual trust and the wisdom of our religious leaders to defuse tensions'.[144] The public is conscious of the MRHA, which members of the majority religion, Buddhism,[145] have invoked as a safeguard against insensitive proselytising and harassment.[146]

B. 2019 Amendments: From Preventive to Punitive and Pastoral Powers

The 2019 amendments, effective 1 November 2022,[147] updated the MRHA for the Internet age, enabling swift action against offensive online communications activity.[148] New rules designed to regulate foreign influences in terms of donations or membership in local religious groups were introduced.[149]

The minister, on making an RO, must 'immediately' give the PCRH a copy with supporting facts and grounds (the previous timeline was 30 days).[150] The PCRH now has an enlarged role in making recommendations to the President: the subject of an RO may now, under section 11(1A), make representations before the PCRH within a set time period. The minister is obliged under section 14 to review an RO at intervals of not more than 12 months.

As well as preventive powers, the MRHA now has punitive powers, as Penal Code religious offences have been ported over, in constructing an omnibus religious harmony legislation. Sections 7E and F deal with serious offences attracting a fine or up to 10 years' imprisonment.

Section 17E covers the urging of violence or force against a target person or group in Singapore who are distinguished by characteristics such as religion, ethnicity, language, political opinion or 'any other characteristic'. Section 17F(1) relates to the offence of inciting feelings of enmity, hatred, ill-will, contempt or ridicule against a target group distinguished by religious belief or activity, while section 17F(2) relates to insulting another's religion or wounding religious feelings. The motive of offenders is irrelevant, as only impact matters: section 17(G).

Such laws can restrict religious liberties, given the ambiguity in the scope of offences like wounding religious feelings: for example, if an Islamic teacher says

[144] PM Lee Hsien Loong, National Day Rally Speech, 16 August 2009, www.pmo.gov.sg/.

[145] As of 2020, the religious composition of the population is Buddhism (31%), Taoism (8.8%), Christianity (18.9%), Islam (15.6%), Hinduism (5%), Other Religions (0.6%) and no religion (20%). Census of Population 2020: Religion: www.singstat.gov.sg/-/media/files/visualising_data/infographics/c2020/c2020-religion.ashx.

[146] 'Agree to Disagree: Conversations on Conversion' 18, https://conversion.buddhist.sg/.

[147] MHA Press Release, 'Commencement of the MRHA (Amendment, 2019)' (31 October 2022).

[148] Under s 8(4), the minister is no longer required to give any person notice of his intention to make an RO.

[149] ss 8(2A), 16.

[150] Rajah notes that under the old s 11 MRHA, an RO may be in place for up to three months, 'without even the limited institutional check on state power that the [PCRH] represents': Rajah (n 9) 250.

Jesus is only a prophet and not the son of God, as Christianity teaches, would many Christians find this insulting where the intent was delivering Islamic doctrine?[151]

The MRHA also has a 'pastoral' function, where law is deployed as an instrument of reconciliation when a religious disharmony incident arises. Reflecting a form of legal communitarianism, 'hard' law which imposes rules and penalties and exerts a continuous background pressure is considered necessary but 'not enough'.[152] It works in tandem with 'soft constitutional law'[153] (SCL), which operates through nurturing expectations and aspirations in the religious harmony project. SCL norms are executive-authored or approved, accessible and contained in white papers and declarations.[154] While not formally binding, they have some effect in guiding the behaviour of constitutional actors.

Indeed, a public ritual or practice of apology and reconciliation had organically developed over more than a decade of religious disharmony incidents,[155] producing a protocol for managing such disputes through quiet diplomacy, without invoking MRHA powers. Where a religious disharmony dispute arises and offence is caused, the offending party should apologise and the offended party should accept this; the two parties should meet under the glare of media scrutiny, hug, sing or have a fellowship meal or inter-faith concert to signal the restoration of friendly relations. Reference is made to SCL norms in the MRHWP, such as not denigrating another's religion, which becomes the normative reference point around which expectations are formed. Other religious groups chorus their support for this settlement, after which an uncharacteristically subdued government articulates its approval, indicating a termination of animus and return to harmonious equilibrium. This reflects the goal of relational constitutionalism[156] not only in keeping the peace, but keeping a certain quality of peace, to heal relational rifts and to build an affective solidarity which sustains racial and religious harmony. Implicit in this is a duty to seek pacific dispute settlement and refrain from vengeful, disproportionate actions which sustain hostility.

[151] A question raised by an opposition parliamentarian, Faisal Manap, in response to which the Home Affairs Minister stated that people were free to express their views but had to do so responsibly without denigrating another religion or degenerating into insults or incitement to violence: K Shanmugam, Maintenance of Religious Harmony Amendment Bill 2019, Wrap-up Speech, para 57, https:/www.mha.gov.sg.

[152] Lee Hsien Loong (PAP Secretary General), Speech, PAP Convention, 28 November 2021, para 18, www.pap.org.sg.

[153] Li-ann Thio, 'Soft Constitutional Law in Non-liberal Asian Constitutional Democracies' (2010) 8 ICON 766.

[154] Thio, 'Constitutional "Soft" Law' (n 82).

[155] The Lighthouse Evangelism incident in 2010, where videos placed on a church website apparently upset Buddhists and other citizens, is the first instance where this public ritual began to be developed: see Thio Li-ann, 'Contentious Liberty: Regulating Religious Propagation in a Religiously Diverse Secular Democracy' [2010] SJLS 484.

[156] Li-ann Thio, 'Relational Constitutionalism and the Management of Religious Disputes: The Singapore "Secularism with a Soul" Model' (2012) 1 OJLR 446.

Building on this public ritual, section 16H to some extent formalises it and empowers the minister[157] to offer the alleged offender[158] an opportunity to take remedial actions as part of a Community Remedial Initiative (CRI); this pivots from criminal prosecution towards 'restoration and rehabilitation'[159] and the de-escalation of animosities. The offender may voluntarily choose to enter a CRI agreement, and the minister will decide what process of reconciliation and contrition rituals are appropriate; these could involve a public or private apology or visiting the aggrieved religious community to learn about their faith, soothe wounded feelings and restore or build friendly relations.[160]

When a CRI agreement is in force, an offender cannot be prosecuted for the alleged offence; if the offender fails to comply with the terms of the agreement, the minister can terminate the CRI and refer the offender to the PP under section 16H(7). Offenders completing the CRI will not be subject to criminal prosecution.

Here, law and the RoL can serve not only to control, but also to operate as an instrument of reconciliation.[161] 'Law' fades into the background to create a non-law space where emotions can be taken seriously[162] and where 'apology and forgiveness are possible',[163] dampening vengefulness and healing community relations. Section 16H provides an institutional 'nudge'[164] rather than a shove; it guides parties in a 'non-legal way'[165] to act in a desirable manner and preserve solidarity as a public good, through informal methods of resolving disputes, which legal sanctions cannot engender. This recognises the utility and limits of the rule and role of law. Further, human dignity and spiritual autonomy are also secured as the CRI is voluntary, with the government sensitive to not wanting to coerce people to do 'what their faith militates against them doing',[166] such as

[157] Making a CRI agreement may interfere with the Public Prosecutor's independent exercise of discretion. Indeed, declining a CRI agreement is a relevant consideration in deciding whether to pursue prosecution or issue a conditional warning. The Law Minister stated it was inappropriate to leave the power to initiate a CRI in the AG's hands, as CRIs are meant to be a voluntary, community-based way of dealing with issues: Wrap-up Speech (n 151) [85]–[86].

[158] The CRI will not be offered where egregious, violent conduct is involved. If someone has caused disquiet carelessly, an educative moment is possible, assuming both parties are 'willing to meet to mend relations': ibid [86].

[159] K Shanmugam (Law Minister), Second Reading, Maintenance of Religious Harmony (Amendment) Bill, 7 October 2019, [71], www.mha.gov.sg.

[160] 'Blogger Sheen Phua Apologises to Sikh Community over "Misinterpreted" Instagram Post' (*Yahoo News*, 23 September 2019). This was discussed during parliamentary debates: Shanmugam (n 159) [72].

[161] Antonio Buti, '"Reconciliation": Its Relationship and Importance to Law' [2018] 43(1) University of Western Australia Law Review 107; Lorna McGregor, 'Reconciliation: Where Is the Law?' in Scott Veitch, Emilios Christodoulidis and Sharon Cowan (eds), *Law and the Politics of Reconciliation* (Routledge 2007) 111–218.

[162] Meghan Clarke, 'Polarization: The Role of Emotions in Reconciliation Efforts' (2009) 72(2) Law and Contemporary Problems 27, 3.1.

[163] ibid.

[164] Richard H Thaler and Cass R Sunstein, *Nudge* (Yale University Press, 2008).

[165] Wrap-up Speech (n 151) [89].

[166] ibid [86].

visiting another religion's place of worship. This reflects the government ethos of carefully finding concrete solutions to problems.

Further, improvement in the alleged offender's understanding and conduct should not be by way of 'forcing someone through the law to "reform"'.[167] This reflects a Confucianist understanding that all people are educable, that education opens the door to developing moral virtues and character through internalising social values.[168] Law can extract external conformity in terms of behaviour and speech, but cannot change the heart. However, law can, through promoting dialogue, interaction and conciliatory processes, facilitate human relating and support personal transformation. While the CRI process can be abused by the insincere, it may provide a useful inflection point for the offender in making amends and better grasping local sensitivities. Through this, the good citizen who values and abides by the communitarian value of racial and religious harmony is cultivated.

The modern secular state thus has a suite of tools to advance the religious harmony project, without exclusively relying on courts and enforceable remedies, while using the binding force of the law to 'nudge' persons towards desirable behaviour. Maintaining religious harmony contours the scope of religious freedom, and the role of law as a tool of reconciliation may help promote the ordered liberty and sense of community needed to sustain a religiously plural democratic society. The good faith of governors and governed is needed for this to be viable, avoiding the extremes of autocratic rule and anarchic animosities.

IV. THE LAW ON PUBLIC ASSEMBLY: MANAGING DEMOCRACY AND CORNERING SPEAKERS

Singapore citizens have the right under Article 14(1)(b) of the Law of Public Assembly 'to assemble peaceably and without arms' subject to restrictions Parliament considers 'necessary or expedient' on grounds of security or public order. Foreign critics, opposition politicians and domestic civil society activists have long been critical of the law governing public assemblies, where a licence is generally required to speak or demonstrate in public.[169]

This form of prior restraint arguably denudes Article 14 of any substantive content, as does the discriminatory application of licensing laws to deny

[167] ibid [87].

[168] Rita Ng, 'College and Character: What Did Confucius Teach Us about the Importance of Integrating Ethics, Character, Learning, and Education?' (2009) 10(4) Journal of College and Character 1.

[169] JB Jeyaretnam, 'Rule of Law' motion, 71 SPR, 24 November 1999, col 597; Chiam See Tong, cols 583–84; James Gomez, 'Restricting Free Speech: The Impact of Opposition Parties in Singapore' (2006) 23 Copenhagen Journal of Asia Studies 105, 110.

civil society activists permits.[170] Stating their disbelief of being granted permits, several activists have given public speeches without a permit, facing arrest, fines and imprisonment. The official stance is that the police have 'approved permit applications regularly'.[171] The lived experience of activists is that this is an illiberal regime where civic space is 'repressed',[172] given the extensive discretion under public assembly laws and weak judicial protection. This is deleterious to the RoL and the right to political participation.

Today, the centrepiece of this regulatory framework is the Public Order Act (POA), introduced in 2009 to rationalise precursor legislation.[173] Lord Denning observed that English common law has long recognised the right to demonstrate and protest on matters of public concern, provided no wrongful act is done. It 'is often the only means by which grievances can be brought to the knowledge of those in authority – at any rate with such impact as to gain a remedy'.[174]

The closely associated rights of free speech and peaceful assembly enable citizens 'to voice criticisms, air grievances and seek redress', including venting unpopular minority views, as 'tolerance is a hallmark of a pluralistic society'.[175] The ability to organise and protest is an important vehicle for holding the government responsible as a facet of extra-parliamentary politics; a demonstration or process as 'an assembly in motion' can give views a 'wide exposure'. This may be an effective form of communication,[176] albeit in terms of slogans rather than reasoned debate, but is nonetheless a useful indicator of public sentiment.[177]

However, in Singapore, where 'effective, efficient and speedy' government action is imperative, the government frowns on street protests[178] and holds that lobby groups are not to 'intervene with the Executive … on any debate',[179] as a duly elected government acting with parliamentary oversight must not be

[170] Report of the Committee on International Human Rights of the Association of the Bar of the City of New York, 'The Decline of the Rule of Law in Malaysia and Singapore – Part II – Singapore' (1991) 46 The Record 7; the court in *Chee Soon Juan v PP* [2003] 2 SLR(R) 445, [21] dismissed the bare allegation that denying a licence to hold a rally was discriminatory.

[171] Mark Jeyaretnam (Ministry of Law), Letter to the Chairman, Human Rights Institute Council, International Bar Association (UK) 9 April 2008 (LAW/06/021/026), [41], www.mlaw.gov.sg.

[172] 'The Singapore Authorities Continues Its Use of Restrictive Laws to Harass Critics and Activists and Stifle Protests' (*Civicus Monitor*, 20 December 2022) https://monitor.civicus.org/explore/singapore-authorities-continues-its-use-restrictive-laws-harass-critics-and-activists-and-stifle-protests/.

[173] Public Entertainments Act; Public Entertainment and Meetings Act; Miscellaneous Offences Act.

[174] *Hubbard v Pitt* [1976] QB 142, 212.

[175] *Leung Kwok Hung v HKSAR* Final Appeal Nos 1 & 2 of 2005 (Criminal), Judgment of 8 July 2005, [1]–[2].

[176] ibid [3].

[177] 'New Forms of Tribalism Can Take Root and Affect Politics in Singapore: Lawrence Wong' *Straits Times* (24 November 2021).

[178] K Shanmugam (Minister of Law), New York State Bar Association Rule of Law Plenary Session, 28 October 2009, [54(3)].

[179] ibid [57].

obstructed from implementing its policies. Some even view engaging in cause advocacy as a form of 'political transgression'.[180]

This cautious approach towards politically driven public assemblies reflects the official association of the RoL as an instrument for maintaining law and order. Within a communitarian setting in a 'small city with a dense population', the 'rights of society' to law and order are 'given significant weight',[181] facilitating the execution of 'all our plans on governance'.[182]

The fear of peaceful protests or assemblies degenerating into mob violence, as in 'many supposedly mature societies',[183] is top of mind. The official discourse addresses assemblies not in terms of rights but in terms of risk assessment, given that riots and violence will inflict slow-healing community wounds and impair 'public confidence in our stability and security'.[184] In other countries, assemblies as assertions of power may intimidate others from expressing contrarian views, as evident in the pro-terrorist Hamas rallies in the West after 7 October 2023. Mutual deplatforming and social unrest ensues.[185] From local history, the trauma of 'the 1950s Maria Hertogh riots and the 1964 race riots' which started as peaceful assemblies but 'ended up with 54 dead, 736 injured and significant damage to property'[186] persists, which courts and politicians regularly recite.[187] This sustains the view that people's politics are a form of chaos to be restrained, underscoring the circumspection towards outdoor street protests, as distinct from containing demonstrations within stadiums or indoor venues.[188]

However, the government's decision in 2000 to undertake a liberalising experiment or, alternatively, an 'exercise in tokenism' was reflective of paternal democracy.[189] Hong Lim Park was designated as 'Speakers' Corner', where speeches and demonstrations could be made without a licence, subject to certain conditions. This reflects the model of managed democracy which we now examine in relation to laws regulating public assembly, where incremental changes are made in response to endogenous and exogenous factors without ceding strong regulatory control.

[180] Rajah (n 9) 264.

[181] 'Singapore's Government's Response to the White Paper by Amsterdam & Peroff' (11 November 2009) [46], www.nas.gov.sg/archivesonline/data/pdfdoc/20091118008.htm.

[182] Jeyaretnam, Letter to the Chairman (n 171) [52].

[183] Wong Kan Seng (Deputy PM and Home Affairs Minister), 84 SPR, 28 February 2008, cols 1153–55.

[184] ibid.

[185] Noah Feldman, 'Protest Is Legal, Intimidation is Different' (*Bloomberg.com*, 17 August 2017).

[186] Jeyaretnam, Letter to the Chairman (n 171) [41].

[187] *Vijaya Kumar v AG* [2015] SGHC 244, [33], [49]. Grace Fu (Minister for Culture, Community and Youth), 'Restricting Hate Speech to Maintain Racial and Religious Harmony in Singapore', 94 SPR, 1 April 2019.

[188] Wong Kan Seng (n 183).

[189] Li-ann Thio, 'Speakers' Cornered? Managing Political Speech in Singapore and the Commitment "To Build a Democratic Society"' (2003) 3 ICON 516.

A. Facilitative or Obstructive? Laws Regulating Public Assembly before the Public Order Act

Opposition politicians and civil society activists have long decried the over-restrictive or discriminatory application of licensing laws, contrary to the RoL value of equal treatment, which unduly limits civil-political rights in the face of statist-oriented judicial review.[190] They consider it 'nonsensical' in a 'modern democratic society based on the RoL' for 'the demonstration of opposition to the actions of the Government to be an offence'.[191]

Pre-POA legislation provided that any assembly of five or more designed to attract attention to a cause, possibly being a public disturbance, required a police permit,[192] and that certain gatherings of four or more needed to obtain an entertainment licence.[193] 'Public entertainment' was broadly defined to include 'any lecture, talk, address, debate or discussion',[194] capturing a Labour Day rally at the Istana, when the grounds of the President's official residence were open to the public.[195] Potentially grouping political speeches with funfairs somewhat trivialises political communication.

Public assembly legislation has been challenged on grounds of according 'absolute discretion' to the permit issuer. As assembly rights are not absolute, the courts have affirmed that 'licensing and permit schemes' are integral to the government's 'ability to efficiently regulate public behaviour'[196] to secure public order where mischief is caused by participants, onlookers or conflict agitators. Courts have upheld such laws by pointing out there was no complete ban[197] on assemblies, nor was discretion unfettered. There was 'nothing' to prevent one from making a permit application[198] under the statutory procedure, nor was it 'inherently wrong or unreasonable' to require permission to hold a public meeting where this was merely 'a facilitative arrangement'.[199] Further, police

[190] The International Bar Association (Human Rights Institute) has noted a 'tendency for the PEMA' (the POA's precursor) to be 'applied rigorously to opposition candidates': 'Prosperity versus Individual Rights? Human Rights, Democracy and the Rule of Law in Singapore' (2008) 63.

[191] *Chee Soon Juan v PP* [2011] 3 SLR 50, [35].

[192] Miscellaneous Offences (Public Order and Nuisance) Act (Cap 184, 1997 rev edn Singapore), Rule 5 was considered to be pre-emptive, leaving the permit issuer to assess disorder risks. The test is that of intent to attract public attention, not success in doing so: *PP v Chong Kai Xiong* [2010] 2 SLR 355, [10].

[193] Public Entertainments and Meetings Act (Cap 257, 2001 rev edn Singapore) (PEMA). For a list of PEMA infringements by opposition parties, see Gomez (n 169) 111, Table 1. In 2000, fines for holding public talks were doubled from $5000 to $10,000. Under s 141 of the Penal Code, an 'unlawful assembly' is one where five or more persons had a common object to eg commit mischief.

[194] PEMA, Schedule, s 2(m). See *Jeyaretnam JB v PP* [1990] 3 Mal LJ 411, where Chan J affirmed that the validity of licensing decisions were subject to *GCHQ* principles of administrative legality.

[195] *Chee Soon Juan v PP* [2003] 2 SLR(R) 445.

[196] *Ng Chye Huay v PP* [2005] SGHC 193, [39].

[197] *Chee Soon Juan v PP* [2011] 2 SLR 940, [10]; *Yap Kheng Ho v PP* [2011] 3 SLR 32, [21].

[198] *Ng Chye Huay* (n 196) [44].

[199] *Chee Siok Chin v MHA* [2005] SGHC 216, [53].

decisions could be challenged through judicial review,[200] even if there was no appeal mechanism like that under the Miscellaneous Offences (Public Order and Nuisance) Act (MOA). Under Rules 2 and 5 of the MOA (Public Order and Nuisance) (Assemblies and Processions) Rules, participants in a public assembly to support or oppose the views or actions of a person, knowing they had no permit, were guilty of an offence even if these activities did not threaten public order.[201]

However, if permit applications were not mere formalities but were subject to assessments which veer sharply towards caution and denial for political reasons, this would support the suspicions of non-government activists of a discriminatory policy against them or a policy not to grant actors like political parties any permits at all. The valorisation of public order considerations[202] is evident where the police denied the Open Singapore Centre's application for 20–30 persons to run to mark Human Rights Day on 10 December 2000, ending at Hong Lim Park, where an anti-ISA demonstration would be held. In response to parliamentary questions, the Home Affairs Minister stated that even if 30 persons were permitted to proceed with this run, the numbers could swell where supporters or opponents of the cause gathered, which in the police's view could cause potential (one may argue, highly speculative) law and order problems.

It emerged that the police took 'a more cautious approach' towards outdoor activities organised by political parties, which posed a greater risk to public disorder. An opposition politician argued this placed a 'sweeping ban' on 'outdoor political activities' that was 'harsh, arbitrary, disproportionate and inconsistent with the RoL'.[203] Arguments against such policies have been raised in court but were unsubstantiated,[204] or raised in cases where permits were not even applied for. Thus, any alleged discriminatory licensing policy would not affect someone convicted for having a public assembly without a permit,[205] irrespective of whether a permit refusal would contravene the equality guarantee.[206]

An example of alleged discrimination was the complaint of the secretary-general of the Singapore Democratic Party (SDP), Chee Soon Juan, about the SDP's unsuccessful application for a permit to hold a *Tak Boleh Tahan* 'protest rally'

[200] *Ng Chye Huay* (n 196) [39].

[201] *Chee Soon Juan v PP* [2011] 3 SLR 50.

[202] Open Singapore Centre (Application to mark human rights day), Oral answers to questions, 72 SPR, 22 February 2001, col 1448.

[203] Ho Peng Kee (for DPM and Home Affairs Minister), 83 SPR, 27 August 2007, col 1138, cited in *Yap Kheng Ho v PP* [2011] 3 SLR 32, [12]. A general policy that considered political activities posed a greater threat to public order than commercial activities was not offensive under administrative law, provided discretion was not fettered: *Chee Soon Juan v PP* [2011] 3 SLR 50, [40].

[204] *PP v Chong Kai Xiong* [2010] SGHC 101, [13]. It was also argued there was an unconstitutional policy not to issue permits for outdoor political activities in *Chee Soon Juan v PP* [2011] 3 SLR 50, [38], but no evidence of unlawful discrimination in showing the SDP was treated differently from other opposition parties, was offered: [41].

[205] *Chee Soon Juan v PP* [2011] 2 SLR 940, [11], [14]. Under PEMA, providing entertainment without a licence was a 'strict liability' offence: [16].

[206] *Yap Kheng Ho v PP* [2011] 3 SLR 32.

on 15 March 2008 at Parliament House. It was announced on the SDP website that the rally would proceed, and the public were invited to join and 'demonstrate your anger in a peaceful manner' against the PAP government's 'exploitative price hikes'.[207] The rally coincided with World Consumer Rights Day: while the Consumer Association of Singapore (CASE), run by PAP MPs, was permitted to conduct a protest outside Parliament House against marketing unhealthy food to children, activists participating in the SDP rally were arrested.[208] The activists had 'deliberately planned to break the law' by holding a rally without a permit, and their convictions and sentences were upheld. In response, Chee penned an open letter to the Chief Justice, Law Minister and AG asserting that if the judiciary did not intervene to protect citizen rights, but enabled the use of law to buttress the ruling party's power while 'suppressing the political opposition and civil society', the RoL would be 'just a buzz phrase used to prop up a façade'.[209]

While the constitutionality and exercise of powers under public assembly legislation are subject to judicial review, this is a relatively weak mode of accountability. The RoL is seen as an instrument for law and governance, as evident in Choo J's comment that Article 14 did not create 'unbridled rights' as 'the RoL requires protection of the law to be extended to all and civil liberties cannot be very civil if in exercising them one disturbs the peace others enjoy'.[210]

The applicable test to review discretion is *Wednesbury* unreasonableness;[211] there is no reasonableness test in assessing the constitutionality of laws, nor need restrictions satisfy a minimum impairment requirement.[212] Article 14(2) empowers Parliament to impose restrictions it considers 'necessary or expedient' in the interests of public order and security, which confers 'an extremely wide discretionary power' to achieve Article 14(2) purposes. Parliament may take a 'prophylactic approach in the maintenance of public order',[213] provided it can show a nexus between the relevant law and any 'permissible restriction' in Article 14(2).[214] Once legislation satisfies this nexus test,[215] it is balanced against

[207] ibid [6].

[208] It was unclear whether CASE had a permit or whether it fell under Rule 2(1)(f) of the MOA which exempts any assembly or procession 'under the direction or control of the Government' from needing a permit. See 'Chee Soon Juan responds to Chief Justice, Attorney-General and Law Minister', SDP website, 7 January 2009, https://yoursdp.org/2009/01/06/perspectives-chee_responds_to_cj_ag_and_law_minister-2-1-0-112/. Chee wanted to question the licensing officer on this point: above n 207, [12].

[209] ibid.

[210] *PP v Chong Kai Xiong* [2010] 3 SLR 355, [13].

[211] ibid [93].

[212] Rejecting the Canadian approach in *Vancouver (City) v Zhang* [2010] BCCA 450, discussed in *Chee Soon Juan v PP* [2011] 2 SLR 940, [9].

[213] *Chee Siok Chin* [2005] (n 199) [50].

[214] ibid [49].

[215] In *Chee Soon Juan v PP* [2003] 2 SLR(R) 445, [20] Yong CJ said it was 'eminently clear' that PEMA was enacted for purposes of public order under Art 14(2(a), being 'fully within' legislative power.

assembly rights which must be exercised responsibly by citizens in a context where Parliament has 'placed a premium on public order, accountability and personal responsibility';[216] as such, individual interests are 'subordinated to the wider community's interests' in service of 'the common welfare and good'.[217] Here, 'balance' appears to entail no more than a judicial ratification of the legislative balance, provided the nexus test is satisfied; this form of weak review does not evaluate the reasonableness or proportionality of the legislative restrictions.

B. The Public Order Act

The POA was introduced in 2009 after the World Bank–International Monetary Fund (WB–IMF) 2006 Summit in Singapore drew local protests led by Chee Soon Juan, which garnered international media attention.[218] Chee and his fellow protesters were confined to Speakers' Corner by a 30-strong police barricade and not allowed to leave during the Summit.[219] Chee was later charged under the Public Entertainments and Meeting Act (PEMA) for handing out flyers and holding a public procession without a permit.

International civil society activists accustomed to more lax assembly regulations were greatly disgruntled by the strict Singapore regulations. Top WB and IMF officials expressed their disquiet when 28 accredited activists were banned from entering Singapore because they were 'disruptive characters' and were unhappy about the venues provided for protestors. Some 1500 foreign activists staged their protests on the nearby Indonesian island of Batam, while 80 NGOs announced a boycott of the official meeting.[220] Given militant protests experienced at earlier meetings, some thought Singapore was chosen owing to its authoritarian reputation and ability to maintain law and order.[221]

To avoid the impression that 'foreigners have more rights than Singaporeans', only indoor demonstrations were permitted, thereby 'sterilising public space from any resistance'.[222] Activists were confined to a roped-off corner in the Suntec Convention Centre lobby, where the Summit was staged. The functioning of the city was not to be disrupted. Rather than a blanket ban on protests, strict restrictions applied: activists could shout, but without amplifiers. Police guidelines instructed against the burning of placards, which may cause alarm

[216] *Chee Siok Chin* [2005] (n 199) [135].
[217] ibid [53].
[218] 'Singapore Deters IMF Protestors' *New York Times* (17 September 2006).
[219] 'Singapore Stand-Off to Last "until Tuesday"' (ABC News (Australia), 17 September 2006).
[220] 'NGOs Boycott World Bank Meetings' *The Guardian* (14 September 2006); 'IMF and World Bank Rebuke Singapore' *Financial Times* (9 September 2006).
[221] DPM and Home Affairs Minister Wong Kan Seng, 'IMF and World Bank Group Meetings in Singapore (Contingency plans to deal with militant protestors)', 80 SPR, 6 January 2006, col 2107.
[222] RH Honggare, 'Uncornering Speakers: On Political Speech in Singapore', The Avery Review, https://averyreview.com/issues/22/uncornering-speakers.

and breach the peace or 'offend religious or racial and ethnic sensibilities'. The police provided free plastic placards for writing slogans on, but disallowed the 'dangerous' hosting of banners on metal or wooden poles.[223]

The need to regulate public assemblies is shaped by Singapore's aspiration to be a hub for hosting large-scale events[224] to economic benefit, such as the 2009 APEC meeting, with the reputation for managing demonstrations and ensuring meetings are not disrupted.[225] The POA was meant to be 'part of the continuum of … measured changes to our framework for political space', to ensure 'adequate space' for political expression without compromising social stability.[226] In Singapore, this balance incorporated considerations of population density, racial and religious diversity and the conviction that stability in socio-economic terms was 'an existential issue'.[227] Singapore's 'intense focus on stability' and its high rankings on international political risk surveys were key competitive advantages in attracting foreign investment. The optimal balance in Singapore was thus predisposed towards according 'greater weight' to stability, while appreciating the need for 'greater political space'.[228]

The POA, which rationalises the PEMA and MOA, is 'not quite new law', though the government described it as 'a substantial relaxation of the current position'.[229] Critics, however, have labelled expansive POA powers as 'draconian',[230] which could be 'systematically' used to 'clamp down' even on solo peaceful protests.[231] Its impact on peaceful public demonstrations is 'extraordinarily strict', with courts not providing a 'significant counterweight' to executive overreach.[232] In 2020, several UN special rapporteurs expressed concern that the POA was used to prosecute legitimate exercises of free speech and assembly.[233]

The POA regulates assemblies and processions in public spaces, and section 2(1) defines 'assembly' broadly as 'a gathering or meeting (whether comprising any lecture, talk, address, debate or discussion)' to support or oppose the views or actions of any person, group or government, to publicise a cause or campaign,

[223] 'Singapore Blocks IMF Street Protests' *New York Times* (4 September 2006).

[224] Rajah (n 9) 261.

[225] Citing events in Thailand, where international leaders had to hurriedly leave a conference by helicopters, the Second Home Affairs stated this showed 'the need for this legislation' as Singapore could not 'afford the luxury of having these meetings disrupted:' K Shanmugam (Second Minister, Home Affairs), Public Order Bill, 85 SPR, 13 April 2009, cols 3656, 3657.

[226] ibid col 3658.

[227] ibid col 3659.

[228] ibid col 3660.

[229] ibid cols 3744–45.

[230] 'The Singapore Model: Advocacy in an Authoritarian State' *The Diplomat* (6 February 2020).

[231] 'The Singapore Authorities Continues Its Use of Restrictive Laws to Harass Critics and Activists and Stifle Protests' (*Civicus Monitor*, 20 December 2022) monitor.civicus.org.

[232] Human Rights Watch, 'Kill the Chickens to Scare the Monkeys: Suppression of Free Expression and Assembly in Singapore' (12 December 2017) 61–88.

[233] Special Rapporteurs, 'Freedom of Peaceful Assembly and Association, Freedom of Opinion and Expression and Situation of Human Rights Defenders', AL SGP/3/2020 (12 October 2020).

or to commemorate any event. It goes beyond prior legislation by explicitly including 'a demonstration by a person alone', and may be considered too restrictive of civil liberties compared to the common law requirement that an unlawful assembly minimally involves three persons. Gatherings of more than five are addressed under the MOA, whereas the PEMA applies for groups of less than five.[234] The minister stated it was 'more logical' to adopt an effects-oriented approach to regulate all public cause-based activities, and to focus on whether an activity was disruptive rather than to choose an 'artificial numerical criterion', as a group of four could be more disruptive than a group of 20 peaceful protesters. This would halt the 'endless farcical antics' where activists gathered in groups of four to evade permit requirements, as during the 2007 ASEAN Summit, distracting the police from security maintenance tasks.[235] Nonetheless, opposition MPs saw this as 'tightening up on small groups',[236] with there being convictions for unlawful single-person assemblies.[237]

A public assembly is an assembly in a public place where the public are invited, induced or permitted to attend. While 'cause-related' public assemblies require a police permit, the POA exempts activities conducted by statutory boards or certain charities which are social, recreational and commercial in nature; thus, 50 per cent of activities formerly requiring permits no longer do.[238] The Police Commissioner under section 7 may grant or refuse to grant a permit for a proposed assembly or procession, and to assemble without a permit is an offence under section 16.

Section 7(2) sets out seven grounds for refusing a permit if the Commissioner apprehends on 'reasonable grounds' that it might occasion public disorder or nuisance, damage public property, jeopardise any person's safety or cause feelings of enmity between different groups, for example.[239] A 2017 amendment allows the Commissioner to reject a permit where foreigners are involved in using such events for political ends, such as shaping opinion on public controversies.[240] A permit may be granted with conditions, such as engaging sufficient security

[234] Shanmugam, Public Order Bill (n 225) col 3745.

[235] ibid col 3746.

[236] Sylvia Lim, Public Order Bill, 85 SPR, 13 April 2009, cols 3656, 3762.

[237] 'Singaporean Artist Jailed after Peaceful Protest' (Al Jazeera, 12 October 2018); 'Activist Gilbert Goh Convicted of Taking Part in Public Assembly without a Permit' *Straits Times* (26 July 2022).

[238] Shanmugam, Public Order Bill (n 225) col 3665. See First Schedule, Public Order (Exempt Assemblies and Processions) Order 2009 No S 489.

[239] Report of the special rapporteur on the rights to freedom of peaceful assembly and of association, Maina Kiai, May 2012, UN Doc A/HRC/20/27, [32] (stating some level of disruption had to be tolerated, or the right would be deprived of substance).

[240] s 7(2)(h) relates to assemblies directed towards a political end involving non-Singaporean entities and non-Singaporeans. See Home Affairs Minister, K Shanmugam, 94 SPR, 3 April 2017, cited in *Wham Kwok Han Jolovan v PP* [2021] 1 SLR 476, [47]. Human Rights Watch considers this deprives the ability of foreigners residing in Singapore to exercise freedom of assembly: Human Rights Watch (n 232) 65. However, this discounts the fact that non-citizens enjoy only a common law liberty to free speech: *Wham Kwok Han Jolovan v PP* [2021] (idem) [48]; *Review Publishing v Lee Hsieng Loong* [2009] 1 SLR 177, [257].

officers to keep good order, requiring adherence to a specified number of participants or stipulated the size for displays (section 8). The Commissioner may cancel the permit on specific grounds under section 10.

The apex court upheld the POA's constitutionality in *Wham Kwok Han Jolovan v PP*,[241] where Wham was charged with violating section 16(1)(a) for holding an assembly without a permit. Wham had organised an event at a public venue called 'Civil Disobedience and Social Movements' and invited a non-citizen to speak via video link from Hong Kong. This took the event outside the scope of recognised permits exemptions.[242]

The court adopted an objective approach, affirming that permissible restrictions under Article 14(2) could not 'undermine entirely' the right to peaceful assembly under Article 14(1)(b). The POA satisfied the nexus test as the legislative purpose objectively related to 'public order', there being a need to strike 'a balance ... between the competing interests at stake'.[243] Bearing in mind that earlier decisions[244] would consider a statute unconstitutional for conferring absolute discretion on a decision-maker, the Court of Appeal (CA) underscored that there was no blanket prohibition on political assemblies or those involving foreigners; it was restricted by the need for the Commissioner's permission. Depending on POA guidelines and case circumstances, the Commissioner could grant a permit, indicating his discretion was 'not an untrammeled and arbitrary one'.[245] Even if a listed circumstance exists, the Commissioner could still grant a permit if the assembly, speaker or topic did not imperil public order.[246] It was 'wholly reasonable' for Parliament to adopt a licensing scheme and confer discretion on the Commissioner, whose knowledge of local conditions made him well-placed to assess permit applications.[247] This could also help prevent disorder as opposed to stopping disorder after the fact. As such, the court could not see how a 'more fundamental deprivation' of the right was involved. A ministerial appeal under section 11 could be brought against the Commissioner's decision, as well as judicial review on grounds of bad faith or improper purposes.

The POA thus sets a clearer regulatory framework, identifying public order grounds for approving or rejecting an application and providing statutory remedies. This promotes the RoL virtues of clarity and transparency.[248] However, other broad POA powers which consolidate executive power nurture

[241] *Wham Kwok Han Jolovan v PP* [2021] (n 240).

[242] Indoor public assemblies involving only Singaporeans would be exempt from the permit requirement – see First Schedule Public Order (Exempt Assemblies and Processions) Order 2009 No. S 489; *Wham Kwok Han Jolovan v PP* [2021] (n 240) [18].

[243] *Wham Kwok Han Jolovan v PP* [2021] (n 240) [33].

[244] *JB Jeyaretnam v PP* [1989] 2 SLR(R) 419, [27].

[245] *Wham Kwok Han Jolovan v PP* [2021] (n 240) [36].

[246] ibid [48].

[247] ibid [50].

[248] Shanmugam, Public Order Bill (n 225) col 3757.

accountability concerns. The minister can effectively cancel any previous permit granted under section 13 by prohibiting an assembly in the 'public interest', and under section 12 can declare by Gazette order any public place to be a prohibited area for public assemblies. This could include sites like Parliament House or the Istana, which may be the most effective sites for holding demonstrations.[249]

Under sections 35–36, police sergeants and above may issue 'move-on' directions to a person or group where there is a reasonable suspicion of interference with the orderly conduct of an event. Such an order must be 'reasonably necessary' for public safety, order or protecting the rights of other persons,[250] and may involve leaving a regulated place for 24 hours or moving from it for 'a stated reasonable distance in a stated direction'. A certain level of formality and certainty avails insofar as the direction must be in writing. While it could theoretically be inappropriately deployed, for example, for neighbour disputes, the intent was that there should be a 'sufficient public order basis', subject to police protocols.[251] The justification was giving police pre-emptive powers to deal with cause-related activism and new security threats: rather than outright arresting someone involved in an illegal assembly, a person issued with a 'move-on' direction could choose to cooperate and thereby 'prevent a situation where there is illegal conduct from escalating'.[252] This person would not have an adverse antecedent record. This 'more calibrated approach',[253] drawn from Australia, was meant to be a 'very low key' power,[254] although non-compliance is a new offence under section 37.

Nonetheless, critics consider the POA regulatory regimes makes it 'almost impossible to hold a public protest relating to anything remotely political anywhere other than in Hong Lim Park', the site of Speakers' Corner. Under section 14, this is recognised as an 'unrestricted area', where the notice and permit requirements for holding public assemblies or processions do not apply. Although activists may apply for a permit beyond Speakers' Corner for cause-related assemblies, it is generally believed this would not be approved;[255] and while assemblies may be held at Speakers' Corner, geography matters, as activists desire to demonstrate 'within sight and sound',[256] such as protesting outside

[249] Thio Li-ann (Nominated Member), Public Order Bill, 85 SPR, 13 April 2009, cols 3656, 3716.
[250] s 36(2), (4).
[251] Shanmugam, Public Order Bill (n 225) col 3760.
[252] 'Singapore's Government's Response (n 181) [46].
[253] Shanmugam, Public Order Bill (n 225) col 3617.
[254] ibid col 3760.
[255] Human Rights Watch (n 232) 68. A list of the routine detail of permits for politically focused assemblies is provided at 68–69, including advocacy for migrant worker rights, minimum wage, LGBT and women's rights. A list of prosecutions may be found at 69–71, relating to a march to celebrate social protests and Guy Fawkes Day, a group of Indian nationals protesting a ban on the practice of Jallikattu in Tamil Nadu, a silent anti-ISA protest on an MRT train and a candlelight vigil supporting the family of a man facing execution.
[256] Report of the special rapporteur on the rights to freedom of peaceful assembly and of association, Maina Kiai, April 2013, UN Doc A/HRC/23/29, [69].

the relevant embassy when Indonesia is about to execute someone,[257] or urging China to stop violent policing.[258] It was arguably an unreasonable restriction to limit protests to venues far away from the targets of those protests.[259] There is concern that criminal penalties are imposed for non-disruptive protests without a permit under section 16, and that fining participants and organisers $3000 and $5000 respectively is disproportionate. However, the new POA penalties regime sought by applying stiffer penalties to repeat offenders (including imprisonment for organisers), a 'recalibration' according to an 'individual's regard for the RoL'[260] in the thin sense of rule-compliance.

There have been allegations of unequal treatment in prosecuting unlawful assembly offences, including single-person protests, influenced by political affiliation. For example, a coalition of local NGOs expressed concern that activist Jolovan Wham served a 15-day prison sentence in lieu of a fine for holding an A4 paper sheet outside the State Courts (a restricted area under Part III of the Public Order (Prohibited Areas) Order 2009 Schedule) in 2018, calling for criminal defamation charges against two people to be dropped.[261] A photograph of Wham holding the sign was uploaded to his Facebook account. This was found to be an 'assembly' under section 15 POA, with Wham demonstrating opposition to their prosecution. The High Court affirmed there was no statutory requirement that 'assembly' relate only to disruptive acts posing a de minimis public order risk.[262] In contrast, no action was taken against Louis Ng, a PAP MP, who a few weeks later posed with hawker stalls holding an A4 sheet saying 'support them' next to a smiley face;[263] this was seen to express care for hawkers so prosecution did not serve the public interest. Activist Kirsten Han said surveillance footage showed that apart from Wham's friend taking the photograph, no one had noticed Wham's presence. Although Ng's action did not take place within a prohibited area, Han concludes the POA was weaponised to suppress assembly rights, signalling that pro-establishment messages would be excused, while even brief protests would be prosecuted as public order threats.[264] Wham was later investigated for demonstrating without a police permit by holding a smiley face sign to support two climate activists investigated for holding placards calling

[257] Quoting Rachel Zeng of the Singapore Anti-Death Penalty Campaign, Human Rights Watch (n 232) 69.

[258] 'Woman under Investigation for Allegedly Protesting outside Chinese Embassy' *Straits Times* (30 November 2022).

[259] Human Rights Watch (n 232) 69.

[260] Shanmugam, Public Order Bill (n 225) col 3666; 'Serial Protester Gets Maximum Fine, Jail for Staging Illegal Protest outside US Embassy' *Today* (20 October 2023).

[261] 'Jail Term Reduced to Fine for TOC Editor and Contributor Who Defamed Cabinet Members' *Straits Times* (4 May 2023); 'Rights Groups "Deeply Troubled" by Charges against Activist Jolovan Wham, Call for Review of Laws' *Today* (27 March 2019).

[262] *Wham Kwok Han Jolovan v PP* [2022] SGHC 241.

[263] 'Louis Ng Public Assembly Investigation: Dos and Don'ts under the Public Order Act' *Straits Times* (4 March 2021).

[264] Kirsten Han, 'Singapore's Elastic Band of a Public Order Act' (2022) 51(4) Index on Censorship 34.

for action,[265] which some considered 'regulatory overkill',[266] as no one's daily life was disrupted. Some view police investigations into persons holding emoji signs as 'absurdist humour rather than regulation'.[267]

However, the government has unapologetically affirmed its 'zero-tolerance approach' to illegal demonstrations; the Law Minister rhetorically asked whether allowing protests beyond Speakers' Corner should be pegged at '1, 2, 3, 50, 100, 200, 5000', and how to tell which protests will be peaceful and which violent.[268]

Ultimately, the POA approach is largely reflective of legal communitarianism in 'seeking a balance'[269] between liberty and maintaining order, while unequivocally prioritising security and development interests, including staging major conferences without distracting demonstrations.[270] In defence of an alternative philosophical approach to power[271] based on a neo-Confucianist presumptive trust in governors, the Law Minister noted according 'substantial power' to the executive 'has worked for us quite stunningly'. While broad, not absolute, discretion must be exercised efficiently based on legal principle, this is not to devolve into 'a rule by man as opposed to rule in accordance with law',[272] and it falls ultimately to the people 'to judge whether the Government has acted properly'.[273]

This suggests modest rather than robust accountability mechanisms as, presumptively, executive decision-makers, 'consistent with the RoL, act in accordance with the law'.[274] An idealistic strain is evident in parliamentary discussion about POA powers authorising certain police officers to issue 'cease filming' orders where this jeopardises ongoing enforcement operations, or to destroy or surrender the film, provided this does not extend to filming abuses of police power. It is an offence under section 38(4) not to comply with such an order,[275] with the government underscoring this was more narrowly scoped than the 2008 UK Counter Terrorism Act, which creates a general offence of filming.

In relation to the Commissioner's power to direct the destruction of such films, the concern was raised that police may order on-the-spot deletion to avoid being second-guessed. However, the Home Affairs Minister stated that this

[265] 'Singapore "Smiley-Face" Activist in One-Man Protest Charged with Unlawful Assembly' *The Guardian* (24 November 2020).

[266] Cherian George, quoted in Stefania Palma, 'Smiley Faces Lead to Frowns under Singapore's Protest Laws' *Financial Times* (18 March 2021).

[267] Palma (n 266).

[268] K Shanmugam, 'Why Good Governance Is Key to Maintaining Public Order' *Straits Times* (4 March 2020).

[269] Shanmugam, Public Order Bill (n 225) col 3747.

[270] ibid col 3750.

[271] ibid col 3749.

[272] ibid.

[273] ibid.

[274] *Wham Kwok Han Jolovan v PP* [2020] 3 SLR 1180, [29].

[275] 'Singapore's Government's Response (n 181) [48].

flowed from the philosophical assumption that police officers would behave illegally, consonant with the liberalism of fear, whereas the local presumption was that 'our officers are fundamentally honest'.[276]

However, when it comes to citizens, idealism fades in the official refusal to remove the permit system and trust all citizens to be law-abiding.[277] Trusting citizens to exercise their rights responsibly appears a glacial process; part of this responsibility may entail underwriting the costs of employing security officers, as section 8 may require. There is little discussion of positive government obligations to take reasonable measures to enable lawful assemblies to proceed peacefully by minimising traffic disruption and public inconvenience; in Hong Kong, this extends even to a government duty to ensure demonstrators may proceed without fear of physical violence by opponents and claiming damages for reasonably foreseeable police negligence if demonstrators are injured.[278] This reflects the low weightage given assembly rights, with government action confined to regulation, not facilitation.

In sum, political assemblies are allowed in designated places and cannot be held elsewhere without a police permit. This cabining of assembly rights is mitigated in part by the alternative avenues available for publicising a cause, whether at Speakers' Corner or online.[279] The reasonableness or proportionality of the Singapore regulatory model will be contoured by the primacy given to 'the societal need for law and order' and determination not to allow demonstrations to disrupt community life or cause economic loss. The RoL is invoked here to ensure 'all persons, politicians or otherwise', should obey the law of the land, for if the law is breached with impunity because an assembly carries a political message, 'the RoL will be fatally undermined'.[280] Views critical of the government may be expressed, but their manner of expression, which may affect their impact, remains regulated.

C. Speakers' Corner: Exemption from Public Assembly Laws and a Free Speech Oasis?

In 1999, LKY, in an interview with William Safire,[281] mooted the idea of having a Speakers' Corner modelled after London's Hyde Park Corner. He raised the example of opposition politician Chee Soon Juan, who engaged in sustained acts of civil disobedience by conducting speeches without a permit in public

[276] Shanmugam, Public Order Bill (n 225) col 3768.
[277] ibid col 3750.
[278] *Leung Kwok Hung v HKSAR* (2005) 8 HKCFAR 229; *Chan Hau Man Christina v Commissioner of Police* [2009] 4 HKLRD 797; *Robinson v CC of West Yorkshire Police* [2018] UKSC 4.
[279] Shanmugam, Public Order Bill (n 225) col 3747.
[280] 'Singapore's Government's Response (n 181) [30], [33]–[34].
[281] 'The Dictator Speaks' *New York Times* (15 February 1999).

places and was arrested under the Parliamentary Elections Act (PEA). These acts,[282] designed to raise the profile of greater free speech demands, apparently wrested a political concession from the PAP government[283] insofar as Lee decided to implement the idea of having a dedicated space 'where people gathered to hear speakers sound off freely'.[284] This would soften the heavy-handed approach towards controlling political dissenters.

This was a controlled experiment in opening up political space established by executive order under subsidiary legislation – the Public Entertainments (Speakers' Corner) (Exemption) Order 2000. The physical space delineated by the boundaries of the centrally located Hong Lim Park was to be exempted from PEA licensing requirements. Surrounded by busy roads, this site has historically seen many passionate political speeches. It opened on 1 September 2000.

Nevertheless, critics decried this as symbolic tokenism,[285] a 'complete farce'[286] and 'pretence'[287] of expanding expressive freedoms, a 'human rights joke'[288] and a place to corner speakers within an 'illiberal democracy'.[289] The government approached the matter not in terms of rights enjoyment but in terms of risk assessment; the idea was worth trying, given 'the support it has attracted from civil society groups'.[290]

Singaporeans could speak on any issue at an outdoor venue without needing a licence. Minimal restrictions would be imposed, such as a 7 am to 7 pm opening time and requiring speakers to register at a nearby police post to prove their citizenship and to sign a form taking note of speaking conditions.[291] The only off-limits topic were religion and themes that may provoke hostile feelings between racial or religious groups.[292] The general law of the land, such as that covering defamation, applied, and police would deal with complaints about

[282] Timeline of events leading to establishment of Speakers' Corner: www.facebook.com/yoursdp/posts/time-line-of-events-leading-to-the-establishment-of-speakers-corner-dr-chee-soon/10151533465418455/.

[283] 'Chee: Civil Disobedience Led to Creation of Speakers' Corner' (*TOC*, 2 November 2017) www.theonlinecitizen.com/2017/11/02/chee-civil-disobedience-led-to-creation-of-speakers-corner/.

[284] 'The Dictator Speaks' (n 281).

[285] Catherine Lim, Open Letter to the PM, 26 November 2007, www.theonlinecitizen.com/2007/11/26/catherine-lims-open-letter-to-the-prime-minister/.

[286] Chee Soon Juan, quoted in 'Singapore Speakers' Corner Draws Crowd' (Associated Press, 31 August 2001).

[287] JB Jeyaretnam, Speakers' Corner Adjournment Motion, 72 SPR, 22 May 2000, col 307.

[288] Chee: Civil Disobedience' (n 283).

[289] Sinapan Samydorai (Think Centre), quoted in 'Speakers' Corner Fails to Fuel Public Debate – but Four Years on, the Government still Portrays It as an Outstanding Success' *South China Morning Post* (7 September 2004).

[290] Wong Kan Seng (Home Affairs Minister), 'Speakers' Corner', 72 SPR, 25 April 2000, cols 20, 21.

[291] Wong Kan Seng (Home Affairs Minister), 'Speakers' Corner', 72 SPR, 9 May 2000, col 101.

[292] When Chee Soon Juan spoke on the religiously sensitive tudung issues (religious headwear) at Speakers' Corner in February 2002 without a permit, he was convicted for breaching the PEA and fined $3000: 'SDP Chief Fined and Barred from Next GE' *Straits Times* (31 July 2002) H2.

disturbances to the peace.[293] Amplification devices were not permitted and non-compliance with these conditions could attract fines up to $10,000 or a 30-day suspension from speaking at the Corner.

In inception and execution, this was a managed free speech corner subject to temporal, subject matter and volume restrictions; calls to open other speakers' corners in neighbourhood parks were rejected, limiting protests to one venue.[294] Its status as an 'unrestricted area' under section 14 POA, exempt from notice and permit requirement for assemblies, is revoked once elections are called, and reinstated after the campaigning period.[295]

The performative limits of what was permissible beyond oral communication were unclear. When, in March 2001, an online photograph of more than five people at the Corner chanting 'abolish ISA' with raised clenched fists appeared, the police investigated this as a possible illegal assembly, but let the participants off with a warning.[296] What emerged was that demonstrations could not be conducted without a permit, and free speech excluded shouting slogans or making wild gesticulations.[297] The initial surge of interest in this 'free speech zone' petered off,[298] although NGO members and opposition politicians did choose to speak there;[299] it was dubbed a failed civic space[300] and the 'Sleepy Corner' some eight years later.[301] In 2010, Senior Minister (SM) Goh Chok Tong noted of the Corner that it was 'mostly dormant, but good to have',[302] allowing citizens to air their views. Thus far, the experiment has shown that relaxing free speech rules does not entail chaos where rights are exercised responsibly, even if public interest has been lukewarm.[303]

Over time, the restrictions were relaxed, and permit requirements were removed first for performances and exhibitions in 2004, then later (in 2008) for assemblies and processions. The intent was to 'find ways to allow people to let off steam a little bit more safely', by allowing outdoor public demonstrations,

[293] Public nuisance offences apply within the confines of the Speakers' Corner: *PP v Han Hui Hui* [2016] SGDC 225, [110].

[294] 'Opening Up: Opposition MPs Want More' *Straits Times* (25 August 2004); 'Rise and Rise of Speakers' Corner' (AsiaOne, 26 July 2014).

[295] 'Speakers' Corner Restrictions to Be Gazette once Elections Called' (*CNA.com*, 15 March 2011).

[296] Ho Peng Kee (Minister of State, Home Affairs), 'Speakers' Corner', 73 SPR, 5 March 2001, col 68.

[297] 'The Evolution of S'pore's Speakers' Corner' *Today* (21 October 2016).

[298] eg there were 395 applications to speak in September 2000, falling to 11 in August 2001: Chee Soon Juan (n 286).

[299] 'Speaker's Corner Fails to Spark Public Debate' *South China Morning Post* (7 September 2004).

[300] 'Sporeans Not Keeping Mum but Are Speaking Up Elsewhere' *Straits Times* (12 August 2003).

[301] 'Sleepy, Opps, Speakers' Corner' *Straits Times* (29 August 2008).

[302] 'Mostly Dormant, but Good to Have; SM Goh Chok Tong on Speakers' Corner, Which Turns 10 amid Falling Applications' *Today* (11 September 2010). Minister Vivian Balakrishnan said in 2006 that the Corner was not successful because 'Singaporeans are sensible people and have decided that there's not much point going up there standing on a soapbox yelling at the mosquitoes and flies': 'Speakers' Corner or Sneakers' Corner' *New Paper* (18 April 2006).

[303] 'Where Have All the Speakers Gone?' *Straits Times* (31 August 2001) 2; 'Speakers' Corner: Has It Run Out of Steam' *Straits Times* (12 November 2000).

which would 'liberalise our society', with the promise to 'progressively open up our system even more'.[304] In 2008, the administration of the Corner was transferred from the police to the National Parks Board (NParks), which may indicate 'the comfort level of the police with citizens' ability to organise themselves peacefully' – a calculated risk taken after 'eight years of calm'.[305] The Corner would be open 24/7, and placards, banners and handheld amplification equipment could be used between 9 am and 10.30 pm. CCTVs were put up in the Corner in 2009 in the interests of security, which critics argued would discourage participation.[306]

Permitting demonstrations at Speakers' Corner was a political gambit; some MPs voiced caution, referencing how demonstrators in 2008 barged into the office grounds of the Thai PM. SM Goh, however, considered this unlikely, that things would not 'get out of hand' provided the government was 'good and fair' and produced results. People were unlikely to confine their demonstrations to a single park if the government was incompetent and corrupt. He opined that demonstrators wanted to draw attention to 'maybe the animal lovers' cause or the green movement', but initial public and media interest would 'eventually die down'. He agreed that this move towards political openness was done out of 'necessity' as oppressive control would drive the people away, 'so we have to move with the times'.[307]

Persons wanting to hold demonstrators could now conveniently register with NParks online, testing the ground to see how the authorities would handle and frame the limits for peaceful protests. The only application rejected was for someone wanting to speak on the absence of Tamil language on public signs, with the applicant advise to air his grievances elsewhere.[308] A journalist mused: 'What if a fledging Gay Pride March comes up against a rival protest organized by Christians who are against homosexual activity?'[309] A analogous scenario did materialise in 2014, discussed below.

The 2008 relaxation gave rise to an increase in applications and activities, on a wide range of topics, some attracting large crowds. This included economically oriented hot button topics of failed structured financial products misleading investors, led by former CEO of NTUC Income and future presidential candidate, Tan Kin Lian.[310] More than 2000 people attended a series of protests against the Central Provident Fund (national pension plan)

[304] PM Lee Hsien Loong, National Day Rally 2008, www.pmo.gov.sg/Newsroom/National-Day-Rally-2008.

[305] 'Sleepy, Opps, Speakers' Corner' (n 301).

[306] Human Rights Watch (n 232) 91; Singapore Democrats news release, 'Police Put Up Camera at Speakers' Corner' (23 July 2009) https://yoursdp.org.

[307] 'Good Govt Needn't Fear Demos: SM' *Straits Times* (28 August 2008).

[308] 'A New Buzz at Hong Lim' *Straits Times* (1 November 200)8.

[309] 'Sleepy, Opps, Speakers' Corner' (n 301).

[310] 'Hearty Buzz at Speakers' Corner' *Straits Times* (2 November 2008); 'Rare Singapore Protests Flags Investor Anger in Hyflux Slump' *The Malaysian Reserve* (1 April 2019).

in 2014, and thousands protested against the Population white paper in February 2013.[311]

The first demonstration was staged by Hearer of Cries, a maid welfare advocacy group. Corner users have been commended for 'exemplary' self-policing, there being no complaints about excessive noise or fights.[312] Clearly, the Corner was given a new lease of life, most significantly through becoming a site for political resistance – in particular, the annual concert and picnic advocating for homosexual or LGBTQ rights, known as Pink Dot.[313] This started in 2009 with some 2500 people, ballooning to 26,000 by 2014. It has been described as the 'most massive social movement in Singapore',[314] attracting the corporate sponsorship of Google in 2011.[315] Consequently, after Pink Dot 2016 attendance exceeded Hong Lim Park's capacity, receiving foreign sponsorship from the likes of multinational corporations and global tech companies, the POA was amended to exempt Singapore entities, local companies and NGOs from the need for a permit to organise Speakers' Corner events. However, after an online petition in June 2016 called for the government to prevent foreign intervention in local politics, the existing rules were amended to underscore that 'Speakers' Corner was set up primarily for Singaporeans';[316] the police had, for example, rejected permit applications by non-Singaporeans to organise Bersih-related (clean elections in Malaysia) events at the Corner.[317] The amendments prohibit foreign entities from sponsoring such events or interfering with domestic issues, particularly 'controversial social issues with political overtones', like 'LGBT issues'.[318] Conditions applicable to public speaking were extended to teleconferencing or pre-recorded messages.[319] From 2017, foreigners were not permitted to assemble at Speakers' Corner; if they did, both foreigner and organiser could be prosecuted and fined up to $10,000 or face six months' imprisonment.[320] The notice period NParks required was extended to 28 days and the police were to be informed of the expected turnout.[321]

[311] 'Hundreds Attend CPF Protest' *Straits Times* (13 July 2014) 15; 'Rare Mass Rally over Singapore Immigration Plans' (BBC News, 16 February 2013).

[312] 'A New Buzz' (n 308).

[313] 'Birth and Evolution of Speakers' Corner' *Straits Times* (4 October 2014).

[314] '6 Things That Prove Pink Dot Has Perfected the Art of Organizing a Mass Movement' (*Mothership.sg*, 28 June 2014).

[315] 'Pink Dot Movement Marks 10 Years' *Straits Times* (22 July 2018).

[316] Home Affairs Ministry, 'Review of Speakers' Corner Rules' (21 October 2016) www.mha.gov.sg/.

[317] K Shanmugam (Minister for Home Affairs and Law), Public Order (Amendment) Bill 2017, 3 April 2017, [52].

[318] Home Affairs Ministry, Statement on Foreign Sponsorship for Pink Dot 2016, 7 June 2016.

[319] '"Singapore Entity" Rule (Dubbed Pink Dot Amendment) Imposed on Use of Speakers' Corner' *The Independent* (21 October 2016). The Bloomberg news agency released a supportive video fronted by Michael Bloomberg.

[320] POA, s 7(2)(g) provides the Commissioner may refuse to grant a permit for a proposed assembly if it is 'directed towards a political end and involves non Singaporean citizens or a non-Singaporean entity'.

[321] Public Order (Unrestricted Area) Amendment Order (2016).

Critics argue this is onerous, as organisers must bear the self-policing costs of barricades and hiring security staff to conduct identity and bag checks to ensure no foreigners enter the Corner for the event's duration.[322] Nonetheless, the homosexual rights group Pink Dot Sg secured the sponsorship of 120 local companies to defray their expenses.[323]

It is clear that Speakers' Corner has opened up a new political and social space for civil society activists seeking to advance their cause, or for citizens seeking apolitical gatherings to memorialise K-Pop stars[324] or express investor grievances.[325] This limited reform reflects the tension in engaging in 'calibrated liberalization',[326] without ceding too much control in the face of a more assertive civil society. In tandem with indoor and online sites, activists use the Corner to agitate, indicating that at least one sector of the Singapore population is not politically apathetic.

A broad diversity of topics have been canvassed: these including promoting environmental issues and opposing the consumption of shark's fin soup,[327] immigration policies,[328] tax hikes, reserved presidential elections[329] and the death penalty;[330] more direct politicised challenges include the call by some 400 people to investigate whether PM Lee abused his power in a feud with his siblings over what to do with their late father's house.[331] There are demonstrations directed at transnational matters, in support of democracy movements in Malaysia and Hong Kong[332] and in opposition to conflict in Gaza in 2014, for which a permit was granted.[333]

[322] Kirsten Han, 'Pink Dot, Speakers' Corner and the Death of Singapore's Only Space for Dissent' (*The New Lens (International Edition)*, 31 May 2017).

[323] 'Security Personnel for Pink Dot Tripled Ahead of Event' *Today* (29 June 2017); 'Pink Dot 2017 to Have Barricades, ID Checks by Security Personnel' (*CNA.com*, 30 May 2017).

[324] 'Grieving Fans Throng Hong Lim Park to Mourn K-pop Star', *New Paper* 21 December 2017).

[325] 'Hearty Buzz' (n 310); 'Angry Investors Turn Up at Hong Lim Park to Seek Redress' (*TOC*, 12 October 2008); 'Hyflux Investors to Stage Protest at Speakers' Corner on March 20' (*Independent.sg*, 26 March 2019).

[326] Luke Stephens, 'Contentious Acts in Controlled Spaces: A Protest Event Analysis of Singaporean Demonstrations' [2023] Journal of Contemporary Asia 1, 4.

[327] 'Rally against Shark Fin Consumption' (World Entertainment News Network, 21 April 2009).

[328] 'Rare Mass Rally over Singapore Immigration Plans' (BBC News, 16 February 2013) (showing displeasure at government predictions that the population would grow by 30% to 6.9 million by 2030, with immigrants making up nearly half that figure).

[329] 'Silent Protest Held at Hong Lim Park Against Reserved Presidential Elections' (*CNA.com*, 16 September 2017) (attended by Tan Cheng Bock and Tan Jee Say, two former presidential candidates).

[330] 'Death Penalty Protest at Speakers' Corner as It Reopens 2 Years after Covid-19 Closure' *Straits Times* (3 April 2022); '300–400 People Attend Candlelight Vigil at Hong Lim Park for M'sian Drug Traffickers on Death Row' (*Mothership.sg*, 26 April 2022).

[331] 'About 400 Showed Up at Speakers' Corner to Protest Against PM Lee Hsien Loong' (*Mothership.sg*, 16 July 2017).

[332] 'Vigil at Hong Lim Park to Back Protesters' *Straits Times* (2 October 2014).

[333] 'Speakers' Corner Rally for Gaza' (AsiaOne, 29 July 2014). No rallies were permitted after 7 October 2023: Singapore Police Force, 'Advisory on Events and Public Assemblies in Relation to IsraelHamas Conflict', 18 October 2023).

Speakers' Corner has been variously utilised; causes are advanced through petition-signing, talks and performative acts; confrontational protest rallies are staged, and community-bonding picnics with free ice cream are held, such as that staged by Stand Up for Singapore. While all these activities involve citizen participation,[334] the government as the dominant political actor prefers those movements aligned with its 'desire for a civic society, rather than a politicised civil society'.[335] This is evident in the staging of the first 'purple parade' for disabled persons, convened by a Voluntary Welfare Organisation and the Central Singapore Community Development Council, whose mayor is a government MP and President of the Autism Resource Centre. Some 5000 supporters signed pledges to support Singapore's 2012 accession to the Convention on the Rights of Persons with Disabilities. Several Cabinet ministers attended the event, and in 2023, 13,000 people attended the 2023 annual parade at Suntec City, where Deputy PM Lawrence Wong spoke. While the government would take the lead in implementing policies for the disabled, he urged every Singaporean 'to do their part … to show more acceptance and kindness to our fellow Singaporeans'.[336] This movement complements rather than confronts government policy. So, too, government ministers and parliamentarians attended the first Singapore Climate rally run by young activists, with some 2000 people in attendance.[337] This called for reducing greenhouse gas emissions and staged self-indulgent performative acts in the form of a 'die-in', where participants fell to the ground to mourn the potential harms of 'climate warming'. Such acts, which attracted some online derision,[338] focus on awareness-raising rather than substantive discussion of a complex issue; nonetheless, they allow politicians to take the 'youth' pulse and build future political support.

Most notably, demonstrating public relations acumen, the now annual Pink Dot event, running since 2009, provides a masterclass on how to frame what many in socially conservative Singapore[339] consider a far-reaching, radical social agenda in appealing, non-threatening terms. This event is primarily responsible for the Corner's surging popularity as a protest venue.

However, unlike the aggressive campaigns and near obscene displays of sexualised activity in LGBT pride parades conducted elsewhere, 'protest with Singapore characteristics' is presented as an innocuous activity, taking the sterilised form of a communal picnic wrapped in fluffy pink hues. Stephens has noted 'the more overt celebration of sexuality seen in other places is also largely removed, instead the demonstrations are promoted as family events centred on

[334] 'Two Hong Lim Park Events, One S'pore' *Straits Times* (5 May 2013).

[335] Stephens (n 326) 11–12.

[336] Over 13,000 People Turn Up at the annual Purple Parade to Support People with Disabilities' *Straits Times* (4 November 2023).

[337] 'Big Turnout at Hong Lim Park for First Singapore Climate Rally' *Straits Times* (22 September 2019).

[338] 'S'poreans Didn't Take SG Climate Rally Seriously Despite Climate Emergency. Here's Why' (*Mothership.sg*, 6 October 2019).

[339] Conservative S'pore 'Not Ready for Same-Sex Marriage' *Today* (5 June 2015).

themes of love and acceptance'.[340] Public visibility and friendly media coverage have helped this cause, with the number of supporters growing from 1000 in 2009 to 28,000 in 2015. This indicates swelling support for the agenda to socially mainstream homosexualism. In contrast, the largest non-Pink Dot protest – an anti-immigration protest – attracted only 4000 participants.[341]

Though unable to undertake a gay pride march beyond Corner boundaries, this social movement attained a high public profile, pressurising the government to engage with their agenda, which reflects the 'growth of civil society as a competitive actor'.[342] The annual visible meetings at the Corner legitimated an alternative view, as distinct from the anonymous world of social media. The physical meeting is considered important to outreach efforts, being a 'safe' space where young people can bring their parents.[343]

However, a lack of even-handedness in allowing the expression of counter-views or counter-demonstrations in the same manner is evident. A licence was denied Touch Family Services, a voluntary welfare organisation chaired by Pastor Lawrence Khong of Faith Community Baptist Church, who wanted to hold a 'Red Dot Family Moment' picnic at the nearby Padang, an open playing field where many national ceremonies are conducted, on the same day as the Pink Dot meeting in June 2014. Presumably, there were fears of escalating social conflict, given the rise of a rare Muslim–Christian alliance against the Pink Dot homosexual agenda. Ustaz Noor Deros had asked Muslims to avoid Pink Dot and to wear white garments for Ramadan evening prayers, which coincided with the day Pink Dot was scheduled.[344] This was to symbolise purity, a 'return to fitrah' (Arabic for 'natural') and the Muslim community's opposition to homosexuality. This grassroots 'Wear White' campaign was supported by the Love Singapore church network, which showed solidarity in supporting pro-family values as integral to public morality.[345] Thousands of adherents turned up in churches and mosques, which are indoor venues, wearing white.[346] Ministers merely urged 'balance and restraint' when religious groups expressed their opposition to the homosexualism agenda, to 'avoid dividing society' over a polarising issue.[347] An iteration of Wear White (We.Wear.White) was held again

[340] Stephens (n 326).

[341] '4000 Turn Up at Speakers' Corner for Population White Paper Protest' (Yahoo Newsroom, 16 February 2013).

[342] Stephens (n 326) 20.

[343] 'Speakers' Corner, 14 Years On' (*CNA.com*, 1 September 2014).

[344] 'Religious Teacher Launches "Wear White" Online Campaign' (n 114); 'A Group of Muslims Have Organized a "Wear White" Movement to Protest Against S'pore's LGBT Movement' (*Mothership.sg*, 19 June 2014).

[345] Thio Li-ann, 'Ambivalence, Accommodation, Antipathy and Anxiety: The State of Religion within Singapore's Secular Democratic Order' in Vidhu Vema (ed), *Religion and Democracy* (Oxford University Press (India), 2019) 75–76.

[346] 'Thousands of Singaporean Christians Wear White to Protest Pink Dot Gay Rally' (Yahoo Newsroom, 29 June 2014).

[347] 'A Dialogue Should Occur between Wear White Movement and the Pink Dot Organisers. Sooner than Later' (*Mothership.sg*, 28 June 2014).

in 2016, coinciding with the Pink Dot rally and led by Pastor Khong in calling all Singaporeans to support 'pro-natural family values';[348] while Ustaz Noor Deros expressed support for this, his focus had turned to Islamic youth educational programmes, rather than campaigning.[349]

The Pink Dot movement ensured that activism 'stays within the law',[350] in their strategy to win hearts and minds. Sociologists have described Pink Dot movements as 'warm and positive' rather than 'angry and volatile';[351] the former is the tenor of Singapore-style 'picnic'-type activism, a fun event 'everyone is happy to go to … wear pink, and party … eat pink muffins and pink cakes … as a show of solidarity'.[352] This is in contrast with 'very confrontational civil disobedience types of actions' other activists prefer.[353] This form of 'pragmatic resistance'[354] has yielded success for Pink Dot activism, which saw its key demand to repeal the law criminalising sodomy achieved in 2022, an expression of social rather than political liberalisation.

This 'picnic activism' now targets Article 156 of the Constitution, which protects the traditional definition of marriage, through indirect attempts to redefine 'family'.[355] However, PM Lawrence Wong has promised that the traditional definition of marriage between a man and woman would not change 'under my watch', nor would laws and policies based on this definition.[356] That politicians from various political parties attended the 2023 Pink Dot[357] demonstrates that views within a single party are not monolithic, and that 'unthreatening' demonstrations are accepted as a legitimate form of civic engagement.

The use of Speakers' Corner is likely to continue as a space for civil society activism. Through calibrated control and strategic liberalisation designed to manage social tensions and reduce challenges to what is perceived and experienced as authoritarian rule,[358] the government allows non-disruptive political activities which do not directly challenge their political dominance.

[348] '"Traditional Values" Wear White Campaign Returning on Pink Dot Weekend' *Today* (23 May 2016).

[349] 'Wear White Campaign Organisers Engages ex ISA Detainee for Anti-LGBT Seminar' *The Independent* (26 March 2022).

[350] Quoting a Pink Dot Spokesmen, 'MHA Says Foreign Sponsors Not Allowed for Pink Dot, or Other Events, at Speakers' Corner' *Straits Times* (2 June 2022).

[351] 'When Protests Cross the Line' *Straits Times* (4 October 2014).

[352] Jolovan Wham describing Pink Dot in *Wham Kwok Han Jolovan v PP* [2020] 3 SLR 251, [47].

[353] ibid [48].

[354] Lynette Chua, 'Pragmatic Resistance, Law and Social Movements in Authoritarian States: The Case of Gay Collective Action in Singapore' (2012) 46(4) Law & Society Review 713.

[355] 'In Post-repeal Singapore, LGBTQ Activists Work to Expand Family Structure' *The Diplomat* (22 June 2023).

[356] 'No Change to Marriage Definition "Under My Watch" as Next PM if PAP Wins Next GE: DPM Lawrence Wong' *Today* (22 August 2022).

[357] 'Thousands Throng Hong Lim Park to Celebrate First Pink Dot SG Rally Since s377A repeal' *Straits Times* (25 June 2023).

[358] Stephen Ortmann, 'Policy Advocacy in a Competitive Authoritarian Regime' (2012) 44(6) Administration & Society 13S, 17S.

D. Conclusion

Singapore laws on public assembly provide some space to highlight causes, particularly through Speakers' Corner, which enables civil society to influence socio-political discussions by advancing ideas and gauging the extent of support or opposition to them; through it, activists may be the bellwether of the next political cause, rather than consigned to the political margins. Speakers' Corner has become the focal point for civil society activism, accommodating while containing the demand for greater expressive freedoms, advancing a brand of politics based on ideology rather than party loyalties.

The POA allows the government to tighten its control over other public spaces beyond Speakers' Corner. Other channels for public political protests remain subject to strict restrictions. Nonetheless, the urge to protest outside the Corner persists, such as where workers protested the non-payment of salaries outside an industrial building, eliciting Manpower Ministry intervention.[359] South Koreans protesting near St Regis Hotel where Kim Jong-Un was staying were deported.[360] Singaporean activists who knowingly stage illegal protests have been criticised as 'posturing for the Western press, portraying themselves as martyrs for human rights', lacking genuine concern for the public good.[361] Activists demur and protest their intent is to 'draw attention to the overbearing and draconian ways of the Singapore government', who are 'blinded by their command-and-control mindset that prefers maximum response to the slightest provocation';[362] being arrested or investigated for illegal assemblies may earn a sort of oppositional bona fides.

The Singapore approach has been criticised as falling short of international standards[363] and certainly would be at odds with the non-binding General Comment No 37 of the Human Rights Committee on the right of peaceful assembly.[364] This precludes one-person assemblies, requires content-neutral restrictions on assemblies and enables assemblies to be conducted within sight and sound of their target audience.[365] The General Comment favours subsequent penal sanctions rather than prior restraints as regulatory methods, frowns on place restrictions, presumptively considers assemblies to be peaceful and

[359] 'Ang Mo Kio Worker Protest: MOM Probes 2 Building Firms, Helps 5 Workers Get Paid Salary Owed to Them' *Today* (21 October 2022).

[360] '5 S Korean Women Protesting near Kim Jong-Un's Hotel Deported, Given Stern Warning: Police' *Today* (13 June 2018).

[361] Former AG Walter Woon, 'When Protests Cross the Line' *Straits Times* (4 October 2014).

[362] Jolovan Wham, quoted in 'Singapore "Smiley-Face" Activist in One-Man Protest Charged with Unlawful Assembly' *The Guardian* (24 November 2020). See 'Activist Jolovan Wham Fined $8000 over Protest on MRT Trains Three Years Ago' *Straits Times* (15 February 2021).

[363] Federation Internationale pour les droits humains (Fidh) Press Release, 'Government Fails to Address Key Human Rights Concerns during UN Review' (8 February 2016) www.fidh.org/en/region/asia/singapore/government-fails-to-address-key-human-rights-concerns-during-un.

[364] CCPR/C/GC/37. Singapore is not a party to the ICCPR.

[365] ibid [13], [22].

considers requirements that participants contribute to policing and security costs to be incompatible with Article 21 of the International Covenant on Civil and Political Rights (ICCPR).[366] Foreign NGOs have also criticised the differentiated treatment of citizens and foreigners, consonant with Article 14, which only applies to citizens.[367]

The RoL is here based on the 'rule-book' conception, where law is deployed as part of a regulatory architecture devoted to securing stability, while permitting some concessions to assembly rights. This is presented as a substantial liberalisation of the political space, allowing grievance ventilation and cause advocacy. This reflects paternal democracy and legal communitarianism, as demands for political participation increase; rights remain more akin to defeasible interests than a trump, requiring specific authorisation before the freedom may be enjoyed. Zero tolerance towards illegal protests is maintained, based on the conviction that where the majority considers a system generally fair, 'the actions of a disaffected few should not be allowed to threaten the rights of the majority to live in a stable, peaceful society'.[368]

V. REGULATING INTERNET SPEECH: THE PROTECTION FROM ONLINE FALSEHOOD AND MANIPULATION ACT AND SUSTAINING DEMOCRACY IN THE INTERNET AGE

As a significant amount of news consumption and democratic discourse has pivoted away from print and broadcast media towards online sites or private messaging groups,[369] Singapore has emerged as a front-runner in the global move towards regulating these new forms of communications technology,[370] through legislation, non-binding codes with some legal effect[371] and the promotion of digital literacy,[372] to foster 'a well-informed and discerning citizenry, equipped with tools to combat online falsehoods'.[373] While likening the Internet to the 'wild wild west'[374] and appreciating the impossibility of effective censorship, the

[366] ibid [17], [37], [56], [64].

[367] Fidh, 'Cornered: Repression of the Right to Freedom of Peaceful Assembly in Singapore' (2022) www.fidh.org/IMG/pdf/singapore786ang.pdf.

[368] 'Hong Kong's Example Shows Singapore's Strict Stance against Illegal Protests Is Warranted: Shanmugam' *Today* (22 March 2020).

[369] More than 50% of Singapore resident use these mediums to communicate and share information: Speech, Minister S Iswaran, Second Reading, POFMA Bill, 8 May 2019, [4] www.mci.gov.sg/.

[370] Thio Li-ann, 'Public Law' in A Phang, S Chesterman and Y Goh (eds), *Law and Technology in Singapore* (Academy Press, 2021) 577–626.

[371] eg if Internet content providers breach the Internet Code of Practice issued under s 6 of the Broadcasting Act, their class licence may be cancelled or suspended under s 12.

[372] 'Singapore's Move to Regulate Online Safety Faces Challenges, but Society Can Help: Commentary' *Today* (28 June 2022).

[373] Iswaran (n 369) [35].

[374] 'Internet Ruling for Civil Servants Absolutely Necessary: PM' *Today* (9 June 2016).

government symbolically banned 100 pornographic sites 'as a statement of our values'.[375]

The Internet is a boon to democracy in terms of greater informational flows; it helps to coordinate common causes and lowers barriers for participation in public debate, within one of the world's most heavily Internet-penetrated countries,[376] where political apathy is waning.[377] However, this comes with a dark side beyond hacking government services or paralysing financial systems: misinformation and disinformation may undermine democratic discourse, which can also be disrupted by bots creating false perceptions and bullies who use anonymous abusive speech to silence opposing views. Rather than exposure to diverse viewpoints, a person can curate and read only preferred views, creating echo chambers which confirm biases and insulate beliefs from challenge. This spawns a 'politics of polarization and misinformation over one of cohesion and reason',[378] making it harder to generate national consensus. Big Tech social media companies can exercise ideological discrimination in amplifying or suppressing views; governments may collude with Big Tech to control narratives and suppress critical voices,[379] impacting electoral outcomes and thwarting democratic processes.[380]

Initially, existing legislation applicable to traditional print and broadcast media like the Broadcasting Act and Telecommunications Act were 'updated' to apply online.[381] After a Select Committee on Deliberate Online Falsehoods was convened in 2018, the government proceeded to craft bespoke legislation with extraterritorial effect, reaching persons and Internet intermediaries based beyond Singapore. The goal was to address the threat communications technology posed to democracy, given its 'virulence and virality',[382] volume, reach and longevity, chiefly in the form of online falsehoods and foreign intervention in local politics. The Protection from Online Falsehood and Manipulation Act (POFMA) and Foreign Interference (Countermeasures) Act (FICA) were respectively adopted in 2019 and 2021, POFMA being the focus here.

[375] Lee Yock Suan (Minister, Information and the Arts) 73 SPR, 9 March 2001, col 557.

[376] As of January 2017, some 84% of Singaporeans are Internet users: '4.83 Million Singaporeans Are Now Online' *Singapore Business Review* (30 January 2018). The mobile population penetration rate of about 150% is 'among the highest in the world' and the wireless penetration rate, over 200%: Iswaran (n 369) [6].

[377] 'Are Singaporeans Really Apathetic?' *Today* (8 April 2021).

[378] K Shanmugam (Minister for Law), Second Reading, POFMA Bill, 94 SPR, 7 May 2019, [213], www.mlaw.gov.sg.

[379] 'Former Twitter Execs Tell Republicans They Erred on Hunter Biden Laptop Story' (Reuters, 9 February 2023); 'Biden Admin Pushed to Bar Twitter Users for COVID 'Disinformation', Files Show' *New York Post* (26 December 2022).

[380] 'Twitter Chief Executive Jack Dorsey Says Company Was Wrong to Block New York Post Hunter Biden Story' (*abc.net.au*, 17 October 2020).

[381] David Tan and Jessica Teng, 'Fake News, Free Speech and Finding Constitutional Congruence' (2020) 32 SAcLJ 207.

[382] Iswaran (n 369) [14].

The objects of regulation are both content-creators and forwarders, as well as the 'larger tech platforms'[383] which host them and are gatekeepers to the information superhighway, operating like 'functional sovereigns'.[384] It was decided not to outsource the responsibility of monitoring and filtering content affecting the national interest to private companies[385] as they could be excessively cautious, profit-motivated or politically biased.[386] Instead, ministers would assume this responsibility and give companies clear directions to implement, on pain of financial sanctions. The government stressed it would not unduly impair international connectivity or informational flows, recognising that tech companies are key parts of Singapore's business ecosystem and digital economy; government overreach would be checked by the scrutiny of a 'highly connected citizenry' and technology and media companies who appreciated the public interest.[387]

From the outset, POFMA was presented as a form of 'calibration for the internet age',[388] to target online falsehood 'with speed, with proportionality and with the Courts given greater powers'.[389] While existing legislation was 'a blunt instrument',[390] POFMA would provide for a 'narrower set of powers' with 'calibrated remedies'.[391] Although it was accompanied by the promise of 'greater judicial oversight',[392] any additions to the regulatory architecture which enhance state powers helmed will attract criticism about the danger of 'chilling' political dissent. A key liberal value is the right to criticise the government without fear of retribution, which promotes political accountability and a culture of justification.

As Hannah Arendt noted, the 'most essential political freedom' is 'the right to unmanipulated factual information'.[393] POFMA sought to address the impact of spreading falsehoods through digital technology to severely attack 'the foundations of democratic society' by undercutting 'the cornerstone of our infrastructure of fact' and undermining trust in public institutions that deliver public goods and are 'the building blocks of democratic societies'.[394]

[383] ibid [93].

[384] 'Mark Zuckerberg Runs a Nation-State and He's the King' (*Vox*, 10 April 2018).

[385] Iswaran (n 369) [34].

[386] Shanmugam, Second Reading, POFMA Bill (n 378) [214]–[215].

[387] The Law Minister noted that they did not take money from Big Tech lobbyists and insisted that Big Tech 'do business with us honourably. Singapore provides a proper rule of law framework for everyone': ibid [239]–[240].

[388] K Shanmugam (Minister for Home Affairs and Law), Second Reading, Foreign Interference (Countermeasures) Bill, 4 October 2021, [159], www.mha.gov.sg.

[389] Shanmugam, Second Reading, POFMA Bill (n 378) [38].

[390] ibid [36]: under the Broadcasting Act, any statement, true or false, fact or opinion, may be ordered to be taken down, subject to judicial review, if it is objectionable against public interest and national harmony.

[391] Shanmugam, Second Reading, POFMA Bill (n 378) [31].

[392] ibid [25].

[393] Hannah Arendt, *Crises of the Republic* (Harvest, 1972) 45.

[394] Shanmugam, Second Reading, POFMA Bill (n 378) [52].

Where society is rifted and the political centre hollowed out, people would be 'driven to extremes'; as democratic discourse depends on 'trust, free speech infrastructure of fact',[395] discussion and compromise without a shared reality would be 'very difficult'.[396] Insofar as Singapore still ranks highly on the 2019 Edelman Trust Barometer in relation to trust of government, scoring 67 points above the average of 47 of 26 countries surveyed, this legislative initiative was pre-emptive.[397]

As politically and judicially affirmed, there is no human right to misinformation,[398] which undermines free speech rationales by hampering truth-seeking and erodes democratic processes by skewing public debates and impacting electoral outcomes. False statements subvert the citizen's positive liberty of informed participation in public debate and negative liberty of transmitting accurate information. Falsehood could hamstring the government's ability to govern, discrediting its reputation and legitimacy and undermining the preferred neo-Confucianist vision of the trustworthy governor. The CA opined that false statements 'can contribute little to the marketplace of ideas', questioning whether it warranted constitutional protection under Article 14.[399]

POFMA was designed to send a 'positive signal'[400] about what society values by preserving 'the local emphasis on honesty and integrity in public discourse'[401] and promoting rational debate 'where we keep the lies out'.[402] POFMA would enable swift government action 'to prevent' and 'to counteract the effects' of communicated falsehoods.

POFMA is presented as a safeguard for democracy, although democracy covers diverse values, such as participation, transparency and popular sovereignty. POFMA is selective in which democratic values it espouses and, while the injurious impact of falsehoods on democratic debate is accepted, valid concerns arise as to who is the arbiter of truth and falsehood, what criteria are used and questions of oversight. The absence of a Freedom of Information Act (FIA) undergirds an environment of informational asymmetry from the citizen's perspective, as citizens can only rely on officially released information, which may be presented in a politically advantageous manner or biased in supporting a preferred narrative. This can hinder public scrutiny over policies and actions.

The official view is that the average person has no interest in an FIA, that it would spawn frivolous fishing for information for personal benefit or to damage

[395] ibid [89].
[396] ibid [163], referenced in *TOC v AG* [2021] 2 SLR 1358, [148].
[397] ibid [59].
[398] Lord Hobhouse, *Reynolds v Times Newspaper* [2001] 2 AC 127, referred to in *TOC v AG* [2021] 2 SLR 1358, [58].
[399] Citing the minority judgment in *AG v Ting Choon Meng* [2017] 1 SLR 373 [115], *TOC v AG* [2021] (n 398) [58].
[400] Report of the Select Committee on Deliberate Online Falsehoods – Causes, Consequences and Countermeasures, Parl 15 of 2018, 19 September 2018, [385].
[401] *Review Publishing v Lee Hsien Loong* [2010] 1 SLR 52, [268]–[271].
[402] Select Committee Report (n 400).

government reputation and that it would hinder internal debate, as government officials will not want to put anything on paper lest somebody obtains it under the Act.[403] Such a posture assumes or asserts the need to trust governors and give them broad leeway in governance. Further, as ministers decide what is 'fake news', POFMA only applies to citizens; if a government minister or official propagates falsehoods, the POFMA office, situated in the Infocomm Media Development Authority (IMDA), does not handle this. The only checks available to deal with official falsehoods would be through parliamentary questions,[404] which may not be robust, and ultimately the check of the ballot box in a polity which has yet to experience political turnover.[405]

The CA upheld the constitutionality of POFMA in *The Online Citizen (TOC) v AG*[406] and situated this law, which restricts Article 14(1) expressive freedom, as one which Parliament considered 'necessary or expedient' in the interests of national security and public order,[407] under Article 14(2). The CA affirmed a capacious understanding of 'public order' beyond physical disturbance to impacting intangible values relating to 'a general disturbance of public tranquility' affecting communal life.[408] As Rajah J opined, public order could be harmed and threatened by 'disseminating false or inaccurate information or claims'.[409] It would be 'simply incompatible' with core democratic principles for elections or referenda to be secured by online falsehoods, which would shake 'the foundations of a democratic society to its very core'.[410]

This section evaluates how POFMA has operated against RoL values like the need for certainty to guide conduct, sufficient rights protection and accountability to stave off regulatory overreach; any party empowered to unilaterally determine what is true or false may potentially alter the balance of political discourse to advantage.

A. How the Protection from Online Falsehood and Manipulation Act Works

POFMA provides a suite of tools allowing for a range of remedial responses to an online falsehood; these have graduated impact on curtailing liberties,

[403] Shanmugam, Second Reading, POFMA Bill (n 378); Select Committee Report (n 400) [315]–[316].

[404] ibid [314].

[405] Muralli Pillai, 94 SPR, 8 May 2019: 'Ultimately, we must all remember our fellow Singaporeans are looking at us and they would be holding the Government to account through the ballot box.'

[406] *TOC v AG* [2021] (n 398).

[407] ibid [89].

[408] *Sudhir Kumar Saha v Commissioner of Police Calcutta* AIR 1970 SC 814, cited in *Re Tan Boon Li* [1976] 2 Mal LJ 83, referenced in *TOC v AG* [2021] 2 SLR 1358, [98]. Although the court applied the three-step test in *Jolovan Wham v PP* [2021] 476, [29]–[32], it focused on a nexus test rather than reviewing the balance struck by the legislation, unlike in *Wham*: see Marcus Teo, 'Constitutional Implications of the First POFMA Judgement: *TOC v AG*' [2022] SJLS 177, 188.

[409] *Chee Siok Chin v MHA* [2006] 1 SLR(R) 582, [135].

[410] *TOC v AG* [2021] (n 398) [100].

depending on the gravity of the harm, without immediate resort to the nuclear option of total censorship.

Part 3 of POFMA deals with the communication in Singapore of false statements of fact and is addressed primarily to persons, within or outside Singapore,[411] while Part 4 addresses Internet intermediaries and mass media services providers. Under section 10, a minister may instruct the POFMA Office to issue a Part 3 Direction if certain conditions are met: that a 'false statement of fact' (the subject statement) has been communicated in Singapore and the minister considers it in the 'public interest' to issue a Direction. These may be in the form of a section 11 Correction Direction (CD) which acts like a 'warning labels', or a section 12 'stop communication' directions (SC) in the form of a 'ban' to ensure the non-availability of the statement to Singapore end users.[412] Non-compliance with Part 3 Directions is an offence for which individuals may be fined up to $20,000 and/or up to 12 months imprisonment; in other cases, fines are capped at $500,000: section 15(1). The Minister may direct the IMDA to issue an Access Blocking Order to an Internet service provider, where a POFMA order is not complied with.[413]

Internet intermediaries may be subject to Part 4 Targeted Correction Directions (TCDs) or General Correction Directions, under sections 21 and 23 respectively. This essentially requires a notice that a subject statement is false and a reference to a specified location where a specified statement of fact is found. A Disabling Direction under section 22 obliges Internet intermediaries to disable access to Singapore end users of the relevant subject material. Non-compliance with Part 4 may attract fines of $20,000 for individuals and in other cases fines not exceeding $1 million, under section 27. Tech companies like Google take the position they will comply with directions regarding what a legal authority determines to be false content, as they do not feel equipped to be truth arbiters.[414]

The minister is empowered under section 32 to declare an online site is a Declared Online Location (DOL) if it has issued three or more statements communicated in Singapore and which are subject to an active Part 3 or 4 Direction within six months before the date the DOL is made. The owner or operator may be obliged to notify Singapore end users that the online location has been declared a DOL; non-compliance with this requirement attracts fines of up to a $40,000 or three years' imprisonment for individuals and fines of up to $500,000 for other entities. It is an offence to receive financial or material benefit from operating a DOL site or by selling advertising space on it; service

[411] POFMA, s 13(1).
[412] POFMA, s 12(5).
[413] POFMA, ss 16, 28, 33.
[414] 'Deliberate Online Falsehoods: Social Media Giants Say They Are Not in a Position to Be "Arbiters of Truth"' (*CNA.com*, 23 March 2018).

providers are obliged to take reasonable steps to ensure any paid content in a DOL site is not communicated in Singapore.[415] For example, TOC, a political news blog, was declared a DOL by the Ministry of Communications and Information (MCI) in July 2023 for a two-year period, for allegedly carrying multiple falsehoods; this is not subject to judicial oversight.[416]

B. Discretion and Oversight

To issue a POFMA direction dealing with the communication of false statements of fact in Singapore, two conditions must first be met: first, there must be a 'false statement of fact', which excludes opinion and satire: section 2(2). However, the loose drafting and vague terms have created concerns over how to determine whether a statement is 'false or misleading'. Second, it must be in the public interest, as defined in section 4, which includes 'not diminishing public confidence in the government'. This raises the fear that bona fide criticism of a government, which must exist in any free society,[417] would be caught.

Accountability in exercising POFMA powers was to be balanced against the need for swift action against online falsehoods. Power is vested in portfolio ministers, drawing on their 'deep domain knowledge' to expeditiously assess whether to issue an order,[418] supported by ministry officials and resources.[419] A direction recipient who disagrees with it must first comply with it, before making a ministerial appeal to cancel or vary the order, under section 19. When this is exhausted, aside from the 'parallel track' of judicial review on *GCHQ* grounds, 'which operates separately',[420] one may resort to the bespoke statutory appeal procedure[421] to the High Court within a prescribed period under section 17. This is designed to be fast and inexpensive, uniquely incorporating some degree of judicial oversight over the ministerial decision. This limited appeal is not a full rehearing akin to a superior court hearing an appeal from an inferior court.[422] Theoretically, the courts, as the final arbiters of truth and

[415] POFMA, ss 36, 37.

[416] See 'Singapore: Anti-Fake News POFMA Law Used to Block News Outlet, Target Critics as Another Law to Regulate Online Content Is Passed' (*Civicus Monitor*, 18 August 2023) https://monitor.civicus.org/explore/singapore-anti-fake-news-pofma-law-used-to-block-news-outlet-target-critics-as-another-law-to-regulate-online-content-is-passed/.

[417] Dennis LP Tan (NCMP) 94 SPR, 8 May 2019.

[418] Iswaran (n 369) [18].

[419] The power to block funding and access to online locations under Part 5 is reposed only in the Minister for Communications and Information.

[420] Murali Pillai, 94 SPR, 7 May 2019; *TOC v AG* [2021] (n 398) [173].

[421] s 17 is a statutory mechanism delineated by 'its particular statutory prescription, context and intent': *TOC v AG* [2021] (n 398) [176]–[177], cited in *The Inquiry Pte Ltd v AG* [2023] SGHC 247, [58].

[422] *TOC v AG* [2021] (n 398) [172]–[176].

falsehood, can hear a case as early as nine days after the first appeal to the minister who issued the POFMA order. Court fees are waived for the first three days of the case.[423]

The High Court, which usually sits in chambers,[424] may confirm or set aside the direction on three grounds specified in section 17(5), determining the relevant facts afresh: that the person did not communicate the subject statement in Singapore; that it was not a statement of fact or was a true factual statement; or where compliance with the direction is technically impossible.

The official view is that 'very clear due process'[425] prevents the minister from 'having excessive powers',[426] as the prospect of enhanced judicial scrutiny 'is a sword hanging over with the Courts'. A minister who makes a mistake risks jeopardising his personal and political reputation and being 'publicly embarrassed', which urges prudential self-restraint.[427] However, the High Court cannot evaluate if the direction was proportionate or made in the public interest, which requires considering the potential for harm, as identified in sections 4(a)–(f).[428] The discretion to issue a CD or SC direction 'clearly lies with the Minister alone'.[429]

The courts are thus 'barred from asking the most significant question', and instead are engaged in making 'almost absurdly meticulous assessments' about whether a statement is factually false.[430] On these significant questions, reliance is placed on faith in ministerial self-restraint, rather than external judicial assessment.[431] Proposals for an independent council or ombudsman which would evaluate issued directions at first instance[432] were dismissed as

[423] 'Appeal Process under Fake News Law Will Be Simple, Fast: Shanmugam' *Straits Times* (8 May 2019).

[424] *Singapore Democratic Party v AG* [2022] 2 SLR 977, [48]–[49].

[425] Iswaran (n 369) [20].

[426] ibid [20f].

[427] Shanmugam, Second Reading, POFMA Bill (n 378).

[428] 'This relates to (a) security (b) public health or finances, public safety and tranquility; (c) friendly relations with other countries; (d) to prevent electoral influence; (e) to prevent incitement of feelings of enmity, hatred or ill-will between different groups of persons and (f) to prevent diminution of public confidence in the exercise of power or performance of duty by the government or government organ': *TOC v AG* [2021] (n 398) [104].

[429] ibid [130].

[430] Lasse Schuldt, 'In Singapore's War on Fake News, the Constitution Is Not an Obstacle' (*verfassungsblog.de*, 16 November 2021). Opposition MP Sylvia Lim noted that the Court on appeal 'cannot ask important questions such as: (a) Is the Minister over-reacting? (b) Did the direction impose obligations on the communicator which are excessively onerous or harsh? (c) Does the public interest require the Direction to be issued?' 94 SPR, 8 May 2019.

[431] The Law Minister asserted that restraint had to be shown under existing analogous laws like the Broadcasting Act. Since its inception in 1996, only 39 take-down notices had been issued and the law had 'no impact' on what the people on the street had been saying, with most orders relating to pornographic, religiously offensive and extremist content: Shanmugam, Second Reading, POFMA Bill (n 378).

[432] 'NMPs Suggest 4 Amendments to Fake News Bill, Including Having Independent Council to Review Govt Decisions' *Straits Times* (1 May 2019).

'unnecessary bureaucratic bloat', as such functions could be achieved 'under the current structure of the Executive and Parliament'.[433]

C. Judicial Oversight, Correction Directions and the Scope of Free Speech

The CA in *TOC v AG* laid down a five-step analytical framework[434] in considering appeals from two cases relating to CDs issued under section 17)(5)(a) or (b), the 'primary tool' under POFMA.[435] These pertained to inaccurate employment figures of locals asserted by the SDP, and the allegedly brutal methods for implementing the death penalty in an article by Malaysian NGO Lawyers for Liberty, published by TOC, a political news blog.

Consistent with precedent,[436] rights-oriented proportionality review was rejected. The court noted that an idiosyncratic proportionality test was baked into section 4, which asks whether it is 'necessary or expedient' in the public interest to issue a direction.[437] There was no basis for reading in a requirement that the minister applies the 'least restrictive means' in counteracting false statement of facts.[438] Liberal critics attribute the absence of proportionality review to Singapore's adherence to a 'thin' RoL where, within a 'Westminster like arrangement', courts have weak review powers.[439] The effectiveness of the judicial check turns on how POFMA is interpreted, the width of ministerial discretion and whether sufficiently clear guidelines are provided to communicators.

The five-step test involves: (i) determining the meaning of the subject statement; (ii) interpreting the subject material to determine if it contained the subject statement; (iii) determining if the subject statement was a statement of fact; (iv) and, if so, whether it was false; and (v) determining if the subject statement communicated had been accessed in Singapore: section 10(1)(a). Several points relating to broad discretionary powers are worth underscoring.

First, the minister must identify the false statement of fact (subject statement) from the subject material in sufficient detail; it is not for the court to identify possible false meanings and uphold a Direction on that basis,[440] but to strictly hold the minister to the identified subject statement to give effect to a CD recipient's right to seek relief under sections 17 and 19.[441] In other words, it

[433] Shanmugam, Second Reading, POFMA Bill (n 378). See 'In Focus: Has POFMA Been Effective? A Look at the Fake News Law 1 Year Since It Kicked In' (*CNA.com*, 3 October 2020).

[434] *TOC v AG* [2021] (n 398) [163].

[435] Edwin Tong (Senior Minister of State, Law), Second Reading, POFMA Bill, 94 SPR, 7 May 2019.

[436] *Chee Siok Chin* [2006] (n 409) [87].

[437] *TOC v AG* [2021] (n 398) [309].

[438] ibid [112].

[439] *TOC v AG* [2021] (n 398).

[440] ibid [125].

[441] ibid [125], [127]–[129].

is for the court to apply an objective interpretation in considering the minister's intended meaning in framing the subject statement. Where there are 'multiple reasonable ways' to interpret the subject material, it would be most consistent with POFMA purposes if Part 3 measures could be taken if 'at least one of the reasonable interpretations amounts to a false statement of fact'.[442]

Second, the section 17 proceeding applicant bears the burden of proving on a prima facie case of reasonable suspicion that section 17(5)(a) or (b) grounds are made out, ie that the person did not communicate the subject statement in Singapore, it is not a statement of fact or it is a true factual statement. The evidential burden then shifts to the minister to show these grounds are not made out. The court considers the totality of evidence and makes the final determination based on the balance of probabilities.[443]

In rejecting an argument that the burden fell on the minister to prove the legal requirements for issuing a Direction, the CA noted that Parliament had not articulated any concern for informational asymmetry and if the complainant of a CD is not required to show 'some objective basis' for the complaint, this could open the 'way for abuse' through frivolous challenges. The administrative law presumption of legality of executive action applied[444] and the minister was obliged to provide the basis for determining the subject statement to be false beyond a 'mere assertion',[445] on the basis of which the CD recipient would explain why those grounds were being challenged. Critics consider placing the burden of proof on the accused, not the accuser, as 'clear violations of the liberal rule of law',[446] discounting the statutory scheme where, in section 17 proceedings, the applicant is the plaintiff and the minister, whose section 10 decision is challenged, is the effective defendant.[447]

Third, POFMA targets 'false statements of facts', not 'statement[s] of opinions',[448] which are evaluative or satirical.[449] Section 2(2)(a) defines a statement of fact as one which 'a reasonable person seeing, hearing or otherwise perceiving it would consider it to be a representation of fact', suggesting an objective approach.[450]

What constitutes a fact as distinct from an opinion was left to analogous case law in defamation, for example, although this is not always clear-cut and

[442] ibid [150]. The CA stated the 'single meaning' rule applying to defamation torts did not apply in the POFMA context.

[443] *TOC v AG* [2021] (n 398) [180]–[184].

[444] Citing *Muhammad Ridzuan v AG* [2015] 5 SLR 1222, *TOC v AG* [2021] 2 SLR 1358, [180].

[445] *TOC v AG* [2021] (n 398) [182]; POFMA Regulations, regulation 6(b).

[446] S Ortmann, 'Liberal Vestiges in an Illiberal Regime: The Case of Singapore (2023) 60 Society 28, 30.

[447] *TOC v AG* [2021] (n 398) [176].

[448] see Ministry of Law, 'How the Protection from Online Falsehoods and Manipulation Act Applies', <www.mlaw.gov.sg/files/news/others/HowPOFMAApplies.pdf.

[449] 'Erroneous to Suggest POFMA Covers Satire: Shanmugam on Media Literacy Council Post' (*CNA.com*, 13 September 2019).

[450] *TOC v AG* [2021] (n 398) [158].

is perhaps best seen as a 'continuum'[451] rather than in binary terms.[452] While a deductive process extrapolating from a lecture about projected population density would render a subject statement an opinion, a report of what was said at the lecture would be a statement of fact.[453] The former is evaluative, the latter, descriptive. The indeterminacy involved in distinguishing fact and opinion presses hard upon a judge's 'common sense',[454] and the courts have gone into granular detail to ascertain whether the impugned statement is false.

Fourth, it is possible that a statement could carry a range of meanings or be apprehended differently by different people. Section 2(2)(b) provides that a statement is false 'if it is false or misleading, *whether wholly or in part*, and whether on its own or in the context in which it appears' (emphasis added). Implicit in this is the understanding that where reading a statement may give rise to different meanings, this 'does not negate its falsity on at least one of the meanings'.[455] Even if interpretations of the same statement may render it true, the legislative intent is that the court not 'ignore the potential ways in which a statement of fact may be false', given the 'speed and scale' at which falsehoods may spread online in the guise of news reports.[456] This reflects the 'effects orientation' of POFMA, where intent is irrelevant[457] and impact is all.

As the focus is on preventing and taking countermeasures against the 'deleterious effects' of online falsehoods to the public, POFMA captures both authors and those who forward false information,[458] while being agnostic about its veracity. There is no defence of 'neutral reportage'.[459]

From reading section 2(2)(b), it appears a statement which is 99 per cent true and one per cent false may be caught within its ambit, and that statements taken out of context may also be caught, even if given a meaning not intended by its author. This is a broader approach than the defamation law requirement of taking a publication in its entirety, following the 'bane and antidote' rule.[460]

[451] Michaele Sanders, 'The Fact/Opinion Distinction: An Analysis of the Subjectivity of Language and Law (1987) 70 Marquette Law Review 673, 680.

[452] Whether the 'invasion' of Vietnam into Cambodia in 1979 or Indonesian into East Timor in 1975 is a statement of fact or opinion may depend on the audience. Whether the term 'cult' was a statement of fact or comment depended on the context and how the statement was made: *Chen Cheng v Central Christian Church* [1998] 3 SLR(R) 236, [33]–[38]. See Rodney Wott, 'Fact and Opinion in Defamation: Recognizing the Formative Power of Context' (1990) 58(4) Fordham LR 761. The Law Minister gave examples of fact and opinion which provides some guidance on how Part 3 Directions would be exercised: 'Fact or Opinion? Shanmugam Explains Difference with 5 Examples' *Today* (7 May 2019).

[453] *Singapore Democratic Party (SDP) v AG* [2022] 5 SLR 650, [56], [60].

[454] *Chen Cheng v Central Christian Church* [1998] SGCA 51, [33].

[455] *TOC v AG* [2021] (n 398) [151].

[456] ibid [242].

[457] POFMA, ss 11(4), 12(4): a CD recipient does not need to know or have reason to believe the statement is false: *TOC v AG* [2021] (n 398) [151].

[458] Inviting readers to access a hyperlink is equivalent to republishing an entire article: *SDP v AG* [2020] SGHC 25, [56].

[459] *TOC v AG* [2021] (n 398) [161].

[460] *SDP v AG* [2020] SGHC 25, [69].

It gives rise to the risk that partisan considerations may slip into the exercise of discretionary powers. The CD may overreach in discrediting the whole statement, even if it is partially true. Whether a statement taken out of context is harmless to public order depends on its substance and scale of publication,[461] which invites a case-by-case approach.

The bulwark against a descent into the tendentious perspectives of eg conspiracy theorists is that it must be a 'reasonable' interpretation of the statement from the perspective of the 'ordinary reasonable reader'. The minister must determine the range of the reasonable, and prudence alone dictates against too low a bar in balancing the importance of preventing falsehoods from circulating and protecting free speech,[462] given the inevitability of making erroneous statements in free debate.[463]

When considering the audience, the court must find 'at least an appreciable segment or a particular class of the potential readership' would 'construe the subject material as containing the subject statement or regard the subject statement as a reasonable interpretation of the subject material'.[464] The 'segment' is referred to 'in the context of an objective standard of reasonableness'; so a detailed recounting of allegations, such as those made by Lawyers for Liberty on the brutal execution process, as distinct from vague conjectural assertions, make it more likely the ordinary reasonable reader would consider the statement a 'representation of fact'.[465] However, a concession is apparent where it is assumed the audience is composed not of the 'reasonable person', but rather, the ideological or gullible man, a class of potential readers who are 'inherently more inclined to believe certain falsehoods' demarcated by 'clearly identifiable characteristics',[466] such as socio-political beliefs,[467] or who may take the subject statement out of context owing to factors like 'clickbait, deceptive headlines … or the use of outsized graphics'.[468] Articles must be read at the level of impression, not undertaking 'fine-grained or unduly technical analysis',[469] and the court should not accept what is 'nothing more than theoretically possible interpretations of the subject matter'.[470] Thean J in *The Inquiry Pte Ltd v AG* observed that both alternatives were 'elucidations' of directing the interpretive

[461] *TOC v AG* [2021] (n 398) [108].

[462] ibid [151].

[463] The US approach is that erroneous statements in free debate warrant protection 'if the freedoms of expression are to have the "breathing space" they "need … to survive"': *NAACP v Button* 371 US 415, 433, cited in *New York Times Co v Sullivan* 376 US 254 (1964) 272.

[464] *TOC v AG* [2021] (n 398) [136].

[465] ibid [243]. While Lawyers for Liberty provided no basis for its allegations, the Singapore Prison Service provided an affidavit categorically refuting the allegations: [244].

[466] *The Inquiry* (n 421) [33].

[467] eg those with similar political inclinations as Jom publications, which had 'a critical attitude towards the Singapore Government': ibid [31].

[468] *TOC v AG* [2021] (n 398) [157].

[469] ibid [136], [210]–[211].

[470] ibid [157].

exercise 'toward a reasonable interpretation held by a sufficiently large number of readers'.[471] Some measure of a need for a 'reasonable balance' between guarding against communicating falsehoods and free speech is reflected in the concern that statements construed in a false sense 'by an insignificant segment of the public or class of persons' are not 'culled from the public discourse'.[472]

If a subject statement was 'within an outer range of reasonable meanings',[473] an unequivocal disavowal or addendum, which is the author's response to the CD, would clarify the author's intent in disassociating from the meaning the minister gave the subject statement. While disavowals would not ensure readers were given full information, the minister could consider this in a section 19 hearing.[474]

Whether false statement targeted by a CD attracts the protection of the Article 14 free speech guarantee is noteworthy, bearing in mind the rationales of the argument from truth and democratic deliberation have been judicially affirmed.[475] The court has stated that misinformation 'is of little, if any, value'[476] in the context of the Protection from Harassment Act (POHA) regime. Similar to POFMA, POHA orders dealing with the spread of falsehoods include stop communication, correction and disabling orders. While judicially determined falsehoods under the POHA regime are not protected under Article 14, ministerial determinations that a statement is false under POFMA remain protected, as the minister may be 'mistaken'. The veracity of a statement is subject to a final judicial determination 'based on the evidence'.[477]

The CA, considering the design and operation of a CD issued under section 11, held it did not curtail Article 14. A CD recipient must communicate at least two things: first, a correction notice in Singapore 'in the specified form and manner' as the minister may formulate,[478] containing a statement that the subject statement is false or that the subject material contains a false statement of fact; and second, a specified statement of fact or a reference to where this may be found, such as providing a hyperlink to the government's fact-checking website, 'Factually',[479] containing the state's version of the truth. This seeks to make a trusted centralised depository a source of reliable information, setting forth

[471] *The Inquiry* (n 421) [33].
[472] *TOC v AG* [2021] (n 398) [156].
[473] ibid [155].
[474] The CA in *TOC v AG* [2021] (n 398) opined that using addenda in such situations where the statement-maker would have no interest in allowing a misperception to persist could be a 'possible balance' between an objective reading of the subject statement from the perspective of the potential readership in Singapore and an interpretation based on the statement-maker's intended meaning: [155]. Unequivocal disavowals would be needed, not just bare denials: *The Inquiry Pte Ltd v AG* [2023] SGHC 247, [68].
[475] *Lee Hsien Loong v Ngerng Yi Ling Roy (Damages)* [2016] 1 SLR 1321, [96]–[107].
[476] *Ting Choon Meng* (n 399) [112]–[113].
[477] *TOC v AG* [2021] (n 398) [61].
[478] ibid [64].
[479] See www.gov.sg/factually.

'full information … as a countermeasure';[480] the CD enables a minister to debunk a communicated falsehood through the less intrusive route of 'counter-speech'[481] rather than censorship, to 'inoculate' the public' against falsehoods.[482]

Internet intermediaries must ensure such notices are 'easily perceived'.[483] In practice, a correction notice is usually posted on top of the offending post, though it can be a new post on the website or on Facebook.[484] This was criticised as a potential overreach[485] and justified by the need to 'reach at least as large a readership as the original falsehood' in trying to stem the multiplication of lies and promote 'the correct understanding of the facts', which is shaped by 'the design of the feed and website'.[486]

The CA in *TOC v AG* held that free speech was not curtailed as a CD recipient had the option to modify the subject statement's content or continue to publish the alleged falsehood, provided he communicates, without having to assert the truth of, the point of view set out in the CD.[487] Indeed, he could express disagreement with the correction notice and had 'the freedom to qualify it appropriately' in an 'equally visible manner'.[488] The CD allows the minister 'to state all the relevant facts' and 'to highlight' through a hyperlink to another website 'the full facts for readers to come to an informed conclusion'. The original statement is not censored or blocked and remains alongside the correction, which old and new readers can continue to access. The CD as a 'warning label' did not 'inhibit free speech' since the statement-maker still maintains 'the original text of its published material'.[489]

Belinda Ang J drew an analogy in *The Online Citizen Pte Ltd v AG*[490] between the CD and the 'right to reply', noting that this facilitates the search for truth. Such right is 'a very practical way of demonstrating a commitment to accuracy' in print or virtual media.[491]

[480] *The Inquiry* (n 421) [63].

[481] GS Hans, 'Changing Counterspeech' (2021) 69 Cleveland State LR 749. In US jurisprudence, this was established by Justice Brandeis in *Whitney v California* 274 US 357, 377 (1927), where the remedy for falsehood was 'more speech, not enforced silence'.

[482] Shanmugam, Second Reading, POFMA Bill (n 378) [303].

[483] POFMA, s 24.

[484] *TOC v AG* [2022] SGHC 177, [60].

[485] Pritam Singh (Opposition Leader) argued it sufficed to have the CD on the article itself to indicate the flagging out of the article; if the CD was on the main webpage, 'which has nothing to do with the article at hand', it may convey the impression that it relates to every article on the Asia Sentinel website: 95 SPR, 3 August 2023.

[486] Janil Puthucheary (Senior Minister of State: MCI), 'Inclusion of POFMA Correction Direction on Main Page of Asia Sentinel Website and Page Hosting Art with False Statement of Fact', 95 SPR, 3 August 2023.

[487] [2021] 2 SLR 1358, [71]–[72], [77]–[78].

[488] ibid [72].

[489] *TOC v AG* [2022] (n 484) [36].

[490] ibid [37].

[491] Mediawise Trust, October 2004 submission to consultation conducted by the UK Department of Culture, Media and Sport, quoted in 'Revisited: An Article 10 Right to Reply' (*The International Forum for Responsible Media Blog*, 17 October 2020).

The CD effectively institutionalises the right to reply, which has juridical status in some human rights instruments,[492] something the government used to demand from foreign print media.[493] It is far cheaper to include a notice in a digital article and a link to the government's perspective.

The government can thus disrupt the narrative by providing information so the reader can assess the accuracy of the facts, promoting a 'balanced inquiry' through the principle of 'audi alteram partem'.[494] This is premised on the view that counter-narratives neutralise bad speech and promote responsible public discourse, insofar as statement-makers verify their claims and readers act like rational persons who take pains to access the corrective materials and evaluate competing accounts.[495] This can encourage 'a more honest and open discussion'[496] and 'a more vigorous online discourse', allowing readers to 'decide for themselves'.[497] This is distinct from an ideologically closed-minded person, who rejects all views challenging his preferred narrative.

While the positive right to free speech is not impacted, it was argued that the negative right not to be required to speak was affected.[498] Having to put up a correction notice compelled a CD recipient 'to express views or opinions' not held, in 'admitting' a false statement of fact was made.[499] Without definitively deciding whether the US doctrine of compelled speech as set out in *Wooley v Maynard*[500] applied in Singapore, the CA held in the instant case that speech was not compelled as the CD recipient could express disagreement and make clear 'in a factually accurate manner'[501] that it was challenging the CD. Negative liberty was not impugned, based on the distinction between communicating a point of view and asserting its truth.[502]

While there is weight to the argument that a right to reply can support the marketplace of ideas, this is based on the assumption of the citizen as a 'rational person' who seeks truth, as distinct from other legislation which

[492] American Convention on Human Rights (1969), Art 14, UNTS No 17955, 143.

[493] Tommy TB Koh, 'Singapore Believes Freedom of Press Must Be a Two-Way Street' *New York Times* (25 February 1987); 'Press Can Criticize, but Govt Expects Right of Reply' *Straits Times* (28 October 2009) A8.

[494] Thio Li-ann, *A Treatise on Singapore Constitutional Law* (Academy Publishing, 2012) para 14.013, cited in *TOC v AG* [2020] SGHC 36, [37].

[495] In contrast, a Must Carry Direction issued under FICA obliges communicators or platforms to tag content to indicate it is part of a 'hostile information campaign' (HIC), with the intent that readers will reject the HIC content and accept the truth of the government narrative, promoting transparency as to who the content is from and whether it is persuasive: Muhammad Faishal Ibrahim (Minister of State, Home Affairs) 95 SPR, 4 October 2021.

[496] Shanmugam, Second Reading, POFMA Bill (n 378) [283].

[497] Iswaran (n 369) [16].

[498] *TOC v AG* [2021] (n 398) [68].

[499] ibid [69].

[500] 430 US 705 (1977), discussed in *TOC v AG* [2021] 2 SLR 1358, [70]. The UK decision of *Lee v Ashers Baking* [2018] 3 SLR 1294 (UKSC) was discussed, [73].

[501] *TOC v AG* [2021] (n 398) [78].

[502] The CA in *TOC v AG* [2021] (n 398) [70] preferred this minority view in *Wooley v Maynard* 430 US 705 (1977).

treats the citizen as an 'emotional man' whose racial or religious feelings can be wounded.[503] In this context, ideological bias can preclude a commitment to deliberation.

Further, one should be conscious that the CD as an institutionalised digital right to reply is an exercise of state power, allowing the government not only to rebut a falsehood, but also to elaborate upon its case. The CD is a form of privileged access which disrupts the insularity of an echo chamber or biased news source; however, the availability of alternative views does not guarantee the hearer will reflect on both sides and reach the right conclusion. The CD may draw more attention to the false statement, on top of any notoriety gained from news reporting. Conspiracy theorists or the ideologically biased may believe a vehemently debunked statement is true.

A CD may delegitimate the communicator and buttress the perception of the government as a carrier of authentic information and corrector of falsehoods, elevating the high degree of trust Singaporeans generally have for the government.[504] While the CD recipients may register disagreement, they may be unable to pursue the matter at depth or to assert the truth of the original statement[505] without attracting another CD, as the government may issue multiple orders concerning the same false statement.[506] Presumably, recipients can give reasons why they disagree with the CD or why they believe the factual statement is true, assuming they have the needed facts or figures at their disposal; the expression of such opinions may have some utility beyond a bare declaration of belief. If the subject statement is true, the CD can be set aside under section 17.

Regardless of arguments that speech is restricted by a CD as the communicators' 'freedom to choose the appearance, context and effect of the statement' is impacted,[507] a CD has been held to be constitutional in allowing the recipient to express qualifications about the correction notice he is required to put up. This is less intrusive than a ban. The same analysis may not apply to a more restrictive Stop Communications Direction, which effectively bans speech.[508]

[503] Li-ann Thio, 'Apollonian Restraint and Dionysian Impulse: Law, Freedom and Religious Feelings' in Li-ann Thio and Jaclyn Neo (eds), *Religious Offences in Common Law Asia: Colonial Legacies, Constitutional Rights and Contemporary Practice* (Hart Publishing, 2021) 75–102.

[504] 'Government Remains Most Trusted Institution in Singapore, Amid Global Trend of societal Polarisation: Survey' (*CNA.com*, 15 March 2023).

[505] Marcus Teo, 'Constitutional Implications of the First POFMA Judgment: *TOC v AG*' [2022] SJLS 177, 185.

[506] Lim Tean communicated the same statement relating to the government's expenditure on foreign students on two occasions: 12 December 2019 and 1 July 2020. Both were subject to POFMA orders: 'Defiant Lim Tean Calls POFMA Correction Order "a Pathetic Demand" as He Considers Legal Options' (*The Independent.sg*, 16 December 2019); 'POFMA Correction Directions Issued to Peoples Voice Party's Facebook Page and Lim Tean's Youtube Channel' *Straits Times* (2 July 2020).

[507] Lasse Schuldt, 'In Singapore's War on Fake News, the Constitution Is Not an Obstacle' (*verfassungsblog.de*, 16 November 2021).

[508] Gary KY Chan, 'Online Falsehoods, Constitutional Free Speech and Its Limits: *TOC v AG*' [2022] SJLS 166, 173.

D. How it has Functioned

In practice, resort is had to 'warning label' CDs before issuing orders to stop communications or disable access to online falsehoods, as more restrictive orders are for 'extreme cases' where 'serious harm' is threatened.[509] From 2019 to 2023, 91.5 per cent of POFMA orders were in the nature of 'warning' labels,[510] with CDs being the 'primary tool'. About 3.7 per cent of POFMA orders (7/189) involve taking down or blocking access to content and were issued to Alex Tan, who runs the States Time Review, Lawyers for Liberty and Asia Sentinel. An order to the East Asia Forum was rescinded after the offending article was retracted, with an apology.[511]

Big Tech companies have largely complied with POFMA orders, showing the efficacy of financial sanctions, which have also been deployed against traditional print media.[512] A day after the States Time Review Facebook page, owned by Alex Tan, who lives in Australia, falsely stated that a whistleblower had been arrested for exposing the religious affiliations of a PAP electoral candidate, Facebook received a TCD to publish a correction notice on the post or be fined up to $500,000.[513] Facebook acceded and issued a statement stating it was 'legally required to tell you that the Singapore government says this post has false information'. It similarly complied when it received a TCD to block access to another Alex Tan Facebook page,[514] but protested that Singapore's use of POFMA was 'severe', potentially curtailing the 'fundamental human right' of expressive freedom which Facebook claimed to work hard to defend globally.[515] Facebook also complied with an order to block Singapore end users from accessing the States Times Review Facebook page after it was labelled a DOL, while protesting this was disproportionate.[516]

The deployment of CDs to swiftly address public health matters during the COVID-19 pandemic, sometimes as fast as within a day of publication, has

[509] Iswaran (n 369) [16].

[510] POFMA Statistics, 'POFMA Action Taken Up to 30 September 2023', www.pofmaoffice.gov.sg/stats/permalink/.

[511] The East Asia Forum, an Australia-based platform, was blocked on 16 September 2023 for an article published on 18 August with access restored on 22 September 2023: 'MCI Restores Access to East Asia Forum after Cancellation of Pofma Order' *Straits Times* (22 September 2023); 'NUS Academic Truly Sorry for Flawed and Biased Article on Recent Political Controversies, Retracts It from Website' *Today* (19 September 2023).

[512] Sanctions under the Newspaper and Printing Presses Act included restricting circulation and blacking out advertisements: see Cherian George, *Freedom from the Press: Journalism and State Power in Singapore* (NUS Press, 2012).

[513] 'Govt Directs Facebook to Run Correction Notice on States Times Review Power, after Page Owner's Non-compliance' *Today* (29 November 2019).

[514] MCI Press Release, '"National Times Singapore" Facebook Page Made a Declared Online Location under POFMA' (28 May 2020).

[515] 'Facebook Slams Singapore's POFMA Laws as "Severe" after Being Ordered to Geo-block Certain Pages' *The Independent* (3 June 2020).

[516] 'Facebook Blocks Access in Singapore to States Times Review Page for Breaching Pofma' *Straits Times* (20 February 2020).

been lauded,[517] as has using CDs to disrupt attempts to exploit racial and religious faultiness. However, there are concerns of the politicised used of CDs where, between 2019 and 2023, it was estimated that more than 75 per cent of CDs issued were directed at opposition politicians, civil society activists and alternative media platforms.[518] For example the Ministry of Manpower (MOM) issued five POFMA correction notices in relation to comments by opposition politician Paul Tambyah at a forum, which drew criticism for using POFMA inappropriately. Tambyah had commented that without the advice of medical professionals, MOM had sent an e-advisory to employers on testing migrant workers for COVID-19. These comments were carried in a Channel News Asia article, a Facebook post and video from TOC, an audio recording by New Naratif and a video from the National University of Singapore Society; all correction notices were complied with. MOM and the Ministry of Health (MOH) stated that Tambyah had said that employers would lose their work pass privileges if they brought their workers for testing, and that the MOM 'actively discouraged' testing workers, which were false allegations. Tambyah denied making these statements. While Tambyah implied in the videos that MOM did not consult MOH before sending the e-advisory, a minister later clarified in a Facebook post that the MOM advisory was sent out at MOH's request. As Tambyah's statement was based on the fact that MOM warned employers via email not to send their migrant workers for testing, a petition was launched asserting it was an 'affront to common sense and logic' to classify what Tambyah said, which was accurate, as a falsehood.[519] Instances like this raise the suspicion that POFMA may be used to quell political dissent by accusing opposition politicians of distorting the truth,[520] particularly where the Manpower Minister, the subject of criticism, is empowered to decide on appeal whether to cancel the CD.

The perception that POFMA is being used to protect the government or establishment figures may not conduce to maintaining public trust in institutions. For example, the Ministry of Finance intervened to issue four POFMA orders[521]

[517] 'Wuhan Virus: Government Will Not Hesitate to Use Pofma on Fake News Regarding Viral Outbreak, Says Iswaran' *Today* (27 January 2020).

[518] S Ortmann, 'Liberal Vestiges in an Illiberal Regime: The Case of Singapore' (2023) 60 Society 28, 34; Nicholas Tan Junda, 'Saving Democracy? Singapore, The Digital Public Square and the Regulation of Online Speech', NUS University Research Opportunity Programme, para 57, Figure 4 (breakdown of affiliation of POFMA targets who received more than one order between 2019 and 2023, eg TOC (22), Alex Tan (17), Kenneth Jeyaretnam (10), Goh Meng Seng (9), Lim Tean, The Independent Singapore (7), Kirsten Han, Singapore Democratic Party and Wake up Singapore (5), New Naratif, Iris Koh, Yeo Lam Keong, East Asia Forum (4)).

[519] Petition to Lew Chuen Hong (IMDA CEO), 6 July 2020, 'POFMA Issued to Professor Tambyah on MOM Is Ridiculous and Abuse of POFMA', www.change.org (this obtained over 15,000 signatures).

[520] 'PAP Using Old Tactic of Accusing SDP of Distorting the Truth, Says Chairman Paul Tambyah' *Malay Mail* (6 July 2020).

[521] 'Four Pofma Corrections Issued over Claims that Ho Ching's Annual Salary at Temasek Is "Around $100 Million"' *Straits Times* (19 April 2020).

relating to Ho Ching, the wife of PM Lee and Chief Executive of Temasek Holdings (a government investment arm), and her supposed annual salary of 'around $100m'.[522] This allegation could have been handled in a more muted fashion by a clarificatory statement on the Temasek corporate website; instead, the POFMA orders inadvertently elevated the profile of this claim. Further, the non-provision of the 'real figure' may potentially 'erode public trust' as 'it will breed more speculation, to no constructive end'.[523]

In contrast, a call for a POFMA order to clarify what could cast Madam Ho in a bad light was rejected. The *Straits Times* had apparently reported inconsistently on whether Temasek had participated in two or three rounds of fundraising by FTX Trading Ltd, a leading cryptocurrency exchange that went bankrupt in November 2022 after its owners misused customer funds. One article[524] reported that Temasek had participated in two rounds, in October 2021 and January 2022, and another[525] reported that Temasek had also participated in the July 2021 round. If the latter were true, this would have been under Ho Ching's watch, before she stepped down in October 2021,[526] significant in that $377 million was lost for a poor investment in the now insolvent company.

E. Conclusion

While the Internet and social media have democratised communication, this has had both positive and negative repercussions. POFMA, through 'calibrated regulatory interventions'[527] rather than an immediate flight to censorship, seeks to promote sustainable democracy by preserving honest public discourse and trust in public institutions.

That said, concerns of abuse of powers persist, as the executive rather than the courts has the power at first instance to determine what an actionable

[522] POFMA Office, 'Minister for Finance Instructs POFMA Office to Issue Correction Directions' (19 April 2020) www.pofmaoffice.gov.sg.

[523] Leon Perera (Non-Constituency), 'Issuance of POFMA Correction Direction for Online Commentaries on Compensation of Temasek Holdings CEO' 94 SPR 5, May 2020.

[524] 'Crypto Exchange FTX Raises $566m in Funding Round Co-led by Temasek' *Straits Times* (22 October 2021).

[525] 'Temasek to Write Down $377 Million in FTX, Says Belief in Bankman-Friend Appears to Be "Misplaced"' *Straits Times* (17 November 2022).

[526] Jeff Ho, 'Open Letter Asking If Temasek's FTX Investment in July Last Year Was Made under Then-CEO, Mdm Ho Ching's Watch?' (*TOC*, 17 November 2022).

[527] Iswaran (n 369) [13]. Since October 2019, the POFMA office has received 22 pieces of feedback and enquiries, rising to 435 in 2020 and 345 in 2021. The 'vast majority' of public complaints of alleged falsehoods were not actionable as 'false statements of facts', being opinions and criticisms. Seven POFMA directions were issued flowing from nine pieces of public feedback about falsehoods: 'Statistics and Outcome of Public Complaints Received Each Year since Enactment of POFMA', 95 SPR, 12 January 2022.

falsehood is. If a statement of fact could be both true and false, depending on context or whether it is read wholly or in part, this points to broad executive powers and the lack of clear guidance on what constitutes a falsehood. Uncertainty can breed self-censorship when whether to issue a POFMA order turns on the minister's subjective assessment. The fear is that POFMA could become 'a proverbial Damocles' sword' over members of the public who 'do not support the Government's narrative or tow the Government's party line'.[528]

There is some degree of judicial oversight, but this is limited to a stipulated set of issues and may not be sufficiently muscular. For example, a statement which could be read in a variety of ways should not be removed from public discourse if only an insignificant segment of the public might construe the subject statement as false. This may have some tempering effect, but the ministerial assessment of what the public interest requires is subject only to the checks associated with political constitutionalism within a dominant party state. During the COVID-19 pandemic, POFMA allowed for swift action against fabricated rumours which could trigger public panic; however, POFMA can also be deployed to advance government narratives on matters like vaccine safety and to marginalise dissenting voices raising alternative views on contestable issues, which the mainstream media largely ignores.[529] This reflects both the utility and dangers of the POFMA regime.

The official view is that POFMA was a 'right step' to take as it does not appear to have curtailed criticism or civil society's involvement in public discourse, as POFMA order recipients 'have continued to air their views online', or put up a correction notice while making new posts to the effect the POFMA notice is misleading.[530] Perhaps the greatest indicator that POFMA has become accepted as part of the regulatory landscape is that Singaporeans have apparently bought into the system: the public actively writes to the POFMA office to flag falsehoods,[531] and becoming 'POFMA-ed' has become a rite of passage or even a badge of credibility, eliciting defiance rather than submission. For example, a TikToker received two POFMA orders within three days, one for claiming in a video the government could trace voting choices from polling card serial numbers and penalise the voter. The TikToker stated he was bringing forth 'coffee shop talk' and would not stop or be intimidated 'by nobody because

[528] Pritam Singh (Opposition Leader), POFMA Bill speech, 7 May 2019, www.wp.sg/protection-from-online-falsehoods-and-manipulation-bill-speech-by-pritam-singh/.

[529] Thio, 'Legal Communitarianism' (n 21) 433.

[530] This is what Lee Hsien Yang did in relation to his Facebook comment on the Ridout Road saga, accusing two ministers of getting preferential treatment in renting state bungalows. The Law Ministry indicated the post had three untrue statements. The matter was investigated and the ministers exonerated: 'Ridout Road Rentals: CPIB Finds no Corruption or Wrongdoing by Shanmugam, Vivian' *Straits Times* (28 June 2023).

[531] 'Time Has Shown Pofma Was the "Right Step", Hasn't Curtailed Public Debate: Janil Puthucheary' *Today* (28 January 2022).

I only answer to my Creator'.[532] This is consonant with politics in a post-deferential era. To the extent receiving POFMA orders does not 'chill' speakers, it may have the salutary effect of requiring corrections to genuine falsehoods while not unduly deterring debate; among good faith interlocutors or journalists, it could spur conscientious attempts at verifying accuracy, serving the free speech rationales of truth-seeking and democratic deliberation.

[532] 'TikToker gets Pofma-ed Twice in 3 Days: I'm Not Going to Apologise or Get Intimidated by Nobody' (*Stomp*, 21 August 2023) https://stomp.straitstimes.com/.

5

Judicial Review and the Administrative State

I. INTRODUCTION

THE EXPANSIVE REACH of the modern regulatory state in its project of social organisation is facilitated by the public service or bureaucracy; this administrative branch is staffed by civil servants who implement the policies and programmes of elected officials in their exercise of statutory and common law powers. The Singapore public service employs some 150,000 public officers who work in 16 ministries and on more than 50 statutory boards.[1]

Much of the angst in other jurisdictions relates to whether the administrative state, vested with the Diceyan nightmare of extensive discretionary powers, subverts the RoL or is able to vindicate it,[2] with administrative law requiring reasonableness and fairness in the decision-making process. The administrative state, where administrators also wield legislative and quasi-judicial powers through delegated legislation and administrative tribunals,[3] may distress adherents to the strict separation of powers (SoP), but is a feature of the modern state.

Within a strong state with an active developmentalist strategy, authority is centralised in cabinet government. Each ministry is headed by a minister, such that regulatory action executed by technocratic bureaucrats comes under political supervision. This may strengthen effective internal checks and balances, which is not ideal in terms of transparency.

The Singapore administrative state does not give rise to concerns about an emerging 'veritable fourth branch of government',[4] as in the USA, which acts independently of the executive and in disregard of constitutional values like democratic accountability and due process.[5] The Singapore legal system is renowned for its efficiency, and the concern here is to ensure not only the

[1] The Public Service, www.careers.gov.sg/.

[2] eg Cass Sunstein and Adrian Vermeule, *Law and Leviathan: Redeeming the Administrative State* (Harvard University Press, 2020).

[3] Richard Magnus, 'Transparent, Fair and Impartial: A Snapshot of Tribunals in Singapore' [2004] 84 Australian Law Reform Commission Reform Journal 33.

[4] *FTC v Ruberoid Co* 343 US 470, 487 (1952) (Justice Jackson dissenting).

[5] Neomi Rao, 'The Hedgehog & the Fox in Administrative Law' (2021) 150(3) Daedalus 220.

realisation of legitimate government policy objectives, but also citizen access to justice to remedy public wrongs. Administrative law typically deals with 'low politics' and extends protection beyond constitutional liberties to a variety of public law rights and interests such as licences.

As the Court of Appeal (CA) affirmed, 'Behind every theory of administrative law there lies a theory of the state'.[6] This underscores the importance of understanding the socio-economic and political context of a particular jurisdiction, to apprehend the nature and scope of judicial review as an external mechanism for controlling the administrative state. In Singapore, the context is framed by a non-liberal democratic setting and practice of legal communitarianism.

While communitarianism encompasses a family of theories, each one revolves around a vision of the community, the common good and the good citizen. Key aspects of Singapore communitarianism include trust in an activist government aided by an efficient bureaucracy, where social harmony and community interests are prioritised. Here, the instrumental role of law as a tool for effective governance is emphasised, moderated by an appreciation of the formal RoL in having clear rules and judicial review exercised by general courts,[7] which underpins legal and social order.

Through a top-down managerial style, the government has achieved stunning economic growth and human development, helming an extensive apparatus regulating life from the womb to the tomb. This economic development imperative, with the state playing the role of 'entrepreneur, regulator, venture capitalist and facilitator'[8] in facilitating industrialisation, international trade and attracting foreign investment, has been rendered a 'shared national aspiration for all sectors of Singaporean society'.[9] The integrity, competence and relatively low corruption associated with public institutions and the bureaucracy has won international praise[10] and broad domestic trust[11] in the interventionist state. Like well-oiled machinery, it is considered rational for government agencies to 'adopt an integrated and holistic approach' towards formulating and implementing government policies.[12]

[6] Carol Harlow and Richard Rawlings, *Law and Administration*, 3rd edn (Cambridge University Press, 2012) 1, cited in *Jeyaretnam Kenneth Andrew v AG* [2014] 1 SLR 345, [50].

[7] Supreme Court of Judicature Act (1969), First Schedule, s 27; Rules of Court 2021, Order 24 (Prerogative Orders).

[8] Connie Carter, *Eyes on the Prize: Law and Economic Development in Singapore* (Kluwer Law International, 2002) 126.

[9] Jolene Lin, 'The Judicialisation of Governance: The Case of Singapore' in Tom Ginsburg and Albert HY Chen (eds), *Administrative Law and Governance in Asia: Comparative Perspectives* (Routledge, 2009) 288.

[10] 'Singapore Ranked 5th least Corrupt Country in 2022' (*CNA.com*, 31 January 2023); 'HDB Wins International Award for Public Sector Innovation in Service' *Straits Times* (13 October 2014).

[11] PM Lee Hsien Loong described Singapore as a 'high trust society' where a system that 'delivers results for Singaporeans' gives people 'good reason to trust the government': Speech, PAP Convention, 28 November 2021, www.pap.org.sg.

[12] *City Developments Ltd v Chief Assessor* [2008] 4 SLR(R) 150, [17].

Writing in 2009, Lin suggested that the courts showed 'significant self-restraint' and 'great reluctance' to interfere with executive decisions, such that the 'judicialization of governance' was 'yet to come'.[13] The weak demand for external checks on the government through judicial control may reflect a conviction that the executive should enjoy maximum powers and the RoL serve primarily as an instrument of governance to advance the developmentalist agenda through clear rules and consistently enforced laws. Chinkin suggested in 1985 that the judiciary was 'well attuned' and supportive of government national policy goals. It was acceptable, for example, to weaken protection of individual rights to render effective schemes for the systematic development of land under the Land Acquisition Act, for the 'greater benefit of the community … leading to housing, employment and economic progress'.[14] Indeed, the High Court in 2006 noted that, given land scarcity, government authorities enjoyed great latitude and flexibility in determining land usage for public benefit. Courts would not 'sit as makers of policy', although discretionary powers were not limitless and stop 'where abuse of power begins' to ensure 'the very idea as well as ideal of the RoL' is not undermined, as such abuses are 'inherently repugnant to the very concept [and] practice of justice and morality itself'.[15]

This concern with the law's internal values is emblematic of the shift away from evaluating law in statist terms of efficiency and convenience, even at the expense of constitutional rights,[16] that was evident up until the early 2000s. Chief Justice Chan in his 2006 welcome reference underscored that efficiency was to be balanced against justice in service of the RoL. Attention was drawn to values including 'due process or procedural fairness, equal protection of the law, consistency and proportionality in sentencing, and rationality in decision-making'.[17] However, in times of emergencies, such as the COVID-19 pandemic, RoL values may be compromised where exigencies demand flexible and efficient decision-making. As such, government instructions may be ambiguous or found in instruments of questionable juridical status, such as press statements and website advisories. This does not augur well for legality and the capacity of rules to guide conduct.[18]

Arguments have been made to explain the relative 'dearth of administrative litigation' deemed 'somewhat surprising' given 'the high degree of regulatory

[13] Lin (n 9) 288.

[14] Christine Chinkin, 'Abuse of Discretion in Malaysia and Singapore' in Andrew Harding (ed), *The Common Law in Singapore and Malaysia* (Butterworths, 1985) 267.

[15] Phang J, *Teng Fuh Holding Pte Ltd v Collector of Land Revenue* [2006] 3 SLR(R) 507, [5], [36].

[16] In relation to an order to ban publications by the Jehovah's Witnesses publishing arm, the High Court stated 'any order other than a total blanket order' would be 'impossible to monitor administratively'. *Colin Chan v PP* [1994] 3 SLR(R) 209, [72].

[17] Welcome Reference, 22 April 2006, reprinted in (May–June 2006) *Inter Se* 07.

[18] BJ Ong, 'The Ideals of Law in a Health Crisis: Singapore's Legitimate Responses to COVID-19' (2020) Law and COVID-19 147, https://ink.library.smu.edu.sg/sol_research/3236.

activity by the numerous agencies',[19] for example, the 'relatively high regard'[20] in which the civil service is held, and the public perception that it was almost indistinguishably fused with the ruling government. However, this is not compelling today, given the uptick in the number of significant judicial review cases from 2010, which has continued with more people 'for a spectrum of reasons' seeking judicial review over decisions impacting their rights. The 'increasing complexity of regulatory environment' has also engendered 'closer scrutiny of how regulators exercise public power'.[21] Cases have been brought against professional bodies, private clubs, government ministries and statutory boards.[22]

While a central aspect of the judicial role in maintaining RoL to sustain a pro-business environment remains, the 'paucity of reported cases' involving administrative law principles and the 'less activist' approach towards ouster clauses that Chinkin wrote of in 1985 are no more.[23] The judicial mood has shifted away from a languorous attitude and the cursory application of British common law principles. Rather than 'formal lip service', there are efforts to create a 'distinctive'[24] theory and practice of administrative law, to indigenise public law 'sensitive to the needs and mores' of Singapore society.[25]

The courts have demonstrated caution towards administrative legal developments in other common law jurisdictions with a liberal bias. The 'foundations of the Singapore law on judicial review' are 'the common law principles developed in England prior to the influence and impact of European Union law'. Thus, circumspection is directed towards post-1972 Europeanised English administrative law, which has transformed into a more rights-oriented intensive degree of judicial scrutiny, as influenced by the European Court of Human Rights. Wariness is accorded to decisions from jurisdictions where judicial review is based on specific statutory regimes, such as the Australian Administrative Decisions (Judicial Review) Act 1977.[26]

Singapore courts have referenced Harlow and Rawlings'[27] traffic light metaphor, which explains judicial attitudes towards judicial review, and have identified themselves with the 'green light' approach, which is 'presently the most accurate reflection of the socio-political attitude in the existing Singapore milieu'.[28] This is contrasted with the English 'red light' model, where courts are

[19] Lin (n 9) 306.
[20] ibid 290.
[21] AG VK Rajah, 'Judicial Review – Politics, Policy and the Separation of Powers', Lecture, Singapore Management University, 24 March 2016, [2].
[22] eg *Chiu Teng v Singapore Land Authority* [2013] SGHC 262; *UDL Marine (Singapore) Pte Ltd v Jurong Town Corp* [2011] 3 SLR 94; *Tan Seet Eng v AG* [2016] 1 SLR 779.
[23] Chinkin (n 14) 264, 267.
[24] ibid 269.
[25] *Tang Kin Hwa v TCMPB* [2005] 4 SLR(R) 604, [27].
[26] *Yeap Wai Kong v Singapore Exchange Securities Trading Ltd* [2012] 3 SLR 565, [4].
[27] Harlow and Rawlings (n 6) 22–40.
[28] *Nagaenthran v AG* [2018] SGHC 112, [123].

the primary adversarial checks against administrative lawlessness.[29] This chapter examines the nature of the 'green light' model in Singapore administrative law and how it shapes the scope of judicial review, questions of standing and intensity of review where fundamental rights are concerned, in a context where the constitution, not Parliament, is supreme. The RoL as a constitutional norm is a strong candidate for grounding judicial review, as moderated by its interactions with other constitutional principles like democracy and SoP.

II. FORGING AHEAD, LOOKING BEHIND: THE PERSISTENT LEGALITY/MERITS DICHOTOMY AND THE GCHQ SECURITY BLANKET

Singapore's adoption of the 'green light' approach emphasises that the primary role of administrative law is not 'to stop bad practices' but to 'encourage good ones'.[30] However, while seeking to tread a distinctive path, the courts have not quite cut the umbilical cord in relation to the English ultra vires theory that the basis of judicial review is to enforce parliamentary intent.[31] This is evident in the invocation of the legality/merits dichotomy and the distinction between judicial review and appeal, where appellate courts enjoy a wider scope in evaluating the merits of a decision. Judicial review 'hinges on the legality of the decision', examining whether jurisdiction is exceeded, whether discretion has been abused or whether the tribunal has acted in bad faith, has acted irrationally or has breached natural justice.[32]

The legality/merit dichotomy is problematic as the difference is wafer thin[33] when it comes to accepted heads of substantive review like *Wednesbury* unreasonableness[34] or evaluating whether a decision-maker has properly directed

[29] *Jeyaretnam* (n 6) [49].

[30] AG Lucien Wong, 'The Rule of Law and the Duty of the Legal Service' Opening of the Legal Year, 9 January 2023, [26].

[31] *Cheng Vincent v MHA* [1990] 1 SLR(R) 38, [26].

[32] *Wong Keng Leong Rayney v Law Society of Singapore* [2006] 4 SLR(R) 934, [97].

[33] Thio Li-ann, 'The Theory and Practice of Judicial Review of Administrative Action in Singapore: Trends and Perspectives' in TM Yeo et al (eds), *SAL Conference 2011: Developments in Singapore Law between 2006 and 2010 – Trends and Perspectives* (Academy Publishing 2011), [56]. The problem is compounded insofar as the *GCHQ* categories sometimes bleed into each other. For example, 'illegality' is traditionally understood as derived from standards in the empowering statute and includes tests such as 'relevant consideration'. However, in *City Development Ltd v Chief Assessor* [2008] 4 SLR(R) 150, [17], relevant considerations could also derive from fairness, personal hardship or the general public interest. See Daniel Tan, 'An Analysis of Substantive Review in Singaporean Administrative Law' (2013) 25 SAcLJ 296; Jeffrey Jowell and Anthony Lester,'Beyond Wednesbury: Substantive Principles of Administrative Law' [1987] PL 368.

[34] As formulated by Lord Diplock in *CCSU v Minister for Civil Service* [1985] AC 374, 410G-H, irrationality referred to decisions 'so outrageous in defiance of logic and accepted moral standards', which opens the door to considering the merits or underlying policy, as some value judgement is involved in evaluating morality: Paul Daly, 'Wednesbury's Reason and Structure' [2011] PL 238.

itself on the facts.[35] In applying these tests, Singapore courts have evaluated the 'merits'[36] in the sense of weighing and balancing the evidence.[37] Thus, the dichotomy has been criticised as a slogan[38] unable to provide operative content. However, it continues to persist in the legal imagination, obscuring the competing principles and factors at play in appropriately scoping judicial review. Despite its fictive or rhetorical nature, it may have some utility as a reminder to exercise self-restraint in remembering who the primary decision-maker is. Its invocation is typically framed thus:

> [I]n judicial review the court is not concerned with the merits or correctness of the decision under review [and does not] substitute its own judgment for that of the decision-maker. In the exercise of its supervisory jurisdiction, the court confines itself to reviewing the decision making process, to ensure that the process met the standards of legality, rationality and procedural propriety …[39]

The courts are thought to violate the SoP in reviewing the 'merits' of a decision, going beyond the traditional '*GCHQ* grounds'[40] (illegality, irrationality, procedural impropriety) which reviews the decision-making process. If Parliament accords decision-making power to a tribunal, parliamentary intent would be subverted, not implemented, if the courts substituted their decision for that of the tribunal. This is orthodoxy where Parliament is supreme,[41] but its force is diminished where the Constitution is supreme. The ultra vires theory cannot account for the expansion of the supervisory empire over non-statutory bodies with the requisite public element, as in the seminal decision of *Datafin*,[42] which was judicially endorsed in *Yeap Wai Kong*;[43] nor can it justify the review of informal rules like circulars and guidelines, which the courts consider reviewable on

[35] Citing Lord Wilberforce, *SS for Education and Science v Tameside MBC* [1977] AC 1014, 1047D in *Re Fong Thin Choo* [1991] 1 SLR(R) 774, [27].

[36] On the possible meaning of 'merits', this could mean the 'weight' given a factor, examining the substance of a decision, evaluating whether evidence supports a conclusion or the remaking of the first instance decision by the court: see Paul Craig, 'The Nature of Reasonableness Review' (2013) 66 Current Legal Problems 131.

[37] It has been argued that by issuing a mandatory order in specific terms, the courts reviewed the case merits: see Kenny Chng and Andrea Soon, 'Revising Remedies and the Legality–Merits Distinction in Singapore Administrative Law: CBB v Law Society of Singapore [2021] SGCA 6' (2022) 22(1) OUCLJ 108.

[38] BJ Ong, 'The Unmeritorious 'Legality/Merits Distinction in Singapore Administrative Law' (2021) 16 AJCL 1, 3. See also Swati Jhaveri, 'Revisiting Taxonomies and Truisms in Administrative Law in Singapore' [2019] SJLS 351, 375 (calling for a presumption of reviewability).

[39] *Yeap Wai Kong* (n 26) [3]. This is rooted in *Chief Constable of the North Wales Police v Evans* [1982] 1 WLR 1155, which should arguably be read narrowly as attempting to confine the scope of natural justice, rather than as an organising administrative law principle: Ong (n 38) 5.

[40] Lord Diplock (n 34).

[41] Parliamentary supremacy is itself challenged by common law constitutionalism: see TRS Allan, *Constitutional Justice: A Liberal Theory of the Rule of Law* (Clarendon Press, 2003); *R (Jackson) v AG* [2006] 1 AC 262.

[42] *R v Panel on Take-overs and Mergers, ex parte Datafin plc* [1987] QB 815.

[43] [2012] 3 SLR 565.

grounds of unreasonableness, fettering discretion and providing actual notice to affected persons.[44] This reflects the RoL value that rules must be able to provide guidance, which justifies the common law precept that ignorance of the law is no excuse,[45] on the basis that the law is available and known. It is a constitutional requirement that delegated legislation be published in the official gazette, ensuring constructive notice.[46]

Where fidelity to parliamentary intent cannot serve as the sole basis for review, review may be justified by the RoL, abuse of power or fairness, for example. The CA in *Starkstrom v Commissioner for Labour*[47] identified three justificatory principles for the traditional threefold *GCHQ* grounds of review: first, the constitutional doctrine of SoP where judicial review of administrative legality is premised on a 'proper understanding' of the roles of the respective government branches 'in a democracy where the Constitution reigns supreme'; second, the need to uphold Parliament's intent where a statute confers executive powers; and third, the pragmatic concern about institutional competence and restraint over decisions with polycentric political considerations. Parliament's intent is important, but not determinative, in a constitutional order based on parliamentary primacy rather than supremacy.[48] To the extent the ultra vires theory grounded in parliamentary supremacy still lingers, this has somewhat restricted the trajectory in developing new grounds or robust review standards based on constitutional principles.

III. GOING GREEN?

In a 2010 extrajudicial speech, Chan Sek Keong CJ sought to allay a perceived 'sense of unease' about the 'dormant state of judicial review', stemming from a 'judicial partiality' to 'protect the mistakes of public authorities at the expense of the public'.[49] Apart from citing statistics and the common sense proposition that the party with the better case in law and on the facts wins,[50] Chan CJ noted that judicial review was 'a function of socio-political attitudes in the particular community'; he considered the 'green light' approach to be 'more appropriate

[44] *Lines International v STPB* [1997] 1 SLR(R) 52, [74], [78]. See Kenny Chng, 'Reconsidering the Legal Regulation of the Usage of Administrative Policies' [2022] PL 76.

[45] *Cheong Seok Leng v PP* [1988] SLR 565, [57], discussing *Blackpool Corp v Locker* [1948] 1 KB 349, 361.

[46] Constitution, Art 58. See *Cheong Seok Leng* (n 45) [61]. For Singapore legislation, see https://sso.agc.gov.sg.

[47] [2016] 3 SLR 598, [58].

[48] Kenny Chng, 'The Theoretical Foundations of Judicial Review in Singapore' [2019] SJLS 294, 301–02.

[49] Chan Sek Keong, 'Judicial Review – From Angst to Empathy' (2010) 22 SAcLJ 469, [12], [14].

[50] Of the 79 judicial review cases reported between 1957 and 2010, 27.8% of applicants were successful: ibid [14].

for Singapore'[51] than the combative executive–judiciary 'red light' approach. This ultimately boils down to whether state power is negatively or positively viewed.[52]

Judicial review protects legal rights, promotes good governance and is the 'principal engine of the RoL'.[53] The RoL ideal hosts a number of values which can be secured by judicial review. The 'red light' approach emphasises the importance of judicial review as constraining abuses of administrative power in rule-making or individualised decisions, resolving controversies according to 'the applicable rules of adjectival and substantive law'.[54] The UK courts developed a strong body of principles and robust judicial review to protect citizen rights from the intrusive actions of the expansive welfare state, in light of the perceived ineffectiveness of traditional institutional remedies such as 'ministerial responsibility, parliamentary oversight committees and public inquiries'.[55] When the UK Human Rights Act came into force in 2000, UK courts were empowered to issue declarations of incompatibility in evaluating statutes against European Convention of Human Rights norms and have developed more liberal rights-oriented interpretive approaches.

Judicial review as constraint is important in Singapore, although more modest than in the UK, as the recognised review grounds are less intrusive and the standing rules less liberal. 'Green light' judicial review upholds the RoL 'by articulating clear rules and principles which the Government may abide by', with the courts playing a 'supporting role in promoting good governance'.[56] Failed policies adopted by bad government are dealt with by general elections, while judicial review deals with bad governance.[57] Control should first come 'internally from Parliament and the Executive, by the Government holding itself to high standards',[58] placing emphasis on political checks 'through the political process and public avenues',[59] rather than aggressive judicial review on the merits. The emphasis on the role and sufficiency of non-judicial checks through political oversight or self-regulation downplays the protective role of judicial review over exercises of power. Indeed, it was suggested that there are fewer court cases given 'how the Government organizes its legal work', by regularly seeking the advice of the Attorney-General (AG) on the legality of their actions before making a decision or implementing a policy. As the government acts 'only when the green light is given', fewer wrong decisions are made.[60] Further, a

[51] ibid [29].
[52] ibid [37].
[53] Laws LJ, *R(Cart) v Upper Tribunal* [2010] 1 All ER 908, [34].
[54] *Tan Seet Eng v AG* [2016] 1 SLR 779, [1].
[55] Chan Sek Keong (n 49) [28].
[56] ibid [44].
[57] ibid [6].
[58] ibid.
[59] ibid [29].
[60] ibid [15].

public authority, in its relentless quest for perfection, will likely conduct a 'post-mortem' if it loses a case, to avoid future errors.[61]

As a descriptor of practice, the 'green light' approach views state power positively as a vehicle to give progressive effect to social policies; where trust in a responsive government which delivers socially desirable results is high, the need for active, intensive judicial scrutiny is less compelling. The courts, by providing guidance through articulating norms of good administration, play a complementary role in the governance project. In interpreting written law, statutory language is taken seriously in service of promoting the legislative purpose,[62] reflecting the primacy of parliamentary intention. Constitutional and common law norms must be factored into the interpretive process as, ultimately, the justification for judicial review is to uphold the rule of constitutional law and supremacy;[63] as Menon CJ noted, 'the legality of every exercise of power is ultimately referable to the Constitution',[64] which is 'emphatically the province and duty'[65] of the judiciary to expound.

IV. THE GREEN LIGHT THEORY AND ATTITUDES TOWARDS JUDICIAL REVIEW

The Singapore courts as the guardians of the RoL prevent government bodies 'from acting beyond' their constitutional powers, through exercising their Article 93 power 'to review the legality of legislative and executive acts'.[66] This is a key facet of legal constitutionalism which is moderated by the green light theory's predilection towards political constitutionalism, which foregrounds political forms of accountability and downplays the role of unrepresentative courts.

This attitude is evident in Chan Seng Oon J's provisional views in *Nagaenthran v AG*[67] on whether all errors of law are jurisdictional; if so, all ouster clauses would be ineffective as illegalities render a purported decision a legal nullity. This would 'effectively be facilitating the judicial review of administrative actions tainted by all errors of law',[68] disregarding ouster clauses. Chan J did not consider this consistent with the 'green light' approach, which he accepted as an accurate descriptor of Singapore socio-political attitudes. Presumably, if there were more types of reviewable errors, the number of judicial review challenges

[61] ibid [6].
[62] Interpretation Act 1965, s 9A.
[63] *Colin Chan v PP* (1994) 3 SLR(R) 209, [50]; *Nagaenthran v PP* [2019] 2 SLR 216, [74].
[64] Sundaresh Menon, 'Executive Power: Rethinking the Modalities of Control' (2019) 29 DJCIL 277, 294.
[65] ibid, citing *Marbury v Madison* US 137, 177 (1803) 294.
[66] *Law Society of Singapore v Tan Guat Neo* [2008] 2 SLR(R) 239, [143].
[67] [2018] SGHC 112.
[68] ibid [123].

would increase, promoting litigiousness and judicial overextension. However, the green light approach does not provide any specific guidance on developing review grounds or calibrating review intensities. It indicates a deferential attitude to considerations of institutional competence and propriety, informed by democracy and the SoP. This sustains the disposition to maintain the legality/merits dichotomy, even if thinking in terms of a legality–merits spectrum is apposite, for fear of judicial intrusion into the autonomy of political institutions. This attitude draws strength from the general social trust in authority and the belief that a strong government is needed to run a well-regulated, prosperous society. Thus, a higher level of trust in the government appears to translate into a less intrusive form of judicial review.

Here, the RoL's value is measured primarily not in terms of effective constraints, but in terms of the law as 'a trusted pragmatic tool' the strong state wields to achieve 'the pragmatic goals of the enterprise, Singapore Inc'. As such, Carter considered the RoL in Singapore 'has become rule *by* law', where law exhibits more holistic, communitarian, duty-based tendencies than rights-based, individualistic Western law.[69] Legal communitarianism appreciates the utility of law as a governance tool, and its normative orientation is seen in the premium placed on public order. Consensus-seeking through persuasive dialogue is officially prized over adversarial litigation and aggressive lobbying, consistent with the supporting role of judicial review in providing clear guidance for decision-makers to follow.

V. CASTING A GREEN PALLOR TOWARDS MORE INTRUSIVE GROUNDS OF JUDICIAL REVIEW

Singapore courts apply the traditional grounds of illegality, irrationality and procedural impropriety as categorised by Lord Diplock in the *GCHQ* case,[70] which may be influenced by constitutional norms such as equality guarantees.

Courts repeatedly insist they do not substitute their judgment for that of the executive, demonstrating fidelity to the SoP and recognising that the executive, with its democratic mandate, is ultimately responsible for making policy decisions. Each of the *GCHQ* grounds 'leaves wide latitude to the Executive'.[71] These three heads of review define the test for the 'lawfulness of an exercise of administrative discretion', engaging 'the *manner* in which the power is exercised'; as such, the scope of judicial intervention has traditionally 'been thought of as a limited one'.[72]

[69] Carter (n 8) 263.
[70] Lord Diplock (n 34) 410D–411B.
[71] Edwin Tong (Second Law Minister), 'Rule of Law, Judicial Review and the Sunlight of Scrutiny', 95 SPR, 4 March 2021.
[72] *Starkstrom* (n 47) [56]–[57].

As courts are experts on questions of procedure, and as the executive tends not to be threatened by corrected procedural mistakes, the courts have demonstrated a high level of comfort in vigorously discussing and developing aspects of natural justice, with individual judges differing on tests like the rule against bias.[73] A more conservative approach is taken with other *GCHQ* heads, particularly irrationality or *Wednesbury* unreasonableness, which stands on its own feet, distinct from 'illegality'.[74] The CA in *Tan Seet Eng v AG*[75] noted that a more deferential, less intensive standard of review to matters like national security was not antithetical to judicial scrutiny.[76]

A decision may be 'legal' in being 'within the legislative scheme' but may still be 'impugned for being substantively unlawful'.[77] Irrationality applies even if the decision-making process passes the hurdle of 'illegality', where the decision-maker acted within the scope of his statutorily conferred power, in good faith, satisfying the test of 'purpose' and 'relevant considerations'. Irrationality, however, is 'a more substantive enquiry' which 'seeks to ascertain the range of legally possible answers', asking whether an answer falling within that range 'is so absurd that no reasonable decision-maker could have come to it' after 'considering the correct factors'.[78] This clearly engages the merits of a decision, assessing the evidential basis and whether relevant factors were duly weighted,[79] while adhering to the principle of non-substitution,[80] where the courts do not replace the decision-maker's decision for their preferred choice.[81]

Rather than thinking of 'legality' and 'merits' in binary terms, it is more accurate to see it in a context-sensitive manner in terms of degrees of acceptable judicial intervention. The threshold for judicial intervention on ground of irrationality is 'relatively high'[82] as it applies only to decisions 'so outrageous

[73] See Phang JC, *Tang Kin Hwa v TCMPB* [2005] 4 SLR(R) 604; Menon JC, *Re Alan Shankar* [2007] 1 SLR(R) 85. The CA, comprising both these judges, pronounced authoritatively on this issue in *BOI v BOJ* [2018] SGCA 61.

[74] *Tan Seet Eng v AG* [2016] 1 SLR 779, [77]–[80].

[75] [2016] 1 SLR 779, [137]–[142].

[76] ibid [95], [105], citing Aileen Kavanagh, 'Defending Deference in Public Law and Constitutional Theory' (2010) 126 Law Quarterly Review 222, 241.

[77] ibid [80].

[78] ibid.

[79] The CA in *AG v Ng Hock Guan* [2004] 3 SLR(R) 253, [27] considered that the judge had not given undue weight to some offending phrases in a police disciplinary report, upholding the finding that the relevant officer had a prejudiced mind that was irrational. See *Lines International* [1997] 1 SLR(R) 52, [85] [89], where a factor which influenced the guidelines was not 'really substantial', so the guidelines were not irrational. The merits are considered to the extent needed to determine the decision's legality.

[80] *Tan Seet Eng* (n 74) [97].

[81] The High Court effectively held that the Strata Title Board's decision to fix a hearing on a date after the expiry of its mandate was irrational as an exercise in futility. This goes to the substantive wrongness of the decision itself, not how it was made: *Mir Hassan bin Abdul Rahman v AG* [2009] 1 SLR(R) 134.

[82] *Vijaya Kumar v AG* [2015] SGHC 244, [48].

in its defiance of logic or of accepted moral standards'[83] that no sensible person could have arrived at it. Reasonableness does not entail 'a single inevitable approach', there being an 'inherent latitude' in assessing reasonableness,[84] as there is room for reasonable people to differ on which possible course of action to take.

A. Proportionality

As 'irrationality' is an established ground of review, one might see it as the outer limit courts consider acceptable in applying review which purports not to engage with the merits. This is evident in rejecting proportionality review, which the CA in *Chng Suan Tze v MHA*[85] and *Chan Hiang Leng Colin v Minister for Information and the Arts* subsumed and treated as 'an adjunct of irrationality',[86] to operate as a factor which helps sketch out the parameters of the reasonable, rather than a determinative, structured test.[87]

Rajah J in *Chee Siok Chin v MHA* noted that proportionality was a Continental European concept imported into English law by dint of UK treaty obligations. It was thus never part of the common law or Singapore law.[88] Proportionality review was 'a more exacting requirement than reasonableness' where courts sometimes substituted their own judgment 'for that of the proper authority'.[89] The CA in *Chan Hiang Leng Colin*[90] noted Lord Ackner's observation that in investing the proportionality test 'with a higher status than the *Wednesbury* test' inquiring into the merits was unavoidable,[91] requiring the court 'to balance the reasons, pro and con',[92] for a decision, evaluating the weight assigned to competing interests. Proportionality review would propel the court towards acting as primary decision-maker, closer towards 'the forbidden appellate jurisdiction'[93] than irrationality review would. Where rights are concerned, even if less restrictive methods are available, this disproportionate method does not render a decision irrational unless it can be shown that no

[83] Lord Diplock (n 34) 410.
[84] *Chee Siok Chin v MHA* [2006] 1 SLR(R) 582, [95].
[85] [1988] 2 SLR(R) 525, [121].
[86] [1996] 1 SLR(R) 294, [38].
[87] Proportionality review allows a court to examine 'whether legislative interference with individual rights corresponds with a pressing social need; whether it is proportionate to its legitimate aim and whether the reasons to justify the statutory interference are relevant and sufficient': *Chee Siok Chin* (n 84) [87]. This three-step test is more precise than the amorphous *Wednesbury* test.
[88] Hong Kong courts recognised proportionality as having roots dating back to Magna Carta: Bokhary J, *Leung Kwok Hung v HKSAR* [2005] HKCFAR 37 (8 July 2005), [169].
[89] *Chee Siok Chin* (n 84) [87].
[90] *Chan Hiang Leng Colin* (n 86) [40]–[41].
[91] *R v SS for the Home Department, ex parte Brind* [1991] 1 AC 696, 762.
[92] *Chan Hiang Leng Colin* (n 86) [44].
[93] Lord Lowry in *Brind* (n 91) 766.

reasonable decision-maker 'would use the proverbial sledgehammer to crack the figurative nut'.[94]

The purposeful subsuming by Singapore courts of proportionality review under irrationality review reflects a local sensitivity against juristocracy and the view that proportionality analysis contradicts the SoP.[95] There is also the fear that accepting proportionality review may increase the number of judicial review challenges, which would be 'inevitable if the threshold of unreasonableness is lowered', leading to costs in terms of time and money for litigants and courts, which negatively impacts the public.[96]

B. Substantive Legitimate Expectations

In discussing the suggestion of the High Court in *Chiu Teng v Singapore Land Authority*[97] to recognise substantive legitimate expectations (SLEs) as a ground of review, the CA in *Starkstrom v Commissioner for Labour*[98] opined this posed a severe constraint on policy-making and would entail a disruptive shift in the constitutional balance of power between the executive and courts.

Essentially, the idea of an SLE is that a public authority may be required to honour an unequivocal promise of a substantive benefit given to a group of people who detrimentally and reasonably relied upon it. When that authority changes policy, it is not allowed to renege if frustrating the expectation is 'so unfair' as to be tantamount to 'an abuse of power'. The court must then weigh what fairness requires against whether there is a 'sufficient overriding interest' to justify departing from what was promised.[99] This entails judicial concern over the substantive fairness of the outcome itself, not fair process,[100] in balancing the public interests and the applicant's private interests to decide 'the weightier concern'.[101] Were the judicial role extended to decide issues with polycentric considerations affecting third parties, this would require revisiting extant understandings of the SoP; whether the courts or executive should undertake this balancing exercise in protecting SLE was reserved for later determination.[102]

Both proportionality review and SLE, adopted in England but not all other common law jurisdictions, are products of the 'red light' approach, 'where there is a strong culture of challenging executive decisions in the court'.[103] While

[94] *Chan Hiang Leng Colin* (n 86) [46].
[95] *Xu Yuanchen v PP* [2023] SGHC 123, [84].
[96] *Brind* (n 91) 766, cited in *Chan Hiang Leng Colin* (n 86) [42].
[97] [2014] 1 SLR 1047.
[98] *Starkstrom* (n 47).
[99] *R v North and East Devon Health Authority ex p Coughlan* [2011] QB 213, 241H–242H.
[100] *Starkstrom* (n 47) [38], referring to Lord Woolf, *ex p Coughlan*, [65], [67], [70].
[101] ibid [62].
[102] ibid [62].
[103] Chan Sek Keong (n 49) [10].

unwilling to adopt these more intrusive review grounds, Singapore courts have shown receptivity to their underlying values, while seeking to accommodate this within the *GCHQ* framework. 'Proportionality' has been subsumed under irrationality, tempering the intensity of the independent proportionality review, which may 'require attention to be directed to the relative weight accorded to interests and considerations'.[104]

In staking out a middle ground between 'merits review' and 'no review', the CA noted that SLE values could be protected by preventing a public authority from ignoring a clear representation reasonably relied upon, but within 'the traditional framework of illegality, irrationality and procedural impropriety'. This could be done by means of a mandatory relevant consideration, where the decision-maker must confirm he has considered its representation in the balancing process, or through a duty to give reasons for how the public interest and legitimate expectation were assessed. This would fall under 'illegality' and 'procedural impropriety' respectively;[105] the *GCHQ* framework apparently is the judicial comfort zone, the site built on the premise that the SoP is respected insofar as the legality/merits dichotomy is maintained in fact, or as aspiration.

VI. FUNDAMENTAL RIGHTS AND REVIEW

There is a consciousness that more intensive scrutiny of executive action is warranted where fundamental rights are concerned, such as proportionality review would provide. English courts have developed a common law 'most anxious scrutiny' approach to address the gravity of interests involved, such as where life is at risk.[106] Thus, a lower standard of irrationality is applied in rights cases.

The CA in *Syed Suhail bin Syed Zin v AG*[107] stated the court had to be 'searching in its scrutiny'[108] where executive action affected life and personal liberty. Thus, the degree of scrutiny varies with the subject matter. In *Suhail*, the issue was whether Article 12 (equality) was violated in the scheduling of executions.

The decision clarified the applicable test was not that of 'deliberate and arbitrary discrimination', which connoted treating individuals in a manner lacking rationality. Rather, the test was whether there were legitimate reasons for treating two similarly situated persons differently. In other words, it was 'whether the differential treatment was reasonable'.[109]

104 Lord Steyn, *SS for the Home Department ex p Daly* [2001] UKHL 26, [27].
105 *Starkstrom* (n 47) [63].
106 *R v SS for the Home Department, ex parte Bugdaycay* [1987] AC 514, 531.
107 [2021] 1 SLR 809.
108 ibid [63].
109 ibid [61].

The test of reasonableness applicable to constitutional rights was distinct from the administrative law test, as treating individuals without rationality would 'fall foul of the ordinary principles of judicial review for irrationality or for taking into account irrelevant considerations'. Article 12(1) prohibited 'impermissibly discriminatory' acts and should be susceptible to challenge beyond ordinary judicial review grounds,[110] to provide enhanced review where constitutional rights were implicated. The CA was confident there were 'readily available standards' for assessing reasonableness in this context:[111] differential treatment would be legitimate only if it bore a rational relation to statutory purpose; legitimate reasons would be absent if differential treatment 'is based on plainly irrelevant considerations or is the result of applying inconsistent standards or policies without good reason'.[112] While relevant considerations falls within the *GCHQ* ground of 'illegality', it remains unclear whether what one might call a principle of consistency, which has not received extensive judicial attention, will develop as a stand-alone ground or as an aspect of rationality review whose intensity is varied according to context.[113] Incorporating consistency into the *GCHQ* ground of rationality, understood not to be a monolithic standard, may alleviate fears of cultivating over-intrusive judicial review which unduly fetters administrative discretion. This may help develop the standard of 'searching scrutiny' where rights are involved, which is meant to be more intensive than contextualised *Wednesbury* unreasonableness but less intrusive than structured proportionality review, which unabashedly entails merits review.

VII. THE GREEN LIGHT THEORY: CITIZEN PARTICIPATION AND STANDING IN PROMOTING GOOD GOVERNANCE

The degree to which a citizen is able to participate in the administrative decision-making process reflects the nature of democracy in a polity, affecting related RoL values like transparency and accountability. How judges develop the common law doctrine of standing will be shaped by the socio-political context.

If the green light approach emphasises seeking redress for administrative abuse outside the courts, one would not anticipate liberal standing rules in Singapore, akin to the Indian practice of public interest litigation. As noted in *Wong Souk Yee v AG*,[114] an applicant 'not seeking to protect some private

[110] ibid [57].
[111] ibid [61].
[112] ibid.
[113] See Thio Li-ann, 'Of Variable Standards of Scrutiny and Legitimate Legal Expectations: Article 12(1) and the Judicial Review of Executive Action' [2022] SJLS 1.
[114] [2019] 1 SLR 1223, [92].

interest' is 'unlikely' to have standing; if an applicant asserts a public right, he must demonstrate suffering 'special damage'.[115] In the main, standing requires individuals to have 'sufficient stakes'[116] in the case. Exceptionally, standing may be accorded where there is an egregious breach of a public duty which does not generate correlative private rights,[117] to avoid a detrimental legal lacuna where courts would be unable to 'vindicate the RoL and get the unlawful conduct stopped'.[118]

In the UK, 'public-spirited citizens and public interest groups' can 'effectively challenge executive decisions despite not having a direct interest in the outcome' through the 'sufficient interest' test, which focuses on the merits of a complaint.[119] Through lower standing requirements and legal aid, 'UK law incentivises and encourages administrative actions',[120] contributing to 'the robust state of judicial review litigation there'.[121]

In contrast, the concern in Singapore is that 'too many unmeritorious cases' may 'seriously curtail'[122] executive efficiency by devouring time and diverting resources from governing the country to defending judicial review applications. Taxpayer costs may rise if a legal system has to handle more cases, worthy or otherwise. What is to be avoided is seeking social reform through litigation, which opens the door to the influence of well-funded interest groups not necessarily reflecting 'the interests of the majority of ordinary people'.[123]

Under the 'green light approach', courts promote the public interest by 'applying a more discriminating test of locus standi' in balancing individual rights and 'the rights of the state in the implementation of sound policies in a lawful manner'.[124] The legality/merits dichotomy re-emerges in the scoping of standing rules primarily to address personal grievances, on the conviction that courts should not extrapolate upon policy matters which 'rightfully remains in the remit of proper political process',[125] underscoring the adversarial ethos of the legal system. It remains to be seen whether more relaxed standing rules will be developed in the future, to enable a politically maturing citizenry a greater role in containing government abuses.

In Singapore, there are no formal rights to be consulted on matters such as environmental governance; nor is there a US-style 'notice and comment'

[115] *Vellama v AG* [2013] 4 SLR 1, [33].
[116] *Jeyaretnam* (n 6) [63].
[117] ibid [64].
[118] *Jeyaretnam* (n 6) [60]–[61], citing Lord Diplock in *R v Inland Revenue Commissioners ex p National Federation of Self-employed and Small Business Ltd* [1982] AC 617, 644.
[119] Chan Sek Keong (n 49) [33].
[120] *Wong Souk Yee v AG* [2019] 1 SLR 1223, [93].
[121] Chan Sek Keong (n 49) [34].
[122] ibid [33].
[123] Wong (n 30) [28].
[124] Chan Sek Keong (n 49) [34].
[125] ibid [56].

guarantee of citizen participation in the formal rule-making process,[126] which courts enforce in promoting democratic values. Citizen participation is mainly channelled through informal consultations and government-hosted dialogue sessions seeking public feedback on policy proposals.[127] Individuals may approach their MPs with their concerns at 'meet the people' sessions, either virtually or in person,[128] in the posture of a supplicant rather than litigant. Civil society groups may prefer to stay on the track of informal consultation rather than alienating the authorities through confrontation, although petition may sometimes succeed, such as where environmental activists got the government to 'change its reclamation plans to preserve Tanjong Check Jawa', after being persuaded of 'the exceptional value of the site'.[129]

Given the asymmetries of powers between the state and citizen, the prospect of abuse can never be eliminated; however, governors and administrators who act in good faith, who course-correct and are willing to comply with the RoL when they lose judicial review cases and who are able to sustain socio-economic development and peace may earn enough trust to perpetuate the social compact. This may enable the green light approach of modest judicial review to sustain good governance, though this depends as much on having a good system of checks and balances as it does on good governors, which law cannot guarantee.

VIII. CONCLUSION: REDDISH STREAKS AND AMBER HUES

Singapore courts disavow the view of confining the judicial role to 'verifying as a clerical matter'[130] that a decision-maker has complied with statutory requirements. While adhering to the principle of non-substitution, this is distinct from judicial scrutiny of executive power, where the RoL requires the court 'to determine whether any public authority has crossed the line of legality'[131] and to invalidate unlawful decisions.

The courts are loath to abdicate the field and leave an applicant bereft of remedy. Even in the face of clauses that would limit proceedings against the Public Prosecutor to the two specified grounds of bad faith and malice under section 33(4) of the Misuse of Drugs Act, the court has rejected a literalist

[126] Li-ann Thio, 'Courts and Judicial Review' in Peter Cane et al (eds), *Oxford Handbook of Comparative Administrative Law* (Oxford University Press, 2020) 728–30.

[127] 'Our Singapore Conversation Themes Identified, Dialogue to Continue' *Today* (15 July 2013).

[128] 'Meet-the-People Sessions Go Hybrid: MPs Adapt as Engagement with Residents Shift Online' (*CNA.com*, 14 January 2022).

[129] PM Lee Hsien Loong's Harvard Club Speech, 6 January 2004, reproduced in *Petir*, 6 January 20024, https://petir.sg/2004/01/06/pm-lees-2004-harvard-club-speech-is-a-harbinger-of-his-vision-for-singapore/; see also Climate Conversations, 'How Passionate Activism Protected Chek Jawa's Wildlife' (10 September 2019) https://climateconversations.sg.

[130] *Tan Seet Eng v AG* [2016] 1 SLR 779, [97].

[131] Chan Sek Keong (n 49) [6].

reading. Aside from violating constitutional norms, which always frame statutory interpretation, the CA 'intuitively' deemed it 'inconceivable' that an applicant be 'left without a remedy' where evidence substantiates a public authority had considered irrelevant considerations.[132]

The courts have rejected more intrusive grounds of review, staying within the comfort zone of the *GCHQ* framework. Presumably, this is thought to shore up the legality/merits dichotomy, while being open to variable intensities of review, depending on the subject matter, such as national security or fundamental rights.

Perhaps the Singapore approach to legal communitarianism, judicial review and the administrative state is better captured by the 'amber light' descriptor, where a continual tussle exists over whether review should be muscular or restrained. This approach views state power positively, appreciating the need for both efficient and accountable governance. The courts play an important role in developing administrative principles and procedures to 'supplement the democratic, political controls over those who exercise state power',[133] seeking an optimal balance between the green light bent towards internal political controls and the red light preference for external legal checks to advance the rule of administrative law.

[132] *Muhammad Ridzuan v AG* [2015] 5 SLR 1222, [72].

[133] L Boulle, B Harris and C Hoexter, *Constitutional and Administrative Law: Basic Principles*, 19th edn (Juta, 1989) 80–83.

6

Judicial Review and Rights Jurisprudence

I. INTRODUCTION

IN A RULE of law (RoL)-governed society, the courts, in protecting rights, moderate the asymmetries of power in state–citizen relations. The preamble to the Universal Declaration of Human Rights (UDHR), which Singapore endorses, states 'human rights should be protected by the RoL'. Courts in Commonwealth jurisdictions are protective towards individuals in interpreting fundamental rights generously, to ensure they are fully enjoyed.[1]

This chapter examines judicial review as a legal mechanism for protecting rights. The Court of Appeal (CA) has linked both the government of constitutional institutions by the RoL and the guarantee of constitutional liberties to constitutional supremacy.[2] Both legislation and executive action which violate fundamental liberties may be directly challenged.[3] Critics have argued, with some justification, that judicial rights protection has been somewhat lacking, and at times parsimonious and parochial in rejecting rights-expansive arguments drawn from transnational sources, privileging statist values of efficiency and public order.[4] The perception is that aggrieved applicants are 'denied their rights' because courts are 'submissive to the Executive'.[5]

Singapore courts have rejected the values of liberal individualism and the heightened weight attributed to rights by European Convention of Human Rights (ECHR)-influenced English common law norms.[6] Liberal commentators have disparaged Singapore as a 'laggard state'[7] for rejecting intrusive

[1] *Ong Ah Chuan v PP* [1979–1980] SLR(R) 710, [23].
[2] *Tan Eng Hong v AG* [2012] SGCA 45, [60].
[3] *Colin Chan v PP* [1994] 3 SLR(R) 209, [50]; *Syed Suhail bin Syed Zin v AG* [2021] 1 SLR 809 (CA), [40]–[41].
[4] Li-ann Thio, '"Beyond the Four Walls" in an Age of Transnational Judicial Conversations: Civil Liberties, Rights Theories and Constitutional Adjudication in Malaysia and Singapore' (2006) 19(2) CJAL 428.
[5] Chan Sek Keong, 'Judicial Review – From Angst to Empathy' (2010) 22 SAcLJ 469, [14].
[6] *Chee Siok Chin v MHA* [2006] 1 SLR(R) 582, [87].
[7] Alec Stone Sweet and Jud Mathews, 'Proportionality and Rights Protection in Asia: Hong Kong, Malaysia, South Korea, Taiwan – Whither Singapore?' (2017) 29 SAcLJ 774, [51].

proportionality review, with a questionable commitment to the RoL and government accountability.

However, rejecting a Dworkinian 'rights-based' conception of the RoL[8] does not necessarily entail rejecting the RoL or adopting a Laodicean 'rule-following' version which merely affirms power. The idea of rights as autonomy-maximising trumps is not universally accepted,[9] under which courts seek to 'capture and enforce moral rights' grounded in community understandings, rather than metaphysics. Dworkin's theory rests on a vision of substantive justice, which is not uncontroversial; further, it is unclear why judges rather than elected legislators are better equipped to ascertain community understandings over intractable moral questions associated with fractious rights disputes.

Juristocracy is disdained, reflected in the judicial self-admonition not to be a 'mini-legislature' or 'super-legislature',[10] as it is 'undemocratic' and 'antithetical to the RoL' for judges to enact their 'personal values of what is just and desirable into law'.[11] The judicial tendency is to be 'leery'[12] of going beyond the constitutional text in the absence of constitutional norms like the US Ninth Amendment, which contemplates the possibility of unenumerated rights. Through the expansive development of the substantive due process doctrine in seminal cases like *Griswold v Connecticut*,[13] the US Supreme Court had moved to 'the center of the culture wars', finding unenumerated privacy or liberty rights, such as the right to abortion in *Roe v Wade*[14] and *Casey v Planned Parenthood*.[15] Not all courts are comfortable with such a position.

In what Justice Scalia trenchantly described as 'the passage that ate the RoL',[16] Justice Kennedy in *Casey* rooted liberty in 'the right to define one's own concept of existence, of meaning, of the universe and of the mystery of human life';[17] this manifests an 'insipid New Age solipsism' underlying the 'modern make-it-up-as-you-go-along judicial decision-making' that hides behind the 'living Constitution' euphemism.[18] Singapore courts stoutly

[8] Ronald Dworkin, *Taking Rights Seriously* (Harvard University Press, 1977) 272–73.

[9] *Shadrake Alan v AG* [2011] SGCA 26, [43], noting the 'clear and present danger' test was an outlier within Commonwealth jurisdictions.

[10] *Lim Meng Suang v AG* [2015] 1 SLR 26, [70], [77]. [82], [84], [93], [101], [173], [189]; *Chiu Teng v SLA* [2014] 1 SLR 1047, [113].

[11] *Yong Vui Kong v PP* [2015] 2 SLR 1129, [73], [75]; *Tan Seng Kee v AG* [2022] 1 SLR 1347, [245].

[12] Sundaresh Menon, 'Executive Power: Rethinking the modalities of control' [2019] 29 DJCIL 277, 297–98.

[13] 381 US 479 (1965).

[14] 410 US 113 (1973). This was struck down in *Dobbs v Jackson Women's Health Organisation* 597 US 215 (2022), where the Supreme Court held there was no constitutional right to abortion, returning the matter to state regulation.

[15] 505 US 833 (1992).

[16] *Lawrence v Texas* 539 US 558, 588 (2003).

[17] *Casey v Planned Parenthood* (n 15) 851.

[18] Edward Whelan, 'The Meta-Nonsense of *Lawrence*' (2006) 115 Yale LJ, http://yalelawjournal.org/forum/the-meta-nonsense-of-lawrence.

repudiate outcome-oriented 'living tree' legal interpretive approaches[19] based on (preferred) moral values. This undermines the RoL, as judicial partiality wrecks judicial legitimacy.

This stance that the judicial role is to 'say what the law is'[20] and not to be 'a front-runner for social change' is informed by the practical possibility of constitutional amendment to reflect 'the prevailing social mores as well as aspirations of Singapore society',[21] as the People's Action Party (PAP) government commands the required two-thirds parliamentary majority. The courts appreciate the creative nature of interpretation and 'making' law interstitially, through incremental common law development, but refrain from amending the Constitution by interpretation, effectively creating new constitutional rights.[22]

While authoritarian rule threatens constitutionalism, the High Court has observed that permitting 'unfettered individual rights' is 'the antithesis of the RoL – a society premised on individualism and self-interest'.[23] Adjudication involves a 'delicate balancing exercise' between rights and 'societal values, pluralism, prevailing social and economic considerations as well as the common good of the community'.[24] Communitarianism[25] as a local value is invoked as resistance against excesses of Western individualism and social decline.

The Attorney-General (AG) described 'freedom from crime' as a 'societal right', where 'the communitarian value of promptness and efficiency' in crime investigation is prioritised over the immediate right to counsel of the accused, while ensuring proper oversight over executive abuses.[26] If Singapore followed Western jurisdictions in prioritising the rights of the accused 'without balancing the rights of the society', it would not have 'the safe and crime-free society we have today'.[27] To unjustifiably impugn the integrity of public institutions harms a national good, such as when the people helming the Central Provident Fund were harassed by demonstrators. This would undermine the 'hard-won national dignity and a reputable international identity' Singapore 'public governance'[28] has earned. This vision of community interest may slide into an apology for the political status quo.

[19] *Tan Seng Kee* (n 11) [112].

[20] ibid [14].

[21] *Lim* [2015] (n 10) [92]; *Xu Yuanchen v PP* [2023] SGHC 123, [88].

[22] *Yong Vui Kong v PP* [2010] 3 SLR 489, [59].

[23] *Chee Siok Chin* (n 6) [52].

[24] ibid.

[25] White paper on Shared Values (Cmd 1, 1991) [24]. See Jothie Rajah, 'Punishing Bodies, Securing the Nation: How Rule of Law Can Legitimate the Urbane Authoritarian State' (2011) 36(4) Law & Social Inquiry 945, 960–63.

[26] VK Rajah SC, 'Judicial Review – Politics, Policy and the Separation of Powers', Guest Lecture, Singapore Management University, 24 March 2016, [23].

[27] K Shanmugam (Home Affairs and Law Minister), Second Reading, Foreign Interference (Countermeasures) Bill, 4 October 2021, [347], www.mha.gov.sg.

[28] *Chee Siok Chin* (n 6) [133].

Even if communitarianism is opposed to the organicist state, there is always a danger it may be invoked to smuggle in statist values. Communitarianism poses a limit to state power, where mediating institutions like families, religious groups, trade unions and professional associations come between the state and individual. Communitarianism envisages that these various communities will seek consensus about the common good, rather than through top-down diktat. In tandem with the developmentalist imperative, 'communitarianism' is associated with prioritising community interests in a disciplined social order over civil-political rights, to maintain the political stability needed for economic growth. However, it was appreciated that with development, a 'more differentiated political system' would emerge, but not necessarily in the Western liberal democratic image.[29] There may be common conceptions of ideals like the RoL and democracy but variable conceptions of RoL values and how these are implemented.

Today, as one of the richest countries in the world, ranking 10/191 on the 2021 Human Development Index,[30] Singapore is undergoing a modest degree of political liberalisation, in response to growing desires for 'a greater diversity of views in politics'.[31] In relation to defences to political libel, the courts are open to recalibrating the balance and providing greater rights protection if there is 'sufficient evidence' of changing socio-political values, manifested in laws and institutions providing 'greater accountability and transparency' and encouraging 'democratic participation' in Singapore political affairs.[32]

In assessing the development of rights jurisprudence, it is important to note there have been three 'waves' of approaches towards constitutional interpretation, which are not necessarily linear, as mentioned in chapter one.[33] In brief, the first wave was driven by judges, for whom constitutional law was 'little more than an extension of English administrative law, transposed to suit local conditions'.[34] The second wave marked the shift from thinking *administratively* to thinking *bureaucratically*, where Yong CJ demonstrated an eclectic methodology in embracing and disdaining extra-textual interpretive approaches but was ideologically consistent in his statist predilection and forging of public order trumps. The third wave, in the twenty-first century's

[29] Wong Kan Seng (Foreign Minister), 'The Real World of Human Rights' (World Conference on Human Rights, 16 June 1993) Press Release No 20/JUN09-1/93/06/16/, 8.

[30] Global Finance, 'Richest Countries in the World 2024' (30 January 2024) https://gfmag.com/data/richest-countries-in-the-world/; UNDP Human Development Reports: https://hdr.undp.org/data-center/human-development-index#/indicies/HDI.

[31] Indranee Rajah, Ministerial Statement, 'Duties and Privileges of the Leader of the Opposition', 31 August 2020.

[32] *Review Publishing Co v Lee Hsien Loong* [2010] 1 SLR 52, [274].

[33] Li-ann Thio, Principled Pragmatism and the "Third Wave" of Communitarian Judicial Review in Singapore in Jaclyn Neo (ed), *Constitutional Interpretation in Singapore: Theory and Practice* (Routledge, 2016) 78–89.

[34] Kevin YL Tan and Thio Li-ann, *50 Constitutional Moments that Defined a Nation* (Marshall Cavendish 2015) 20.

first decade, marks the beginning of a maturing, autochthonous public law, when the Bench, headed by Chan CJ and Menon CJ, showed they were thinking *constitutionally*, in articulating rights theory and declaring unwritten constitutional norms shaping the scope of judicial review. Judgments today regularly engage with international and comparative law, attempt to frame balancing along more structured lines and seek to apply greater judicial scrutiny in fundamental rights cases.[35]

Part II of this chapter examines the general rights jurisprudence, focusing on how open-textured norms are construed, when rights may be implied, whether transnational influences buttress rights-based arguments and the 'balancing' approach adopted in constitutional adjudication. It examines whether there has been a shift from a statist to a more communitarian review able to adequately secure rights, or whether rights are treated as defeasible interests. It considers if the era of under-theorised decisions has yielded to an RoL culture of judicial reason-giving. Part III focuses on the scope of political speech through the lens of political libel and the common law offence of 'scandalising the court', which was placed on a statutory footing in 2016 under the Administration of Justice (Protection) Act (AJPA). These two topics have attracted the most criticism, with charges that a 'compliant' judiciary has dampened political dissent.[36] Many of these critiques have not assessed latter-day developments, and the question of whether these changes sufficiently safeguard political speech, defrosting the 'chilling' effect, is investigated.

II. RIGHTS JURISPRUDENCE IN GENERAL: PROTECTING RIGHTS, ESCHEWING RIGHTISM

The Part IV chapter on fundamental liberties in the Constitution is an abbreviated list of rights drawn from the Malaysian bill of rights,[37] itself influenced by the Indian Constitution.[38] It contains only civil-political rights, as socio-economic rights were considered non-justiciable;[39] issues like homelessness are thus addressed in the political arena.[40]

[35] *Syed Suhail bin Syed Zin* (n 3) [63].

[36] The allegations of judicial bias could stem from 'the very high number of cases won by the Government or members of the ruling party' in contempt proceedings or defamation suits, 'brought against critics of the Government, be they individuals or the media': Param Cumaraswamy, Report, Special Rapporteur on the Independence of Judges and Lawyers, Commission on Human Rights, 52nd Sess, 18, UN Doc E/CN.4/1996/37, [218].

[37] *Yong* [2010] (n 22) [61].

[38] *Sugumar Balakrishnan v Pengarah Imigresen Negeri Sabah* [1998] 3 Mal LJ 289, 307H–I.

[39] 'Indians Ask for Seven Basic Rights in S'pore Charter' *Straits Times* (3 March 1966) 5.

[40] Destitute Persons Act (Welfare Homes), 84 SPR, 22 January 2008, col 305; 'Addressing Homelessness Problem as Reported in Study of over 1000 People Sleeping in the Rough', 94 SPR, 6 January 2020.

Malaysia's Article 13, requiring adequate compensation for compulsorily acquired property, was excised from the Singapore Constitution. This was to facilitate the agenda of the developmentalist state through extensive acquisition powers, to achieve the objective of universal homeownership and to manage land to promote economic activity and build public services. Removing property rights is considered to be inconsistent with the RoL[41] but justified in terms of elevating 'the public interest above individual property rights'; compensation for property acquired for a 'public purpose' is handled by a tribunal under the Land Acquisition Act. As such, the land 'actually went towards public usage, as opposed to into private pockets', admittedly 'a classic example of socialism'. This policy was a determinative factor in Singapore's success, allowing rational land-use planning, which has led to 77 per cent of the resident population living in public housing built on acquired land, of which about 90 per cent own their homes, building world-class infrastructure and facilitating manufacturing industries.[42] This is integral to the right to development, which Singapore considers inalienable.[43]

A. Rights by Implication

The right to own property was one of four rights the 1966 Constitutional Commission proposed for constitutional incorporation, along with the prohibition against torture or inhuman treatment (PATI), the right to elect a government by secret vote and the right to a judicial remedy for rights violations.[44] While the last right is in practice enjoyed through judicial review, the right to vote has been recognised as an implied constitutional right, whereas PATI has not. The judicial reasoning on when unwritten rights will be recognised is instructive.

First, the courts have rejected the idea of unenumerated rights, associated with 'first principles of natural law'; this is envisaged as appealing to subjective normative preferences associated with Enlightenment naturalism, rather than an objective natural rights theory based on practical reason in the stream of perennial jurisprudence.[45] There was no 'natural law' basis in *Yong Vui Kong v PP*[46] (*Yong* [2015]) for reading in PATI, there being no singular view of what natural law requires of judges.

[41] World Justice Project Rule of Law Index (2010).

[42] Speech, Home Affairs & Law Minister K Shanmugam, Judicial Executive Programme, 21 November 2022, [55]–[64], www.mlaw.gov.sg.

[43] eg ASEAN Human Rights Declaration (2012), [35], https://asean.org/asean-human-rights-declaration/.

[44] *Report of the Constitutional Commission* (Singapore National Printers, 1966) 10–12, [40]–[44].

[45] Stephen Hall, 'The Persistent Spectre: Natural Law, International Order and the Limits of Legal Positivism' (2001) 12(2) European Journal of International Law 269, 273–79.

[46] *Yong* [2015] (n 11) [73].

Second, the CA in *Daniel de Costa Augustin v AG* recognised the right to vote as a constitutional right anchored in the text, derived from 'construing' the constitution 'in its entirety' or through 'necessary implication' from Articles 66 and 39(1), which relate to elections.[47] The right to vote was implied as it was necessary to operationalise a parliamentary system based on competitive elections. In suggesting the right to vote could be part of the Singapore Constitution's 'basic structure', the CA in *Yong* [2015] noted that in 2011 the government had acknowledged that the right to vote was 'implied within the structure of our Constitution' and 'is fundamental to a representative democracy'[48] embodied in Singapore Westminster parliamentarianism.[49] It is unclear whether 'basic structure' refers to a foundational aspect of the constitutional order or an immutable feature, after the Indian basic features doctrine,[50] which the courts have not accepted.

The CA opined that something must be 'fundamental and essential to the political system'[51] to be part of the basic structure. Conceptually speaking, the constitution is a power-limiting tool and the CA approvingly quoted an opinion that fundamental rights were not part of the basic structure as they relate to individual rights, rather than defining 'the powers of and checks on each organ of the State'.[52] In this sense, the 'basic structure' was no more than a truism that 'the Constitution rests on an overarching principled framework embracing the precepts of the RoL and the SoP [separation of powers]'.[53] The CA in *Yong* [2015] concluded there was 'nothing inherent' in the constitutionally established government system 'which requires a finding that the PATI forms part of its basic structure'.[54]

If the criterion for being part of the basic structure is that a constitutional norm is power-limiting, this reasoning is unconvincing, as fundamental liberties limit both executive and legislative power. More likely, a distinction has been drawn between rights associated with the workings of a constitutional institution and more 'free-standing' rights pertaining to the individual. If a more

47 [2020] 2 SLR 621, [9].

48 Wong Kan Seng (Home Affairs Minister), 73 SPR, 16 May 2001, col 1725, cited in *Yong* [2015] (n 11) [69].

49 *Vellama v AG* [2013] 4 SLR 1, [79].

50 *Kesavananda v State of Kerala* AIR 1973 SC 1461, referenced in *Yong* [2015] (n 11) [69].

51 *Yong* [2015] (n 11) [71]. In *Ravi v AG* [2017] 5 SLR 489, [69], [73], the High Court opined that an unqualified right to stand for public office was not 'fundamental and essential' to the constitutionally established political system. This was raised to challenge the onerous Art 19 qualifications to run for the elected presidency. See *Wong Souk Yee v AG* [2019] 1 SLR 1223 for the possible existence of an implied right to be represented by a full slate of members in a multi-member constituency, noting it did not follow that there was a 'particular form of representation' which could not be departed from: [72], [76], [78].

52 Citing Calvin Liang and Sarah Shi, 'The Constitution of Our Constitution, A Vindication of the Basic Structure Doctrine' *Singapore Law Gazette* (August 2014) 12, [38], [46]; *Yong* [2015] (n 11) [71].

53 *Ravi* (n 51) [66].

54 *Yong* [2015] (n 11) [72].

cosmopolitan approach were adopted, rights such as the PATI, which the 1966 Constitutional Commission identified as a 'fundamental human right',[55] could well be considered part of the basic law. The CA has recognised that the PATI is an international peremptory norm in *Yong* [2015],[56] or it could be viewed as a right which positive instruments recognise rather than create, being 'inherent and fundamental to democratic civilised society'.[57]

Article 9(1) of the Constitution provides that no person shall be deprived of life or personal liberty 'save in accordance with law'. An argument to read into 'law' an inhuman punishment prohibition to challenge the mandatory death penalty (MDP) in *Yong Vui Kong v PP* (*Yong* [2010])[58] was rejected, by reference to constitutional history. The 1966 Constitutional Commission had recommended such a prohibition in a proposed Article 13. Although the government stated in principle that no one should be subjected to torture, without specifically referring to inhuman punishment, Article 13 was, for reasons unknown, not included. It was reasonable to assume there was no overlap between Article 13 and Article 9(1), otherwise the latter would be redundant.[59] The court could not, 'under the guise of constitutional interpretation',[60] read into Article 9(1) a right the government 'decisively rejected' in 1969; the proper route would be to amend the Constitution. The CA underscored that the government had stated that torture was wrong and was a crime, without commenting on whether imposing the MDP for drug-trafficking offences constituted inhuman punishment.[61]

Thus, constitutional rights may only be implied where needed for the workings of the government system. The government has declined to expressly enact a right to vote, on the basis that it is now well established and that its suggested entrenchment in 1966 was because Singaporeans then had little experience of general elections and did not sufficiently cherish choosing their governors.[62] If an express right were adopted, this could give rise to constitutional issues, as the electoral scheme for multi-member constituencies designed to secure multiracial representation may contravene the equality clause, as acknowledged by the notwithstanding clause in Article 39A(3).

As things stand, a litigant is obliged to establish the 'precise content' of a right to vote and to demonstrate it is violated; while the CA in *de Costa*[63] accepted that elections should be free and fair, what this constituted was

[55] *Report of the Constitutional Commission* (n 44) [40].
[56] *Yong* [2015] (n 11) [27].
[57] Lord Cooke, *R (Daly) v SS for the Home Department* [2001] 2 AC 532, 548, dealing with access to legal advice.
[58] *Yong* [2010] (n 22).
[59] ibid [64], [71]–[72].
[60] ibid [122].
[61] ibid [75].
[62] K Shanmugam (Law Minister), 'Legal Status of the Right to Vote and Entrenchment', 85 SPR, 13 February 2009, cols 3157–61. See Thio Li-ann, 'Westminster Constitutions and Implied Fundamental Rights: Excavating an Implied Constitutional Right to Vote', [2009] SJLS 406.
[63] *de Costa* (n 47).

'contestable'; the appellant had to specifically show that a pending election was conducted 'in a constitutionally impermissible manner'.[64] This cannot be ideal, as it is not clear what standards a litigant might reference in contending unfairness, rising to a rights violation. An enacted right, complete with normative standards of fairness, which could be judicially developed, would provide greater protection. Regrettably this has not been the path taken for this fundamental political right.

B. Interpreting Rights and Transnational Influences

The impact of international and foreign legal sources on expansive rights interpretation is minimal owing to the nationalist approaches towards construing Part IV of the Constitution. Despite affirming that the Constitution should be read 'primarily … within its own four walls',[65] the courts have regularly looked to foreign cases for inspiration, as anti-model and as an interlocutor, such as when considering whether the Euro-American doctrine of compelled speech should apply to Protection from Online Falsehoods and Manipulation Act (POFMA) Correction Directions.[66] This is further explored in discussing contempt and political libel cases.

Foreign constitutional cases are of persuasive value, and courts are aware these may be selectively cited to bolster a legal argument. For example, pointing to developments in other jurisdictions in relation to decriminalising sodomy was unhelpful as 'such examples can be countered by examples of areas where there are shifts in the opposite direction'. As an 'independent nation with its own unique history, geography, society and economy', Singapore would find its own way over fractious issues implicating social mores,[67] with Parliament taking the lead over issues involving moral questions, which call for 'continued discussion and open-ended resolutions', rather than the 'win–lose outcomes' of adversarial litigation.[68]

Resistance has been demonstrated towards Europeanised English cases as well as cases from the Caribbean, whose constitutions were modelled after the ECHR; while the ECHR was applicable to Singapore and Malaysia during British colonial rule, it ceased to apply upon Independence. Unlike Caribbean constitutions, the Singapore Constitution does not contain an inhuman punishment prohibition; as such, Caribbean 'inhuman punishment' cases are irrelevant to interpreting 'law' under Singapore's Article 9.

[64] ibid [13].
[65] Thomson CJ, *Government of the State of Kelantan v Government of the Federation of Malaya and Tunku Abdul Rahman* [1963] Mal LJ 355, 358, approvingly cited in *Colin Chan* (n 3) [51].
[66] *TOC v AG* [2021] SGCA 96, [68]–[80].
[67] *Lim Meng Suang v AG* [2013] 3 SLR 118, [133].
[68] *Tan Seng Kee* (n 19) [4]–[5], [7]–[8], [14].

Nonetheless, the courts do demonstrate a non-parochial awareness of competing foreign standards, such as when considering whether caning as corporal punishment constitutes 'torture', which imports a greater intensity of suffering than 'inhuman punishment'.[69] In *Yong* [2015], the CA considered a wide range of cases brought to their attention, concerning what international courts identified as 'torture'. This included extra-legal acts of abuse committed by public officers to extract information from detained individuals, subjecting victims to electrocution, severe beatings, sodomy by object and 'Palestinian hanging', which the European Court of Human Rights (ECtHR) and the International Criminal Tribunal for the Former Yugoslavia considered torture. The level of physical and mental suffering 'seemed to us to far exceed that caused by a sentence of caning'.[70] Judicial corporal punishment was considered to be inhuman punishment in cases from Zimbabwe, Namibia, South Africa and Zambia; the ECtHR in *Tyrer v UK*[71] found juvenile birching – the whipping of a boy's clothed posterior with a light cane – to be 'degrading punishment'.[72]

Comparatively, Singapore practice was considered less severe than how corporal punishment was inflicted in Trinidad and Tobago and the Sudan. In *Caesar v Trinidad and Tobago*,[73] a person convicted of attempted rape was subject to 15 lashes with a cat-o'-nine-tails, while in *Curtis Francis Doebbler v Sudan*,[74] two female students received 25–40 lashes each with a wire and plastic whip for 'immorally' talking with boys and wearing trousers. In *Caesar*, the lashing was expressly considered torture, while in *Doebbler*, Article 5 of the African Charter on Human and Peoples Rights, which prohibits 'torture, cruel, inhuman or degrading punishment and treatment', was found violated, although the African Commission mostly spoke of 'inhuman punishment'.

Bearing in mind the Singapore Constitution does not prohibit inhuman punishment, the CA in *Yong* [2015] noted that, unlike these cases, caning was administered in private, with a cane of a specified diameter, on the prisoner's buttocks to minimise injury risks to the bones and organs. Strokes were meted out at regular intervals in a measured, controlled manner, and under medical supervision.[75] Caning in Singapore was thus 'less severe than the flogging in *Caesar*' and 'different from the public lashing of the female students in *Doebbler*';[76] the CA considered that the safeguards attending caning ensured it did not 'breach the high thresholds of severity and brutality' to be regarded as torture.[77]

[69] *Ireland v UK* [1978] ECHR 1, [167], cited in *Yong* [2015] (n 11) [83].
[70] *Yong* [2015] (n 11) [85].
[71] [1978] ECHR 2, cited in *Yong* [2015] (n 11) [86].
[72] ibid [86].
[73] Series C, No 123, Judgment of 11 March 2005 (Inter-American Court of Human Rights), cited in *Yong* [2015] (n 11) [87].
[74] (2003) AHRLR 153 (African Commission on Human and Peoples Rights), cited in *Yong* [2015] (n 11) [88].
[75] Cited in *Yong* [2015] (n 11) [89]–[90], [99].
[76] Cited in ibid [90].
[77] Cited in ibid [99].

As for international law, Singapore courts espouse a dualist approach under which international law and domestic law are seen as two separate legal systems. Treaties are not self-executing and need to be legislatively enacted to have domestic application. Treaties such as the Convention for the Elimination of All Forms of Discrimination against Women would not automatically introduce new prohibited grounds of discrimination under Article 12(2), for example.[78]

Thus, their transformative potential in relation to rights litigation is dulled where legislation is not adopted to give 'horizontal' effect to treaties[79] relating to discrimination against women, racial discrimination or the rights of children or disabled people. Either Singapore law is presumed to already be consistent with international standards or treaty norms are implemented through policies and 'soft' codes.[80] Courts reference human rights treaty norms to demonstrate that these reiterate domestic rules, such as Article 18 of the Convention on the Rights of the Child, which resonates with section 46(1) of the Women's Charter, relating to joint parental responsibility.[81]

Customary human rights norms must be recognised by courts to have domestic legal effect,[82] and courts must be satisfied that any customary international law (CIL) rule is 'clearly and firmly established before its adoption by the courts'.[83] The courts have noted there is no CIL general prohibition against the death penalty, citing UN reports listing the number of retentionist and abolitionist countries,[84] manifesting a lack of 'the extensive and virtually uniform'[85] state practice needed for a norm to have CIL status. The same was demonstrated by pointing to the continuing use of the MDP for drug-related offences by a 'significant number of states'; the court did not accept there was a CIL norm prohibiting the MDP as inhuman punishment.[86]

This is consonant with the government's view that the death penalty may have a role in securing the sanctity of life and the larger societal interest in safety and security, where strictly applied in a context with 'an unwavering commitment to the RoL' based on independent courts observing due process. The death penalty has enabled Singapore to successfully fight the drug problem by treating drug trafficking as a most serious crime with due

[78] *Lim* [2015] (n 10) [188].

[79] Only the Convention on the Prevention and Punishment of the Crime of Genocide, acceded to in 1995, has been domestically enacted –as s 6B of the Penal Code in 2007 – which has little quotidian significance.

[80] Li-ann Thio, 'Reception and Resistance: Globalisation, International Law and the Singapore Constitution' (2009) 4(3) NTU L Rev 335.

[81] *CX v CY (minor: custody and access)* [2005] 3 SLR 690, [26].

[82] *Yong* [2010] (n 22) [91].

[83] *Nguyen Tuong Van v PP* [2005] 1 SLR(R) 103, [88]. See generally, Thio Li-ann, 'International Law in the courts of Singapore: Still a Little Island?' (2013) 19 Asian YBIL 1.

[84] *Nguyen* (n 83) [92].

[85] *North Sea Continental Shelf Cases* [1969] ICJ Rep 3, [74].

[86] *Yong* [2010] (n 22) [96], [98]. The AG noted 31 states applied the MDP to drug-related and serious offences: [94].

consideration accorded to 'its impact on the immediate and third party victims, as well as on society at large'. This balance reflects the commitment to legal communitarianism, buttressed by high public support for such laws. International consensus is lacking 'for or against the death penalty' such that sovereign states should determine what criminal law model serves the people's welfare.[87]

Thus, where there is no clear CIL norm or disagreement over the content of an established CIL norm,[88] invoking international law will not assist a rights claim. Where the executive considers religious freedom does not encompass conscientious objection to military service, the courts will defer to such assessment.[89] Where a clear CIL exists, Singapore courts will presumptively interpret domestic law consistently with Singapore's international legal obligations; for example, caning in Singapore must not violate the international law prohibition against torture, 'absent express legislative provision'.[90] This is subject to 'inherent limits',[91] such as where the constitutional text or history militates against incorporating a human rights norm, unless Parliament amends the Constitution or enacts new law needed for the courts to give 'full effect' to international human rights norms. Further, even if there was a CIL inhuman punishment prohibition a Singapore statute contravened, CIL norms are incorporated as part of domestic common law, ranking below statutes. At best, invoking a human rights violation may have moral influence in demonstrating non-compliance with international obligations. Indeed, even *jus cogens* norms, like the prohibition against torture embodied in Article 5 UDHR, only have the rank of common law norms upon reception. The CA stated it would be undemocratic to accord constitutional status to international norms, as this would allow other states to dictate the Constitution's meaning 'regardless of what the people of Singapore, expressing their will through their elected representatives, think'.[92] Insofar as respecting international human rights obligations is part of the RoL, this is qualified by considerations of popular sovereignty.

[87] MFA Press Release: Transcript of Minister Vivian Balakrishnan's Intervention at the High-Level Side Event at UNGA, 'Moving Away from the Death Penalty: Victims and the Death Penalty' (21 September 2016) www.mfa.gov.sg/.

[88] eg the CA in *Nguyen* (n 83) [91]–[92] did not find a specific CIL prohibition against hanging as a mode of execution.

[89] Singapore Statement, General Debate on Item 2, 48th Regular Session of the Human Rights Council, 14 September 2021, www.mfa.gov.sg/Overseas-Mission/Geneva/Mission-Updates/2021/09/Statement-by-Singapore-HRC48-14-September-2021. The High Court in *Colin Chan* (n 3) [66] affirmed the government position that the Enlistment Act mandating compulsory military service for all male citizens does not recognize conscientious objection.

[90] *Yong* [2015] (n 11) [98].

[91] *Yong* [2010] (n 22) [59]. See Thio Li-ann, 'Reading Rights Rightly: The UDHR and Its Creeping Influence on the Development of Singapore PL' [2008] SJLS 264.

[92] *Yong* [2015] (n 11) [38].

C. Interpreting Open-Textured Rights and Rights Expansive Standards

Singapore judges avoid values-oriented interpretive methods which connect the law with their perception of evolving social values.[93] This can breed 'rightism', where courts are seen to intervene in the political decision-making process, inaugurating a 'rule by judges' which may impose rights-oriented, subjective value preferences through a covert liberal theory of the good.[94] This brand of philosophical liberalism is distinct from classic liberalism, as the state is remoralised[95] and ideologically prescriptive, rather than 'neutral' towards competing conceptions of the good.

'Rightism' is manifested firstly, by courts effecting rights proliferation through declaring unwritten rights or reading rights expansively through a 'living tree' methodology; and secondly, through an intensive brand of review which accords heavy or determinative to rights. Such courts are heroes or villains, depending on one's ideological orientation.

In Singapore, the involvement of courts in the culture wars is negatively viewed as judicial intrusion into the legislative province; a rights-centric approach driven by liberal individualism which valorises choice over what is chosen sits at odds with Singapore's mix of legal and political constitutionalism, manifesting communitarian, statist and liberal values which support an overt conception of communal solidarity and the common good.

This is illustrated by the judicial restraint when courts interpret broad terms like 'personal liberty' and 'life' under Article 9(1), which can be deprived 'in accordance with law'. The term 'law' is conditioned by standards like the fundamental rules of natural justice (FRNJ). The CA stated that Article 9(1) does not impose affirmative state duties,[96] stressing the importance of examining the historical precursor provisions to understand how Article 9(1) is appropriately contoured today. Article 9(1)'s genealogical origins were traced back to clause 39 of the Magna Carta by way of the US Constitution's 5th and 14th Amendments, Article 21 of the Indian Constitution and Article 5(1) of the Malaysian Constitution.

The CA rejected the expansive approaches Indian courts apply in construing 'life' to encompass rights to livelihood, health, medical care, education and

[93] Exceptionally, the CA in *UKM v AG* [2019] 3 SLR 874 took sides in the culture war, in assuming rather than interrogating what the child's best interest was, regarding a homosexual man desiring to adopt his biological son by a surrogate mother in the USA. See Tan Seow Hon, 'Surrogacy, Child's Welfare and Public Policy in Adoption Applications', [2019] SJLS 263.

[94] See Thio Li-ann, 'Rightism, Reasonableness and Review: Section 377A of the Penal Code and the Question of Equality – Part One' (2022) 34 SAcLJ 180, [59].

[95] eg the Indian courts have spoken in terms of promoting a substantive ideology in terms of a 'cult of egalitarian liberalism': *Navtej Singh Johar v UOI* AIR 2018 SC 4321; Writ Petition (Criminal) No 76 of 2016, [86]–[87].

[96] *Yong* [2015] (n 11) [16].

even a clean environment,[97] underscoring 'their unique social, political and legal circumstances'.[98] Although 'life' has not been authoritatively interpreted, Singapore courts consider the narrow reading given 'personal liberty' equally applicable, cabined by Article 9's context and structure.[99] The historical intent underlying the clause was underscored, such as where the Indian drafters of Article 21 inserted the word 'personal' before 'liberty' to prevent 'liberty' from being construed 'very widely' to encompass other freedoms, like expressive freedom, which had its own dedicated clause.[100]

The content of other Part IV liberties do not overlap with the ambit of Article 9(1). Article 9's five sub-clauses all contain procedural safeguards relating to arrested or detained persons, such as the right to counsel or habeas corpus.[101] The history, text and structure thus supports reading Article 9(1) to encompass only 'freedom from unlawful deprivation of life and unlawful detention or incarceration'.[102]

Thus, 'personal liberty' did not include a right to economic liberty able to prevent an *en bloc* condominium sale,[103] nor did it contain a right to erotic liberty so as to invalidate laws criminalising sodomy. The latter claim invoked 'privacy, human dignity, individual autonomy and the human need for an intimate personal sphere',[104] which is exemplary of an 'empty container' approach, filling terms like 'personal liberty' with the preferred philosophy *du jour*. The CA rejected the argument that a law criminalising sodomy was invalid because personal liberty included a 'limited right to privacy', which encompassed 'a right of personal autonomy allowing a person to enjoy and express affection and love towards another human being'. Equating 'love' with erotic love does not capture all forms of love.[105] The court noted this vague claim contained the 'seeds of an unlimited right' which could potentially 'encompass as well as legalise all manner of subjective expressions of love and affection'; this implicated 'broader societal morality',[106] better suited for legislative determination.

Nonetheless, the CA in *Yong* [2015] considered that limiting Article 9(1) to protection from unlawful execution, incarceration or detention was too 'parsimonious'. To enlarge it beyond the ambit of physical bodily restraint, it looked back into history and, engaging Blackstonian theory, found that 'personal

[97] eg *Bandhua Mukti Morcha v UOI* AIR 1984 SC 802, cited and followed in *Tan Tek Seng v SPP* [1996] 1 Mal LJ 261 (Malaysian CA).
[98] *Lim* [2015] (n 10) [48].
[99] ibid [45].
[100] *Yong* [2015] (n 11) [19].
[101] *Tan Seng Kee* (n 19) [248].
[102] ibid [252], affirming *Lim* [2015] (n 10) [45].
[103] *Lo Pui Sang v Mamata Kapildev Dave* [2008] 4 SLR(R) 754, [3], [6].
[104] *Tan Eng Hong v AG* [2012] 4 SLR 476, [120].
[105] For a discussion on love as *eros*, *storge*, *philia* and *agape*, see CS Lewis, *The Four Loves* (Mariner Books, 1971).
[106] *Lim* [2015] (n 10) [49].

liberty' also encompassed protections against the unlawful use of force to interfere with a person's bodily integrity.[107]

Consonant with the emphasis on text, history, precedent and theory as interpretive methods, the courts have refused to treat FRNJ as the local equivalent of the US substantive due process doctrine, the gateway to judicial activism. The Privy Council in the 1980 decision of *Ong Ah Chuan v PP* had affirmed that 'law' in Westminster constitutions referred to 'a system of law which incorporates those FRNJ forming part and parcel of the English common law' operating in Singapore when the Constitution commenced.[108] It was initially unclear what the content of FRNJ was, apart from vague guidelines that criminal trial procedures should not be 'obviously unfair'. In ascertaining this, a broad palette of sources could be canvassed, including the UDHR, the ECHR and inquisitorial legal systems; practices should not be viewed in isolation but considering their role in the complete judicial process.[109]

Earlier decisions have been ungenerous towards fundamental liberties in refusing to recognise a right to be told of the existing Article 9(3) right to counsel, which would have facilitated its enjoyment.[110] The courts have refused to construe 'law' in Article 9(1) as importing substantive standards like humane treatment, which would have precluded imposing the death penalty after undue delay ('death row phenomenon').[111]

This does not mean a formal positivist approach, which confines the courts to ensuring that law as *lex* is duly enacted and complied with rather than deploying a more justice-oriented conception of law as *jus*, is adopted. The CA in *Yong* [2015] clarified that FRNJ related to procedural rights or norms, not substantive rights, aimed at securing a fair trial and which ordinary legislation cannot abrogate. It would include the narrower common law prohibition of using torture to secure evidence to ensure conviction, but would not extend to punishing convicted criminals, which the international legal prohibition of torture covers.[112]

Today, it is acknowledged that the words 'in accordance with law' go beyond 'formal validity' to incorporate a modest set of standards: that legislation must be consonant with securing a fair trial, not be *ad hominem* or absurd or arbitrary, nor contravene the RoL by precluding access to justice.[113] The court clarified that 'absurdity' as a test lacked substantive content and a statute would fall short if it 'could not be understood or complied with'.[114] FRNJ are understood

[107] *Yong* [2015] (n 11) [15]–[18].
[108] *Ong Ah Chuan* (n 1) [26].
[109] *Haw Tua Tau v PP* [1981–1982] SLR(R) 133, [8], [24]–[25].
[110] *Rajeevan Edakalavan v PP* [1998] 1 SLR(R) 10, [19].
[111] *Jabar v PP* [1995] 1 SLR(R) 326.
[112] *Yong* [2015] (n 11) [64].
[113] *Tan Seng Kee* (n 19) [254].
[114] ibid [259], [265]. The CA opined that even if absurdity was a substantive test, invalidating a law 'if it is so abhorrent that no reasonable person can contemplate it as being morally justified' [266], it

to be universal rules which apply at all times and cannot be abrogated; thus, a putative rule that the death sentence required an unanimous verdict, originating from 'medieval England', was not a FRNJ as it was 'too particular and too idiosyncratic to the jury system' to have universal import. As such, Parliament was entitled to allow judges to return majority verdicts in capital cases, after criminal trials by jury were abolished in 1971.[115] Thus, what FRNJ rules constitute have been developed in a disciplined, if limited, manner.

D. Judicial Balancing

'Rightism' is not a current concern in Singapore; the predominant contrary reservation is that rights are insufficiently protected, under-theorised and subordinated to collective interests.

However, there has been a shift from the nadir of statist interpretive approaches in the second wave decision of *Colin Chan v PP*.[116] This concerned the restriction of the Article 15 right to religious freedom of Jehovah Witnesses (JWs) for possession of religious publications prohibited under the Undesirable Publications Act. The JWs had been deregistered under the Societies Act in 1972 because their pacifist refusal to perform military service rendered their existence 'prejudicial to the public welfare and good order in Singapore'.[117] Article 15(4) provides that religious freedom may be limited in the interests of public order, morality and health.

Although Yong CJ spoke in terms of balancing rights, he effectively fashioned an extra-textual public order trump in declaring the 'sovereignty, integrity and unity of Singapore' to be the 'paramount mandate of the Constitution' such that 'anything, including religious beliefs and practices which tend to run counter to these objectives must be restrained'.[118] This statist disposition is evident in Yong CJ's approving reference to an Australian World War Two decision where legislative restrictions on advocating religious convictions prejudicial to the persecution of war was upheld.[119] In addition, the High Court carelessly equated 'public order' with 'national security' considerations, with the latter term associated with anti-subversion legislation under Article 149. The elevation of order-centric considerations is evident in characterising the rationale for deregistering the JWs as the need to avoid 'absolute freedom of religion', which could create 'a complete denial of a government's authority' and ability

would not be satisfied on the facts as parliamentary debates indicated that many people considered the anti-sodomy law justified on grounds of societal morality: [268].

[115] *Kho Jabing v PP* [2016] 3 SLR 135, [98], [111].

[116] *Colin Chan* (n 3) 209.

[117] MHA Press Statement, 14 January 1972, referenced in ibid [3].

[118] *Colin Chan* (n 3) [64]. See Thio Li-ann, 'The Secular Trumps the Sacred' (1995) SLR 26.

[119] *Adelaide Co of Jehovah's Witnesses v The Commonwealth* (1943) 67 CLR 116, cited in *Colin Chan* (n 3) [60].

to govern religious entities.[120] This speculative musing is not rigorous judicial reasoning.

Similarly, in other cases of that vintage, while the High Court noted that a 'balancing exercise' was involved in reconciling Article 14 expressive guarantees and 'broader societal concerns such as public peace and order', no actual balancing took place. Yong CJ in *Chee Soon Juan v PP*[121] noted that in any society, 'democratic or otherwise', free speech was not an absolute right, before proceeding to make a bare assertion that he did not find the provisions of the Public Entertainment and Meetings Act (PEMA) requiring a licence for public speaking (which had not been obtained on the facts) to be 'in any way contrary to our Constitution'. Since the PEMA was designed to promote public order, and since public order was one of eight permissible grounds of derogation from free speech in Article 14(2)(a), the enactment of the PEMA was 'fully within the power of the legislature'. In other words, so long as a statute stated it related to a ground within the derogation clause, it was valid and the courts would ratify the legislative balance struck between liberty and restriction. This is a toothless form of review.

This statist bias was further affirmed in *Chee Siok Chin v MHA*,[122] where the High Court, paying close attention to the free speech clause's textual formulation, rejected the two-step Indian 'reasonableness' approach and the three-step European proportionality review test towards construing the scope of this freedom in justifying the 'extremely wide discretionary power' Parliament enjoyed in enacting restrictions.

Article 14(1)(a) from the outset expressly subjects the right of free speech to any law Parliament considers 'necessary or expedient in the interests of … public order', as set out in Article 14(2)(a). This has elsewhere been described by the CA as a 'subsidiary right', distinct from more heavily weighted 'fundamental' or 'preferential' rights.[123] The judicial task was confined to ascertaining 'whether an impugned law is within the purview' of the Article 14(2)(a) restrictions by establishing a 'nexus' between both ('nexus test'). The government had to prove Parliament had a 'factual basis' when considering it 'necessary or expedient' to enact the law 'in the interest of' an Article 14(2)(a) purpose, and the court should construe such parliamentary intent generously, not pedantically, as the 'presumption of legislative constitutionality will not be lightly displaced'.[124] Owing to the phrasing, incidental measures in the interests of public order not confined to maintaining public order allowed Parliament to adopt a 'prophylactic approach'.[125] Unlike Indian courts, Singapore courts will not question

[120] *Colin Chan* (n 3) [78].
[121] [2003] 2 SLR 445.
[122] *Chee Siok Chin* (n 6).
[123] *Review Publishing* (n 32) [286]–[289].
[124] *Chee Siok Chin* (n 6) [49].
[125] ibid [50].

whether the legislation is 'reasonable', which is what the former would do after establishing a nexus,[126] let alone apply proportionality review, which is 'more exacting' than a reasonableness test.[127] Article 14(2)(a) precluded any 'minimum impairment requirement',[128] as applied to an equivalent Canadian clause.[129]

However, there are signs that the 'third wave' courts are reading down statist considerations and have shifted from *faux* to actual balancing, where rights are taken a little more seriously. Three key developments support this view.

First, the CA adopted a structured three-step approach in *Jolovan Wham v PP*,[130] where the constitutionality of the Public Order Act, which regulates the Article 14 freedom of assembly through licensing requirements, was challenged. It declared that an objective approach was necessary as a subjective one would render the right 'wholly toothless' by giving Parliament unlimited powers to restrict the right, provided correct procedure was followed. An interpretive approach could not 'undermine entirely' the right to peaceful assembly, rendering it 'purely symbolic'.[131] While recognising the Constitution vests primary decision-making power in Parliament, the courts were to objectively review the legislation and legislative materials to ascertain whether 'the statutory derogation is within the permitted space provided for this purpose in the Constitution'.[132] The courts would apply the maxim '*omnia praesumuntur rite esse acta*' ('all things are presumed to have been done rightly and regularly'),[133] which comports with the neo-Confucian tenet of treating governors as trustworthy, 'honourable gentlemen'.[134]

While agreeing with the 'nexus' test in *Chee Siok Chin*, the CA made a welcome clarification, as noted in *Saravanan v PP*,[135] that the presumption of constitutionality in ascertaining legislative validity is 'no more than a starting point that legislation will not presumptively be treated as suspect or unconstitutional'; otherwise, it runs the risk of 'presuming the very issue which is being challenged'. Taken to its extreme, the government could just sit back and see what argument a challenger puts forth, rather than present some justificatory basis for its action. Hence, the Court must apply 'applicable principles' in determining the constitutionality of a challenged law[136] or the validity of acts of high

[126] ibid [49].
[127] ibid [87].
[128] Expressive freedoms under the Canadian Charter may be subject under s 1 to 'such reasonable limits prescribed by law … in a free and democratic society', which imports the 'minimal impairment requirement': *R v Oakes* [1986] 1 SCR 103, discussed in *Chee Soon Juan v PP* [2011] 2 SLR 940, [9].
[129] Referencing *Vancouver (City) v Zhang* [2010] BCCA 450 in *Chee Soon Juan* (n 128) [10].
[130] [2021] 1 SLR 476.
[131] ibid [22].
[132] ibid [24].
[133] *Ramalingam v AG* [2012] 2 SLR 49, [45].
[134] White paper on Shared Values (n 25) [41].
[135] [2020] 2 SLR 95.
[136] ibid [154].

public office-holders.[137] These principles include the SoP, in recognising each government branch has 'its own role and space', and the RoL, which ensures the 'nexus' test is met.[138]

The first step considers whether the legislation restricts the constitutional right; if so, the second step is to ascertain whether Parliament considered it 'necessary or expedient' to serve an Article 14(2)(b) enumerated purpose. Thirdly, the court must analyse objectively whether the legislative purpose for restricting the right bears a 'nexus' to one of the 'relevant and permitted purpose' under Article 14(2)(b). Finally, it is 'imperative' to appreciate 'that a balance must be found between the competing interests at stake',[139] although it is not clear whether the legislator or the court should evaluate whether the balance struck is appropriate. Contrary to some academic wishful thinking,[140] which views this three-step approach as an incipient form of proportionality review, it is clear that judicial efforts have been made to delineate a more structured form of judicial inquiry without acceding to the normative liberal agenda and methodology of proportionality review.

Aedit Abdullah J in *Xu Yuanchen v PP* underscored that proportionality analysis would contravene the SoP on grounds of institutional competence and propriety.[141] Proportionality analysis would be 'alien to the text', and arrogate to the courts 'a limitation on the breadth of action of the Legislature' uncontemplated by the constitutional text.[142]

The second development relates to the abandonment of the public order trump as a form of categorical balancing proclaimed in *Colin Chan v PP* in 1994. While subsequently invoked as a determinative mantra,[143] when *Chan* was invoked in the 2015 case of *Vijaya Kumar v PP*,[144] concerning the regulation of religious processions, it was for the proposition that the 'clear and immediate danger' test did not apply in evaluating restrictions on Article 15 religious freedoms.[145] This may disappoint liberals, for whom such test alone would satisfy. For communitarians, judicial engagement in a genuine balancing exercise framed within the distinctive historical and cultural context is a positive development. In assessing the constitutionality of conditions barring the playing of music during the Hindu Thaipusam religious procession, the court went into granular detail to find the police had 'legitimate public order concerns';

[137] *Syed Suhail bin Syed Zin* (n 3) [63].
[138] White paper on Shared Values (n 25) [27]–[28].
[139] *Jolovan Wham* (n 130) [30]–[33].
[140] See Marcus Teo, 'A Case for Proportionality Review in Singaporean Constitutional Adjudication' [2021] SJLS 174; Alec Stone Sweet, 'Intimations of Proportionality? The Singapore Constitution and Rights Protection' [2021] SJLS 231.
[141] *Xu Yuanchen* (n 21) [85].
[142] ibid [88].
[143] *Nappalli v ITE* [1998] SGHC 351, [46] (HC), [1999] 2 SLR(R) 529, [26] (CA).
[144] [2015] SGHC 244.
[145] ibid [32].

the measures undertaken were designed to protect 'higher order'[146] public order concerns arising from religious processions, compared to cultural parades, given Singapore's history of riots from a 1964 religious foot procession.[147] Considering the number of devotees, the duration and the route passing by two churches and a mosque, the High Court found the risk of public disorder 'not unreal'.[148] The connection between the music restrictions and public order were 'neither illogical nor unreasonable'.[149] Further, no blanket music ban was imposed, as the police allowed religious hymns to be sung and permitted the transmission of music through a public audio system at three points, demonstrating it had 'nuanced its approach over time' in dialogue with the Hindu community.[150]

In other words, the court found the police's reasons to be reasonable; their 'calibrated approach to the music use' showed the police gave 'due regard' to Article 15 rights, balanced against public order – a communitarian society seeks a reasonable accommodation of both. What might be termed a 'reasonableness' approach enhances a culture of reason-giving and promotes RoL values of accountability and transparency, distinct from cursory, opaque judgments.

Lastly, there is evidence that when executive decisions affect constitutional rights, scrutiny is intensified, as evident in Article 12 equality cases, as discussed in chapter five. Indeed, the High Court, while not advocating a shift to US-style tiered scrutiny, which entails a judicially authored hierarchy of values attracting variable degrees of scrutiny, said it was natural to accord very careful scrutiny to legislation which apparently discriminated on factors 'like race or religion' or affected Part IV fundamental liberties.[151] The CA in *Syed Suhail bin Syed Zin v AG*[152] also underscored that where an executive decision is directed at an individual rather than being a general policy, and where life and liberty are at stake, the court would be 'searching in its scrutiny' to ensure individuals enjoyed the 'full measure' of Article 12 rights.[153]

Cumulatively, these developments evidence a shift, if too modest for some, towards genuine contextualised balancing of fundamental liberties, where rights are viewed as part of, not antithetical to, the common good, and where law and the values it espouses are taken seriously.[154] While this recalibration rejects the idea of 'rights as trumps', it thankfully seems to have rejected categorical order-centric trumps and hollowed out conceptions of rights which are subordinated to any competing interests and effectively demoted to common law liberties.

[146] ibid [44].
[147] ibid [33], [49].
[148] ibid [35].
[149] ibid [35].
[150] ibid [38].
[151] *Lim* [2013] (n 67) [113].
[152] *Syed Suhail bin Syed Zin* (n 3) 809. See Kenny Chng, 'A Reconsideration of Equal Protection and Executive Action in Singapore' (2021) OUCLJ 1.
[153] *Tan Seng Kee* (n 19) [326].
[154] Peter Cane, 'Taking Law Seriously: Starting Points of the Hart/Devlin Debate' [2006] Journal of Ethics 21.

Whether the courts will settle on reasonableness review or a more structured inquiry which construes restrictions sufficiently rigorously remains to be seen. What is clear is that in its search for an autochthonous public law, just as there was no 'liberal moment'[155] in constitution-making, so too the courts have not sought to read and remake the Constitution in a liberal image after the rights-oriented court-centric model. As Menon CJ stated extrajudicially, 'Public confidence in the rule of law – rather than the rule of the courts – is what we should be striving for'.[156]

III. POLITICAL SPEECH – LIES, SCANDAL AND JUDICIAL REVIEW

Criticisms about the RoL are predominantly directed at public law cases, where cultural particularities are invoked; the RoL in the field of commercial law is set aside for praise.[157] The central allegation is that a compliant judiciary suppresses political speech through speech-restrictive readings of political libel and contempt of court laws, as recognised grounds of derogation under Article 14(2)(a). This is inferred from the high number of such cases won by government members,[158] where the weak protection of political speech in favour of protecting reputation and the high damages awarded for political defamation have a 'chilling' effect. This section examines whether 'third wave' judicial developments have ameliorated such concerns.

A. Scandalising the Court

The rationale of the common law contempt of 'scandalising the court', a species of criminal contempt, is to secure public confidence in the administration of justice (PCAOJ), which upholds 'the very structure of ordered life'.[159] The Supreme Court's jurisdiction to punish for contempt, which is 'a public injury rather than a private tort',[160] flows from its inherent jurisdiction as a superior court.[161]

Contemptuous statements in newspapers or private Facebook posts include allegations that a subservient judiciary constrains international media

[155] Chan Sek Keong, 'The Courts and the Rule of Law in Singapore' [2012] SJLS 209, 216.

[156] 'Court's Role Is to Apply Law Impartially, Not Be Front Runners for Social Change: CJ Menon' *Straits Times* (22 September 2023).

[157] Jack Lee, 'Shall the Twain Never Meet? Competing Narratives and Discourses of the Rule of Law in Singapore' [2012] SJLS 298.

[158] Cumaraswamy (n 36).

[159] Lord Morris, *AG v Times Newspaper* [1974] AC 273, 302, cited in *Pertamina Energy Trading Ltd v Karaha Bodas* [2007] 2 SLR(R) 518, [22].

[160] *Shadrake Alan v AG* (n 9) [21].

[161] The Supreme Court of Judicature Act, s 7(1) gives statutory expression to this power: *Sebastian v Sembcorp Marine Ltd* [2013] 2 SLR 256, [64].

reporting[162] or that a litigious government could rely on courts to bankrupt and disqualify opposition politicians from contesting general elections.[163] Singapore has attracted some notoriety for such allegations.[164]

While judicial independence and legitimacy requires public respect and support, judges are not infallible and the right to criticise the judiciary's work is 'part of the freedom of speech and expression the citizen enjoys in a democracy';[165] this is a form of public review which helps prevent 'lawless courts and irresponsible judging',[166] which immunity from scrutiny may engender. Indeed, some consider that 'scandalising the court' offences have no role in modern democracies, where public institutions are subject to criticism. However, there has been judicial recognition that the offence is not incompatible with expressive freedoms provided restrictions are proportionate and 'reasonably justifiable in a democratic society'.[167]

Before the law on contempt for scandalising the court was placed on a statutory footing in 2016, the courts had developed a weak test of 'inherent tendency' in balancing speech and concerns with judicial reputation in the 1991 case of *AG v Wain*;[168] the CA replaced this in 2011 with the more rights-protective 'real risk' test in *Shadrake Alan v AG*.[169]

Contempt laws are not designed to protect the judge personally nor to restrict 'honest criticism based on rational grounds'[170] on how judges discharge their function. Such criticism provides some accountability, which may impact the role of courts in upholding the RoL. However, the right to fair criticism of the judiciary, as part of Article 14 and long recognised by the common law,[171] is exceeded if speech 'impugns the integrity and impartiality of the court',[172] where intent is relevant only to the question of punishment.[173] Thus, 'criticism

[162] *Li Shengwu v AG* [2019] 1 SLR 1081. AJPA, s 19 provides a person is not guilty of a s 3(a) or (b) contempt if he did not know or have reason to believe that the publication, published outside Singapore, would be seen or heard by people in Singapore.

[163] *AG v Lingle* [1995] 1 SLR(R) 199. This concerned an IHT 'Opinion' article of 7 October 1994 called 'The Smoke over Parts of Asia Obscures Some Profound Concerns'. While not specifically referring to Singapore, the High Court found that an ordinary reasonable reader knowing the extrinsic facts – that some widely reported 11 High Court defamation suits were brought against opposition politicians – would reasonably conclude the words referred to the court: [25]–[26].

[164] The AG argued that Lingle, in referring to an 'intolerant regime' in his article, knew he was referencing Singapore as there were no other countries with a large number of defamation suits where government politicians successfully sued opposition politicians: ibid [24], [34].

[165] Chan Sek Keong, 'Securing and Maintaining Judicial Independence' (2021) 22 SAcLJ 229, [21].

[166] ibid.

[167] *Dhooharika v Director of Public Prosecutors* [2014] UKPC 11.

[168] [1991] 1 SLR(R) 85.

[169] *Shadrake Alan v AG* (n 9).

[170] Rich J, *R v Dunbabin, ex p Williams* (1935) 53 CLR 434, 442–43.

[171] eg Lord Atkin, *AG of Trinidad and Tobago* [1936[AC 322, 335; *Lingle* (n 163) [11].

[172] *Lingle* (n 163) [13]. In contrast, 'intent' is relevant to a finding of contempt in Canada, where the common law offence was revised to give due weight to the free speech guarantee under the Canadian Charter of Rights and Freedoms: *Regina v Kopyto* 47 DLR (4th) 213 (Ontario CA).

[173] The only mens rea needed is that publication was intentional: *Shadrake Alan v AG* (n 9) [55].

of judgments' should not devolve into 'denigration of judges',[174] and making 'irresponsible accusations'[175] which erode PCAOJ diminishes this prized aspect of socio-political stability.

The balancing of free speech and judicial reputation is predicated on two key factors: first, whether the public is gullible or discerning; and second, whether judges are to be treated as 'men of fortitude, able to thrive in a hardy climate'[176] or whether more tender men need greater reputational insulation. While 'scandalising the court' had become obsolete in England at the end of the nineteenth century, the British thought it was needed in the 'small colonies, consisting principally of coloured populations', to preserve 'the dignity and respect for the Court',[177] for fear that immature colonised people might be 'goaded into madness', seek vigilante justice or even riot where they disrespected the administration of justice.[178] While criticism of courts in England could be left to public opinion, there is a racist undertone in assuming the colonised would lack similar discernment and restraint.

In 2011, the CA in *Shadrake Alan v AG*[179] acknowledged that an impugned statement may elicit different responses; the court, from the average reasonable person's perspective, as opposed to a less rational person, would make an 'objective decision' whether the statement would undermine PCAOJ.[180] This may be unrealistic or difficult in an age where common sense is less common and where an appreciable segment of the community may be more prone to conspiracy theories, as acknowledged in the POFMA context.[181]

The *Wain* speculative 'inherent tendency' test indicates the need to accord greater weight to the public interest in maintaining PCAOJ over free speech rights.[182] Anything can bear a tendency which may not become an eventuality; the 'real risk' test was rejected, with 'real' connoting an evidentiary base. Presumably the US 'clear and present danger' test against a 'serious substantive evil'[183] or the Canadian need for an 'imminent danger',[184] both of which

[174] Chan Sek Keong, 'Securing and Maintaining Judicial Independence' (n 165) [21].
[175] *Lingle* (n 163) [11].
[176] Brennan J, *New York Times v Sullivan* 376 US 254 (1964) 274, discussing criminal contempt in *Bridges v California* 314 US 252 (1941).
[177] *McLeod v St Aubyn* [1899] AC 549, 561.
[178] ibid 554.
[179] [2011] 3 SLR 778.
[180] The High Court judge in *AG v Shadrake Alan* [2011] 2 SLR 445, [52] suggested that the public included persons 'less rational' or possibly 'more discriminating' than the average reasonable person, citing *Secretary for Justice v Oriental Press Group Ltd* [1998] HKC 267 (Hong Kong).
[181] *The Inquiry Pte Ltd v AG* [2023] SGHC 247, [34].
[182] The CA in *Shadrake Alan v AG* (n 9) [56] considered the apparent distinction between the inherent tendency test and real risk test a 'legal red herring', suggesting the judge in *Wain* did not intend to divorce the inherent tendency test from its actual or potential impact on public confidence in the courts.
[183] *Bridges v California* 314 US 252 (1941) 270.
[184] *Kopyto* (n 172).

underscore the importance of free speech, would be unacceptable. This discounts the concern that restricting speech to shield judges from criticism 'would probably engender resentment, suspicion, and contempt much more than it would enhance respect'.[185]

Sinnathuray J in *Wain* justified the test by invoking 'local conditions', without explaining what these were.[186] He noted the disutility of English cases after the 1981 Contempt of Court Act altered the English common law to give effect to ECHR values, modifying it 'in a liberal direction'.[187] After jury trials were abolished, Singapore judges became triers of both fact and law, and thus Sinnathuray J considered any imputation of judicial wrongdoing which strikes the core function of judges 'must be firmly dealt with'.[188] The counter-argument is the more power a judge wields, the more important it is to ensure accountability. The 'inherent tendency' test was affirmed as best suiting a 'small island',[189] and was even subsequently celebrated as having 'two advantages': first, it allowed finding contempt without detailed proof a publication would impair PCAOJ and; second, it enabled courts to act pre-emptively.[190] This may be criticised as unduly restricting socially valuable speech that exposes judicial misconduct.

The CA in *Shadrake Alan v AG*[191] affirmed the High Court's holding[192] that the applicable test was at 'real risk' of undermining PCAOJ. After a comprehensive review of Commonwealth cases, policy and first principles,[193] Loh J pointed to the weakness of the inherent tendency test, which was 'susceptible of controversy and misunderstanding' as it 'tends to obscure the fact that a contextual analysis is actually required'; 'inherent' in indicating something 'intrinsic' apparently excluded extrinsic factors.[194] Conversely, the real risk test 'precisely conveys' to layman and lawyer 'what the law is concerned with',[195] as distinct from 'a remote and fanciful possibility' of undermining PCAOJ, or finding this only in 'the most serious situations'.[196] Disagreeing with an observation in *AG v Hertzberg*, Loh J stated that drunken dinner party rants against the judiciary posed no 'real risk' and should be ignored as trifling matters only an 'overzealous judiciary' would take 'serious notice'[197] of.

185 *Bridges* (n 183) 271.
186 *Wain* (n 168) 85.
187 ibid [34].
188 ibid [38], [53].
189 *AG v Chee Soon Juan* [2006] 2 SLR 650, [25]–[27].
190 *AG v Hertzberg* [2009] 1 SLR 1103, [33].
191 [2011] 3 SLR 778, [57].
192 [2011] 2 SLR 445, [50].
193 eg the real risk test was adopted in *Times Newspaper* (n 159) 298–99.
194 [2011] 2 SLR 445, [50].
195 ibid [50].
196 *Shadrake Alan v AG* [2011] 3 SLR 778, [36].
197 [2011] 2 SLR 445, [47].

The CA expressly rejected that 'real risk' be read as importing the 'clear and present danger' test, which was an 'extremely stringent standard'[198] associated with the 'unique culture'[199] and constitutional position of the US First Amendment, an outlier within the Commonwealth, apart from a solitary Canadian decision.[200] While the parochial US approach accorded paramountcy to free speech, the Singapore approach was one of balance, where rights are not absolute as this could be prone to 'untrammeled abuse', and be 'a negation of the right itself'.[201]

The CA treated fair criticism as an element of liability, rather than a defence;[202] the party relying on it bears the evidential burden, while the respondent bears the legal burden of proving beyond a reasonable doubt that the impugned statement was not fair criticism.[203] This was thought to appropriately calibrate the tensions between the competing interests.[204]

The High Court and CA in *Shadrake* approvingly referenced Prakash J's exposition on what fair criticism entailed in *AG v Tan Liang Joo*, being made in good faith, in a temperate, respectful manner, supported by argument and evidence. Unlike vilification, which only seeks to abuse, such criticism 'allows for rational debate',[205] and could enhance the administration of justice.

This links the value of speech to democratic theory and practice; such theorising is a positive development in ensuring both sides of the balance are duly weighted. Judges should not be 'so complacent' as to assume their infallibility or imperviousness to human sentiment,[206] and the public interest is served 'in rooting out bias and impropriety where it in fact occurs'. Prakash J rejected that speech imputing improper motives or impugning a judge's impartiality was automatically contemptuous,[207] as over-restrictive substantive limits. Consonant with Commonwealth authority, the CA in *Shadrake* accepted that limiting fair criticism to criticism which did not question 'the independence, impartiality and integrity' of a court 'overly limited its ambit' as most allegedly contemptuous statements would 'by their very nature' question these things.[208]

Although *Shadrake* shifted the constitutional balance in favour of expressive rights, this was legislatively rolled back by the AJPA, which provides legal certainty by placing contempt on a statutory footing, which the Chief Justice

[198] *Shadrake Alan v AG* (n 9) [39].
[199] ibid [41].
[200] *Kopyto* (n 172).
[201] *Shadrake Alan v AG* (n 9) [17].
[202] ibid [58]–[80].
[203] ibid [78].
[204] Belinda Ang J, *AG v Au Wai Pang* [2015] 2 SLR 352, [11].
[205] [2009] 2 SLR(R) 1132, [19].
[206] ibid [22].
[207] *Tan Liang Joo* (n 205) 1141, [22]. Quentin Loh J agreed with this view in *AG v Shadrake Alan* [2011] 2 SLR 445, [70]–[71], while Tay J had taken the view that alleging judicial impartiality could never be fair criticism in *AG v Hertzberg* (n 190) [54].
[208] ibid [84].

called for in 2010.[209] Section 3(1)(a) AJPA provides that a contempt is committed where any person scandalises the court by intentionally publishing any matter or doing any act that (i) imputes improper motives or impugns the integrity, propriety or impartiality of any court and (ii) poses a risk that PCAOJ would be undermined. Explanation 1 provides that 'Fair Criticism of a Court' does not constitute scandalising contempt under section 3(1)(a).

This codification of the common law shows the judiciary would have permitted a broader latitude of criticism than what Parliament, from its 'larger policy perspective', considered appropriate. It legislatively overruled the 'real risk' test, which the courts struck in their commitment to ensure that neither free speech, 'which is the rule', or the offence of contempt, 'an exception to the rule', would be defined in a manner rendering the other 'otiose'.[210] The rationale for the statutory test of 'risk' was to afford greater protection to the courts against constant attacks of bias and corruption; a communitarian orientation is evident in balancing 'some people's desire to launch personal attack against judges' and the prioritised value of 'the confidence reposed in the Judiciary'.[211] Critics argued this was an unnecessary, self-serving lowering of the threshold of what amounts to scandalising the courts.[212]

Ensuring the integrity of the judiciary is 'pristine', though the 'risk' test would give Singapore a 'strong anchoring in the RoL', buttressing faith in the role of courts in a 'well-functioning democracy'. Building on the existing 'highest esteem' for courts and their authority[213] as part of the 'fundamental public good', the AJPA was part of the bigger project of helping Singapore become the 'pre-eminent vibrant legal centre in the region', standing out in Asia as a jurisdiction of 'unchallenged independence', reflected in the quality of the legal profession and 'the international work it gets' which is economically beneficial. This ties the commercial RoL to developmentalist imperatives. Protecting the reputation of eminent foreign judges helps secure their agreement to sit on the Singapore International Commercial Court, and Singapore's reputation for the RoL also enables it to host the top Asian arbitration body, the Singapore International Arbitration Centre.

In weighing the 'tremendous positive impact' on the economy of making Singapore a legal hub as a public good against proscribing allegations that a judge is biased, the Law Minister considered 'the balance is quite clear'.[214] In response to the British High Commissioner, who urged the abolition of scandalising the

[209] 'New Laws for Contempt' *Straits Times* (9 January 2010).

[210] Loh J, *AG v Shadrake Alan* [2011] 2 SLR 445, [57].

[211] K Shanmugam (Minister for Law), Administration of Justice (Protection) Bill, 94 SPR, 15 August 2016.

[212] Sylvia Lim (Workers Party), Speech, Administration of Justice (Protection) Bill, 15 August 2016, www.wp.sg/administration-of-justice-protection-bill-speech-by-sylvia-lim/.

[213] According to a Law Ministry survey, 92% of Singaporeans said they trusted the legal system and 96% agreed Singapore was governed by rule of law: Shanmugam (n 211).

[214] ibid.

court, the Law Minister pointed out that Britain was not a model, given the 'coarsening of society' and loss of public respect for their judiciary, which was 'not protected', was 'underpaid' and where judges felt 'undervalued'.[215]

Judges, who cannot defend themselves in discharging their professional duties, must be shielded from the odium that 'illusory truth' engenders, lest repeated false statements in Goebbelsian fashion become accepted as truth. The maximum penalties were substantially raised to a $100,000 fine and three years' imprisonment, compared to the imposition of six weeks and a $20,000 fine in *AG v Shadrake*, where Shadrake showed no remorse in 'the worst cases of scandalising contempt' to come before Singapore courts,[216] implicating passages in Shadrake's book – *Once a Jolly Hangman: Singapore Justice in the Dock.*[217]

Nonetheless, criticism conveyed through fair and accurate reporting, as distinct from self-indulgent journalistic diatribe, such as Hong Kong newspapers describing the evils of 'swinish, white-skinned judges', was not precluded, just regulated in a 'stricter' fashion. Judges could be criticised for personal conduct, the conduct of trials or judgments, provided no improper motives are ascribed. Further, section 16 AJPA provides an additional route of accountability, where a good faith report made to the Chief Justice is not contemptuous if it discloses grounds which, if unrebutted, would be a sufficient basis to investigate alleged misconduct.

Case law is still useful in developing the content of 'fair criticism', the 'full latitude' of which is to be preserved under the AJPA as an aspect of liability, reflecting the CA's view in *Shadrake*.[218] The AG must prove the impugned statement is not fair criticism.[219]

The first prosecution under section 3(1)(a) AJPA related to a Facebook post of 27 April 2018 by activist Wham, stating: 'Malaysia's judges are more independent than Singapore's for cases with political implications.' On 6 May, Tan made a public post containing a link to Wham's Facebook profile, stating: 'By charging Jolovan for scandalising the judiciary, the AGC [Attorney-General's Chambers] only confirms what he said was true.' Both Wham and Tan were convicted of scandalising the judiciary.

The CA in *Wham Kwok Han Jolovan v AG*[220] held that Wham's post (and Tan's re-post) was objectively contemptuous, there being only one reasonable way to interpret the post: that one would more likely succeed in bringing a

[215] ibid.
[216] *Shadrake Alan v AG* (n 9) [153]. Before the AJPA, the punishment for the offence of scandalising the court was unlimited, being the only criminal law based on case law: noted by Shanmugam (n 211).
[217] Alan Shadrake, *Once a Jolly Hangman: Singapore Justice in the Dock* (Strategic Information and Research Development Centre, 2010).
[218] Shanmugam (n 211); *Shadrake Alan v AG* (n 9) [80].
[219] AJPA, s 28 sets the test at 'beyond reasonable doubt'.
[220] [2020] 1 SLR 804, [32].

constitutional challenge in Malaysia than in Singapore as Singapore judges in politicised cases were not independent.

In applying the risk test, the CA noted that Parliament's intent was to introduce a test that could be 'applied more expediently and pragmatically' without having to make 'hair-splitting or fine distinctions' regarding the level of risk to be satisfied. This flowed from a 'considered policy choice'[221] to strongly favour judicial integrity and standing, diminishing free speech protections. The 'risk' test requires the court to ask: 'Is the risk one that the reasonable person coming across the contemptuous statement would think needs guarding against so as to avoid undermining PCAOJ?' Both the content and context of the alleged contemptuous statement may be relevant, in asking this question.[222] The CA found the risk present on the facts, as the content objectively was 'among the most serious attacks', going to 'the very heart and essence of the judicial mission and oath'.[223] It was contained in a public post accessible to the world at large and to Wham's 7000 Facebook followers, made by Wham, who held himself out as a knowledgeable social commentator. Being published on Facebook did not render it 'so fanciful or self-evidently unreliable' that no risk of undermining PCAOJ arose.[224] The degree of harm caused by a publication could be assessed in quantitative and qualitative terms, such as reach and whether the platform of publication burnished the publication's journalistic gravitas.[225]

Further, 'fair criticism' was not made out for Wham or Tan's posts which lacked 'objective or rational basis'; Wham made 'a bald and outrageous assertion without reference to any supporting facts'.[226] The court examined the rationale proffered for the statement in granular detail, such as where Wham claimed his post was informed by at least three specific case examples where Malaysian courts had adopted a 'less conservative approach' than their Singapore counterparts.[227] However, these cases were not comparable, as they dealt with different subject matters and legislation, not least because one decision was delivered a week after Wham's post was published. This gave the appearance of being an afterthought, as Wham equivocated about whether he, lacking legal expertise, had read the cases or read about them.[228] Nothing in the case pairs could 'reasonably' lead to the conclusion that Singapore judges were more prone than Malaysian judges to decide 'political' cases 'otherwise than in accordance with the merits'.[229]

[221] ibid [36].
[222] ibid [38].
[223] ibid [32]–[33].
[224] ibid [39].
[225] *Xu Yuan Chen v AG* [2022] 2 SLR 1131, [52]–[53], [58]–[59].
[226] *Wham* (n 220) [51].
[227] ibid [41]–[42].
[228] ibid [44].
[229] ibid [47].

Wham and Tan were both fined \$5000. Tan's request for a more onerous imprisonment sentence, to avoid being disqualified from contesting parliamentary elections by being fined more than \$2000 under Article 45, was denied.[230] Offenders should not be allowed to choose particular sentences based on their political aspirations, as this entailed deciding the case other than on the merits, the very thing Wham and Tan had accused the judiciary of! As for Wham, the CA declined to impose an apology order under section 12(3) AJPA; he had refused the AGC's demand for a public apology, as this entailed succumbing to 'the culture of fear' and being 'humiliated into submission'.[231] While the court recognised that apology orders for scandalising contempt could serve 'signaling, educative and corrective functions', possibly retribution and deterrence, a signal did not need to be sent in every case.[232] Coerced apologies would be a bridge too far in terms of the cost to human dignity; being insincere, they could diminish the standing of the judiciary, and should only be exceptionally required. In addition, a cease-publication injunction under section 9(d) AJPA was imposed: Wham's post was still online and had been referenced in his other posts so that it had not 'faded from the public consciousness'; it was thus still a continuing publication, which could actively resurface in newsfeeds. As this contemptuous statement was of little value, there was no reason not to require its removal, which would not be 'disproportionately costly or technically difficult'.[233]

Civil society activists view scandalising contempt offences as a form of judicial harassment, even if not officially prosecuted. In *Han Li Ying Kristen v AG*, the AG found Han's Facebook post of 10 May 2022 to be contemptuous under section 3(1)(a) AJPA in asserting that high costs orders created a climate of fear that deterred lawyers from representing death row prisoners, making the occurrence of wrongful executions more likely. Han was called down to the police station on 21 October 2022, where she received a conditional warning and no answer when she asked which parts of her post scandalised the judiciary. Han viewed this decision as 'harassment and intimidation from the Attorney-General's Chamber, using the Singapore Police Force as their messenger to do so'. Her application to quash the conditional warning failed as it has no legal effect and is not subject to judicial review.[234]

Speech critical of the judiciary can impair PCAOJ, but unduly restricting speech can also erode public confidence. Free speech, which includes criticisms of judicial reasoning and conduct, must be sufficiently protected to adequately promote democratic and RoL values of accountability. The current balance errs

[230] To the argument that allowing Tan to run for public office might be an overriding public interest in promoting democratic processes, the answer was the public interest is served only if electoral candidates are not disqualified under Art 45: ibid [62]–[63].

[231] Wham's 20 January 2020 Facebook post: ibid [16].

[232] ibid [71], [75].

[233] ibid [80]–[82].

[234] [2023] SGHC 137, [6]. See 'Activist Receives Conditional Warning for Social Media Post' (*Civicus Monitor*, 20 December 2022) https://monitor.civicus.org/.

on the side of protecting judicial reputation while keeping the door open for temperate, reason-based criticisms of the judiciary.

B. Political Speech – Defamation and Politicians

Perhaps the most notorious RoL-related critique directed at Singapore is the judicial treatment of political speech in relation to political libel. This hits at the heart of free speech rationales relating to truth and democracy, with fears that insufficient protection sustains autocratic governance.

The charge is typically framed in terms of judicial bias, which services government lawfare to 'harass and prosecute critical voices'[235] through civil defamation suits to cripple political opposition by bankrupting opponents and disqualifying them from contesting general elections.[236] This stifles dissent, creates a culture of fear and nurtures the hegemonic dominance of the ruling elite. Further, the 'very high number of cases won by the Government or members of the ruling party',[237] the 'slim likelihood' of mounting a successful defence and the 'extraordinary high damages awarded in defamation cases involving PAP officials'[238] cast doubt on judicial independence.

In response, judges have stated that there are 'no private directives to a judge from the executive' on how to conduct a case, and that Singapore had 'an open system of justice' where court hearings, records and judgments are open to public scrutiny.[239] Empirically, political opponents have been subject to debilitatingly high damage awards,[240] and critics have, with reason, lamented the 'judicial normalization of a statist rule of law'.[241]

[235] Human Rights Watch 2022 Annual Report, 'Singapore: Events of 2021', www.hrw.org/world-report/2022/country-chapters/singapore.

[236] The Lawyers Rights Watch Canada has opined that 'the twin swords of defamation and bankruptcy law effectively allow the PAP to silence and eliminate members of the opposition'. 'Rule of Law in Singapore: Independence of the Judiciary and the Legal Profession in Singapore' (17 October 2007) 5, www.lrwc.org.

[237] Cumaraswamy (n 36) [218].

[238] International Bar Association (IBA) Human Rights Institute, 'Prosperity versus Individual Rights? Human Rights, Democracy and the Rule of Law in Singapore' (IBA, 2008) 1. See Kanishka Jayasuriya, 'The Exception Becomes the Norm: Law and Regimes of Exception in East Asia (2001) 2 Asian-Pacific Law & Policy Journal 108, 111–12.

[239] Rajendran J, *Goh Chok Tong v JB Jeyaretnam* [1997] 3 SLR(R) 46, [31]–[32]. This concerned Jeyaretnam, the Workers' Party (WP)'s secretary-general, who allegedly defamed the PM and PAP secretary-general at a 1997 election rally by stating that Tang Liang Hong, his fellow WP member, whom PAP leaders had smeared as an 'anti-English educated and anti-Christian' Chinese chauvinist, had handed him two police reports made against Goh and other PAP members. The media republished this verbatim. This was considered defamatory by innuendo. The High Court's award of $20,000 damages was increased to $100,000 on appeal: *Goh Chok Tong v JB Jeyaretnam* [1998] 2 SLR(R) 971, [53], [57], [59].

[240] eg Amnesty International, 'Singapore: JB Jeyaretnam – Defamation Suits Assault Freedom of Expression' (22 July 1998) AI Index: ASA 36/05/98; Human Rights Watch, 'Singapore: End Efforts to Silence Opposition' (17 October 2008).

[241] Cameron Sim, 'The Singapore Chill: Political Defamation and the Normalization of a Statist Rule of Law' [2011] 20 Pacific Rim Law and Policy Journal 319, 352. Sim notes at 320 that PMs

First and second wave cases may be criticised for undervaluing speech and valorising reputational rights – while the common law 'presumes the good reputation of the plaintiff', it nonetheless lacks constitutional status.[242] A bloated conception of reputation may be attributed to cultural norms of deference and honour. The under-protection of expression operates at two levels: first, narrowly scoping defences to political libel; and second, hefty damages awards.[243] This must be investigated in the light of 'third wave' developments in free speech jurisprudence, where efforts to recalibrate balances for defences and damages are discernible.

Case law developments since the 2009 decision of *Review Publishing v Lee Hsien Loong*[244] must be evaluated to determine if enough has been done to allay the 'most feared punishment' of the defamation lawsuit, 'which may cause permanent financial ruin'.[245] While inadequate free speech protections arrest democratic development, the cure is not necessarily a liberal rights approach. While a statist RoL may be an apology for power, in 'buttressing state power and immunizing governors from all critique',[246] a 'communitarian' RoL may offer a third way, provided communitarian values are a product of authentic deliberative dialogue and social consensus, not disguised statist values.

(i) Balancing

The offence of criminal defamation is recognised under section 499 of the Penal Code, while the civil wrong of defamation is a common law tort, which the Defamation Act partially modifies.[247] Damages are awarded for successful civil suits, while criminal sanctions include fines or imprisonment for two years.

The 'qualified privilege' defence to civil defamation is designed to serve 'the common convenience and welfare of society',[248] where the speaker has a duty to communicate and the hearer, a reciprocal interest to receive such information. With respect to political defamation, various common law jurisdictions have by

Lee Kuan Yew and Lee Hsien Loong have never lost a defamation suit they brought, listing some 21 cases at fn 6.

[242] The right to be protected from unlawful attacks on reputation is recognised as part of the right to privacy in Art 11 of the American Convention on Human Rights (1969). See also Art 5(1) of the German Basic Law, Art 2 of the Italian Constitution, Art 24(3)(b)((i) of the Tuvalu Constitution and Art 43 of the Burundi Constitution.

[243] Tey Tsun Hang, 'Singapore's Jurisprudence of Political Defamation and Its Triple Whammy Impact on Political Speech' [2008] PL 452; Cassandra Chan, 'Breaking Singapore's Regrettable Tradition of Chilling Free Speech with Defamation Laws (2003) 26 Loy LA Int'l & Comp L Rev 315.

[244] *Review Publishing* (n 32).

[245] Catherine Lim's open letter to the PM, republished in *TOC* (26 November 2007) www.theonlinecitizen.com/2007/11/26/catherine-lims-open-letter-to-the-prime-minister/.

[246] Thio Li-ann, 'Between Apology and Apogee, Autochthony: The "Rule of Law" beyond the Rules of Law in Singapore [2012] SJLS 260, 289.

[247] This was introduced in 1960 as the Defamation Ordinance.

[248] *Toogood v Spyring* (1843) 1 CM&R 181, 149 ER 1044 (Ch) 1050 (Parke B), cited in *Review Publishing* (n 32) [176].

statute or judicial development recognised political speech as a special category deserving robust protection, as the lifeblood of democracy. This may be effected through privileges relating to the media, elections[249] or political information, none of which have been adopted in Singapore. To attract qualified privilege which seeks to balance expressive freedom and reputational interests, 'special facts' must be shown, such as a terrorist threat or distribution of contaminated foodstuffs. The normative orientation of societal values affects this balance, and explains why Singapore courts have rejected the heightened political speech protection in cases raised before the court from the USA, Europe and the Commonwealth.

Given the liberal's fear of power abuses, US and European politicians are expected to be more thick-skinned than private persons, and display a 'greater degree of tolerance' in enduring 'wider' limits of 'acceptable criticism',[250] as they knowingly open themselves to close public scrutiny. The US 'public figure' doctrine[251] is based on elevated free speech interests, where the inevitability of 'erroneous statements' in 'free debate' is accepted[252] and there is a 'national commitment' that public debate should be 'uninhibited, robust and wide-open', including even 'vehement, caustic and sometimes unpleasantly sharp attacks on governments and public officials'.[253] Free speech would be inhibited by 'fear of an award of damages in civil suits', and thus free speech protections extend to defamatory publications concerning the official conduct of public officials or politicians unless 'actual malice' on the publisher's part can be proven.[254]

The public figure doctrine and maximally protecting free speech to facilitate 'unconstrained political debate and effective democracy'[255] were rejected by the CA in the leading second wave decision of *Jeyaretnam Joshua Benjamin v Lee Kuan Yew*.[256] Prime Minister (PM) Lee Kuan Yew, the PAP's secretary-general, sued Jeyaretnam, the WP's secretary-general, for words spoken at an election rally. This related to the suicide of a minister under investigation for corruption. Jeyaretnam's words allegedly injured the PM's reputation by imputing he had advised the minister to commit suicide and did not order an inquiry into how the drug taken by the minister was obtained.

The CA noted the material difference between the formulation and underlying policy of Singapore's Article 14 compared to the US First Amendment and Article 10 ECHR. Article 14 conferred a broad discretion on Parliament to enact restrictive laws against defamation, which did not even have to satisfy the

[249] Persons addressing public meetings like election rallies should exercise care in what they say about their opponents and have no interest in defaming opponents to garner votes: *Bureau v Campbell* [1928] 3 SLR 907, 931–32, cited in *Jeyaretnam v Lee Kuan Yew* [1992] 1 SLR(R) 791, [68].

[250] *Lingens v Austria* App No 9815/82 (8 July 1986), [42].

[251] *Gertz v Robert Welch Inc* 418 US 323 (1974).

[252] *New York Times v Sullivan* 376 US 254 (1964) (Justice Brennan).

[253] ibid.

[254] [1992] 1 SLR(R) 791, [52], discussing various US cases.

[255] ibid [43].

[256] ibid.

test of 'necessary and expedient' applicable to other grounds of derogation in Article 14(2) like public order.[257] In contrast, the First Amendment contains no express limits in prioritising speech, while Article 10(2) ECHR requires limits to be 'necessary in a democratic society', a far more rigorous test than what a statist or even communitarian RoL would require.[258] The nightmare spectre of an absolute right to free speech was invoked, of 'persons recklessly maligning others with impunity', doing the public 'more harm than good'.[259]

Singapore courts have rejected the US public figure doctrine as public office-holders or politicians are 'equally entitled' to the protection private persons enjoy for their reputations, as defamation law 'protects the public reputation of public men'.[260] It would be 'untenable and wrong' to reduce damages in cases with a 'political flavour', as this would violate the equality guarantee.[261]

Citing two pre-Canadian Charter cases in support,[262] one dating to the nineteenth century, the CA in *Jeyaretnam v Lee Kuan Yew* accorded great weight to the reputational interests of public persons and determinative weight to the public interest in the maintenance of public character by ensuring that 'sensitive and honourable men'[263] were not deterred from seeking public office and serving the common weal. This resonates with the government's espoused neo-Confucianist ideal that governors were honourable men '君子' (*junzi*), who could be trusted to act rightly,[264] as distinct from Western distrust of governors. A *junzi* is a noble, moral person who leads by example and, while this is desirable, the danger is that governors are as capable as private persons of being corrupt and self-serving. Although framed as a balance and acknowledging the importance of free speech as a way of 'exposing wrongdoing', the High Court has insisted there is an 'equal public interest' in allowing officials 'to exercise their duties unfettered by false aspersions'.[265] However, one might argue that the CA has subsequently treated reputational interests of politicians as superior interests, downplaying the democratic importance of robust political speech.

However, the common law does not stand still and the courts have intimated in *Review Publishing v Lee Hsien Loong* their willingness to recalibrate balances in favour of free speech if socio-political values have changed in favour of greater political accountability, transparency and democratic participation.[266] The CA noted that the *Reynolds* privilege of 'responsible journalism'[267] was based

[257] *Xu Yuan Chen v PP* [2024] SGCA 17, [56]–[57].

[258] ibid [56].

[259] ibid [61], citing *Post Publishing Co v Hallam* [1893] 59 Fed 530, 540, [65] (US Court of Appeal).

[260] ibid [62].

[261] *Tang Liang Hong v Lee Kuan Yew et al* [1997] 3 SLR(R) 576, [118]–[119].

[262] *Campbell v Spottiswoode* (1863) 32 LJ QB 185; *Tucker v Douglas* [1950] 2 DLR 827.

[263] [1992] 1 SLR(R) 791, [64], Citing *Gatley on Libel and Slander*, 8th edn (Sweet & Maxwell, 1981) 206.

[264] White paper on Shared Values (n 25).

[265] Rajendran J, *Goh Chok Tong v Jeyaretnam JB* [1977] 3 SLR(R) 46, [25].

[266] ibid [274].

[267] This was abolished under s 4(6) of the 2013 UK Defamation Act c 26, which creates a 'public interest' defence under s 4.

on elevating the UK common law right of free speech to constitutional status based on a 'higher legal order foundation'[268] by the Human Rights Act (HRA). Section 12(4)(a) HRA directed the courts to pay regard to the public interest in media publications, shifting the balance by giving 'greater weight' to free speech over reputational rights.[269] The *Reynolds* privilege was clearly 'based … on a "liberalising intention"' even if it did not recognise political speech as a new subject matter category of qualified privilege.[270] Australia and New Zealand have also evolved indigenous balances elevating free speech interests.[271]

Were the courts to adopt the *Reynolds* privilege or its underlying value, it would be on the basis of Article 14 as a constitutional right being part of the supreme law, which is 'of a higher legal order' than the ECHR. The rationale grounding the *Reynolds* privilege of free speech as the rule and restrictions as the exception is 'equally relevant' to Singapore citizens.[272] Any alteration of the 'existing balance' between political speech and protecting reputation would only benefit citizens as the constitution-makers 'did not think it proper or wise to confer constitutional free speech on non-citizens who have no stake in our country'.[273]

One might argue that the 'existing balance' as expressed in *Jeyaretnam v Lee Kuan Yew*[274] is flawed in not taking Article 14 seriously,[275] considering the constitutional framers intended that free speech should be subject to the common law of defamation, effectively treating it as a common law liberty[276] or subsidiary right.[277] Any judicial development which would recognise more robust protection for political speech would be welcome. In this respect, the CA was willing to consider the values underlying the *Reynolds* privilege as fodder for forging a distinctive Singapore approach, to mitigate the 'long recognised …

[268] Lord Steyn, *Reynolds v Times Newspaper Ltd* [2001] 2 AC 127, 207–08, cited in *Review Publishing* (n 32) [197].

[269] *Review Publishing* (n 32) [199].

[270] ibid [205], citing Lord Carswell in *Seaga v Harper* [2009] 1 AC 1, [10].

[271] ibid [216]–[220], [221]–[229].

[272] ibid [265].

[273] ibid [267]–[268].

[274] [1992] 1 SLR(R) 791, [61].

[275] Kevin YL Tan, 'Besmirching Honourable Men: The Defamation of Politicians in Singapore' [2020] IYCL 55.

[276] Art 162 requires that all existing laws be construed with any modifications needed to bring it into conformity with the Constitution, but the CA stated that the law of defamation as modified by the Defamation Act was not inconsistent with Art 14: *Jeyaretnam v Lee Kuan Yew* [1992] 1 SLR(R) 791, [57]–[59]. It later characterised the equivalent of Art 162 as a 'law-enacting provision': *Review Publishing* (n 32) [250]. The constitutionality of retained pre-Independence laws relating to criminal defamation was upheld in *Xu Yuanchen v PP* [2023] SGHC 23, [75] and on appeal [2024] SGCA 17, [61].

[277] A subsidiary right such as that in Art 14(2)(a) 'expressly allows Parliaments to impose restrictions on constitutional free speech' to provide against defamation: *Review Publishing* (n 32) [286].

"chilling" effect of this rigorous reputation protective principle',[278] while recognising that Parliament ultimately determines the balance between the competing interests.[279]

The 'responsible journalism' privilege as a defence was guided by 10 non-exhaustive factors,[280] including taking steps to verify information and to ensure the article contains the gist of the plaintiff's story. However, in striking an autochthonous path, due regard has to be paid to local particularities and political culture. This includes citizens' demand for 'a high level of civility in our public discourse',[281] ensuring 'honesty and integrity in public discourse on matters of public interest'[282] and holding the media to the traditional activities of reporting and commenting, refraining from 'investigative journalism which carries with it a political agenda'.[283] This indicates a lower tolerance for lies and a higher regard for reputation, both as an aspect of dignity and as a form of honour, characteristic of a 'deference society'.[284] This is manifest in how damages are calculated in political defamation suits.

(ii) Quantum and Cultural Context

Singapore has rejected the US 'public figure' doctrine, which requires politicians to be more tolerant of criticism; both public and private persons enjoy equal protection of their reputations. Indeed, even where it is argued that the motive of a high-ranking government official like the PM in bringing a defamation suit in his private capacity was to 'silence his critics', the courts would not limit the rights of injured parties to access the courts to vindicate their interests 'even if they happen to be public figures'.[285]

However, defamed public figures receive greater protection by receiving higher damages. Effectively, reputational interests are treated at least as co-equal constitutional rights, balanced against free speech. The Singapore public figure variant is non-egalitarian and neo-feudalist, with the reputations of government ministers and politicians ranked at the apex of a fourfold tier of defamed plaintiffs, set forth by the CA in *Lim Eng Hock Peter v Lim Jian Wei* (Table 2).[286]

[278] Lord Nicholls, *Reynolds v Times Newspaper* [2001] 2 AC 127, 192, cited in *Review Publishing* (n 32) [175].

[279] *Review Publishing* (n 32) [269]–[271].

[280] Lord Nicholls, *Reynolds v Times Newspaper* [2001] 2 AC 127, 205, cited in *Review Publishing* (n 32) [192].

[281] National Report: Singapore, Working Group, Universal Periodic Review, A/HRC/WG.6/24/SGP/1 (28 October 2015) [117].

[282] *Review Publishing* (n 32) [285].

[283] ibid [272], [278].

[284] Robert C Post, 'The Social Foundations of Defamation Law: Reputation and the Constitution' (1986) 74 California Law Review 691, 702.

[285] *Leong Sze Hian v Lee Hsien Loong* [2019] 2 SLR 591, [4]–[5].

[286] [2010] 4 SLR 357. This drew a distinction between public leaders, in both the public and private sectors, as distinct from people famous in the public eye, who promoted the public welfare, the reputation of professional men and finally that of ordinary individuals.

Table 2 Ranking Reputations for Calculating Damages for defamation

Top tier	Political leaders, where defamation causes injury to both personal reputation and the institutional reputation of government
Second tier	Non-political public leaders who are public figures in business, industry and the professions where their devotion to public service augments public welfare
Third tier	Prominent figures like businessmen who are not national leaders or involved in public affairs, where the business does not serve the public welfare; damages are higher due to the damage done to their professional reputations
Fourth tier	Private individuals

The higher the social status, the heavier the weight of reputation and the greater the damages awarded. Public figures are 'typically awarded substantial damages' if the defamation relates to their 'honesty, integrity or character',[287] including professional reputation.[288] For example, Prime Ministers and senior Cabinet ministers received between SGD$300,000 and $350,000 in damages in *Lee Kuan Yew v Vinocur John*[289] for an International Herald Tribune article alleging political nepotism and corruption. Such charges were 'very grave', and if not challenged would have destroyed the plaintiffs by eroding their moral authority and ability to govern effectively.[290] Thus, the involvement of two 'prominent public figures' with the greater capacity to damage the reputations of those they speak ill of, such as a PM defamed by a prominent opposition politician, translated into higher damages of $300,000 in *Goh Chok Tong v Chee Soon Juan*.[291] Opposition politician Tang Liang Hong was sued by 11 members of the ruling political party for defamatory remarks published in written publications and at an election rally, and had to pay damages to each for a whopping total of $8.075 million.[292] Topping the schedule of damages in *Lee Kuan Yew v Tang Liang Hong*[293] was $600,000 awarded to PM Goh for a single count (Goh received a total of $1.4 million for three counts).

On appeal, the CA in *Tang Liang Hong v Lee Kuan Yew*[294] registered a 'caveat' against the trend of rising 'substantial damages' awarded in defamation cases, which was to be discouraged, otherwise mounting damages would become 'extremely high', akin to the 'grossly exorbitant awards' juries made

[287] *Lee Hsien Loong v Leong Sze Hian* [2021] 4 SLR 1128, [88].
[288] *Lee Hsien Loong v Xu Yuan Chen* [2022] 3 SLR 924, [69].
[289] [1995] 3 SLR(R) 38.
[290] ibid [55], citing *Lee Kuan Yew v Seow Khee Leng* [1988] 2 SLR(R) 252, [25].
[291] [2005] 1 SLR(R) 573, [42], [72].
[292] *Lee Kuan Yew et al v Tang Liang Hong* [1997] 2 SLR(R) 81. This concerned defamatory remarks suggesting that the PM and senior Cabinet ministers acted improperly in receiving developers' discounts for some property purchases.
[293] [1997] 2 SLR(R) 81, [112].
[294] [1997] 3 SLR(R) 576, [158].

elsewhere. While each case turned on its own facts and without prescribing a cap, the CA underscored that damages should fall 'within a reasonable bracket' and be 'a fair and reasonable sum which is proportionate to the harm and injury' suffered by the unjustly defamed. The CA found the awards excessive and sought to moderate the individual awards, so, for example, in Mr Goh's case, the $600,000 award was reduced to $270,000, the $450,000 to $200,000 and the $350,000 to $230,000 (totalling $700,000).[295]

By way of broad comparison, government and opposition parliamentarians have received damages of $120,000[296] to $210,000,[297] while professionals have received sums such as $45,000 (architect), $150,000 (lawyer) and $210,000 (businessman), inclusive of aggravated damages.[298] Private individuals of lesser public standing, such as company employees, have received awards ranging from $20,000 to $80,000.[299] Damages are meant to be compensatory and vindicatory, deterrent not punitive and assessed according to a set of factors, including the plaintiff and defendant's standing.[300] They are not meant to yield a 'cornucopia' nor be merely symbolic.[301]

The courts have appeared defensive towards the perception that excessive damages are awarded in political defamation cases so as to 'chill' public interest debate:[302] they have protested that the issue of quantum 'appears to be continually misrepresented or misunderstood by some sections of the public in Singapore', a misconception that needed clearing up by explaining the basis for the spectrum of differentiated damage awards for 'different classes of plaintiffs'.[303]

Public leaders, including political and non-political leaders in government or the private sector, have consistently been awarded 'higher damages', as they 'devote their careers and lives to serving the State and the public'. This excludes famous persons like entertainers or footballers. Higher damages flow from 'their standing in Singapore society and devotion to public service', and the impact of defamatory statements by which they suffer 'greater damage' not only to their personal reputation but to the reputation of their affiliated institutions. With respect to a Cabinet minister, this would include 'the reputation of Singapore', whose leaders have a global reputation for honesty, integrity and dedicated service.[304] The Singapore public may hold a 'higher regard and respect'[305] for its public leaders than elsewhere, with distrust of politicians becoming endemic in Western liberal jurisdictions.

[295] ibid [159]–[160].
[296] *Chiam See Tong v Ling How Doong* [1996] 3 SLR(R) 942 (where Chaim, the leader of an opposition party, was accused of being a PAP lackey).
[297] *Vasoo v Chee Soon Juan*, Suit No 936 of 1993.
[298] *Lim Eng Hock Peter* (n 286) [15]–[17].
[299] ibid [31]–[32].
[300] ibid [7]–[8].
[301] ibid [6], [10].
[302] ibid [10].
[303] ibid [2].
[304] ibid [12].
[305] ibid [18].

The CA in *Peter Lim* noted there has been no conscious reduction of damages awarded to political figures in jurisdictions like Australia, Canada, New Zealand and the UK 'despite the common law defence of qualified privilege to political speech'.[306] Comparatively speaking, it considered that Singapore damages awards had in the past 'not been excessive' but 'rather moderate',[307] pointing to damages awards elsewhere in the Commonwealth to plaintiffs of lesser standing. It noted that damages in a single suit with respect to the PM or ministers where defamed 'have to date not exceeded $500,000'.[308] In England, author Jeffrey Archer was awarded £500,000 in 1987 by a jury for alleged defamation by a newspaper of a paid sexual encounter; Lord Aldington received £1.5 million for being called a war criminal; and more recently an MP received £150,000 when accused of receiving money from Iraqi President Saddam Hussein.[309]

It appears, then, that damages imposed by Singapore courts do not exceed the range applied in other common law jurisdictions.

The justification for higher damages for government leaders resonates with the neo-Confucianist conception of government by trustworthy, honourable men, although this rationale has never been raised judicially. Instead, Belinda Ang J in *Lee Hsien Loong v Singapore Democratic Party* took inspiration from the teachings of Greek rhetorician Isocrates, noting that 'the stronger a man's desire to persuade his hearers, the more zealously will he strive to be honourable and to have the esteem of his fellow citizens'.[310] A good reputation serves one's personal and professional life as 'people are apt to listen to those whom they trust'.[311] Effective government is tied to moral authority, which is a form of reputational honour.

A hierarchical view of society is also manifest in the discount given when quantifying damages, in examining the status of the defamer, a distinctive local particularity. The higher the standing of the defendant, the greater the weight accorded to his words and consequently the greater the damage to the plaintiff.[312] For example, the fact that the defendant was a prominent public figure, an opposition politician and Singapore Democratic Party secretary-general, was a relevant factor in *Goh Chok Tong v Chee Soon Juan*, where Chee, while campaigning the 2001 General Elections, alleged the PM had mishandled national funds. Damages were quantified at $300,000.[313]

Conversely the 'comparative low standing' of the defendant in *Lee Hsien Loong v Roy Ngerng Yi Ling*,[314] who claimed he was a 'defamer of low

[306] ibid [10].
[307] ibid [14].
[308] ibid [15].
[309] ibid [19].
[310] [2009] 1 SLR(R) 642, [102].
[311] ibid.
[312] *Lee Hsien Loong v Xu Yuan Chen* (n 288) [71].
[313] *Goh Chok Tong* (n 291).
[314] [2016] 1 SLR 1321.

credence'[315] and was less likely to be believed, translated into a 'substantial reduction'[316] in damages. A sum of $150,000 in damages was awarded, which is about a 50 per cent discount from the sum imposed on those defaming the PM during the last 20 years. Ngerng comments on local politics in his private blog and published an article found to defame the PM by alleging criminal misappropriation of moneys paid to the Central Provident Fund. The High Court indicated there was a difference between a flippant post and Ngerng's blog, which had some 400 well-structured articles; thus, it had a greater impact that a 'run-of-the-mill blog' but would be 'less influential than a traditional newspaper'[317] or an institutional site.

This is relevant because the wider the extent of publication and the greater the impact of an article on an objective reader, the greater the damages.[318] Higher damages would be appropriate where an article was published on a site which was not a mere individual blog, such as TOC, an alternative news publication website with a wide following (over 121,000 on its Facebook page), as TOC's 'wide viewership and role' lent credence to that publication, rendering it 'more believable to the ordinary reader'.[319] While TOC was not 'as reputable or influential' as international publications like the International Herald Tribune (IHT), the TOC Chief Editor had a 'higher standing' that the defendant in *Ngerng*. A total of $210,000 in damages was awarded, with the court noting that damage assessment was 'not quasi-scientific', affirming the need 'to guard against the trend' of rising damages with each successive case.[320] In a 2024 decision involving two Cabinet ministers and a defendant (who happened to be the PM's brother) who was active on social media, posting on Singapore matters with 89,000 Facebook followers, the statuses of the parties were significant factors in calculating damages ($200,000 per minister).[321]

Sharing a hyperlink on a 'public setting' Facebook post to an online article alleging the Singapore PM was embroiled in the 1MBD corruption scandal involving the Malaysian PM sufficed to constitute publication in *Lee Hsien Loong v Leong Sze Hian*.[322] Whether a publication is 'substantial' turns on evidence showing a sufficient number of readers to justify awarding damages.[323] While Leong described himself as a 'staunch government critic'[324] and was

[315] ibid [34].
[316] ibid [116].
[317] ibid [55].
[318] *Lim Eng Hock Peter* (n 286) [33].
[319] *Lee Hsien Loong v Xu Yuan Chen* (n 288).
[320] ibid [122]–[124].
[321] *K Shanmugam v Lee Hsien Yang* [2024] SGHC 136, [36]–[40].
[322] *Lee Hsien Loong* [2021] (n 287).
[323] Post (n 283) [36]. The High Court, in *Lee Hsien Loong* [2021] (n 287) [41], rejected the Canadian approach in *Crooke v Newton* [2011] 3 SCR 269, which did not consider bare hyperlinks as publications, preferring to holistically assess facts like the number of Facebook friends, followers and 'likes' a poster had, and the privacy settings of the social media platform: [92].
[324] ibid [91].

involved in politics, he did not have the elevated status of being the 'principal opposition speaker', whose words would attract more weight than a 'lesser individual' in *Lee Kuan Yew v JB Jeyaretnam*.[325] There was a 'qualitative difference' between Leong and individuals who were MPs, holders of public office or editors of influential daily newspapers with an international circulation, like the IHT.[326] Leong's standing was 'roughly comparable' with Roy Ngerng, both being socio-political commentators not holding any public office, with 'some modicum of following' on their social media platforms. Although Ngerng's defamatory article had a broader reach, Leong's defamatory statement was worse, and damages of $133,000 was awarded.[327]

The Confucianist differentiation of persons into categories of the sensitive and honourable *junzi* (君子), as opposed to the disreputable *xiaoren* (小人), a petty person bound by personal prejudices, shows how Singapore cultural conceptions of social hierarchy shape the contours of political libel. This may be mitigated by a growing appreciation of the importance of political speech to democracy and judicial willingness to recalibrate balances in relation to political libel defences or import the values underlying the *Reynolds* privilege to moderate damages – the court may calibrate damages in proportion to 'the degree of care' the defendant took to ensure the accuracy of the publication. This would give expression to a 'new balance' between free speech and reputation, without 'immunising the defendant from liability' in cases where free speech is appropriately accorded precedence over reputational interests.[328] An autochthonous variant of a 'responsible journalism' test is one where the defendant does not 'get off scot-free' for injuring the plaintiff's reputation, maintaining the merit of 'deterring irresponsible journalism',[329] given that falsehoods or misinformation undermine the democratic rationale for free speech, as the House of Lords observed in *Reynolds*.[330]

While the developments in political libel jurisprudence may not yet go far enough to robustly protect free speech, the shift from cursory to reason-giving judgments and the willingness to consider recalibrating defences or moderating damages is an incremental improvement towards developing a due appreciation of political speech. In a post-deferential age, it is clear there is a growing appetite for alternative political views and government accountability; the fact that Ngerng and Leong were able through crowdfunding to pay off the damages awarded against them, of $150,000 and $133,000 respectively, may be evidence of a modest political sea change, of resistance and the broad desire for greater free speech.[331]

[325] [1979–1980] SLR(R) 24, [70].
[326] *Lee Hsien Loong* [2021] (n 287) [91].
[327] ibid [125]–[126].
[328] *Review Publishing* (n 32) [297].
[329] ibid.
[330] *Reynolds v Times Newspaper* [1999] WLR 1010, discussed in *Review Publishing* (n 32).
[331] 'Blogger Roy Ngerng Finishes Paying PM Lee $150,000 for Defamation Using Crowdfunding' *Straits Times* (17 May 2021).

IV. CONCLUSION

While the liberalism of fear may sustain a rights-oriented, court-centric brand of constitutionalism, the communitarianism of mixed trust in authority and fear of disorder generates an approach towards rights which does not sustain an ever-expanding pantheon of rights claims. The concern remains whether the law provides sufficient constraints over political expediency, to prevent the invocation of the RoL from becoming 'empty legalism'[332] in failing to restrain government action by protecting rights.

For Lord Bingham, the 'adequate protection of fundamental human rights' is one of eight principles in his definition of the RoL.[333] While human rights are certainly a worthy object, the ambiguity of the concept, which is contested, opens the door for the RoL to become an umbrella term invoked to house all virtues, effectively to become a theory of the rule of *good* law, which invites controversy in a plural world.

Rights in Singapore jurisprudence do not have peremptory status, being subject to a balancing process in a context where less weight is given to counter-majoritarian institutions than in liberal democracies, where the focus is on preventing majority tyranny and maximising autonomy. The brand of legal communitarianism evolving in Singapore may not be satisfactory to proponents of Western liberal values, but is preferable to the subjugation of rights to statist trumps. It seeks to accommodate collective aspirations to self-government and democratic rule, while sufficiently protecting individual rights.[334] The individual is not atomistic but is situated in the community, where due regard must be given to rights, responsibilities and the common weal in the endless project of seeking the equilibrium of ordered liberty. This is situated somewhere between the abuses of the RoL as juristocracy and the RoL as unmoderated authoritarianism.

[332] Beatrice Frank et al, 'The Decline of the Rule of Law in Singapore and Malaysia: A Report of the Committee on International Human Rights of the Association of the Bar of the City of New York' (The Association, 1990) 17.

[333] Tom Bingham, *The Rule of Law* (Allen Lane, 2010).

[334] Roberto Gargarella, 'Constitutionalism and the Rule of Law' in Jens Meierhenrich and Martin Loughlin (eds), *The Cambridge Companion to the Rule of Law* (Cambridge University Press, 2021) 428.

7

Conclusion: The Future of the Rule of Law in Singapore

THE CONTEXT IN which the rule of law (RoL) operates in Singapore is in a state of flux, given the generational shift and evolving nature of Singapore politics as it enters its 'fourth generation', or 4G.[1] On 15 May 2024, Lawrence Wong became Singapore's fourth Prime Minister (PM), and in an interview with *The Economist*[2] made two key points in relation to the evolving nature of politics and economics in Singapore.

The first was that the days of People's Action Party (PAP) dominance under PM Lee Kuan Yew 'are over, and we cannot go back to that period', and that 'the opposition presence in parliament is here to stay'. PM Wong plans to continue consulting and engaging with Singaporeans by finding 'platforms where people can get involved in decision-making and start shaping the future of our country together'. For a cosmopolitan younger generation that has only ever known peace and prosperity, and which is plugged into cyberspace, global trends and the online morass of information, misinformation and divergent viewpoints, it is dialogue, not diktat, persuasion not fear, that is the expectation. Although unlikely in the mid-term, even the political leadership recognises there might one day be a post-PAP Singapore and the experience of political turnover. As such, paternal democracy is on display, as the governors, through modest social and political liberalisation, accommodate, by institution and practice, the desires of a more demanding citizenry for greater political freedom in a post-deferential era where the PAP no longer enjoy 'the largely unquestioned trust'[3] of times past. To the extent that the 'history of political repression'[4] have been relegated to memory rather than lived experience, this is to be welcomed.

Second, while Singapore has achieved spectacular economic success since 1965, 'the period of effortless growth is over' and, despite an allergy to

[1] James Chin, 'The PAP Model: Can the 4G Hold on to Power' (2023) 112(2) The Round Table 173.

[2] DPM Lawrence Wong's interview with *The Economist* (6 May 2024) pmo.gov.sg.

[3] Sudhir Vadaketh and Donald Low, *Hard Choices: Challenging the Singapore Consensus* (NUS Press, 2014) xi.

[4] Chua Beng Huat, *Liberalism Disavowed: Communitarianism and State Capitalism in Singapore* (NUS Press, 2017) 17.

welfarism, social spending has increased, particularly with regard to healthcare and an aging population. This was 14 per cent of the GDP in 2010, and is expected to rise to 20 per cent by 2030.[5] As of 2024, Singapore ranks as the best country in the World Bank Human Capital Index.[6] Social tensions arising from the sensitive issue of increasing immigration for labour purposes will need to be managed, with foreigners welcomed for the economic benefit they bring, but asked to 'adjust to our social norms'.[7]

What may be anticipated is a period of *controlled* change, where reform will take place at an evolutionary rather than revolutionary pace. Expectations for material prosperity will have to be managed and the economy will undergo 'the process of churn', where non-viable businesses will fade away in the push towards 'the productivity and innovation frontier', as Singapore reinvents itself again.[8] The RoL will continue to underpin the business-friendly environment in the continued search for new investments in what is now, by some metrics,[9] a developed country and by others, a developing country,[10] or somewhere in-between, as a 'more advanced developing country'.[11] It seems that Singapore defies easy categorisation.

Singapore cannot be a mere 'hotel', but must be a home that engenders a sense of belonging, even affective solidarity.[12] This requires a shift to the intangibles, to principles and ideals that bind, to finding common ground in an age of divisive identity politics, the recalibration of the tensions between pragmatism and principle, based on foundational commitments to meritocracy, incorruptibility, tripartism, racial and religious harmony. In 1999, PM Goh Chok Tong spoke of the difficulties of creating the Singapore 'tribe',[13] in the sense of 'an extended Singapore Family with its distinctive core values and social characteristics, and sharing a common destiny'. In an ethnically and religiously plural nation without a shared history, a shared future is what unifies a people. In 2015, when Singapore celebrated her jubilee, PM Lee Hsien Loong spoke of the

[5] 'Singapore Has Achieved Astounding Economic Success' *The Economist* (8 May 2024).

[6] The World Bank in Singapore, www.worldbank.org/en/country/singapore/overview.

[7] Chin (n 1).

[8] ibid.

[9] Singapore is classified a developed country by dint of its high Human Development Index, where it ranks in the top 10: 'Developed Countries 2024', worldpopulationreview.com.

[10] The World Trade Organization considers Singapore a developing country owing to its reliance on global trade: 'Singapore Does Not Take Advantage of WTO Special Provisions for Developing Nations in Negotiating Agreements: MTI' *Today* (27 July 2019). Singapore is not recognised as a developed country under the Paris Climate Accords: 'Grace Fu, Leon Perera Debate over Singapore's Developing Country Status at COP27' *Today* (21 April 2023).

[11] The Organisation for Economic Co-Operation and Development (OECD) so reclassified Singapore in 1995. See Peter Wilson, 'The Dilemma of a More Advanced Developing Country: Conflicting Views on the Development Strategy of Singapore' (2000) 38(1) The Developing Economies 105.

[12] Anna Teo, 'How to Make Singapore a Home Not a Hotel' Business Times (21 June 1991) 26.
Terence Ho, 'Why It's Getting Harder to Make Singapore a Home Truly for All, and yet We Must Persevere' *Today* (8 August 2022).

[13] PM Goh Chok Tong, 'Whither Singapore?' (NTU Students Union, 11 May 1999) nas.gov.sg.

governors and the people, 'the lions and the lion-hearted', partnering to build a nation.[14] He spoke of how, as 'one Singapore family', the mourning of PM Lee Kuan Yew's death that year was a 'shared moment of sorrow' which bonded the people, making the intangible concrete, ending the struggle of finding words 'to define the Singapore spirit or to say what being Singaporean is. Now we know that we are Singaporean.'[15] It was, in a way, a national coming of age, a celebration of past successes and a gearing up for the next set of challenges to scale, in an increasingly volatile and uncertain world.

PM Lawrence Wong has described the transformation of Singapore in the past 60 years as 'nothing short of a miracle', with his mission being 'to make sure our little red dot shines brightly for as long as possible', with the sober apprehension that Singapore remains 'a very tiny little island in a vast and dangerous world'.[16] In his last speech as Prime Minister, Lee Hsien Loong noted that Singapore had made 'exceptional economic and social gains, because our system is exceptional', and that if Singapore politics became like other countries, 'beset by populism, tribalism, nativism or obsessed by short gains', then 'we will certainly be sunk'. He urged Singaporeans to 'uphold this ethos of exceptionalism and excellence', to maintain political stability, while appreciating the system 'will evolve with time', hopefully in a way that 'continues to serve Singapore's interests'.[17]

If the RoL was a key pillar of the developmentalist state in its salad days, underpinning the stellar economic success of the city-state, it is quite clear the RoL will continue to play a central role in seeking to maintain economic success and sustainable development within a highly developed mixed market economy. The situation is different now, as a now mature economy charts a path of continuing economic transformation to meet the exigencies of a global environment, which, after three decades of globalisation, has shifted 'from collaboration to competition'.[18] Restructuring should be along the lines of shared ownership, promoting a strong innovative ecosystem and continuing to be a trusted partner for the world.

The RoL in the future will continue to be a pre-eminent feature of Singapore governance, but the key question is, given the paradoxical nature of the RoL as both a constraint upon and an affirmation of state power, where will the accent lie? Will it veer more closely towards the Lockean or Hobbesian side of the continuum?

The solution to the problem of power is that 'you must first enable the government to control the governed'. The RoL has been deployed in Singapore

[14] PM Lee, 'National Day Message 2015' *Today* (8 August 2015).
[15] PM Lee, 'National Day Rally, 2015', pmo.gov.sg.
[16] Wong (n 2).
[17] PM Lee Hsien Loong, 'May Day Rally, 1 May 2024', pmo.gov.sg.
[18] DPM Heng Swee Keat, 'Reasons to Be Upbeat about S'pore's Prospects, Despite Difficult Challenges Ahead' *Straits Times* (28 February 2024).

to serve this objective, to great effect. However, this raises the very real danger of autocratic rule and authoritarian abuse, and hence this must be moderated by obliging the government 'to control itself'.[19] Undoubtedly, great importance will continue to be given to the instrumental role of the RoL as a tool of governance, to maintain socio-political order and an environment where community life is not disrupted, where business thrives and where human flourishing can take place. However, it appears that greater weight is being given to the role of the RoL in terms of constraining power, through enforcing legal limits to power or protecting rights by judicial review in tandem with political means of accountability. While senior lawyers like Michael Hwang, sometime President of the Law Society, have in times past confessed their lack of courage in seeking judicial review for matters like licence denials, the Chief Justice in a 2010 speech took Hwang's urging that the Bar be 'more proactive in commencing judicial review proceedings' as a good sign of faith 'that the legal system and the operation of the RoL remain functional'.[20] Certainly, from the vantage point of the twenty-first century's third decade, any such diffidence appears to have been expelled in the face of growing activism before the courts.

The RoL in Singapore starts with a thin or formal rule-of-law core, and is thickened by a political and economic philosophy which may be described as producing a form of legal communitarianism; the endgame here is not Western liberal democracy, though it is fair to say that many constitutional governments have mixed elements which are statist, liberal and communitarian. The RoL in Singapore has long supported objects like development, law and order, fair treatment of investors associated with the conservative right in the US estimation, as well as centrists who focus on technocratic ideals pertaining to government accountability, transparency and anti-corruption; increasingly, the RoL is encompassing a concern with rights, fair and equal treatment for all and helping the disadvantaged – concerns which occupy the political left.[21]

While Singapore has long been criticised for being illiberal and authoritarian, this is a temptation all governments are prone to. Indeed, governments in the 'West' which pride themselves as being liberal, have, when mixed with progressivism or faced with exigency, demonstrated distinctly illiberal traits – whether through lawfare and weaponising the use of courts to suppress political opponents, draconian uses of law to detain terrorists without trial or to impose pandemic lockdowns, or other oppressive measures threatening life, bodily integrity, livelihood and freedom of movement in the name of public health. State-sanctioned philosophical liberalism, sometimes related to 'woke ideology', threatens liberties like freedom of speech, conscience and religion or the right of parents to choose their children's education, which are recognised

[19] The Federalist Papers No 51, https://avalon.law.yale.edu/18th_century/fed51.asp.

[20] Chan Sek Keong, 'Judicial Review – From Angst to Empathy' (2010) 22 SAcLJ 469, [12].

[21] Thomas Carothers, 'Rule of Law Temptations' (2009) 33(1) Fletcher Forum of World Affairs 49, 52.

human rights.[22] The RoL is against autocracy and arbitrariness, whether through rulers or rules, and those who wield the power to oppress today may be state or non-state actors, who may form collusive alliances to manipulate public opinion.[23] The inability or unwillingness of certain governments to keep order and the flow of ordinary life in the face of often euphemistically termed 'peaceful protests', which can be intimidating and abusive to other persons and can be disruptive to community life, will continue to be an anti-model as a failure to govern.[24]

The RoL can be violated by diverse means, whether through authoritarian acts and policies, through schemes of distributive justice which accord preferential treatment to sectors of the population, through courts which are partisan to the political branches or through courts which practise juristocratic rule. No country can claim perfect realisation of RoL values, and the project should be to closely approximate their achievement, bearing in mind the prospects for improvement or the possibilities for deterioration are always present.

The study of the RoL in the Singapore context is salutary for a few reasons. First, it shatters the orthodoxy that economic liberalisation and development within an advanced capitalist society, underpinned by juridification and judicialisation, necessarily leads to political liberalisation, after the conception of the RoL associated with Western liberal democracy. Where this view is prevalent, the impulse then is to compare how the RoL in one context measures up to the norms of Western liberal democracy, expressed through the rights-oriented court-centric model of constitutionalism. If countries like Singapore are 'semi-authoritarian' or otherwise less civilised, then Singapore practice is but the way station to some Fukuyaman 'end of history'.

However, the fact that Singapore has achieved economic success and realised at least a formal RoL shows that economic liberalisation is possible without political liberalisation, after the Western liberal model. Authoritarian from the outset, Singapore is undergoing an incremental political liberalisation where the accent remains on political constitutionalism in tandem with a calibrated form of judicial review pursuant to a model based on legal communitarianism, which weighs community values and national interests more heavily than in Western liberal jurisdictions. The key question may be: if economic success can be attained without political liberalisation, can continued economic success in a now developed nation be sustained without authoritarianism? Could the

[22] Hans Clausen, 'The Privilege of Speech in a Pleasantly Authoritarian Country' (2005) 38(2) Vanderbilt Journal of Transnational Law 443; Cathy Young, 'Perils to Free Speech from Woke and Anti-Woke' (Cato Institute Commentary, 11 January 2023).

[23] eg Tim Groseclose, *Left Turn: How Liberal Media Bias Distorts the American Mind* (St Martin's Press, 2011); House Committee on Oversight and Accountability Press Release, 'The Cover Up: Big Tech, the Swamp and Mainstream Media Coordinated to Censor Americans' Free Speech' (8 February 2023) oversight.house.gov.

[24] 'Anthony Albanese Blasts Greens over Blockades on MPs Offices in Heated Row over Gaza Conflict' (*The Nightly*, 5 June 2024); 'Whether It's Campus Rioters or Campus Occupation, the Rule of Law Must Prevail' *Philadelphia Inquirer* (6 May 2024).

Singapore model of the RoL operating within a non-liberal communitarian democracy be a 'stable and self-sustaining' one, rather than 'merely a transit stop on the way from one end of the spectrum to the other'.[25]

There are fears that the Singapore model might be attractive to authoritarian states like China or Vietnam, which could adopt the model as justification for rejecting the claims of Western liberalism in relation to constitutional government. Apologies for authoritarian rule are unfortunately always possible, although the Singapore model should be analytically distinguished from de jure one-party states and brute authoritarianism; while the architects of the Singapore legal and political system hold to its exceptionalism, they have never been prescriptive, owing to the particularities of the city-state. Indeed, the Singapore model is not an arrival to be attained, but a constant journey in the continuing experimental project of good governance, based on 'an effective and responsible interaction between lawgiver and subject' to maintain a healthy legal system.[26] If the practice of RoL in Singapore is accepted as an expression of the RoL rather than an exception to it, this practice can enrich the global discourse of RoL in terms of what it is and what it requires, how it relates to liberty, equality and dignity, and what it is able or unable to accomplish in the enterprise of statecraft.

Second, by decentring the hegemonic RoL model, which is dogmatically conflated with 'thick' values associated with the processes and institutions of liberal democracies, the Singapore model facilitates the pluralisation of the RoL as a universal principle, which may be variously adopted in the task of moderating power. Without discounting the concept of universal justice, this helps avoid a myopic parochialism towards the RoL in a complex, postmodern world. It provides the occasion for interrogating whether RoL values can be meaningfully implemented in different constitutional contexts, particularly of the non-liberal or communitarian variety,[27] where RoL is no mere handmaiden to the authoritarian state.

Third, by engaging the varieties of the RoL beyond the abusive and anaemic conception of law wielded by absolutist states, in appreciating that all substantive theories of RoL draw flesh from disparate political and economic philosophies, we are invited to revisit the realm of normative ideals, to apprehend the universal norm and how it is contextually instantiated in accordance with legitimate cultural particularities.

All versions of the RoL are generally united in opposing the arbitrariness and absolutism which the 'government of man' may engender, being anti-totalitarian

[25] Gordon Silverstein, 'Singapore's Constitutionalism: A Model, but of What Sort? (2015) 100 Cornell Law Review 1, 1.

[26] Lon Fuller, *The Morality of Law* (Yale University Press, 1971) 217.

[27] Randall Pereenboom, 'Varieties of Rule of Law' in R Pereenboom (ed), *Asian Discourses on Rule of Law: Theories and Implementation of Rule of Law in Twelve Asian Countries, France and the US* (Routledge-Curzon 2004) 1–53.

in disposition. They may variously focus on where the RoL may deliver us to ('heaven') or what it may deliver us from ('hell'), or a mixture of both. While the hellishness of legal chaos and anarchy may be universally apprehended, the nature of 'heaven' will be rigorously contested, even if the RoL is the closest thing to a 'universal secular religion'.[28] This draws us back into a broader conversation about constitutionalism, limited government, human flourishing and the type of conditions needed for the RoL to exist and operate with effect. This engages the foundational question that goes beyond the anatomical approach which postulates a set of criteria (which are not self-evident) by which to measure the RoL, to grappling with the more fundamental questions pertaining to the *telos* of law, and how this affects our understanding of the RoL.

[28] Tom Bingham, *The Rule of Law* (Penguin Books, 2011) 196.

Bibliography

BOOKS

Allan, TRS, *Constitutional Justice: A Liberal Theory of the Rule of Law* (Clarendon Press, 2003)

Arendt, Hannah, *Crises of the Republic* (Harvest, 1972)

Ashworth, Andrew and Zedner, Lucia, *Preventive Justice* (Oxford University Press, 2014)

Bagehot, Walter, *The English Constitution* (1867)

Bingham, Tom, *The Rule of Law* (Penguin, 2011)

Blackstone, William, *Commentaries on the Law of England* (Clarendon Press, 1765)

Boulle, L, Harris, B and Hoexter, C, *Constitutional and Administrative Law: Basic Principles*, 19th edn (Juta, 1989)

Carter, Connie, *Eyes on the Prize: Law and Economic Development in Singapore* (Kluwer Law International, 2002)

Chan, Heng Chee, *The Politics of One Party Dominance: PAP at Grassroots* (Singapore University Press, 1976)

Chng Suan Tze et al (eds) *1987 Singapore's Marxist Conspiracy 30 Years On* (Function 8 Ltd, 2017)

Chua, Beng Huat, *Liberalism Disavowed: Communitarianism and State Capitalism in Singapore* (NUS Press, 2017)

Deene, Patrick, *Why Liberalism Failed* (Yale University Press, 2018)

Dicey, AV, *An Introduction to the Study of the Constitution*, 7th edn (Macmillan, 1908)

Dicey, AV, *Introduction to the Study of the Law of the Constitution*, 8th edn (Macmillan, 1915)

Dutton, William H, *The Fifth Estate: The Power Shift of the Digital Age* (Oxford University Press, 2023)

Duwell, Marcus, et al (eds), *Cambridge Handbook of Human Dignity: Interdisciplinary Perspectives* (Cambridge University Press, 2014)

Dworkin, Ronald, *Taking Rights Seriously* (Harvard University Press, 1977)

Dworkin, Ronald, *A Matter of Principle* (Harvard University Press, 1985)

Finnis, John, *Natural Law and Natural Rights* (Oxford University Press, 1980)

Finnis, John, *Natural Law and Natural Rights*, 2nd edn (Oxford University Press, 2011)

Fong Hoe Fang (ed), *That we May Dream Again* (Ethos, 2012)

Freeden, Michael, *Liberalism: A Very Short Introduction* (Oxford University Press, 2015)

Fuller, Lon L, *The Morality of Law* (Yale University Press, 1969)

Gatley, Clement, *Libel and Slander*, 8th edn (Sweet & Maxwell, 1981)

George, Cherian, *Freedom from the Press: Journalism and State Power in Singapore* (NUS Press, 2012)

Hailsham, Lord, *Elective Dictatorship*, Dimbleby Lectures (BBC, 1976)

Han Fook Kwang et al, *Lee Kuan Yew: The Man and His Ideas* (Times Edition, 1998)

Harden, Ian and Lewis, Norman, *Noble Lie: The British Constitution and the Rule of Law* (Hutchinson, 1986)

Harlow, Carol and Rawlings, Richard, *Law and Administration*, 3rd edn (Cambridge University Press, 2012)

Kalb, James, *Tyranny of Liberalism: Understanding and Overcoming Administered Freedom, Inquisitorial Tolerance and Equality by Command*, 2nd edn (Intercollegiate Studies Institute, 2008)

Lewis, CS, *The Four Loves* (Mariner Books, 1971)
Macedo, Stephen, *Liberal Virtues: Citizenship, Virtue and Community in Liberal Constitutionalism* (Oxford University Press, 1990)
Malik, Walled Haider, *Judiciary-Led Reforms in Singapore: Framework, Strategies, and Lessons* (World Bank Publications, 2007)
Meierhenrich Jens and Loughlin, Martin, *Cambridge Companion to the Rule of Law* (Cambridge University Press, 2021)
Pereenboom, Randall (ed), *Asian Discourses of Rule of Law: Theories and Implementation of Rule of Law in Twelve Asian countries, France and the US* (Routledge, 2004)
Pereenboom, Randall, Petersen, Carole J., Chen, HY Albert (eds), *Human Rights in Asia: A Comparative Legal Study of Twelve Asian Jurisdictions, France and the USA* (Routledge, 2006)
Phang, Andrew, *From Foundation to Legacy: The Second Charter of Justice* (Singapore Academy of Law, 2006)
Rajah, Jothie, *Authoritarian Rule of Law: Legislation, Discourse and Legitimacy in Singapore* (Cambridge University Press, 2012)
Rawls, John, *A Theory of Justice* (Harvard University Press, 1971)
Seow, Francis, *Media Enthralled: Singapore Revisited* (Lynne Rienner Publishers, 1998)
Seow, Francis T, *To Catch a Tartar: A Dissident in Lee Kuan Yew's Prison* (Yale Center for International and Area Studies, 1994)
Shklar, Judith *Political Thought and Political Thinkers* (Stanley Hoffman ed, University of Chicago Press, 1998)
Sunstein, Cass and Vermeule, Adrian, *Law and Leviathan: Redeeming the Administrative State* (Harvard University Press, 2020)
Tamanaha, Brian, *On the Rule of Law: On the Rule of Law: History, Politics, Theory* (Cambridge University Press, 2004)
Tamanaha, Brian, *A Realistic Theory of Law* (Cambridge University Press, 2017)
Tan, Kevin YL, *The Constitution of Singapore: A Contextual Analysis* (Hart Publishing, 2015)
Tan, Kevin YL and Lam, Peng Er (eds), *Managing Political Change: The Elected Presidency* (Routledge, 1997)
Tan, Kevin YL and Lee, Terence, *Voting in a Time of Change: Singapore's 2020 General Election* (Ethos Books, 2021)
Tan, Kevin YL and Thio, Li-ann, *50 Constitutional Moments that Defined a Nation* (Marshall Cavendish, 2015)
Tan, Wah Piow, *Smokescreens and Mirrors: Tracing the 'Marxist Conspiracy* (Function 8 Ltd, 2012)
Taylor, Charles, *Modern Social Imaginaries* (Duke University Press, 2004)
Teo, Soh Lung, *Beyond the Blue Gate: Recollections of a Political Prisoner* (Strategic Information, Research & Development Centre, 2010)
Tey, Tsun Hang, *Legal Consensus: Supreme Executive, Supine Jurisprudence, Suppliant Profession of Singapore* (Centre for Comparative and PL, 2011)
Thaler, Richard H and Sunstein, Cass R, *Nudge* (Yale University Press, 2008)
Thompson, Edward P, *Whigs and Hunters: The Origin of the Black Act* (Penguin Books, 1990)
Thio, Li-ann, *A Treatise on Singapore Constitutional Law* (Academy Publishing, 2012)
Vadaketh, Sudhir and Low, Donald, *Hard Choices: Challenging the Singapore Consensus* (NUS Press, 2014)
Woodiwiss, Anthony, *Globalisation, Human Rights and Labour Law in Pacific Asia* (Cambridge University Press, 1998)
Yap, Sonny, Lim, Richard and Leong, Weng Kam, *Men in White: The Untold Story of Singapore's Ruling Political Party*, 2nd edn (Singapore Press Holdings, 2010)

BOOK CHAPTERS

Ali, Mohamad, 'The Religious Rehabilitation Group (RRG): A Community–Government Partnership in Fighting Terrorism' in Zainul Abidin Rasheed and Norshahril Saat (eds), *Majulah: 50 Years of Malay/Muslim Community in Singapore* (World Scientific, 2016) 243–55

Allan, TRS, 'The Rule of Law' in David Dyzenhaus and Malcolm Thorburn (eds), *Philosophical Foundations of Constitutional Law* (Oxford University Press, 2016) 201–20

Burge-Hendrix, Brian, 'The Educative Function of Law' in Michael Freeman and Ross Harrison (eds), *Law and Philosophy* (Oxford University Press, 2007) 243

Chinkin, Christine, 'Abuse of Discretion in Malaysia and Singapore' in Andrew Harding (ed), *The Common Law in Singapore and Malaysia* (Butterworths, 1985) 261–91

Cooter, Robert, 'The Rule of State Law versus the Rule of Law State' in E Buscaglia, W Ratliff and R Cooter (eds), *The Law and Economics of Development* (JAI Press, 1997) 101–48

Fernandez, M and Loh, KS, 'The Left Wing Trade Unions in Singapore, 1945–1970' in M Barr and CA Trocki (eds), *Paths Not Taken: Political Pluralism in Post-War Singapore* (NUS Press, 2008) 206–27

Gargarella, Roberto, 'The Majoritarian Reading of the Rule of Law' in José María Maravall and Adam Przeworski (eds), *Democracy and the Rule of Law* (Cambridge University Press, 2003) 147–67

Gargarella, Roberto, 'Constitutionalism and The Rule of Law' in Jens Meierhenrich and Martin Loughlin (eds), *The Cambridge Companion to the Rule of Law* (Cambridge University Press, 2021) 425–42

Goldoni, Marco and McCorkindale, Christopher, 'Political Constitutionalism' in *Encyclopedia of the Philosophy of Law and Social Philosophy* (Springer, 2018) 1–8

Hickling, RH, 'The Origins of Constitutional Government in Singapore' in *Essays in Singapore Law* (Pelanduk Publications, 1992) 1–51

Hor, Michael, 'Constitutionalism and Subversion: An Exploration' in Li-ann Thio and Kevin YL Tan (eds), *The Evolution of a Revolution: 40 Years of the Singapore Constitution* (Routledge-Cavendish, 2009) 260–87

Hor, Michael, 'Singapore's Anti-terrorism Laws: Reality and Rhetoric' in V Ramraj (ed), *Global Anti-terrorism Law and Policy* (Cambridge University Press, 2012) 271–89

Jaysuriya, Kanishka, 'Corporatism and Judicial Independence within Statist Legal Institutions' in Kanishka Jayasuriya (ed), *East Asia in Law, Capitalism and Power in Asia: The Rule of Law and Legal Institutions* (Routledge, 1999) 147–73

Krygier, Martin, 'Rule of Law' in Michel Rosenfeld and Andras Sajo (eds), *The Oxford Handbook of Comparative Constitutional Law* (Oxford University Press, 2012)

Krygier, Martin, 'Tempering Power' in Anne Meuwese and Ernst Ballin (eds), *Constitutionalism and the Rule of Law*, Maurice Adams (Cambridge University Press, 2017) 34–59

Lau, Kwan Ho, 'A Study in Separate Judgments' in Goh Yihan and Paul Tan (eds), *Singapore Law: 50 Years in the Making* (Academy Publishing, 2015) ch 4

Lee, HP and Pittard, Marilyn, 'The Challenge of Judicial Independence in the Asia-Pacific' in HP Lee and Marilyn Pittard (eds), *Asia-Pacific Judiciaries: Independence, Impartiality and Integrity* (Cambridge University Press, 2018) 398

Lin, Jolene, 'The Judicialisation of Governance: The Case of Singapore' in Tom Ginsburg and Albert HY Chen (eds), *Administrative Law and Governance in Asia: Comparative Perspectives* (Routledge, 2009) 287–311

McGregor, Lorna, 'Reconciliation: Where Is the Law?' in Scott Veitch, Emilios Christodoulidis and Sharon Cowan (eds), *Law and the Politics of Reconciliation* (Routledge 2007) 111–218

Meierhenrich, Jens, 'What the Rule of Law Is … and Is Not' in Jens Meierhenrich and Martin Loughlin (eds), *Cambridge Companion to the Rule of Law* (Cambridge University Press, 2021) 569–621

Munro, Vanessa, 'Feminist Critiques of the Rule of Law' in Jens Meierhenrich and Martin Loughlin (eds), *Cambridge Companion to the Rule of Law* (Cambridge University Press, 2021) 340–56

Neo, Jaclyn, and Lee, Yvonne, 'Constitutional Supremacy: Still a Little Dicey' in Li-ann Thio and Kevin Tan (eds), *Evolution of a Revolution: 40 Years of the Singapore Constitution* (Routledge, 2009) 153–92

Neo, Jaclyn and Tan, Kevin, 'Judicial Minimalism as Towering: Singapore's Chief Justice Chan Sek Keong' in Rehan Abeyratne and Iddo Porat (eds), *Towering Judges: A Comparative Study of Constitutional Judges* (Cambridge University Press, 2021)

Quah, Jon ST, 'Singapore in 1987: Political Reforms, Control and Economic Recovery' in M Ayoob and Ng Chee Yuen (eds), *Southeast Asian Affairs 1988* (Institute of Southeast Asian Studies, 1988) 233–52

Raz, Joseph, 'The Rule of Law and its Virtue' in J Raz (ed), *The Authority of Law: Essays on Law and Morality* (Oxford University Press, 1979) 210–29

Rutter, MF, 'The Future of the Common Law' in *The Applicable Law in Singapore and Malaysia: A Guide to the Reception, Precedent and the Sources of Law in the Republic of Singapore and the Federation of Malaysia* (Malayan Law Journal, 1989) 575

Santos, Alvaro, 'The World Bank's Uses of the "Rule of Law" Promise in Economic Development' in David M Trubek and Alvaro Santos (eds), *The New Law and Economic Development: A Critical Appraisal* (Cambridge University Press, 2010) 253–300

Selznick, P, 'Legal Cultures and the Rule of Law' in M Krygier and A Czarnota (eds), *The Rule of Law After Communism* (Ashgate, 1999) 26

Silverstein, Gordon, 'Singapore: The Exception that Proves Rules Matter' in Tom Ginsburg and Tamir Moustafa (eds), *Rule by Law: The Politics of Courts in Authoritarian Regimes* (Cambridge University Press, 2012) 73–101

Tamanaha, Brian, 'Functions of the Rule of Law' in Jens Meierhenrich and Martin Loughlin (eds), *Cambridge Companion to the Rule of Law* (Cambridge University Press, 2021) 221–36

Tan, Kevin YL, 'As Efficient as the Best Businesses: Singapore's Judicial System' in Juinn-rong Yeh and Wen-Chen Chang (eds), *Asian Courts in Context* (Cambridge University Press, 2014) 228–96

Tan, Kevin YL, 'Is Singapore an Authoritarian Constitutional Regime? So What if It Is?' in Weitseng Chen and Hualing Fu (eds), *Authoritarian Legality in Asia; Formation, Development and Transition* (Cambridge University Press, 2020) 187–202

Ten, CL, 'Constitutionalism and the Rule of Law' in Robert E Goodin, Philip Pettit and Thomas Pogge (eds), *A Companion to Contemporary Political Philosophy* (Blackwell Publishing 1993) 494–502

Thio, Li-ann, 'Religion in the Public Sphere of Singapore: Wall of Division or Public Square' in Bryan S Turner (ed), *Religious Pluralism and Civil Society: A Comparative Analysis* (Bardwell Press, 2008) 73–104

Thio, Li-ann, 'The Theory and Practice of Judicial Review of Administrative Action in Singapore: Trends and Perspectives' in TM Yeo et al (eds), *SAL Conference 2011: Developments in Singapore Law between 2006 and 2010 – Trends and Perspectives* (Singapore Academy of Law, 2011) 714–52

Thio, Li-ann, 'Constitutionalism in Illiberal Polities' in Andras Sajo and Michel Rosenfeld (eds), *Oxford Handbook on Comparative Constitutionalism* (Oxford University Press, 2012) 133–52

Thio, Li-ann, 'The Chan Court and Constitutional Adjudication: A Sea Change into Something Rich and Strange' in Chao Hick Tin et al (eds), *The Law in His Hands: A Tribute to Chief Justice Chan Sek Keong* (Academy Press, 2012) 87–119

Thio, Li-ann, '"We Are Feeling Our Way Forward, Step by Step": The Continuing Singapore Experiment in the Construction of Communitarian Constitutionalism in the 21st Century's First Decade' in Albert Chen (ed), *Constitutionalism in Asia in the Early Twenty-First Century* (Cambridge University Press, 2014) 270–94

Thio, Li-ann, 'Principled Pragmatism and the "Third Wave" of Communitarian Judicial Review in Singapore' in Jaclyn L Neo (ed), *Constitutional Interpretation in Singapore: Theory and Practice* (Routledge, 2016) 75–116

Thio, Li-ann, 'Ambivalence, Accommodation, Antipathy and Anxiety: The State of Religion within Singapore's Secular Democratic Order' in Vidhu Vema (ed), *Religion and Democracy* (Oxford University Press (India) 2019) 54–87

Thio, Li-ann, 'Past Imperfect, Future Tense: The Elected Presidency and the Constitutional Development of an "Ever Evolving Hybrid"' in Jaclyn L Neo and Swati S Jhaveri (eds), *Constitutional Change in Singapore: Reforming the Elected Presidency* (Routledge, 2019) 41–66

Thio, Li-ann, 'Courts and Judicial Review' in Peter Cane et al (eds), *Oxford Handbook of Comparative Administrative Law* (Oxford University Press, 2020) 721–46

Thio, Li-ann, 'Apollonian Restraint and Dionysian Impulse: Law, Freedom, and Religious Feelings' in Li-ann Thio and Jaclyn Neo (eds), *Religious Offences in Common Law Asia: Colonial Legacies, Constitutional Rights and Contemporary Practice* (Hart Publishing, 2021) 75–103

Thio, Li-ann, 'Public Law' in A Phang, S Chesterman and Y Goh (eds), *Law and Technology in Singapore* (Academy Press, 2021) 577–626

Thio, Li-ann, 'Higher Law/Rule of Law: The Sacred Roots and Secular Shoots of the Supreme Law' in Nicholas Aroney and Ian Leigh (eds), *Christianity and Constitutionalism* (Oxford University Press, 2022) 193–215

Thio, Li-ann, 'Legal Communitarianism and Pandemic Regulation in Singapore' in Stefan Braum (ed), *Experimental Law: The Rule of Law and the Regulation of the Corona Pandemic in Europe*, Luxembourg Legal Studies (NOMOS 2023) 383–440

Toth, Gabor Attila, 'Illiberal Rule of Law? Changing Features of Hungarian Constitutionalism' in Maurice Adams, Anne Meuwese and Ernst Ballin (eds), *Constitutionalism and the Rule of Law* (Cambridge University Press, 2017) 389–415

Tushnet, Mark, 'Critical Legal Studies and the Rule of Law' in Jens Meierhenrich and Martin Loughlin (eds), *Cambridge Companion to the Rule of Law* (Cambridge University Press, 2021) 328–39

Waldron, Jeremy, 'The Rule of Law as an Essentially Contested Concept' in Jens Meierhenrich and Martin Loughlin (eds), *The Cambridge Companion to the Rule of Law* (Cambridge University Press, 2021) 121–36

Walker, Graham, 'The Idea of Nonliberal Constitutionalism' in Ian Shapiro and Will Kymlicka (eds), *Ethnicity and Group Rights* (New York University Press, 1977) 154–84

Whalen-Bridge, Helena, 'Access to Justice in Singapore: A Government and Lawyer Dynamic' in Helena Whalen Bridge (ed), *The Role of Lawyers in Access to Justice: Asian and Comparative Perspectives* (Cambridge University Press, 2022) 162–77

ARTICLES

Ackerman, Bruce, 'The New Separation of Powers' (2000) 113(3) Harv L Rev 633

Albert, Richard, 'The Fusion of Presidentialism and Parliamentarianism' (2009) 57 American Journal of Comparative Law 531

Allan, TRS, 'Legislative Supremacy and the Rule of Law: Democracy and Constitutionalism' (1985) 44 Cambridge Law Journal 111

Barlet, Michael, 'Mandatory Mediation and the Rule of Law' (2019) 1(1) Amicus Curiae Series 2 50

Bingham, Tom, 'Rule of Law' (2007) 66 Cambridge Law Journal 67

Buti, Antonio, '"Reconciliation": Its Relationship and Importance to Law' [2018] 43(1) University of Western Australia Law Review 107.

Cane, Peter, 'Taking Law Seriously: Starting Points of the Hart/Devlin Debate' (2006) 10(1) Journal of Ethics 21

Carothers, Thomas, 'Rule of Law Temptations' (2009) 33(1) Fletcher Forum of World Affairs 49
Chan, Cassandra, 'Breaking Singapore's Regrettable Tradition of Chilling Free Speech with Defamation Laws' (2003) 26 Loy LA Int'l & Comp L Rev 315
Chan, Gary KY, 'Online Falsehoods, Constitutional Free Speech and Its Limits: The Online Citizen v AG' [2022] SJLS 166
Chan, Sek Keong, 'Securing and Maintaining the Independence of the Court in Judicial Proceedings' (2010) 22 SAcLJ 229
Chan, Sek Keong, 'Judicial Review – From Angst to Empathy' (2010) 22 SAcLJ 469
Chan, Sek Keong, 'The Courts and the "Rule of Law" in Singapore' [2012] SJLS 209
Cheah, Wui Ling, 'Migrant Workers as Citizens within the ASEAN Landscape: International Law and the Singapore Experient' (2009) 8(1) Chinese Journal of International Law 205
Chin, James, 'The PAP Model: Can the 4G Hold on to Power?' (2023) 112(2) The Round Table 173
Chng, Kenny, 'The Theoretical Foundations of Judicial Review in Singapore' [2019] SJLS 294
Chng, Kenny, 'A Reconsideration of Equal Protection and Executive Action in Singapore' (2021) OUCLJ 1
Chng, Kenny, 'Reconsidering the Legal Regulation of the Usage of Administrative Policies' [2022] PL 76
Chng, Kenny, 'Microcontextual Considerations in Ouster Clause Analysis: A Comparative Study of Parallel Trends in the UK and Singapore' (2022) 20(3) ICON 1257
Chng, Kenny and Soon, Andrea, 'Revising Remedies and the Legality–Merits Distinction in Singapore Administrative Law: CBB v Law Society of Singapore [2021] SGCA 6' (2022) 22(1) OUCLJ 108
Chua, Lynette, 'Pragmatic Resistance, Law and Social Movements in Authoritarian States: The Case of Gay Collective Action in Singapore' (2012) 46(4) Law & Society Review 713
Clarke, Meghan, 'Polarization: The Role of Emotions in Reconciliation Efforts' (2009) 72(2) Law and Contemporary Problems 27
Clausen, Hans, 'The Privilege of Speech in a Pleasantly Authoritarian Country' (2005) 38(2) Vanderbilt Journal of International Law 443
Cohen, J, 'The Chinese Communist Party and "Judicial Independence": 1949–1959' (1969) 82(5) Harv L Rev 967
Craig, Paul, 'Formal and Substantive Conceptions of the Rule of Law: An Analytical Framework' [1997] PL 467
Craig, Paul, 'The Nature of Reasonableness Review' (2013) 66 Current Legal Problems 131
Daly, Paul, 'Wednesbury's Reason and Structure' [2011] PL 238
Daly, Stephen, 'The Rule of (Soft) Law' (2021) 32(1) King's Law Journal 3
Davis, Michael C, 'Constitutionalism under Chinese Rule: Hong Kong after the Handover' (1998) 27 Denver Journal of International Law and Policy 275
Endicott, Timothy, 'The Impossibility of the Rule of Law' (1999) 19 OJLS 1
Frank et al, '"The Decline of the Rule of Law in Malaysia and Singapore Part II – Singapore", A Report of the Committee on International Human Rights of the Association of the Bar of the City of New York' (1991) 46 The Record 65.
Fuller, Lon, 'The Forms and Limits of Adjudication' (1979) 92 Harv L Rev 353
George, Robert, 'Reason, Freedom and the Rule of Law: Their Significance in Western Thought' (2002–03) 15 Regent University Law Review 187
George, Robert, Girgis, Sherif and Anderson, Ryan T, 'What Is Marriage' (2010) 34(1) Harv JLPP 245
Gomez, James, 'Restricting Free Speech: The Impact of Opposition Parties in Singapore' (2006) 23 Copenhagen Journal of Asia Studies 105
Grant, James, 'The Rise of Juristocracy' (2010) 34(2) Wilson Quarterly 16
Green, LC, 'Native Law and the Common Law: Conflict or Harmony' (1970) 12 Mal L Rev 38
Hall, Stephen, 'The Persistent Spectre: Natural Law, International Order and the Limits of Legal Positivism' (2001) 12(2) European Journal of International Law 269

Han, Kirsten, 'Singapore's Elastic Band of a Public Order Act' (2022) 51(4) Index on Censorship 34
Hans, GS, 'Changing Counterspeech' (2021) 69 Cleveland State Law Review 749
Hooker, MB, 'Raffles' Singapore Regulations' (1968) 10(2) Mal L Rev 248
Jayakumar, S, 'Applying the Rule of Law' (2009) 43 International Lawyer 83
Jayakumar, Shashi, 'Research Note: Singapore's "Deradicalisation" Model: Revolution – or Evolutions?' (Spring 2021) 26 Journal for Deradicalisation 227
Jayasuriya, Kanishka, 'The Exception Becomes the Norm: Law and Regimes of Exception in East Asia' (2001) 2 Asian-Pacific Law & Policy Journal 108
Jhaveri, Swati, 'Interrogating Dialogic Theories of Judicial Review' (2019) 17(3) ICON 811
Jhaveri, Swati, 'Revisiting Taxonomies and Truisms in Administrative Law in Singapore' [2019] SJLS 351
Jowell, Jeffrey and Lester, Anthony, 'Beyond Wednesbury: Substantive Principles of Administrative Law' [1987] PL 368
Kauper, Paul G, 'The Supreme Court and the Rule of Law' (1961) 59 Mich L Rev 531
Kavanagh, Aileen, 'Defending Deference in Public Law and Constitutional Theory' (2010) 126 Law Quarterly Review 222
Kavanagh, Aileen, 'Judicial Restraint in the Pursuit of Justice' (2010) 60(1) UTLJ 23
Khaitan, Tarunabh, 'Balancing Accountability and Effectiveness: A Case for Moderated Parliamentarianism' (2021) 7 CJCCL 81
Khng, Nathaniel, 'Judicial Independence and the Singapore Judiciary' (2012) Lawasia Journal 53
Klarman, Michael J, 'What's So Great About Constitutionalism' (1998) 93 NULR 145
Lee, Tsen-Ta Jack, 'Shall the Twain Never Meet? Competing Narratives and Discourses of the Rule of Law in Singapore' [2012] SJLS 298
Liang, Calvin and Shi, Sarah, 'The Constitution of Our Constitution, A Vindication of the Basic Structure Doctrine' [2014] Singapore Law Gazette 12
Lord Diplock, 'Judicial Control of Government' [1979] Mal LJ cxl
Magnus, Richard, 'Transparent, Fair and Impartial: A Snapshot of Tribunals in Singapore' (2004) 84 Australian Law Reform Commission Reform Journal 33
Menon, Sundaresh, 'International Terrorism and Human Rights' (2014) Asian Journal of International Law 1
Menon, Sundaresh, 'The Rule of Law: The Path to Exceptionalism' (2016) 28 SAcLJ 413
Menon, Sundaresh, 'Executive Power: Rethinking the Modalities of Control' (2019) 29 Duke Journal of Comparative and International Law 277
Neo, Jaclyn L, 'Navigating Minority Inclusion and Permanent Division: Minorities and the Depoliticization of Ethnic Difference' (2017) 17(1) Jus Politicum 607
Ng, Rita, 'College and Character: What Did Confucius Teach Us about the Importance of Integrating Ethics, Character, Learning, and Education?' (2009) 10(4) Journal of College and Character 1
Ong, Benjamin Joshua, 'The Ideals of Law in a Health Crisis: Singapore's Legitimate Responses to COVID-19' (2020) Law and COVID-19 147
Ong, Benjamin Joshua, 'The Unmeritorious 'Legality/Merits Distinction in Singapore Administrative Law' (2021) 16 AJCL 1
Ortmann, S, 'Liberal Vestiges in an Illiberal Regime: The Case of Singapore' (2023) 60 Society 28
Ortmann, Stephen, 'Policy Advocacy in a Competitive Authoritarian Regime' (2012) 44(6) Administration & Society 13S–25S
Pereenboom, Randall, 'Human Rights and Rule of Law: What's the Relationship?' (2005) 36(1) Georgetown Journal of International Law 815
Phang, Andrew, Yihan, Goh and Soh, Jerrold, 'The Development of Singapore Law: A Bicentennial Retrospective' (2021) 32 SAcLJ 804
Post, Robert C, 'The Social Foundations of Defamation Law: Reputation and the Constitution' (1986) 74 California Law Review 691
'Practice Statement (Judicial Precedent Issued July 11, 1994)' (1944) 2 SL Rev 689

Prime Minister Lee Kuan Yew, 'Speech at the Opening of the Singapore Law Academy (31 August 1990)' (1990) 2 SAcLJ 155
Quek-Anderson, Dorcas, 'The Evolving Concept of Access to Justice in Singapore's Mediation Movement' (2020) 16(2) International Journal of Law in Context 128
Rajah, Jothie, 'Punishing Bodies, Securing the Nation: How Rule of Law Can Legitimate the Urbane Authoritarian State' (2011) 36(4) Law & Social Inquiry 945
Rajah Jothie, and Thiruvengadam, Arun, 'Of Absences, Masks and Exceptions: Cause Lawyering in Singapore' (2014) 31(3) Wisconsin International Law Journal 646
Rajah, VK, 'Panel Discussion: Measuring the Rule of Law' [2012] SJLS 331
Rao, Neomi, 'The Hedgehog & the Fox in Administrative Law' (2021) 150(3) Daedalus 220
Raz, Joseph, 'The Law's Own Virtue' (2019) 39(1) OJLS 1
Sanders, Michaele, 'The Fact/Opinion Distinction: An Analysis of the Subjectivity of Language and Law' (1987) 70 Marquette Law Review 673
Scalia, Antonin, 'The Rule of Law as a Law of Rules' (1989) 56(4) University of Chicago Law Review 1175
Shugart, Matthew, 'Semi-Presidential Systems: Dual Executive and Mixed Authority Patterns (2005) 3 French Politics 323
Schuldt, Lasse, 'In Singapore's War on Fake News, the Constitution Is Not an Obstacle' (*verfassungsblog.de*, 16 November 2021)
Shanmugam, K, 'The Rule of Law in Singapore' [2012] SJLS 357
Silverstein, Gordon, 'Singapore's Constitutionalism: A Model, but of What Sort?' (2015) 100 Cornell Law Review 1
Sim, Cameron, 'The Singapore Chill: Political Defamation and the Normalization of a Statist Rule of Law' (2011) 20 Pacific Rim Law and Policy Journal 319
Skaaning, Svend-Erik, 'Measuring the Rule of Law' (2010) 63(2) Political Research Quarterly 449–460
Stephens, Luke, 'Contentious Acts in Controlled Spaces: A Protest Event Analysis of Singaporean Demonstrations' [2023] Journal of Contemporary Asia 1
Sternlight, Jean R, 'Is Alternative Dispute Resolution Consistent with the Rule of Law? Lessons from Abroad' (2006–07) 56 DePaul law Review 569
Stone, Adrienne, 'Judicial Review without Rights: Some Problems for the Democratic Legitimacy of Structural Judicial Review' (2008) 28(1) OJLS 1
Sweet, Alec Stone, 'Intimations of Proportionality? The Singapore Constitution and Rights Protection' [2021] SJLS 231
Sweet, Alec Stone and Mathews, Jud, 'Proportionality and Rights Protection in Asia: Hong Kong, Malaysia, South Korea, Taiwan – Whither Singapore?' (2017) 29 SAcLJ 774
Tamanaha, Brian, 'The Dark Side of the Relationship Between the Rule of Law and Liberalism' (2008) 23 NYU JL & Liberty 537
Tamanaha, Brian, 'The History and Elements of the Rule of Law' [2012] SJLS 232
Tan, Daniel, 'An Analysis of Substantive Review in Singaporean Administrative Law' (2013) 25 SAcLJ 296
Tan, David and Teng, Jessica, 'Fake News, Free Speech and Finding Constitutional Congruence' (2020) 32 SAcLJ 207
Tan, Eugene KB, 'Curial Deference in Singapore PL: Autochthonous Evolution to Buttress Good Governance and the Rule of Law' (2017) 29 SAcLJ 800
Tan, Eugene KB, 'Law and Values in Governance: The Singapore Way' (2000) 30 Hong Kong Law Journal 91
Tan, Eugene KB, 'Singapore: Transitioning to a "New Normal" in a Post-Lee Kuan Yew Era' (2012) Southeast Asian Affairs 265
Tan, Junda Nicholas, 'Saving Democracy? Singapore, The Digital Public Square and the Regulation of Online Speech', NUS University Research Opportunity [57]

Tan, Kevin YL, 'Besmirching Honourable Men: The Defamation of Politicians in Singapore' (2020) IYCL 55

Tan, Netina and Preece Cassandra, 'Democratic Backsliding in Illiberal Singapore' (2024) 9(1) Asian Journal of Comparative Politics 25

Tan, Seow Hon, 'Religion in the Abortion Discourse in Singapore: A Case Study of the Relevance of Religious Arguments in Law-making in Multi-religious Democracies' (2010) 26 (2) Journal of Law and Religion 505–539

Tan, Seow Hon, 'Surrogacy, Child's Welfare and Public Policy in Adoption Applications' [2019] SJLS 263

Teo, Marcus, 'A Case for Proportionality Review in Singaporean Constitutional Adjudication' [2021] SJLS 174

Teo, Marcus, 'Constitutional Implications of the First POFMA Judgement: TOC v AG' [2022] SJLS 177

Tey, Tsun Hang, 'Singapore's Jurisprudence of Political Defamation and Its Triple Whammy Impact on Political Speech' [2008] PL 452

Thio, Li-ann, 'The Post-Colonial Evolution of the Singapore Legislature' [1993] SJLS 80–122

Thio, Li-ann, 'The Secular Trumps the Sacred: Constitutional Issues Arising out of Colin Chan v PP' (1995) SL Rev 26

Thio, Li-ann, 'The Right to Political Participation in Singapore: Tailor-Making a Westminster-Modelled Constitution to Fit the Imperatives of "Asian" Democracy' (2002) 6 SJICL 181

Thio, Li-ann, '*Lex Rex or Rex Lex*: Competing Conceptions of the Rule of Law in Singapore' (2002) 20 UCLA Pacific Basin Law Journal 1

Thio, Li-ann, 'Speakers Cornered? Managing Political Speech in Singapore and the Commitment "To Build a Democratic Society"' (2003) 3 International Journal of Constitutional Law 516

Thio, Li-ann, 'Constitutional "Soft" Law and the Management of Religious Liberty and Order: The 2003 Declaration on Religious Harmony' [2004] SJLS 414

Thio, Li-ann, 'Control, Co-optation and Co-operation: Managing Religious Harmony in Singapore's Multi-ethnic, Quasi-secular State' (2005) 33(2/3) Hastings Constitutional Law Quarterly 197

Thio, Li-ann, '"Beyond the Four Walls" in an Age of Transnational Judicial Conversations: Civil Liberties, Rights Theories and Constitutional Adjudication in Malaysia and Singapore' (2006) 19(2) CJAL 428

Thio, Li-ann, 'Reading Rights Rightly: The UDHR and Its Creeping Influence on the Development of Singapore PL' [2008] SJLS 264

Thio, Li-ann, 'The Virtual and the Real: Article 14, Political Speech and the Calibrated Management of Deliberative Democracy in Singapore' [2008] SJLS 25

Thio, Li-ann, 'Westminster Constitutions and Implied Fundamental Rights: Excavating an Implied Constitutional Right to Vote' [2009] SJLS 406

Thio, Li-ann, 'Reception and Resistance: Globalisation, International Law and the Singapore Constitution' (2009) 4(3) NTU L Rev 335

Thio, Li-ann, 'Soft Constitutional Law in Non-liberal Asian Constitutional Democracies' (2010) 8 ICON 766

Thio, Li-ann, 'Contentious Liberty: Regulating Religious Propagation in a Religiously Diverse Secular Democracy' [2010] SJLS 484

Thio, Li-ann, 'Relational Constitutionalism and the Management of Inter-religious Disputes: The Singapore "Secularism with a Soul Model"' (2012) 2 Oxford Journal of Law and Religion 446

Thio, Li-ann, 'Between Apology and Apogee, Autochthony: The "Rule of Law" beyond the Rules of Law in Singapore' [2012] SJLS 269

Thio, Li-ann, 'International Law in the Courts of Singapore: Still a Little Island?' (2013) 19 Asian YBIL 1

Thio, Li-ann, 'Irreducible Plurality, Indivisible Unity: Singapore Relational Constitutionalism and Cultivating Harmony through Constructing a Constitutional Civil Religion' (2019) 20(7) German Law Journal 1007

Thio, Li-ann, 'Ousting Ouster Clauses: The Ins and Outs of the Principles Regulating the Scope of Judicial Review in Singapore' [2020] SJLS 392
Thio, Li-ann, 'Varieties of Constitutionalism in Asia' (2021) 16(2) AJCL 285
Thio, Li-ann, 'Rightism, Reasonableness and Review: Section 377A of the Penal Code and the Question of Equality – Part One' (2022) 34 SAcLJ 180
Thio, Li-ann, 'Of Variable Standards of Scrutiny and Legitimate Legal Expectations: Article 12(1) and the Judicial Review of Executive Action' [2022] SJLS 1
Tushnet, Mark, 'Authoritarian Constitutionalism' (2015) 100 Cornell Law Review 391
Wake, CH, 'Raffles and the Rajas: The Founding of Singapore in Malayan and British Colonial History' (1975) 48(1) Journal of the Malaysian Branch of the Royal Asiatic Society 47
Walid Jumblatt Bin Abdullah, 'The Politics of Compromise: Analyzing the Repeal of Section 377A in Singapore' (2023) 96(1) Pacific Affairs 105–118
Westen, Peter, 'The Empty Idea of Equality' (1982) 95 Harv L Rev 537
Wott, Rodney, 'Fact and Opinion in Defamation: Recognizing the Formative Power of Context' (1990) 58(4) Fordham Law Review 761
Yee Chee Wai, Ho, Monica and Seng, Daniel, 'Judicial Review of Preventive Detention under the ISA' (1989) 10 SL Rev 66
Yoo, Christopher S, 'Free Speech and the Myth of the Internet as an Unintermediated Experience' (2010) 78 George Washington Law Review 697

OFFICIAL REPORTS, WHITE PAPERS

White Papers and Official Reports

Maintenance of Religious Harmony white paper (Cmd 21, 1989)
Principles for Determining and Safeguarding the Accumulated Reserves of the Government and the Fifth Schedule Statutory Boards and Government Companies (Cmd 5, 1999)
Report of the Commission of Inquiry into Allegations of Executive Interference in the Subordinate Courts (Cmd 12, 1986)
Report of the Constitutional Commission (Singapore National Printers, 1966)
Report of the Electoral Boundaries Review Committee 2020 (Cmd 26, 2020)
Report of the Select Committee on Deliberate Online Falsehoods – Causes, Consequences and Countermeasures, Parl 15 of 2018, 19 September 2018
Report of the Select Committee on the Maintenance of Religious Harmony Bill, Parl 7 of 1990, October 1990
Safeguarding Financial Assets and the Integrity of the Public Service, white paper (Cmd 11, 1990)
Salaries for a Capable and Committed Government (Cmd 1, 2012)
Shared Values White Paper (Cmd 1, 1991)
The Jemaah Islamiyah Arrests and the Threat of Terrorism, white paper (Cmd 2, 2003)
White Paper on Singapore Women's Development: Towards a Fairer and More Inclusive Society (2022)

Key NGO Reports and Other Reports

Human Rights Watch, '"Kill the Chickens to Scare the Monkeys": Suppression of Free Expression and Assembly in Singapore' (12 December 2017)
International Bar Association (Human Rights Institute), 'Prosperity versus Individual Rights? Human Rights, Democracy and the Rule of Law in Singapore' (2008)

Param Cumaraswamy, Report of the Special Rapporteur on the AL SGP/3/2020 Independence of Judges and Lawyers, UN Commission on Human Rights, 52nd Sess, UN Doc E/CN.4/1996/37, [218]

Report of the Committee on International Human Rights of the Association of the Bar of the City of New York, 'The Decline of the Rule of Law in Malaysia and Singapore – Part II – Singapore' (1991) 46 The Record 7

Index

www.ingramcontent.com/pod-product-compliance
Ingram Content Group UK Ltd.
Pitfield, Milton Keynes, MK11 3LW, UK
UKHW020804290926
15470UKWH00003B/947

9 781509 951390